HOW THE
NEW
TESTAMENT
CAME TO BE

HOW THE
NEW
TESTAMENT
CAME TO BE

Edited by
Kent P. Jackson and Frank F. Judd Jr.

THE 35TH ANNUAL
BRIGHAM YOUNG UNIVERSITY
SIDNEY B. SPERRY SYMPOSIUM

RSC
B Y U

DESERET®
BOOK

The Sperry Symposium is sponsored annually by Brigham Young University and the Church Educational System in honor of Sidney B. Sperry. In the course of his forty-five-year career as a religious educator, Dr. Sperry earned a reputation for outstanding teaching and scholarship. The symposium seeks to perpetuate his memory by fostering continuing research on gospel topics.

Copublished by the Religious Studies Center, Brigham Young University, Provo, Utah, and Deseret Book Company, Salt Lake City, Utah.

Library of Congress Cataloging-in-Publication Data

Sperry Symposium (35th : 2006 : Provo, Utah)
How the New Testament came to be : the 35th annual Sidney B. Sperry Symposium / edited by Kent P. Jackson and Frank F. Judd, Jr.
     p. cm.
Includes bibliographical references and index.
ISBN-10 1-59038-627-2 (hardbound : alk. paper)
ISBN-13 978-1-59038-627-9 (hardbound : alk. paper)
1. Bible. N.T.—History—Congresses. 2. Bible. N.T.—Canon—Congresses.
3. Bible. N.T.—Criticism, interpretation, etc.—Congresses. 4. Church of Jesus Christ of Latter-day Saints—Doctrines—Congresses. 5. Mormon Church—Doctrines—Congresses.
I. Jackson, Kent P. II. Judd, Frank F. III. Title.
BS2315.S66 2006
225.1—dc22   2006018418

Printed in the United States of America
Worzalla Publishing Co., Stevens Point, WI
10   9   8   7   6   5   4   3   2   1

CONTENTS

INTRODUCTION

The 2006 Sidney B. Sperry Symposium, *How the New Testament Came to Be,* celebrates the writing of the New Testament and the faithful service of those who brought that book of sacred scripture into existence. In the papers contained in this volume, presented on the Brigham Young University campus in Provo, Utah, on October 27–28, 2006, authors explore the New Testament's origin and examine ancient and scriptural evidence on a variety of related topics.

The symposium, held annually and named in honor of pioneer Latter-day Saint scripture scholar Sidney B. Sperry, seeks each year to examine an aspect of the Church's religious and scriptural heritage.

Recently there has been a great deal of interest worldwide in the origin, early history, and reliability of the documents that make up the New Testament. Through popular books, the publication of alternate Gospels, and the continuing popularity of novels and motion pictures that deal with New Testament themes and question biblical claims, readers and viewers have been exposed to many new ideas relating to New Testament studies. This volume, although not seeking to respond directly to any of those works, puts in print the research of faithful Latter-day Saint scholars who have explored the earliest evidence for the New Testament and have asked hard questions concerning it.

Indeed, the New Testament presents us with many questions. Unlike the Book of Mormon, which was written anciently but was preserved for centuries to come forth in its purity in the latter days, the New Testament's early history is in large part unknown. We do not know, for example, when, and under what circumstances, many of the documents were written. Nor do we know all the history of the texts from the time of their composition until many years later when the earliest-known manuscripts were copied. We know that "plain and precious things" were removed from the scriptural text (1 Nephi 13:28), but because the original manuscripts do not exist, is there any way to find out from the earliest preserved documents what those "plain and precious things" were and when they were lost? What does modern revelation contribute to answer questions like this?

Similarly, the New Testament presents us with questions concerning authorship that are unknown from the Book of Mormon. What do we know about the traditional attributions of the Gospels to Matthew, Mark, Luke, and John? What can we say about how those and other books were collected to form the New Testament? Do the ancient manuscripts provide answers? What does modern revelation teach us?

How the New Testament Came to Be does not deal with the life of Jesus Christ or how to become better disciples—topics which we believe are of the greatest worth. Our theme in the volume is the writing and compilation of the New Testament, with a focus on authors and manuscripts. Topics include writing in the ancient world, the work of scribes, the authorship of New Testament books, the occasions for and dating of individual New Testament books, the earliest ancient manuscripts, New Testament textual criticism, the development of the New Testament canon, and contributions of Joseph Smith to our understanding of the New Testament. Readers will see that the authors do not always interpret the evidence in the same way, and we as editors do not always agree with what the authors have written. But such is the nature of scholarly exploration in pursuit of truth, and the book is enhanced by the variety of its contents. What the authors have in common, however, is a commitment to the centrality of the sacred mission of Jesus Christ and a belief that modern revelation is an indispensable guide for reading and understanding the New Testament.

We are grateful to have among our contributors Elder Alexander B. Morrison, whose chapter poses questions and points out uncertainties while at the same time reaffirming the importance of faith and revelation. His chapter begins the book, and subsequent chapters build on the themes he introduces.

The 2006 Sperry Symposium committee consisted of Patty Smith and Professors Clyde J. Williams, Frank F. Judd Jr., and Kent P. Jackson. The editorial responsibilities were carried out by Professors Judd and Jackson. We thank the contributors to this volume and the contributors to the symposium for sharing the fruit of their research. And we thank colleagues at Brigham Young University and elsewhere who reviewed manuscripts and encouraged quality.

Kent P. Jackson

Frank F. Judd Jr.

"PLAIN AND PRECIOUS THINGS": THE WRITING OF THE NEW TESTAMENT

Elder Alexander B. Morrison

I must make it clear that the views presented in this chapter are my own and do not represent the official position of The Church of Jesus Christ of Latter-day Saints. If there are errors of omission, commission, or interpretation, they are mine, and I accept full responsibility for them.

It has been nearly two millennia since the bits and pieces of what would become the most influential book in history were written, over a period of perhaps fifty to seventy years, by obscure and, in some instances, perhaps unknown authors. At first glance, the New Testament tells a fantastic tale. A child is born to a virgin mother and is laid in a manger "because there was no room for them in the inn" (Luke 2:7). He grows to resplendent manhood, the only sinless, perfect soul ever to grace this earth; preaches His message of love, mercy, and forgiveness for three short years; garners a few supporters, though rejected by most of His hearers; and then, condemned to death as a common criminal, dies on a cross suspended between two thieves.

Elder Alexander B. Morrison is an emeritus member of the First Quorum of the Seventy.

And then, wonder of wonders and miracle of miracles, He rises from the dead to become "the firstfruits of them that slept" (1 Corinthians 15:20) and brings universal resurrection to all mankind and the promise of eternal exaltation to those who are faithful to His teachings. His message of love and redemption then is carried by faithful disciples to much of the Roman Empire and ultimately to the whole world.

The story of the life and teachings of Jesus and His Apostles—the "good news" that they bring—is the most oft-told tale in human history. It has had more influence on the thoughts of men and women than any other book, inspiring reverential awe and devotion in untold millions for two millennia. It kept light and truth alive during a long night of spiritual darkness and enlightens, edifies, and lifts up the souls of all who read it with pure intent. It brings its readers to a knowledge of God and His Only Begotten Son. It has permeated the thought, culture, literature, government, and art of the Western world as has nothing else. Yet the story of how it came to be lies squarely in the realm of uncertainty, its details largely covered over by the sands of time, tradition, and the lack of reliable evidence.

It hardly needs repeating that the New Testament did not just appear one day in the form and content so familiar to us today. However, within a few years of Jesus' death and Resurrection, His followers began to write down their accounts of His life and teachings and to record or comment on them in their worship services. Thus, the second-century Christian apologist Justin Martyr, killed at Rome about AD 165, wrote of church services in Rome in his day: "On the day called Sunday, all who live in cities or in the country gather together to one place, and the memoirs of the apostles, or the writings of the prophets are read, as long as time permits."[1]

The motives of those who wrote what came to be considered authoritative and binding on all Christians were, of course, many and varied. Many were motivated by pure love and reverence for their divine Master, filled with sincere desire to tell others about Him and to have His teachings considered authoritative and binding on all who believed in Him. Others wished to be certain that *their* views of what had happened, and what Jesus had taught, were clearly understood by all. The intent to protect a particular political or theological position, while denigrating those of opponents, a wish to defend the truth (as understood by the writer) against heretical views held by others, must have been important motivators, along with a desire to meet the perceived needs of an intended audience.

AGE AND AUTHORSHIP

Well-established techniques of textual criticism are commonly used to estimate the age and authorship of New Testament manuscripts. Experts ask whether the literary style, content, and philosophy of the written material are consistent with other manuscripts generally accepted as having been authored by the individual in question. Are the literary style and substantive content uniform or disjointed? Are historical issues (dates, personalities, and events) mentioned in the manuscript corroborated or denied by independent outside sources? Does the work refer to events that occurred long after the death of the purported author? Is the theology in the manuscript consistent with that presented in other manuscripts generally accepted as having been written by the purported author? These and other related questions tell much about who probably authored a given text, or who did not.

It must be pointed out, however, that textual criticism does not prove anything in the sense that a math or physics problem can be proven. At best, it increases the *probability* that someone wrote or did not write something at a certain time, but that stops short of conclusive proof, as I understand it.

THE FOUR GOSPELS

Whatever the reasons they were written, the four Gospels are, by no means, the unchanged and unadulterated words of biographers or stenographers who followed Jesus around and recorded His utterances verbatim. They probably began, in common with other ancient scriptures, as oral traditions—collections of reminiscences, stories, proverbs, and anecdotes.

Most scholars agree that the first of the three so-called synoptic ("see-alike") Gospels to be written is Mark,[2] composed within a few decades of Jesus' death (c. AD 65–70) at a time when some who knew

Him personally were probably still alive (see Mark 9:1). The author is likely John Mark, the sometime missionary companion of Paul and Barnabas and a reputed acolyte of Peter. Tradition tells us that Mark wrote his Gospel under the direction of Peter, perhaps in Antioch, or even Rome. No one knows for certain. Mark's Gospel, apparently written primarily for a Gentile audience, emphasizes Jesus' activities more than His sayings. It appears to have been cited less often by early Christians than were the Gospels of Matthew and Luke.

Matthew, who was perhaps not the Apostle of the same name who had been a tax collector before his call, is believed to have utilized much source material from Mark in writing his Gospel,[3] the longest and most eloquent of the three synoptic Gospels. Some scholars suggest that the book was written ten to fifteen years later than Mark's Gospel, about AD 80–85. Matthew's Gospel contains many of the same accounts found in the book of Mark but adds, *inter alia,* a detailed genealogy of Jesus, the story of the wise men, the flight to Egypt, and (most importantly) the Sermon on the Mount. It was written, so tradition says, in various places around the Mediterranean basin.

Luke, the biographer of Paul's missionary journeys, was, so tradition avers, a Gentile physician who wrote his Gospel in idiomatic Greek, perhaps about the same time as the Gospel of Matthew may have been written (AD 80–85).[4] Luke emphasizes Jesus' loving-kindness and human understanding (see Luke 15), while underlining His role as the Savior of all humankind. He gives Gentiles a significant place in Christ's ministry, leading some scholars to believe that Luke's Gospel was written for an audience of predominately Greek-speaking Gentile Christians. Luke tells many stories of faithful women about whom nothing is said in the other Gospels, including Mary's cousin Elisabeth, mother of John the Baptist (see Luke 1:5–66); the widow of Nain (see Luke 7:11–17); and the woman (reportedly a sinner) who washed Jesus' feet with her tears (see Luke 7:37–50). In Luke's account, Mary the mother of Jesus, and not Joseph, plays the principal role in the story of Jesus' birth.

Though many modern scholars disagree, Latter-day Saints aver that the Gospel of John, his epistles, and the book of Revelation were written by the Apostle "whom Jesus loved" (John 13:23), perhaps towards the end of the first Christian century (about AD 90–95).⁵ John differs from the other Gospels. It was written for a different audience, addressed to middle-class, literate, Hellenistic members of the new Christian community. It contains numerous accounts not found in the other Gospels, including Jesus' conversation with Nicodemus, the story of the Samaritan woman at Jacob's well, and the raising of Lazarus from the dead. John emphasizes Jesus' divinity and His Resurrection, affirming that He is the Only Begotten Son of the Father. More abstract than the three synoptic Gospels, the Gospel of John begins with a profoundly beautiful statement of Christ's status in the premortal life: "In the beginning was the Word, and the Word was with God, and the Word was God" (John 1:1). Some modern scholars believe John wrote those words, at least in part, to counteract the Gnostic heresy that the spirit of God had descended on a mortal man (Jesus) at his baptism.⁶ John testified that Jesus Christ is real, both fully human and fully divine, not a phantom, as the Docetics falsely claimed. John had seen, heard, touched, and broken bread with Him.

Latter-day revelation confirms the greatness of John, not only in the meridian of time but also in the last days (see 1 Nephi 14:18–27). Perhaps the greatest clarification of John's role is the modern declaration that he did not die but was allowed by Jesus to "tarry until I come in my glory, and . . . prophesy before nations, kindreds, tongues and people" (D&C 7:3; see also 3 Nephi 28:6).

THE REST OF THE NEW TESTAMENT

It generally is agreed that the Acts of the Apostles also was written by Luke. It describes the adventures and tumultuous lives of the earliest Christian missionaries, most notably Peter, the chief Apostle, and Paul, the great missionary to the Gentiles, and provides insights into the struggling branches of the Church established by Paul and others throughout Greece and Asia Minor.

Much of the rest of the New Testament tells the story of the Apostle Paul's struggles to maintain the doctrinal purity of the infant churches he established or was otherwise involved with throughout the various provinces of the Roman Empire, in Corinth, Galatia, Philippi,

Rome, and Thessalonica. Thus, Paul's epistles are not primarily evangelistic but regulatory and doctrinal in nature.

Among scholars, there is general, though not universal, agreement about Paul's authorship of the letters to the Saints at Corinth, Rome, Galatia, Philippi, and Thessalonica.[7] Many scholars believe, however, that 2 Corinthians was cobbled together from two, or perhaps three other letters, now lost, which Paul wrote to the Corinthian Saints.[8] It must be emphasized that Paul's letters were not intended for private use but, in a world where most people were illiterate, were to be read aloud to the congregation. The major portions of Paul's letters apparently were written with secretarial help, with a concluding salutation in the Apostle's own hand. This complicates attribution of authorship, on stylistic grounds if nothing else. Many scholars now believe that the letter to the Ephesians is non-Pauline, its author perhaps being Onesimus,[9] the runaway slave mentioned in Paul's short letter to Philemon of Colossae.

The authorship of other letters commonly attributed to Paul, including Hebrews and the "pastoral" letters to Timothy and Titus, is disputed, as is that of Colossians, upon which Ephesians draws extensively.[10] This uncertainty probably never will be cleared up to everyone's satisfaction. Some scholars (ancient as well as modern) have conjectured, for example, that Hebrews may have been written by Barnabas or Apollos, both of whom were powerful exponents of the gospel and well known to Paul. Similarly, many scholars believe that 1 and 2 Peter, James, and Jude also were written pseudonymously by faithful and admiring disciples and attributed out of respect to the great leaders in the early Church whose names they bear.[11] However, it must be noted the Prophet Joseph Smith said that "Peter penned the most sublime language of any of the apostles."[12] So we should be slow to judge that Peter did not write one or both of the epistles which bear his name. Whether James was actually written by the Lord's brother (see Galatians 1:19) is uncertain. But the admonition that those who lack wisdom should ask God for enlightenment (see James 1:5–6) was instrumental in Joseph Smith's inquiring of the Lord, which ushered in the dispensation of the fulness of times.

To me, at least, the authorship of James, and for that matter the other books of the New Testament as well, is of far less importance than the messages and testimonies of the Holy Messiah which they bear. I honor them as holy scripture, the word of God given for our edification and instruction, "as far as [they are] translated correctly" (Article of Faith 8). The testimony of the Holy Ghost, which teaches us "all things" (John 14:26) and testifies that Jesus is the Only Begotten Son of the Father (John 15:26), is independent of who the author of a particular book was.

Paul's letters to the Saints in Thessalonica[13] are considered to be the earliest of his epistles, dating from late in the fifth decade of the Christian era, and thus are the oldest known Christian texts of the New Testament. They probably were written about AD 49, some twenty years before any of the Gospel accounts of Jesus' life and teachings. The spirit of iniquity was already abroad in the Church: "The mystery of iniquity doth already work," Paul lamented (2 Thessalonians 2:7). By Paul's time—only a few decades after Christ's death and Resurrection—the Church was sliding into apostasy, as many members of the infant Church of Christ were being seduced by heretical movements which pretended to give their adherents access to "special" knowledge restricted to only a few, but which ended up dissembling, deceiving, and destroying the unwary.

It must be acknowledged that in addition to the biblical record as we have it today, there undoubtedly are many lost yet authentic manuscripts which did not survive the tumultuous early years of the Christian Church. We know, for example, that Luke indicates he had consulted the writings of many others before declaring his witness of Jesus (see Luke 1:1–3). And in 1 Corinthians 5:9, which it is agreed was written by Paul, the Apostle mentions another letter written previously which he had sent to the Corinthian Saints. So it is at least possible that there are other authentic Acts of the Apostles, even Gospels, which have been lost, perhaps forever. To speculate as to their possible content would be fruitless.

Many scholars believe that in preparing their Gospels, both Matthew and Luke drew upon an earlier document which no longer exists (or at least has not been found) for many of their distinctive teachings about Jesus. This hypothetical source has been designated as

"Q" from the German word *Quelle,* meaning "source." Thus, "Q" is believed by some scholars to have been the non-Markan "source" for many of the sayings of Jesus found in Matthew and Luke.

It must also be noted, however, that all noncanonical early manuscripts attributed to New Testament characters are, in the views of nearly every scholar, out and out forgeries. The Gospel of Peter, for example, probably written early in the second century AD, and thus clearly not authored by the chief Apostle, contains a fragmentary account of Jesus' trial, death, and Resurrection. It presents vitriolic anti-Jewish views, as well as those which can be considered Gnostic. Indeed, of forty-four apocryphal works cited by Ehrman,[14] most are clearly heretical forgeries, many written by Gnostics, or those seeking to counteract Gnostic influences. Only a handful of these works (most notably the Didache, Epistle of Barnabas, and the Shepherd of Hermas) are proto-orthodox in content, in that they represent what became the dominant mainstream of Christianity. It is noteworthy that even in this latter group none survived to become part of the canon of sacred scripture eventually accepted by most Christians, including Latter-day Saints.

I must not fail to mention the great treasure trove of ancient "Christian" writings found near the village of Nag Hammadi in Upper Egypt in 1945. Many scholars believe that this ancient collection of books—found in an earthenware jar sealed with bitumen—represents the most important group of lost "Christian" writings to be found in modern times. There are twelve leather-bound volumes, and pages of a thirteenth, containing some forty-six papyrus documents. The writing is in ancient Coptic, but many believe the books originally were written in Greek and may have been in existence by the second Christian century. They deal with a vast array of topics relating to doctrine, purported revelations, and mystical speculations.

Perhaps the most well known of the Nag Hammadi texts is the Gospel of Thomas, which consists of 114 purported sayings of Jesus. More than half of these sayings are similar to those found in the Synoptic Gospels, but some are very difficult to understand, to say the least. For example, how does one make sense of the following: "This heaven will pass away, and the one above it will pass away. The dead are not alive and the living will not die. In the days when you ate what is dead you made it alive. When you are in the light what will you do? On the day when you were one you became two. But when you become two, what will you do?"[15]

The author, whoever he was, clearly was not the Apostle Thomas. The Gospel of Thomas is widely believed to be some kind of Gnostic work. At the very least, if one reads the book with a Gnostic mindset and orientation, the probable meaning of some of the purported sayings of Jesus in it becomes clearer. Whatever else it is, the Gospel of Thomas must be considered a heretical forgery.

THE DEVELOPMENT OF THE CANON

In addition to concerns and uncertainties about who is the author of the various books of the New Testament, there is not full agreement among the various "branches" of Christianity as to which books belong in the canon of accepted scripture. The authors of early Christian writings probably were little interested in contributing to a collection of "orthodox" books of doctrine. They were intent on proclaiming the "good news" of Jesus as the redeeming Savior and Son of God, and in strengthening, edifying, and regulating the infant, struggling Christian communities throughout the Roman Empire. But it is believed that by the middle of the second century (and perhaps even earlier), the written Gospels, and other sayings attributed to Jesus, began to circulate among Christians and to be used in their religious meetings. The earliest written Christian document available today is only a tiny snippet, written on papyrus and called the Rylands Fragment.[16] It was found nearly a century ago in Egypt. The fragment is a tiny portion of the Gospel of John, dealing with Jesus' trial before the Jewish Council, and includes Pilate's cynical question, "What is truth?" (John 18:38). Authorities believe it was written about AD 130 and probably came from a Christian meetinghouse. It dates a full century before the oldest known, *relatively* complete texts of books of the New Testament, as we know them, were prepared. For example, the Chester Beatty papyri are a group of manuscripts found in Egypt and acquired by Mr. Chester Beatty, an English industrialist, in 1931.[17] All are incomplete, though several are of substantial size. In addition to portions of numerous Old

Testament books, they include parts of the Gospels, Acts, the Pauline epistles, and Revelation. Eleven chapters of the apocryphal book of Enoch also are included. Many of the Beatty papyri are of third-century origin, a century older than the earliest vellum manuscript.

The oldest vellum manuscript of the New Testament is the famous *Codex Sinaiticus*,[18] perhaps commissioned by the Emperor Constantine early in the fourth century. This codex, found in 1859 in St. Catherine's Monastery at Mount Sinai by Constantin von Tischendorf, a German professor, eventually ended up in Britain, having passed through the hands of the Russian czar. (A codex, unlike a papyrus roll, is put together much like a modern book, with the pages written on both sides and sewn together such that they can be opened and read.) This codex contains the Old Testament as we know it, and the New Testament with the addition of the Epistle of Barnabas and part of the Shepherd of Hermas. These latter books are not found in the King James Bible.

Of roughly contemporary age is the *Codex Vaticanus*,[19] a fourth-century manuscript of the Greek Bible now in the Vatican Library. In the New Testament, all after Hebrews 9:14 has been lost. The *Codex Vaticanus* is made of fine vellum, said to be antelope skin, each page being composed of three columns of over forty lines, and is the work of two unknown copyists. It perhaps was written in Alexandria, supposedly under the direction of Hesychius,[20] purportedly an Egyptian bishop martyred in the Diocletianic persecution, at the beginning of the fourth century AD.

The current Christian canon, in a sense, came into existence as a response to Marcion, a mid-second-century bishop's son and a clever heretic.[21] Marcion believed that of all the early Christian leaders, only Paul got it right. Marcion claimed there were two different Gods: the harsh, demanding God of the Jews, whom he rejected, and the loving God of Jesus. Marcion denied any Jewish connections with Jesus and so, in his list of what he considered to be the authentic writings of the Christian faith, included some, but not all, of Paul's letters and a revision of Luke's Gospel, with careful deletion of all mention of the Jews. Orthodoxy began to be defined, in part, by listing those sacred texts considered acceptable to Christians and excluding all others, including those of heretical sects, such as the Gnostics. And, as always, the winners decided what was orthodox and what was not.

But there still were differences of opinion over the books which should be contained in the canon of scripture. About AD 170, someone in Rome wrote, in Greek, a list of books considered canonical by the Roman church of the day. That list provides the earliest record of canonical books available. Seventy lines of this list, written in very rough Latin probably copied from a Greek version in the eighth century, were found in the Ambrosian library in Milan in 1840. The list is called the Muratorian Canon,[22] since it was found by a man named Lodovicio Muratori. The Muratorian Canon lists the four Gospels and the other books currently in our New Testament, except Hebrews, James, and 1 and 2 Peter. It also includes two other books not currently in the New Testament—the Apocalypse of Peter and the Wisdom of Solomon. The Shepherd of Hermas, the Marcionite epistles of Paul to Laodicia and Alexandria, and various other Gnostic and "heretical" writings were rejected. The Marcionite epistles were clearly forgeries: the Shepherd of Hermas, though "orthodox" in terms of doctrine, evidently was rejected because it was not of apostolic origin.

Writing about AD 300, Eusebius, bishop of Caesarea and revered "Father of Church History," considered Hebrews, James, 2 Peter, 2 and 3 John, Jude, and Revelation to be of questionable status.[23] Agreement on the contents of the New Testament canon, insofar as the Eastern church was concerned, was solidified when Athanasius,[24] then metropolitan (bishop) of Alexandria, recommended a canonical list in a letter sent in AD 367 to church members in North Africa. This list contained all of the books of the current New Testament. A papal decree of AD 403 confirmed the canon of Athanasius for use in the Western church, but it took until the Council of Trent in the sixteenth century for Roman Catholics to decide formally on their canon of scripture, though there had been general agreement among Catholics for centuries.[25]

There is, however, no universally agreed upon canon of New Testament scripture, nor has there ever been one. Some churches, notably the Syrian Orthodox and Chaldean Syrian, continue to reject 2 Peter, 2 and 3 John, Jude, and the Revelation of John. The Greek Orthodox Church has always excluded the Revelation of John, and, at the other extreme, the Ethiopian church includes more than thirty books on its official list of New Testament scriptures. In addition to the twenty-seven books in the King James Version of the Bible, the Ethiopian church includes the Shepherd of Hermas, two epistles of Clement, and a collection of ecclesiastical law called the Apostolic Constitutions.[26] (The Apostolic Constitutions, though written in the names of the Twelve Apostles, dates only from the fourth century and is considered to be a forgery.[27])

The Protestant Reformation of the sixteenth century brought new challenges to the matter of what should be considered in the "orthodox" canon. Martin Luther believed that Hebrews, James, Jude, and Revelation could not be counted among the "true and noblest" books of the New Testament.[28] Some Protestants had considered these books to be apocryphal for nearly a century. In short, the idea that there is one canon of New Testament scriptures acceptable to all Christians simply is not supported by the facts.

COPIES OF COPIES OF COPIES

The problems of deciding who wrote the various books of the New Testament, when they wrote them, and what should be included in the "orthodox" canon of scripture are made much more difficult because we do not have the original manuscripts. They have been lost, without exception, and all we have are "copies of copies of copies," as Professor Bart Ehrman has pointed out.[29] For example, the earliest reasonable, though fragmentary, copy we have of Paul's letter to the Galatians dates to about AD 200—nearly fifteen decades after Paul wrote it.[30] We have no way of knowing how accurately the copy available to us reflects the content or the actual wording of the original, although the two probably are in general agreement. With the exception of the smallest fragments, no two of the over 5,700 New Testament manuscripts in the Greek language alone are exactly alike in all their particulars. No one knows how many variant readings occur among the surviving copies, but, in Ehrman's view, they "must number in the hundreds of thousands."[31]

Most of the changes, as one might expect, are the result of human error, carelessness, or fatigue on the part of the scribe or copyist.

Misspellings and the inadvertent omission or duplication of a word or a line clearly fall into that category. Most copyists in the early centuries of the Christian era were not trained to do the work but were simply the literate members of a congregation. Origen, a third-century Christian Father, complained about the copies of the Gospels to which he had access: "The differences among the manuscripts have become great, either through the negligence of some copyists or through the perverse audacity of others; they either neglect to check over what they have transcribed, or, in the process of checking, they make additions or deletions as they please."[32]

But, Ehrman notes, some changes made by both "orthodox" and "heretical" scribes in the second and third centuries were intentional and deliberate. They were, in the main, intended to make absolutely clear in the printed text what the scribe thought he *knew* the original writer had meant, or *should* have meant. In other words, changes were introduced to defend a particular theological position, while denigrating those in opposition to it. For example, "orthodox" scribes felt it was necessary to defend the "orthodox" position that Jesus was both fully mortal and fully divine against charges that He was not divine but merely a man (as taught by the Ebionites),[33] or that He was inherently divided in Himself, at one and the same time the mortal Jesus and the immortal Christ (as taught by the Valentinian Gnostics).[34] These changes, Ehrman believes, were generally not made maliciously, in that those who altered the text did not change it to say what they knew it did not. But they were anxious to eliminate the possibility that heretics would "misuse" the scriptures. In saying this, we must always keep in mind that in the early centuries of the Christian church there were no printing presses, regulatory agencies to rein in irresponsible authors, or copyright laws to protect against the modification of texts. Furthermore, prophetic guidance from the Lord's Apostles soon disappeared.

Other changes probably occurred when a scribe came across a passage, or even a word, which clearly had been a mistake and needed correcting. But once the change had been made, for whatever reason, it became permanent, unless another copyist "corrected" it again in turn. Ehrman notes that in the *Codex Vaticanus* there occurred in Hebrews 1:3 two different translations. The earliest version reads, as

Christ "*manifests* all things by the word of His power," but a subsequent scribe several centuries later changed the word *manifests* to the word *bears,* thus altering the meaning of the text.[35] Later still, a third scribe erased the word *bears* and rewrote the word *manifests.* Then he added in the margin a stinging rebuke to the earlier scribe: "Fool and knave! Leave the old reading, don't change it!"

In a recent book, *Misquoting Jesus: The Story Behind Who Changed the Bible and Why,*[36] Ehrman expands his contention that mistakes and changes shaped the Bible we read today into a very human document. I think Ehrman goes too far in his critique of the New Testament. He brings undoubted intellectual strength to problems of biblical exegesis, but to me at least, he lacks the full light of the Spirit. The fact that there are no existing original New Testament manuscripts, and many variant readings among those available to us, clearly contributed to what became, for Ehrman, a deep and shattering challenge to his personal religious faith. By his own admission, he now has changed from a fervent evangelical Christian, of the from-God's-lips-to-my-ears school of believers in the inerrancy of the Bible, to an agnostic, who does not know exactly what he does believe.

To Latter-day Saints, the Bible is much more than a "human document." We revere and respect it. We honor it. We recognize that it is not complete nor entirely accurate, but hopefully we never forget that latter-day revelation sustains, supports, and verifies the biblical account of God's dealings with His children.

Ehrman cites numerous examples of changes which apparently have occurred in the biblical text over the years. As an example of many, consider the famous story of the woman taken in adultery, found in John 8:1–12 in the King James Version. The story is well known to all who are familiar with John's Gospel. I have used it many times myself, perhaps most notably in my book, *His Name Be Praised.*[37]

It is an engaging, brilliant story, both captivatingly clever and loving, portraying Jesus as both wise and compassionate. But Ehrman contends it suffers from one enormous problem: it was, he says, not originally in the Gospel of John or in any other of the Gospels.[38] It was added by later scribes. Many scholars do indeed believe that the story was a well-known part of the oral tradition about Jesus and at some point was added to the text of John's Gospel. But it is not found in what Ehrman calls "the oldest and best" manuscripts of the Gospel of John, including all the earliest Greek manuscripts.

The fact that the story does not seem to have been included in "the oldest and best" manuscripts of John's Gospel does not, in and of itself, prove the account is made out of whole cloth, so to speak, that it is false and should be omitted. Any decision about what is "oldest and best" is inherently subjective, given that we have no original manuscripts at all. Further, oral traditions based on eyewitness observations have their legitimate places, and whoever added the story to the printed record may, in fact, have done so under inspiration, thereby not only enriching the record with good intent, but also reflecting an actual event and a solid truth which, though it had not yet been written down, had long been a factual part of the oral tradition widely accepted by Christians. This view is further strengthened by the Joseph Smith Translation of John 8:11, to which the Prophet added this sentence: "And the woman glorified God from that hour, and believed on his name."[39] Surely, if the whole story had been sheer fabrication, Joseph Smith would, under inspiration, have discerned that and thrown it out.

There is yet another possibility which must be considered, though neither it nor any other theory can definitively be proven. It is based firmly on the truthfulness of Nephi's statement that plain and precious truths were maliciously removed from the biblical records by agents of the devil intent on confusing and misleading its readers (see 1 Nephi 13). It is possible, though perhaps not probable (and certainly unprovable), that the story of the woman taken in adultery may have been in the *original* manuscript of John's Gospel, as it fell from the pen of the Apostle. Possibly it was removed by one or more malicious tamperers and *reinserted* at some later date by an unknown copyist acting (whether he knew it or not) under divine inspiration. Many may disagree with this contention in favor of a "rational" approach which does not involve Deity. To those so inclined, my counsel is simple. Be careful: the ability of the Father to protect the record of His Son and to thwart the work of the devil cannot be taken lightly.

As noted, most scholars believe it is more probable that the story of the woman taken in adultery, though true, was *not* in the original

Gospel of John and was inserted by an unknown scribe perhaps as late as the fourth or fifth century AD.[40] We know that divinely approved additions to holy writ have occurred on other occasions. For example, during His ministry to the Nephites, the resurrected Christ discovered that parts of a prophecy by Samuel the Lamanite had not been included in the original Nephite record. He commanded Nephi to amend the record, inserting the missing information (see 3 Nephi 23:7–13). Further, Luke included a sentence in Acts, attributed to Paul, which had been omitted from Luke's Gospel ("Remember the words of the Lord Jesus, how he said, It is more blessed to give than to receive" [Acts 20:35]). Thus, true statements, not originally in sacred records, have indeed been added later, under inspiration, or even divine commandment. In other words, the content of the Christian canon has been influenced by oral tradition, as well as by the written word.

Another example of changes in the biblical record will suffice to make Ehrman's point.[41] In 1515, the Dutch humanist Erasmus produced the first printed (as compared to handcopied) edition of the Greek New Testament. In doing so, he relied heavily on manuscripts which had been produced well over a thousand years after the originals. He did not include an account given in 1 John 5:7–8, because it is not found in any Greek manuscripts prior to the sixteenth century, though it is found in the manuscripts of the Latin Vulgate. (The Vulgate was translated by Jerome at the command of Pope Damasus in the late fourth and early fifth centuries. It was "the Bible" of the Western church for a thousand years.) In the Vulgate, 1 John 5:7–8 reads: "For there are three that bear record in heaven, the father, the word and the spirit; and these three are one; and there are three that bear witness on earth, the spirit, the water, and the blood, and these three are one." Almost exactly the same wording is found in the King James Bible. This is the only passage in the Bible which explicitly presents the doctrine of the Trinity, that there are three personages in the Godhead but they constitute one God. As such, it is dear to the heart of those who believe in the triune God, and was an obvious candidate for inclusion in a version "corrected" by a scribe who wished to make certain readers would have the truth as he saw it. The earliest evidence of a change in the original wording of 1 John apparently comes from a manuscript of Priscillianist provenance, originating in North Africa or Spain.[42] (The Priscillianists were fourth- and fifth-century heretics, condemned by the Council of Braga in 563.) But Erasmus did not find this wording in his Greek manuscripts, which read differently: "There are three that bear witness: the spirit, the water, and the blood, and these three are one." There is no reference in the Greek manuscripts to "the father, the word, and the spirit." Erasmus, of course, did not include "the father, the word, and the spirit" in his Greek text.

As Ehrman recounts the story, a fury broke out among theologians. Erasmus was denounced, accused of tampering with the doctrine of the Trinity. He replied that if the text found in the Vulgate could be found in any Greek manuscript he would be glad to include it in the next edition of his Greek New Testament. Evidently, so Ehrman proclaims, someone manufactured such a text by copying out the Greek text and substituting the Latin text found in the Vulgate for the passage in question, translating it into Greek, of course. This was presented to Erasmus, who dutifully included what scholars call the Johannine Comma in his subsequent editions.[43] Interestingly enough, these Greek texts provided the form of the text used in producing the King James Bible so familiar to us today, even though the Johannine Comma is *not* found in what Ehrman considers to be "the oldest and best" manuscripts of the Greek New Testament.

Of course, it can be argued, as scholars such as Richard Simon, the eighteenth-century French scholar, have done, that the Latin Vulgate text produced by Jerome was, in fact, the better text, and that the Greek texts are inherently inaccurate because they are inherently degenerate. As Simon concluded: "St. Jerome has done the Church no small Service, in Correcting and Reviewing the ancient Latin Copies, according to the strictest Rules of Criticism. This we endeavor to demonstrate in this work, and that the most ancient Greek Exemplars of the New Testament are not the best, since they are suited to those Latin Copies, which St. Jerome found so deleterious as to need an Alteration."[44]

It seems possible, even perhaps probable, that an unknown scribe, attempting to provide proof for the false doctrine of the oneness of the Trinity, altered 1 John 5:7–8 as support for the apostate notion that the Father, Son, and Holy Ghost are one in substance, not separate beings.

It would take the Prophet Joseph Smith to provide restoration of the plain and precious doctrine that the members of the Godhead are separate beings but perfectly one in purpose (see D&C 130:22).

These examples of changes in the New Testament scriptures over the years—and many more could be mentioned—underline what to me is an important issue: scripture itself is not sufficient authority for one's Christian faith. To that must be added at least two things: the whisperings of the Spirit—that Spirit which teaches the truth and testifies of it—and the traditions and teachings of modern-day prophets and Apostles. Perhaps some Latter-day Saints do not accord enough weight to the importance of long-established apostolic teachings, though our Catholic friends certainly do.

THE GREAT AND ABOMINABLE CHURCH[45]

I must part company with Ehrman when he claims that "orthodox" scribes, though they clearly made errors and made some changes deliberately, did not do so out of malice.[46] Nephi wrote that someone, or more likely a group of people, "have taken away from the gospel of the Lamb many parts which are plain and most precious" (1 Nephi 13:26) and that this was done so "they might pervert the right ways of the Lord, that they might blind the eyes and harden the hearts of the children of men" (1 Nephi 13:27). It seems certain that most of the changes that have significantly corrupted the scriptures came early in the Christian era, before the end of the first century, when many variations on the Christian message were widespread. There are, indeed, many allegations by second-century Christian writers that others were corrupting the scriptures, and with malice aforethought. Tertullian, the first Christian Father who wrote in Latin and who lived and worked during the last half of the second and early third centuries, wrote extensively about a number of heretic Christian sects, including that of Marcion. Of Marcion, Tertullian wrote: "[He] expressly and openly used the knife, not the pen, since he made such an excision of the scriptures as suited his own subject matter." "[He]," continued Tertullian, "mutilated the Gospel according to Luke, removing all the narrative of the Lord's birth, and also removing much of the teachings of the discourses of the Lord."[47]

Irenaeus, the bishop of Lyon at the end of the second century AD, claimed that the followers of Valentinus (perhaps the most influential of the Gnostics) changed the scriptures "by transferring passages, and dressing them up anew, and making one thing out of another."[48] Clement of Alexandria (AD 150–215)—the teacher of Origen, a professor at Alexandria, and a man thoroughly infused with Greek philosophy—railed similarly against the Carpocratians, another Gnostic sect.[49] Charges of deliberate falsification of the scriptures flew thick and fast. Dionysius, bishop of Corinth in the late second century, complained that his own epistles had been tampered with and added ruefully, "Small wonder then if some have dared to tamper even with the word of the Lord Himself, when they have conspired to mutilate my own humble efforts."[50]

Without going into more detail, it is clear that allegations of scriptural tampering and downright forgery were common in the second century of the Christian era. No individual or group was immune; not only heretical sects like the Gnostics were implicated, since the group that eventually morphed into "orthodox" Christianity was as well.

How then could the malicious corruption have proceeded? What methods would have been used? They include the following:

Misinterpretation and subsequent wresting of the scriptures. The writer of 2 Peter seems to be alluding to this occurring even in his time: "And account that the longsuffering of our Lord is salvation; even as our beloved brother Paul also according to the wisdom given unto him hath written unto you; as also in all his epistles, speaking in them of these things; in which are some things hard to be understood, which they that are unlearned and unstable wrest, as they do also the other scriptures, unto their own destruction" (2 Peter 3:15–16). Those who do so "have gone far astray," as Alma said to his son Corianton (Alma 41:1).

Reinterpretation of the scriptures, considering them in an allegorical framework rather than as literal truths, was another common fault amongst early Christian writers. It was a manifestation of the internal corrosion that was a real threat to the church and, at least by the third century, of the effects of Greek philosophy on Christian doctrines. Such wresting of the scriptures leads inevitably to the rise of men "speaking perverse things, to draw away disciples after them" (Acts 20:30).

Yet another way to reinterpret scriptural texts is to change the meaning of the words. Professor John Gee points out that this topic has not received the treatment it deserves, but he notes that an example would be the change in the word *mysterion* from "(initiation) rite" to "secret."[51]

Deletion or substitution of words or ideas. This is the fault ascribed by Tertullian to Marcion mentioned above. I have already noted the stinging rebuke from one scribe to another, who had altered the text of Hebrews 1:3: "Fool and knave! Leave the old reading, don't change it!"

Forgery of text. Tertullian discusses forged documents, falsely attributed to Paul, which circulated in his day. This practice seems to have been widespread. It is clear that many heretical groups, striving for credibility, used the name of a revered Christian leader to promulgate false ideas. So perhaps did others, writing pseudonymously, though with doctrinal correctness and out of respect, in the name of Peter, Paul, or some other major leader. Indeed, as noted previously, some scholars believe some such writings (such as Paul's pastoral letters and 2 Peter) have found their way into the New Testament as we know it today in the King James Version of the Bible.

The Nephite record testifies of the nefarious role of a "great and abominable church" in taking away many plain and precious things from the sacred scripture (1 Nephi 13:26). Professor Stephen E. Robinson has discussed the nature of the great and abominable church, the spiritual Babylon, which wars against the Saints of God.[52] It is the church of the devil, the "whore of all the earth" (2 Nephi 10:16), which "seek[s] the lusts of the flesh and the things of the world" (1 Nephi 22:23). Professor Robinson points out that the great and abominable church is "an immense assembly or association of people bound together by their loyalty to that which God hates. Most likely this 'church' is involved specifically in sexual immorality, idolatry (that is false worship), or both." The "great and abominable church" did its dirty work after the Jews had transmitted the Bible in its purity to the Gentiles (1 Nephi 13:24). Furthermore, its darkest deeds probably occurred right after the Apostles had "fallen asleep"—by the end of the first century (D&C 86:3). But make no mistake, whether completed by then or not, its work was well under way in the first century. One of the most significant ways the great and abominable church corrupted the scriptures was to withhold plain and precious parts of the gospel of the Lamb, such that important truths were lost (see 1 Nephi 13:32–34).

Historically, what could be the identity of the great and abominable church which corrupted the scriptures? Could it have been the Jews? That seems highly unlikely. Though the Jews and Christians squabbled and fought often during the first three centuries of the Christian era (and have many times since), it simply does not make sense that the Jews, whose record was taken forth "in purity unto the Gentiles" (1 Nephi 13:25), would tamper with their own record. Furthermore, to even suggest that Judaism has the odious characteristics of the great and abominable church is to indulge in the foulest of calumnies against a great people who have been maligned and persecuted by far too many, Christians included. Well, then, what about the Roman Catholic or Eastern Orthodox churches? Even though these churches have been guilty of many errors over the centuries, the answer must again be a most emphatic "no." The Roman Catholic Church, as we know it, did not even exist in the first two centuries of the Christian era, when the great and abominable church was especially active in corrupting the scriptures. Even if we consider as "Catholic" (that is, universal) the church Constantine sponsored early in the fourth century AD as part of a larger political strategy to bring unity to his troubled empire,[53] it is plain that the changes to the scripture had long since been perpetrated. The church was, by then, already apostate. The injury was already done, long before the "universal" church can be identified as such.

In passing, let us also lay to rest the common misperception that the scriptures were corrupted by malicious medieval monks. During the long centuries before the invention of movable-type printing in the fifteenth century AD, in the days when the Bible was copied by hand in monasteries throughout Europe, mistakes certainly were made by the copyists, as already noted. But those mistakes were, in general at least, accidents, the results of carelessness or ineptitude, often the result, one imagines, from working long hours in cold and fatigue, bent over vellum pages, in the scriptorium of a monastery. We actually owe a great debt to those anonymous copyists, who preserved the Bible for subsequent generations and in the process helped ensure the continuance of Christian culture.

We cannot clearly identify the leaders and members of the great and abominable church, though we understand much of its nature. But that does not mean it was not real. It still exists. Its members are bound by one great loyalty—to Satan and his devilish work. As Stephen Robinson has said: "Membership [in the great and abominable church] is based more on who has your heart than on who has your records."[54] By that reasoning, as Robinson has noted, undoubtedly there are people who call themselves Latter-day Saints who belong to the great and abominable church and there are members of other churches who do not belong, because they strive to follow the Lamb of God and aspire to become like Him.

It is most probable, I believe, that the great and abominable church, which maliciously corrupted the scriptures early in the Christian era, was actually not a single entity but a coalition or at least a conglomerate of people who rebelled against God. Those who called themselves Christian but rebelled against the leaders and quarreled with their fellows, who practiced idolatry, who wallowed in mysticism, who could not fully leave Judaism, who betrayed other Christians (as occurred many times and may have resulted in the death of Peter and Paul[55]), and who responded to persecution by craven recanting of their testimony of Christ—those and others like them ensured that the infant church would receive a fatal blow, such that the "mystery of iniquity" would prevail. The deliberate corrupters of the scriptures surely are found among this group.

CONCLUSION

I finish where I began. Study of the creation of the New Testament is seriously hampered by the passage of nearly two millennia of time, the complete lack of any original manuscripts, our inadequate understandings of the realities of life in the ancient world (including that of early Christians) uncertainties inherent in textual criticism, and considerable evidence that the scriptures have undergone significant changes over the years. Serious doubts exist as to the age and authenticity of many New Testament books. Few scholars believe that the Bible as available to us today is inerrant. Disputes continue about the contents of the canon of scripture.

I believe that for too long Latter-day Saint scholars have not, perhaps, paid as much attention to examining the New Testament as they have to their brilliant analysis and defense of the Nephite record and other aspects of this great latter-day work. We have, I submit, been too content to leave biblical exegesis largely in the hands of others, who however academically brilliant, have not, for a number of reasons, brought the full light of the Spirit to their labors. This must be remedied by Latter-day Saint scholars who combine intellectual rigor and spiritual strength. I believe Brigham Young University has a vital role to play in this endeavor, in providing both the rigorous training needed to prepare scholars and an environment which fosters and encourages Spirit-based scholarship.

As Latter-day Saint scholars accept this challenge, they will be following in the steps of and building on the foundation laid by Professor Sidney B. Sperry, who had both the scholarly credentials and the courage to address questions previous Latter-day Saint scholars had not considered fully. He understood that both our faith and our doctrine encourage us to search for the truth. Truth need never be feared: it is our friend and ally, not our enemy.

I cannot leave this sacred topic without expressing my own deep love for the New Testament. I first read it many years ago as a boy at my mother's knee, and have loved it ever since. In good times and bad, it has been as a lamp unto my stumbling feet, a beacon of hope and love which lights my path, a standard against which I strive to measure all that I do. When sorrow comes, it binds up my broken heart and encourages me to forget my own problems and reach out to raise others to higher ground. My soul is stirred by the soaring majesty of its prose and the glory of its portrayals of the Good Shepherd and those who follow Him.

Above all else, from the New Testament I learn of the wondrous Son of God, who died that I might live and who rose triumphant from the tomb to bring resurrection to all and celestial joy to those who keep

His commandments. He will return again, in power and glory, with healing in His wings, to set His people free. Of that I testify.

———————

NOTES

1. Justin Martyr, in Bart D. Ehrman, *Misquoting Jesus: The Story Behind Who Changed the Bible and Why* (New York: HarperSanFrancisco, 2005), 32.

2. See Bart D. Ehrman, *The New Testament: A Historical Introduction to the Early Christian Writings,* 3d ed. (New York: Oxford University Press, 2004), chap. 6; see Bruce M. Metzger and Michael D. Coogan, eds., *The Oxford Companion to the Bible* (New York: Oxford University Press, 1993), 493.

3. Metzger and Coogan, *The Oxford Companion to the Bible,* 502–3. See also Bible Dictionary, s.v. "Gospels," 683. Many scholars believe that the author of Matthew probably was an unknown Jewish Christian of the second generation, rather than the first.

4. Metzger and Coogan, *The Oxford Companion to the Bible,* 469–74.

5. See Bible Dictionary, "John, Gospel of," 715–16.

6. Elaine Pagels, *Beyond Belief: The Secret Gospel of Thomas* (New York: Random House, 2003), 72–73.

7. See Luke Timothy Johnson, *The Apostle Paul* (Chantilly, VA: Teaching Company, 2005), audiotape.

8. Johnson, *The Apostle Paul.*

9. Metzger and Coogan, *The Oxford Companion to the Bible,* 186.

10. Metzger and Coogan, *The Oxford Companion to the Bible,* 275, 574.

11. Metzger and Coogan, *The Oxford Companion to the Bible,* 584, 586, 340, 397.

12. Joseph Smith, *History of the Church of Jesus Christ of Latter-day Saints,* ed. B. H. Roberts, 2d ed. rev. (Salt Lake City: Deseret Book, 1980), 5:392.

13. F. L. Cross, ed., *The Oxford Dictionary of the Christian Church* (New York: Oxford University Press, 1958), 1346–47.

14. Bart D. Ehrman, *Lost Christianities: The Battles for Scripture and the Faith We Never Knew* (New York: Oxford University Press, 2003), xi–xv. For further information on the Gospel of Thomas, see Pagels, *Beyond Belief.*

15. Marvin Meyer, *The Gospel of Thomas: The Hidden Sayings of Jesus* (New York: HarperCollins, 1992), 25.

16. John Romer, *Testament: The Bible and History* (New York: Henry Holt, 1988), 183–84. The official name of this particular fragment is P^{52}.

17. Cross, *The Oxford Dictionary of the Christian Church,* 270.

18. Ehrman, *Misquoting Jesus,* 119–20.

19. Ehrman, *Misquoting Jesus,* 56.

20. Cross, *The Oxford Dictionary of the Christian Church,* 948.

21. Alexander B. Morrison, *Turning from Truth: A New Look at the Great Apostasy* (Salt Lake City: Deseret Book, 2005), 50–151; see also Ehrman, *Lost Christianities,* 104–9.

22. Cross, *The Oxford Dictionary of the Christian Church*, 934; see also Morrison, *Turning from Truth*, 81–82.

23. Morrison, *Turning from Truth*, 82.

24. Morrison, *Turning from Truth*, 82.

25. Cross, *The Oxford Dictionary of the Christian Church*, 1373–75.

26. Stephen E. Robinson, *Are Mormons Christians?* (Salt Lake City: Bookcraft, 1991), 53.

27. Ehrman, *Lost Christianities*, 10.

28. Robinson, *Are Mormons Christians?* 53.

29. Bart D. Ehrman, *The Orthodox Corruption of Scripture* (New York: Oxford University Press, 1993), 27.

30. The manuscript, contained in what is referred to elsewhere as the Chester Beatty Papyri (P^{46}), is dated to about AD 200 (see Metzger and Coogan, *The Oxford Companion to the Bible*, 488).

31. Ehrman, *The Orthodox Corruption of Scripture*, 27.

32. Quoted by Ehrman, *Misquoting Jesus*, 52.

33. Morrison, *Turning from Truth*, 154–56.

34. Morrison, *Turning from Truth*, 156–57.

35. Ehrman, *Misquoting Jesus*, 56.

36. Ehrman, *Misquoting Jesus*, 32.

37. Alexander B. Morrison, *His Name Be Praised* (Salt Lake City: Deseret Book, 2002), 34–37.

38. Ehrman, *Misquoting Jesus*, 63–65.

39. New Testament Manuscript 2, folio 4, 116; Scott H. Faulring, Kent P. Jackson, and Robert J. Matthews, *Joseph Smith's New Translation of the Bible: Original Manuscripts* (Provo, UT: Religious Studies Center, Brigham Young University, 2004), 459; see Morrison, *His Name Be Praised*, 38.

40. See for example, Thomas A. Wayment: "The Woman Taken in Adultery and the History of the New Testament Canon," in *The Life and Teachings of Jesus Christ: From the Transfiguration Through the Triumphal Entry*, ed. Richard Neitzel Holzapfel and Thomas A. Wayment (Salt Lake City: Deseret Book, 2006), 372–99. Professor Wayment is a faithful and well-trained Latter-day Saint scholar.

41. Ehrman, *Misquoting Jesus*, 80–82.

42. Cross, *The Oxford Dictionary of the Christian Church*, 729.

43. Cross, *The Oxford Dictionary of the Christian Church*, 729.

44. Richard Simon, *A Critical History of the Text of the New Testament* (London: R. Taylor, 1689), preface.

45. Much of the material in this section is taken from my book, *Turning from Truth*.

46. Ehrman, *The Orthodox Corruption of Scripture*, 27–30. The Prophet Joseph Smith allowed for both accidental and intentional changes (*History of the Church*, 1:245).

47. Tertullian, *On Prescription Against Heretics*, in *The Ante-Nicean Fathers*, 3:262; see also *Documents of the Christian Church*, ed. Henry Bettenson, 2d ed. (New York: Oxford University Press, 1963), 37.

48.   Irenaeus, *Contra Haereses,* in *The Ante-Nicean Fathers,* 326.

49.   See Morrison, *Turning from Truth,* 72.

50.   Eusebius, *History of the Church,* 132, in Morrison, *Turning from Truth,* 72.

51.   John Gee, "The Corruption of Scripture in Early Christianity," in *Early Christians in Disaray: Contemporary LDS Perspectives on the Christian Apostasy,* ed. Noel B. Reynolds (Provo, UT: Foundation for Ancient Research and Mormon Studies, Brigham Young University Press, 2005), 179.

52.   Stephen E. Robinson, "Warring Against the Saints of God," *Ensign,* January 1988, 34–39.

53.   Morrison, *Turning from Truth,* 109–30.

54.   Robinson, "Warring Against the Saints of God," 34–39.

55.   Gary Wills, *Papal Sin: Structures of Deceit* (New York: Doubleday, 2000), 280. Wills quotes Clement of Rome, writing near the end of the first century AD, who claimed that Peter and Paul were killed out of a "rivalrous grudge."

2

ASKING RESTORATION QUESTIONS IN NEW TESTAMENT SCHOLARSHIP

Kent P. Jackson

Like other scholars of the Old and New Testaments, Latter-day Saints who engage in academic research of the Bible seek to come to understand its context, history, meaning, and application to the lives of believers. In doing so—if they are to do it right—they must seek out the best possible professional training, use the best academic tools, examine the best available ancient evidence, be aware of the best of current scholarship, and ask the same hard questions that others ask. Ideally, this means that Latter-day Saint Bible scholars must master the historical and cultural sources that pertain to the world in which the Bible came to be, and they must know the languages of the original writers so they can study their words without having to rely on the scholars who translated those words into modern languages.

But for Latter-day Saint scholars, all of that is not enough, even if done extremely well. Unlike their academic colleagues, Latter-day Saints have both additional evidence and additional questions, and their work is not done until that evidence is examined and those questions

---

Kent P. Jackson is a professor of ancient scripture at Brigham Young University.

are asked. The evidence is the flood of new information made available by the Restoration of the gospel through the Prophet Joseph Smith. The questions are those that inevitably flow as a result of the bright light that the Restoration shines on everything important—including the Bible and our understanding of it.

Here are some examples of questions that we must ask: Does the restored gospel have something to say regarding a given matter of biblical interpretation? Does the Book of Mormon reveal things that can enlighten our understanding of the Bible? Do the revelations to Joseph Smith contribute to our knowledge of it? Did the Prophet say or write anything on the topic? Is there—or should there be—a Latter-day Saint point of view on this issue? What are the underlying presuppositions of biblical scholarship, and what do those presuppositions say about conclusions based on them? Are the standard academic assumptions correct? And does the gospel teach us anything about those assumptions?

Another way to ask these questions would be to inquire simply, Is there a Latter-day Saint scholarship of the Bible?

I believe that there is, and must be, a Latter-day Saint Bible scholarship, and I believe that in fundamental ways, it must be different from the scholarship of others. The restored gospel gives Latter-day Saints evidence not available to anyone else, evidence that answers many questions over which students of the Bible have struggled for years, in some cases for centuries. Latter-day Saint Bible scholarship embraces revealed sources and uses them at every stage in the process of understanding and interpreting the words of scripture. Drawing from the Book of Mormon, the Doctrine and Covenants, the Pearl of Great Price, Joseph Smith's New Translation of the Bible, and the Prophet's teachings and writings, Latter-day Saints read the Bible differently from how others read it. Given those additional resources, we are going to see things in the Bible not visible to our friends and colleagues not of our faith.

In studying and understanding the Old and New Testaments in the light of the restored gospel, Latter-day Saints are sometimes accused of "Christianizing" or "Mormonizing" the Bible.[1] But in using modern revelation in their scholarship, Latter-day Saints are simply using all the sources available to them, which is a necessary scholarly practice. To consciously choose not to use all the evidence, including the very best evidence, is to engage in shoddy scholarship. And to ignore evidence made uniquely available by means of the restored gospel is to be unfaithful to the Restoration and its blessings.

WHAT IS IMPORTANT AND WHAT IS NOT

The restored gospel does not give Latter-day Saint scholars an excuse to be smug, lazy, or uninformed. The same qualities and efforts that are required for serious scholarship in the broader academic world are also required of us. Nor do the additional questions we must ask make our task necessarily easier. Latter-day Saint scholars, like others, need to challenge unproven assumptions, question unfounded traditions, and demand evidence for historical and interpretive claims. Where the Restoration provides answers, we must rely on those answers and use them in our continuing quest for truth. We need not believe any tradition simply because it is a tradition, and commonly held assumptions are not part of our religion simply because they are commonly held. This is as true for Latter-day Saint traditions and assumptions as it is for those that come from elsewhere. But where modern revelation gives us a clear view—whether substantiating or refuting customary beliefs—that is where we stand.

Some matters are important and their answers necessary, whereas some are not. For example, the New Testament teaches the Resurrection of Jesus in several passages (see Matthew 28; Mark 16; Luke 24; John 20; 1 Corinthians 15:3–14). The Resurrection is confirmed in modern revelation as well, explicitly and repeatedly (see Helaman 14:15–17; 3 Nephi 11; D&C 138:27; Moses 7:62). With those evidences, the historicity of the Resurrection must be viewed as a truth that is non-negotiable, and Latter-day Saints cannot reject it in good conscience. In contrast, and I select this only as an example, neither the New Testament nor modern scripture identifies Mark as the author of the second Gospel. No scriptural passage says Mark wrote Mark, and the earliest existing written sources that attribute the authorship to him do not come until long after his time.[2] Based on circumstantial evidence and the available tradition, I personally believe that Mark was the author of Mark. But I do not know of any way in which the restored gospel has anything at stake in whether he did or did not. Thus, it seems that this matter—unlike the issue of Jesus' Resurrection—is fair game for continued exploration, interpretation, and examination of evidence. There are many other examples like this. Again, where modern revelation *has* spoken, we embrace the revealed information and bring it into our research and writing.

In this chapter, I will examine three topics of fundamental importance to New Testament research—authorship, dating, and the corruption of the text—to illustrate what the Restoration contributes to creating a Latter-day Saint point of view about the origin and early history of the New Testament.

AUTHORSHIP

The four Gospels were written anonymously, perhaps because the ancient authors did not want to draw attention to themselves and detract from the subject of their writing, Jesus Christ. Early tradition attributed the books to four people known from the New Testament: Matthew, Mark, Luke, and John, attributions that are now rejected by many Bible scholars. Latter-day Saints are under no obligation to accept those identifications simply because they are printed in modern translations. But does the Restoration provide evidence beyond that found in tradition and in the Bible? In some cases is does.

Joseph Smith's translation of the Bible calls the Gospels of Matthew and John "testimonies," but it does not do the same for Mark and Luke.[3] Because Apostles are called to be "special witnesses of the name of Christ in all the world" (D&C 107:23), does the designation of only those two books as "testimonies" suggest apostolic authorship and thus substantiate the traditional designations? I think it does, but the matter is, admittedly, far from certain. At the very least, the designations give authority to the witness of Christ in those books. Joseph Smith added these words to the author's introduction at the very beginning of Luke: "As I am a messenger of Jesus Christ . . . ,"[4] giving authority to Luke's account but not telling us all we might want to know about the author and the nature of his calling.

In the Book of Mormon, an angel taught Nephi about the early history of the Bible. When it went forth, "it contained the fulness of the gospel of the Lord, of whom the twelve apostles bear record" (1 Nephi 13:24). The New Testament would "go forth by the hand of the twelve apostles" (1 Nephi 13:26). It is the record "of the twelve apostles of the Lamb" (1 Nephi 13:39). A visionary record, presumably the book of Revelation, was written by "one of the twelve apostles of the Lamb" named "John" (1 Nephi 14:20, 27). Further, we are to seek Jesus, "of whom the . . . apostles have written" (Ether 12:41). In the Doctrine and Covenants, we learn that we are to say nothing but what "the . . . apostles have written" (D&C 52:9, 36), "as it was written by the . . . apostles in days of old" (D&C 66:2).

These and similar passages are sometimes overlooked, but they tell us important things about the authorship and origin of the New Testament: it would be the Apostles' record, it would contain their writings, and it would go forth by their hand. To be sure, these verses do not answer all our questions, nor can we say exactly what they mean. For example, we might suspect that writings commissioned by, or endorsed by, Apostles might well be included in their record. But at the very least, these verses cast serious doubt on theories that rule out inspiration and apostolic authorship for the Gospels and other New Testament books. Whatever the circumstances were of the writing of the documents of the New Testament, modern revelation testifies that it is indeed the testimony of Jesus Christ that the ancient Twelve created and sent to the world. This may also substantiate the traditional authorship of Mark, as an associate of the Apostle Peter (see 1 Peter 5:13), and of Luke, as an associate of the Apostle Paul (see Colossians 4:14).

But what exactly does "authorship" mean? Examples from modern Church history show us that this matter is not as simple as it may seem.[5]

In 1838 the Prophet Joseph Smith began an autobiography, compiled from his memory, his journals, and the records of others. The first installment was published in a Church newspaper in 1842.[6] When he died, the history had been compiled only to 1838 and was published only to 1831. Assistants carried on the work, both in Nauvoo and in Utah, where installments were published in the *Deseret News* until the completion in 1858.[7] Decades later, Elder B. H. Roberts compiled the history into a six-volume book that is still in print today. He refined it with his own careful editorial hand, and it was published as *History of the Church of Jesus Christ of Latter-day Saints,* with Joseph Smith identified as its author.[8] But did Joseph Smith write it? The *History of the Church* starts with autobiographical material that the Prophet dictated to scribes. It then shifts to the format of an ongoing diary, with his journals providing the framework. The Prophet's journals were intermittent. Some entries appear to have been dictated by him, but much of the journal material was kept independently by his clerks, who recorded his daily activities as they observed them. In the compilation of his history, clerks' entries in the third person were transformed to first person, making the Prophet the speaker. Where there were gaps in the record, passages from the journals of others were added to supply the needed information so none of the significant documented acts or words of Joseph Smith would be excluded. One such entry comes from the diary of Elder Wilford Woodruff: "Joseph Said the Book of Mormon was the most correct of any Book on Earth & the key stone of our religion & a man would get nearer to God by abiding by its precepts than any other Book."[9] Staff members added letters, transcriptions of sermons, and other documents in their proper sequence to make the record as complete as possible. Using today's definitions, we would not say that Joseph Smith "wrote" all of the *History of the Church.* But it was clearly created at his instruction and under his direction, and the historians who continued the process after his death were completing the work he had begun.

In 1938, Elder Joseph Fielding Smith of the Quorum of the Twelve Apostles published *Teachings of the Prophet Joseph Smith,* a collection of the Prophet's writings and sermons, mostly extracted from the *History of the Church.*[10] Because this book collected Joseph Smith's words, he is listed as its author, even though he did not compile it and probably never thought of publishing such a book, and even though it first came out over ninety years after his death. Similarly, in 1994, when I published *Joseph Smith's Commentary on the Bible* from excerpts from primary records of his sermons and writings, I was gratified that the U. S. Library of Congress cataloged it with Joseph Smith as its author—150 years after his death—and with me only in the supporting role of compiler and editor.[11]

These examples, well documented and from recent history, show what cautions we should observe when we speak about the authorship of books of the New Testament—which are neither well documented nor recent. I believe that the biblical Matthew, Mark, Luke, and John wrote Matthew, Mark, Luke, and John. But I cannot say how that authorship process worked nor how the final products compare with what the original writers first said or put into writing.[12]

DATING

Modern revelation provides some answers concerning the dating of New Testament writings. Scholars typically date the composition of the Gospels to about AD 70 or later. In the case of the Synoptic Gospels (Matthew, Mark, and Luke), a substantial reason for doing this is that they contain the Olivet Discourse, Jesus' sermon in which He foretold, among other things, the destruction of Jerusalem and its temple. If one begins with the assumption that no one can see beyond his or her own time, then Jesus' prophecy of Jerusalem's destruction—precisely because it came true—must have been written after the fact, thus after AD 70. Latter-day Saints do not share the assumption that one cannot foresee the future, so we are not bound by the conclusions that necessarily follow from that assumption.[13] But does modern revelation contribute anything to substantiate New Testament accounts of Jesus foretelling events that actually happened after His day? The answer is yes.

The Olivet Discourse is repeated twice in modern scripture: in Joseph Smith—Matthew in the Pearl of Great Price and in section 45 of the Doctrine and Covenants. The Joseph Smith—Matthew account is the Prophet's New Translation of Matthew 24.[14] It is a much-clarified version of the prophecy that not only substantiates the account in Matthew but also improves upon it. Doctrine and Covenants 45 likewise confirms the biblical Olivet Discourse. The Lord told His modern disciples: "Wherefore, hearken and I will reason with you, and I will speak unto you and prophesy, as unto men in days of old. And I will show it plainly as I showed it unto my disciples as I stood before them in the flesh, and spake unto them" (D&C 45:15–16). Then follows a retelling of the sermon, substantiating the historicity of the biblical account and its content.

Many scholars, including some Latter-day Saints, see other features in the Gospels that suggest the passage of some time after Jesus' Resurrection before they were written. But the date of AD 70, mandated by the prophesied destruction of Jerusalem, is not an issue for those who believe in modern revelation.

As we have seen, the New Testament would be the Apostles' record of Jesus and would be taken forth by them (see 1 Nephi 13:24, 26).[15] This provides a fairly narrow time frame during which the documents could have been written. After the original Twelve and Matthias, who was called to replace Judas (see Acts 1:21–26), it is unclear how long the Lord perpetuated the apostleship. Although the evidence is unclear, it appears that only James the brother of Jesus, Barnabas, and Paul became Apostles after that time (see Acts 12:17; 14:14; Galatians 1:19), each called before AD 50. Neither scripture nor tradition mentions any others called to the Twelve. When Clement of Rome wrote around AD 96, he spoke of the Apostles in the past tense and gave no indication of any living at that time. By that point in history, it is likely that only John remained, who at about the same time ended his public ministry. Our evidence suggests that sometime near the middle of the first century, because of apostasy, the Lord ceased calling new members of the Twelve (see 1 Corinthians 4:9). If the New Testament went forth in the hands of the Twelve, as the angel told Nephi, then it had to be done while there were still Apostles in the Church to do it.

THE GREAT AND ABOMINABLE CHURCH AND CORRUPTION OF THE TEXT

When we ask Restoration questions as we study the history of the text of the New Testament, we gain a perspective that is not possible otherwise. Joseph Smith wrote: "Many important points, touching the salvation of man, had been taken from the Bible, or lost before it was compiled."[16] He said further: "We believe the Bible to be the word of God as far as it is translated correctly" (Article of Faith 8), or, concisely, "as it ought to be, as it came from the pen of the original writers."[17]

Because the Prophet appears to have been speaking of more than simply conveying the text from one language to another, the word *translated* in the eighth Article of Faith presumably includes the entire process of transmission from original manuscripts to modern-language printings. On another occasion, he pointed out that there are "many things in the Bible which do not, as they now stand, accord with the revelation of the Holy Ghost to me."[18]

We know little about the history of Christianity in the last four decades of the first century AD.[19] The book of Acts, our major source of historical knowledge from Jesus' resurrection to about AD 63, ends not long before Peter and Paul were executed in Rome, according to tradition.[20] From then until early in the second century, we have few historical sources that tell us of the fate of the Church. Without its two leading personalities, however, it is reasonable to suspect that the Church faced significant challenges. When historical sources begin to reappear near the turn of the second century, they show that much had changed in the Church: Apostles were gone, no others were being chosen to take their place, and Christians longed for the old days when the Lord's servants were still among them.[21] In those early historical sources, it is also evident that the doctrines of the Church had changed as well.[22] The earliest known fragments of New Testament manuscripts date to not long after this time.

Jesus and His Apostles prophesied of a coming apostasy in the Church.[23] The Greek word *apostasía,* inadequately translated as "a falling away" in the King James Version (2 Thessalonians 2:3), means "rebellion," "mutiny," "revolution."[24] It is used in ancient literature with reference to uprisings against established authority, describing well what was prophesied to happen in the Early Christian Church, according to several New Testament passages.[25] The Apostasy, by the very nature of the word itself and as foretold in the New Testament, had to be the work of insiders, not persecutors or external enemies. It was brought about as members of the Lord's Church rebelled against the authority and doctrine of the Apostles and replaced them with leaders and teachings of their own choosing.

Modern revelation, particularly in the Book of Mormon, gives a window from which we can gain glimpses into the earliest decades of

Christianity. The angel taught Nephi about a "great and abominable church" that would bring people "down into captivity." In part, it would do that by removing things "which are plain and most precious" both from the scriptures and from the gospel itself. The New Testament, which would be brought forth by the Apostles, would ultimately not go to the world until "many plain and precious things" in it would be "taken away" as it went "through the hands of the great and abominable church" (1 Nephi 13:4–6, 20–29). The angel's words do not allow us to take this matter lightly: "After these plain and precious things were taken away it goeth forth unto all the nations of the Gentiles. . . . Because of the many plain and precious things which have been taken out of the book, which were plain unto the understanding of the children of men, according to the plainness which is in the Lamb of God— because of these things which are taken away out of the gospel of the Lamb, an exceedingly great many do stumble" (1 Nephi 13:29).

With respect to the New Testament, much of the process of removing "plain and precious things" had to be very early, clearly in the first century AD, because we have evidence that the dissemination of the books of the New Testament was well under way early in the second century.[26] The spread of the New Testament, the appearance of aberrant beliefs very early in the Church, the New Testament prophecies of the Apostasy, and the descriptions of Nephi and his angel-instructor identify the "great and abominable church" of 1 Nephi 13 with the Christian church itself, now dominated by the philosophies, behavioral patterns, and people who rejected, and then supplanted, the Apostles and the gospel in its purity that they had taught.[27] In the hands of individuals clearly intent on altering the apostolic record, the first and most significant changes were made in the New Testament text, as the angel informed Nephi.

Because our informant is an angel in the Book of Mormon, we know that the removal of "plain and precious things" from the original New Testament was a historical reality, and we trust the angel's words that its implications were profound. But we do not know what those changes were. And because that work was done prior to the time in which copies of New Testament manuscripts spread throughout the ancient world, we likely will not learn the content of the original New

Testament texts from the thousands of ancient fragments that have been discovered so far, all of which appear to be copies of copies of copies of texts that had already been altered "through the hands of the great and abominable church" (1 Nephi 13:28).

PROVING TO THE WORLD

A common academic view today is that the New Testament is "a very human book."[28] But when we ask Restoration questions, we come to a Latter-day Saint point of view that the New Testament is a divine work that, like everything else touched by human hands, shows evidence of human fingerprints. Those fingerprints, whether large or small, may provide us with academic questions and historical uncertainties, but they do not negate or devalue either the cumulative product nor the vast majority of its details.

Joseph Smith believed in the Bible "as it came from the pen of the original writers," and so do Latter-day Saints today.[29] But unlike scriptural fundamentalists, we do not believe that the Bible is inerrant, even in its original manuscripts. There are many instances in which the Gospel writers relate events differently or record Jesus saying different words in the identical circumstance. Such differences were probably in the authors' originals. Jesus told His disciples:

> The Son of man shall be betrayed unto the chief priests and unto the scribes, and they shall condemn him to death, and shall deliver him to the Gentiles to mock, and to scourge, and to crucify him. (Matthew 20:18–19)
>
> The Son of man shall be delivered unto the chief priests, and unto the scribes; and they shall condemn him to death, and shall deliver him to the Gentiles: And they shall mock him, and shall scourge him, and shall spit upon him, and shall kill him. (Mark 10:33–34)
>
> All things that are written by the prophets concerning the Son of man shall be accomplished. For he shall be delivered unto the Gentiles, and shall be mocked, and spitefully entreated, and spitted on: And they shall scourge him, and put him to death. (Luke 18:31–33)

These three accounts are not identical, and it may well be that none of them conveys Jesus' words with utter exactness (not to mention the fact that Jesus was not speaking English, the language of this translation, nor Greek, the language in which the Gospel writers wrote His words).[30] The New Testament has many such inconsistencies, but Latter-day Saints are not concerned by them because we recognize that it is the New Testament's message that is sacred, not its precise words, and each of these accounts communicates well the same point, even if the words are different. Variants like these do not harm the integrity of the Gospels nor their message. Even the writers of the Book of Mormon were keenly aware of their own imperfections. The Title Page reminds us, "If there are faults they are the mistakes of men; wherefore, condemn not the things of God."

Some variants in the New Testament text are more difficult to explain. For example, the Synoptic Gospels present the Last Supper as a Passover meal, whereas for John, the Passover began at sunset following Jesus' death on the cross. John also has Jesus nailed to the cross at a different hour of the day. For such questions, scholars employ historical and textual criticism in an attempt to determine historical realities and original words. But even historical puzzles like these are of no consequence to the message of the Gospels. Latter-day Saint New Testament scholars are aware that problems like these exist in the text and have no reason to pretend otherwise. Even though they do not have all the answers to explain them, they are not bothered by them.[31]

The Prophet Joseph Smith endorsed both the New Testament's apostolic origin and its content. In his sermons and writings, he quoted or made reference to over three hundred New Testament passages, attesting to the fact that he ascribed real authority to them.[32] We have no record of any authorship issues being brought to his attention, nor of him questioning the traditional authorship attributions. It appears that he simply took for granted the authorship designations printed in his Bible. He said that Latter-day Saints are "the only people under heaven" who believe in the Bible.[33] He stated: "The fundamental principles of our religion [are] the testimony of the apostles and prophets, concerning Jesus Christ, 'that he died, was buried, and rose again the third day, and ascended up into heaven.'"[34] One of the purposes of the Restoration was that of "proving to the world that the holy scriptures [the Old and New Testaments] are true" (D&C 20:11), something that would make no sense if the Bible were *not* true. Likewise, the prophesied calling of the "choice seer," Joseph Smith, was not only to bring forth new scripture but also "to the convincing them of my word, which shall have already gone forth among them" (2 Nephi 3:11). Certainly, if the Prophet's mission was to convince the world of the truth of the Bible, the Bible must be true, despite whatever imperfections may exist in it.

The scriptures also promise that in the last days, truths lost from the Bible would be restored. The Book of Mormon would reveal "plain and precious" things (1 Nephi 13:35), and it would join with other books of the Restoration to convince people all over the world "that the records of the prophets and of the twelve apostles of the Lamb are true" (1 Nephi 13:39). "These last records," the angel told Nephi, "shall establish the truth of the first, which are of the twelve apostles of the Lamb, and shall make known the plain and precious things which have been taken away from them" (1 Nephi 13:40). I believe that among "these last records" is the Joseph Smith Translation of the Bible, which restores New Testament material that was lost anciently. But probably most of the restoration of the New Testament was actually the restoration of its pure doctrine, brought about by means of the books of modern revelation given to the world through the ministry of Joseph Smith. Reading the apostolic record in the light of that pure doctrine, illuminated by modern scriptures and modern prophets, makes the New Testament whole again and restores its plain and precious truths.

SCHOLARSHIP AND CONSECRATION

Latter-day Saint Bible scholars have a mission different from that of their peers in that they both embrace and use in their research the information obtained through modern revelation. They recognize that the New Testament is not only interesting and influential, but it is also *important.* Thus they understand that although professional training and hard work are necessary requisites for true scholarship, a greater goal is true discipleship. Their research, therefore, is not merely a work of avocation or profession but, indeed, of worship and consecration. And unlike many of their peers who set the agenda for religious discourse in their denominations, Latter-day Saint Bible scholars hold allegiance to the Church as an institution and welcome the continuing guidance of those whom the Lord has called to preside in it.

The restored gospel provides a doctrinal backdrop and perspective to our study of the New Testament that would be impossible without it. Through the Book of Mormon, the Doctrine and Covenants, the Pearl of Great Price, the Joseph Smith Translation of the Bible, and the Prophet's sermons and writings, we have a much better view of the big picture of the gospel and a sharper focus on many of its smaller details. By asking Restoration questions that come from our enhanced vision that modern revelation provides, we are able to see and understand more clearly the critical issues that relate to the early history of the New Testament.

NOTES

1. An example of this notion is Melodie Moench Charles, "The Mormon Christianizing of the Old Testament," *Sunstone,* November–December 1980, 35–39.

2. See Irenaeus, *Against Heresies,* 3.11.8; Eusebius, *History of the Church,* 3.39.14–17.

3. The footnotes at the beginning of Mark and Luke in the 1979 Latter-day Saint edition of the Bible are in error. See New Testament Manuscript 2, folio 1, page 1; 2, folio 2, pages 8 and 45; 2, folio 4, page 105, in Scott H. Faulring, Kent P. Jackson, and Robert J. Matthews, eds., *Joseph Smith's New Translation of the Bible: Original Manuscripts* (Provo, UT: Religious Studies Center, Brigham Young University, 2004), 235, 314, 359, 442.

4. New Testament Manuscript 2, folio 2, page 45, in Faulring, Jackson, and Matthews, *Joseph Smith's New Translation,* 359.

5. The following paragraphs are drawn from a fuller discussion in Kent P. Jackson, *The Restored Gospel and the Book of Genesis* (Salt Lake City: Deseret Book, 2001), 59–61, in the context of a discussion of the authorship of Genesis.

6. See "History of Joseph Smith," *Times and Seasons* 3, no. 10 (March 15, 1842): 726–28.

7. See Dean C. Jessee, "The Writing of Joseph Smith's History," *BYU Studies* 11, no. 4 (Summer 1971): 439–73.

8. Joseph Smith, *History of the Church of Jesus Christ of Latter-day Saints,* ed. B. H. Roberts (Salt Lake City: Deseret News, 1902–12).

9. Recorded November 28, 1841; Scott G. Kenny, ed., *Wilford Woodruff's Journal 1833–1898 Typescript* (Midvale, UT: Signature Books, 1983), 2:139.

10. See Joseph Smith, *Teachings of the Prophet Joseph Smith,* comp. Joseph Fielding Smith (Salt Lake City: Deseret Book, 1938).

11. See Joseph Smith, *Joseph Smith's Commentary on the Bible,* comp. Kent P. Jackson (Salt Lake City: Deseret Book, 1994), copyright page.

12. The obscurity of the men Matthew, Mark, and Luke adds, in my mind, credibility to the attribution of the Gospels to them. If one were to invent authors for anonymous early Christian documents, none of those names would come to mind.

13. See R. T. France, *The Gospel of Mark: A Commentary on the Greek Text* (Grand Rapids, MI: Eerdmans, 2002), 35–41.

14. Including Matthew 23:39.

15. For the complexities involved with the word *apostle,* see Eric D. Huntsman, "Galilee and the Call of the Twelve Apostles," in *The Life and Teachings of Jesus Christ, Vol. One: From Bethlehem through the Sermon on the Mount,* ed. Richard Neitzel Holzapfel and Thomas A. Wayment (Salt Lake City: Deseret Book, 2005), 228–38.

16. Dean C. Jessee, ed., *The Papers of Joseph Smith* (Salt Lake City: Deseret Book, 1989), 1:372.

17. Andrew F. Ehat and Lyndon W. Cook, eds., *The Words of Joseph Smith: The Contemporary Accounts of the Nauvoo Discourses of the Prophet Joseph* (Provo, UT: Religious Studies Center, Brigham Young University, 1980), 256. The editors of the *History of the Church,* either from some other source or from their memory of what the Prophet had said on another occasion, added the following phrase, not found in the original transcript of Joseph Smith's statement: "Ignorant translators, careless transcribers, or designing and corrupt priests have committed many errors" (*History of the Church,* 6:57). Ironically, the history of this phrase illustrates the process of editors (even well-meaning ones) changing a text and reminds us that we must exercise caution and humility when dealing with the history of any ancient writing.

18. Ehat and Cook, *Words of Joseph Smith,* 211; spelling and capitalization modernized.

19. The following discussion summarizes a fuller treatment in Kent P. Jackson, *From Apostasy to Restoration* (Salt Lake City: Deseret Book, 1996), 1–56.

20. See Eusebius, *History of the Church,* 2.25.

21. See Justin Martyr (AD 110–65), *Hortatory Address to the Greeks,* 8; and Hegessipus, in Eusebius, *History of the Church,* 3.32.7. These can be found in A. Roberts and J. Donaldson, eds., *The Ante-Nicene Fathers* (Grand Rapids, MI: Eerdmans, repr. 1951); and P. Schaff and H. Wace, *The Nicene and Post-Nicene Fathers,* 2d series (Grand Rapids, MI: Eerdmans, repr. 1983).

22. See Jackson, *From Apostasy to Restoration,* 23–27.

23. See Kent P. Jackson, "'Watch and Remember': The New Testament and the Great Apostasy," in *By Study and Also by Faith,* ed. John M. Lundquist and Stephen D. Ricks (Salt Lake City: Deseret Book and Foundation for Ancient Research and Mormon Studies, 1990), 1:81–95.

24. See William F. Arndt and F. Wilbur Gingrich, *A Greek-English Lexicon of the New Testament and Other Early Christian Literature,* ed. Frederick W. Danker, 3d ed. (Chicago: University of Chicago Press, 2000), 120.

25. See Matthew 24:5, 9–11; Acts 20:29–31; 2 Thessalonians 2:1–12; 1 Timothy 4:1–3; 2 Timothy 4:3–4; 2 Peter 2:1–3; 1 John 2:18.

26. See Richard D. Draper, "The Earliest New Testament," in this volume.

27. The description of the "great and abominable church" in 1 Nephi 13 is in concrete historical terms pertaining to the demise of the Early Church. In 1 Nephi 14 the term is used in more universal terms, primarily with respect to the latter days.

28. Bart D. Ehrman, *Misquoting Jesus: The Story Behind Who Changed the Bible and Why* (New York: HarperSanFrancisco, 2005), 11.

29. Ehat and Cook, *Words of Joseph Smith,* 256.

30. Some of the word differences we see in the Synoptic Gospels in the KJV are the result of translators' choices, not different Greek words.

31. Bart Ehrman's self-described (but not unprecedented) shift from being a believer in the inerrancy of the Bible to being an agnostic illustrates, in my mind, the inherent dangers in fundamentalism of any sort. See Ehrman, *Misquoting Jesus,* 1–15.

32. See the scripture index in Ehat and Cook, *Words of Joseph Smith,* 421–25. See also Jackson, *Joseph Smith's Commentary on the Bible.*

33. *Elders' Journal,* July 1838, 42.

34. *Elders' Journal,* July 1838, 44.

3

FROM CLAY TABLETS TO CANON: THE STORY OF THE FORMATION OF SCRIPTURE

Kerry Muhlestein

It is difficult for us, in the age of information, to appreciate the impact of both the sweeping movements and technical advances that allowed for the creation of the canonized book we call the Bible. We live in a time when we regularly turn to written documents for the "final word," and we take for granted an astounding volume of written works and easy access to them. Indeed, it has been argued that U.S. culture has been the most textually oriented society in the history of the world.[1] In contrast, for most of biblical history, Israel lacked the ability to create and read texts widely enough to be turned to as *the* source of religious information. Perhaps more importantly, the Israelites generally lacked the cultural concept that such would be desirable. If we want to understand how we received the Bible as we have it—not the process of how certain books were chosen to be in the Bible, but instead how it was decided to *have* a Bible—then we must examine both changes in writing technology as well as cultural concepts of knowledge. These two components interact throughout history in a symbiotic cycle of influence

---

Kerry Muhlestein is an assistant professor of ancient scripture at Brigham Young University.

and impact that eventually culminated in the desire and ability to create a Bible.

To truly appreciate this story, we must divest ourselves of our twenty-first-century worldview and instead enter an era in which authoritative knowledge originated from the spoken, not the written, word. While as Latter-day Saints we are somewhat unique in believing that keeping written records was an activity in Adam's day (see Moses 6:5), we can also acknowledge that this was not a widespread pattern and that the Bible was created in a post-Zion, post-Flood world wherein we are unable to trace the effects of these earliest writers. It is likely that early Israel was a largely illiterate group with little access to or inclination toward large-scale writing.[2] The Israelites learned the word of God as it was spoken to them by His prophets.[3] They were not alone in this: cultural concepts of authoritative knowledge in Israel were indicative of parallel notions among her neighbors in the Near East. The mental framework underlying transmitting knowledge orally and the move toward the textuality that would eventuate in a canon can best be understood in light of the technical components of writing.

THE TECHNOLOGY OF WRITING

My intent is not to provide here a treatise on the development of writing. However, a few background details must be understood. First, the earliest writing systems, those developed in Mesopotamia and Egypt, were both based on *pictograms:* pictures that came to represent sounds (*phonograms*) and sometimes nonphonetic concepts (such as the Egyptian determinative, a *semagram*).[4] In Mesopotamia, each picture became a stylized configuration of wedge-shaped impressions known as *cuneiform.* In Egypt, the pictograms maintained their pictographic nature throughout Egyptian history as *hieroglyphs* but also developed into a parallel tradition of stylized cursive representations. The development of the cuneiform and hieroglyphic traditions was likely influenced by the medium on which the representatives were inscribed.

In Mesopotamia, the primary writing material was the clay tablet. Probably the earliest attempts at writing were the use of fashioned lumps of clay on which marks were made to represent amounts of goods in accompanying commodity shipments.[5] The need to keep track of how many units were being shipped, as well as how many were received, seems to be the impetus for the creation of writing.[6] As writing became more sophisticated, the writing material Mesopotamians used also advanced a little. Instead of roughly shaped clay lumps, they created regular rectangular tablets on which they could make wedgelike impressions with reeds.[7] The ability to indent wet clay with reeds leant itself to the creation of the cuneiform script. If these clay tablets were fired, or were in a building that burned, they became hard enough that many of them survived throughout the millennia, giving modern philologists the opportunity to decipher the writing and learn of the culture.

Egypt was blessed with an abundance of a plant type that would dominate the world of writing west of the Himalayas for thousands of years—papyrus. The Nile and its delta naturally grew great quantities of papyrus. This plant could be interwoven, pressed, and dried into a resilient and supple writing material. The process is difficult, yet the ancient Egyptians mastered it in such a way that even today we cannot create papyrus rolls of such high quality as they did in the glory days of the plant.[8] The strips could be grafted side by side for great length, making the creation of rolls a natural part of the papyrus-making process (the longest-known roll is about 133 feet long).[9] Long rolls became the standard, and if a scribe wanted a small sheet, it seems he would just cut one from a roll.[10] The papyrus roll became the primary writing medium of the ancient Mediterranean world for most of its history.

While clay and papyrus were the most common textual materials, other substances were employed as well. Writing occasionally took place on wood (somewhat commonly in the Hittite Empire),[11] or even linen.[12] Additionally, most ancient cultures used stone for monumental inscriptions. Treated animal skins were also used. From as early as Thutmosis III (c. 1450 BC), we have record of a leather roll being deposited in a temple, but leather generally did not survive for long and was almost certainly an infrequent writing material.[13] Broken potsherds, known as *ostraca,* served as the scratch paper of the ancients. From very early periods, we know of rare instances of Summerian, Phoenician, Akkadian, Hittite, Egyptian, and Israelite writing on metal.[14] In general, the preparation of all these writing materials was difficult and costly. However, despite the resource-intensive process of creating writing materials, other factors proved to be even more limiting in the spread of writing.

The greatest prohibition in writing was the writing system itself. In order to write proficiently with either the hieroglyphic or cuneiform script, one had to master thousands of signs.[15] In our age, when a four-year-old is able to learn to write all twenty-six simple English alphabetic characters in four months, it is hard to imagine how restrictive it was to employ more difficult writing systems consisting of thousands of symbols. We know much about the techniques used to train scribes in Egypt and Mesopotamia. Less is known of their neighbors, but we have enough evidence to be sure that the many cultures that lived between these great empires during their days of power had independent yet similar scribal-training processes. Ancient Near Eastern scribal schools were long and intense. Since the primary purpose of writing was to enable bureaucracy to function, and because training a scribe was so expensive, scribal schools were usually state sponsored. They focused not only on teaching the writing system but on producing scribes who could perform necessary mathematical and diplomatic functions. Thus, scribal schools usually contained the ancient equivalent of courses in distribution logistics, accounting, geometry, diplomatic letter writing, and literature.[16] Much of the schooling process involved copying classic works from a variety of genres. Generally only the elite could afford to send their children to a scribal school, and many of these probably dropped out. The difficulty of the courses and the strictness of the instructors is reflected in an Egyptian text about schoolboys: "Do not spend a day in idleness or you will be beaten. The ear of a boy is on his back, he listens when he is beaten."[17] All of these factors combined to severely limit the number of people who could read or write.

The primary purpose of a scribe was to keep records, not to create great literary works.[18] While some certainly did create such works, the mindset of the societies and their schools was that scribes were primarily functional. In such societies, the locus of authoritative ideas lay in the spoken word, or oral tradition, not the written word.

As true as this mindset was in the great and wealthy societies that arose in the Nile Valley or in Mesopotamia, it was amplified in the Holy Land. There, resources were less plentiful, indigenous papyrus was unavailable, and the inhabitants looked to their great neighbors for guidance in cultural prestige. Eventually, eastern Mediterranean Semitic groups used Egypt's writing system to develop the alphabet,[19] which had the power to democratize literacy. Yet this revolutionary process had to wait for some time, for neither the cultural mindset nor the scarcity of writing materials lent themselves to widespread literacy; thus the idea of turning to texts for authority lay latent.

Here I wish to distinguish between textuality and literacy. While the two concepts certainly impact one another, they are not completely synonymous. *Literacy* has many definitions, but for our purposes we can agree that it means one has achieved a functioning ability to read and write. *Textuality* is a mental orientation toward texts as the most authoritative source of knowledge. While epistemology can take into account many sources of knowledge, we generally place textuality and orality on opposite ends of a continuum.[20] This is not to say that textuality and orality are mutually exclusive, as many assume. Many cultures, including Latter-day Saint culture, look to both oral and textual sources for authoritative knowledge. Yet in the end, one source or the other must gain primacy. For most of Israelite history, texts did not hold the primary position.

ORAL AND TEXTUAL AUTHORITY

Biblical evidence clearly points toward early Israel as a society that looked to oral tradition as its locus of authority.[21] Solomon was said to have *spoken* his three thousand proverbs (see 1 Kings 4:32); he and David *sang* much of their teachings and wisdom (see 1 Kings 4:32 and many of the Psalms); the Lord continually calls for Israel to "*hear*" His word; the oldest texts in the Bible are actually *songs* or *poems;* the Lord *spoke* the Ten Commandments to all Israel before He wrote them (see Deuteronomy 5:22; the Exodus 19–20 account does not mention its being written, *only spoken*); and we could adduce many more examples. It is interesting to note that the Hebrew verb *qr'*, translated as "read," originally meant "call out," or "proclaim."[22] Eventually the word came to mean that a proclamation would be read out loud. It was only after a cultural shift toward textuality that later stages of Hebrew transformed the word to mean "read."[23] Very few could read: scrolls were expensive, and only royal courts (when they existed) had the necessary infrastructure to support writing on a large-scale basis. Since frequently these courts were not looked to as the source of wisdom or inspiration, writing was not turned to as the primary source of valued knowledge. That source was oral tradition. This is not to say that writings and books were not important or sacred to the Israelites; they clearly possessed a long and rich tradition of writing and literary ability. Concomitantly, these early and beautiful texts that we value so highly were largely unavailable (both from lack of manuscripts and lack of literacy) to the average Israelite. It is not a question of whether or not any Israelites engaged in writing; rather, it is a matter of where the Israelites primarily turned for authoritative information. Those who would maintain that because Israel had sacred texts it was a textually based society misunderstand the issue; while Israel certainly had sacred texts demonstrating a sophisticated literary ability, these writings did not hold the same status for them that they do for us.

However, this would not always remain the case. Israel's cultural climate in regard to writing changed in a pattern parallel to the rest of its neighbors. While many minor shifts occurred along the way, some time periods proved to be watershed eras in the movement along the continuum towards textual primacy. One such era was the reign of Hezekiah (c. 725 BC). A brief perusal of Isaiah's writings makes it abundantly apparent that while Israel may have looked primarily to hearing the word of the Lord through His prophets as the source of divine revelation, it had certainly developed high levels of prophetic writing. Yet the presence of such an accomplished and inspired writer among the social elite was only part of the crucial setting of Hezekiah's time. It was during his day that Assyria systematically attacked both the northern kingdom of Israel and the southern kingdom of Judah. As refugees fled from both nations, they gathered to Jerusalem for safety. Both textual and archaeological evidence attest that Jerusalem grew rapidly during this time, nearly tripling in size.[24] The rapid growth carried with it an incumbent need for a larger textually active bureaucracy.[25] It has been said of this time period, "The small, isolated town of Jerusalem mushroomed into a large metropolis. Writing became part of the urban bureaucracy as well as a political extension of growing royal power. These changes would be the catalyst for the collecting and composing of biblical literature."[26] This is not to suggest that no portions of the Bible had been written. Yet it would be simplistic to assume that because there had been writing since the time of Adam, the books of the Bible had been written and collected with focus on creating a canonized compilation. The substance of the Bible itself suggests a fundamental shift hinging on this time period.

It is within Isaiah's generation that we see the creation of the biblical books written by and named after prophets, such as Isaiah, Hosea, Amos, and Micah. Before this time, the biblical tradition knows of great prophets such as Elijah only from later records. A good share of the Bible as we now have it was written or collected at the time of Hezekiah and later. The textual revolution that began at this time was not the genesis of all biblical books, but it was truly the dawn of the concept of biblical literature that would guide Israel for years to come. Even the existing books were probably gathered and rewritten or redacted during this phase.[27] The mere existence of the book of Moses attests that at some point there was a substantial reworking and rewriting of extant books. Undoubtedly the rise of urbanization, and its demand for a literate bureaucracy, is not the sole factor behind the paradigm shift that Israel went through, but it is certainly a major factor.

The trend seems to have climbed steeply upward during the reign of Josiah (c. 640 BC). During this time, we find evidence of a sharp increase in literacy in Judah. While we have insufficient data to arrive at a quantitative assessment of the literacy rate, we can easily ascertain that relative to previous levels, the ability to read and write skyrocketed in Judah. Seal impressions (the marks imprinted in damp clay or wax in order to both seal something and identify it)[28] and official inscriptions attest to growth in official use of writing. Ubiquitous graffiti and ostraca demonstrate a more widespread ability to read and write.[29] Numerous signatures of people without title on various documents also illustrate this fact.[30] A letter found in the Judahite citadel of Lachish seems to indicate something of the status of literacy during this time period. Lachish Letter 3, known as the letter of the literate soldier, is from a junior officer protesting a superior's implication that he would need a scribe to read a letter to him.[31] His protests make it clear that even for a junior member of the military a social stigma would have been attached to illiteracy.[32] A more widespread literacy eventuated in a shift of focus from an oral to a written locus of authority.[33] This is not to imply that the majority of Judahites became literate; such was surely not the case. Yet an increase in literacy created a more widespread use of texts, making them a more pervasive part of life.

We can see evidence of this movement in the book of Jeremiah. His is the first prophetic work which self-referentially describes the creation of the text. Jeremiah was commanded by the Lord to take a roll of a book and record all the words that had been spoken to him (see Jeremiah 36:2). Jeremiah employed a scribe, Baruch, who not only wrote these words but had them read to the king, who burned them. Jeremiah again recited them to Baruch, who rewrote the scroll (from its description of being cut and burned, this was probably a papyrus roll; see Jeremiah 36). From this point forward, the manner in which the Lord's words actually became a text was of increasing concern in Judah.

Another example of the importance placed on sacred texts comes from just before the time of Jeremiah. During Josiah's reign, a "book of the law" was found in the temple (2 Kings 22:8). This book, coming from an earlier time and often identified with parts of the book of Deuteronomy, was deemed so important that Josiah read the book— this time called "the book of the covenant" (2 Kings 23:2)—to all of Judah. Everyone present covenanted to obey that which was written in the book. Here we see Judah turning to a text to know how to keep the law and as a focus of the covenant. Lehi was likely a youth when this book was found and read. He and his descendants seem to reflect this view of the importance of sacred texts as the source of authority on the law and the covenant. The literacy of Lehi and his children also reflects the growing importance of literacy in their generation.

It was shortly after Josiah and Lehi that Jerusalem was destroyed and its inhabitants carried away by the Babylonians (c. 586 BC). The Jews were greatly affected by the Exile in many ways. The loss of their promised land and their captivity in Babylon incontrovertibly created a desire to preserve tradition, and part of the process of preserving tradition was to freeze that tradition in a text. The desire to create, compile, and preserve sacred texts, then, was greatly enhanced by the

Exile. Yet this could not have been the sole cause of the Jews' increasing textuality. In many ways the captive Jews were merely mirroring the Mediterranean world. This axial age was a time of textual turning in many civilizations.[34] It is the era in which we see the rise of the Ionian philosophers in Greece. It is the age of Jeremiah and Ezekiel, writers who convey a focus on texts. Egypt also experienced a resurgence of placing primacy on the written text at this time.[35] In some way, the Mediterranean world during this era was transforming its views on the relative weight of the text, and Judah was caught up in the transition.[36] Clearly, the written word was taking a new cultural place. Evidence for this is seen in the books of Ezra and Nehemiah (c. 450 BC), where scribes and the text hold a primary position. Ezra's authority is not prophetic but rather seems to derive from his position as a preeminent scribe. The later invention of the *genizah,* a place where sacred books could be respectfully buried because nothing so sacred could be destroyed in good conscience, indicates the status the sacred text had assumed. We also find an architectural expression of this shift in attitude. While early synagogues did not have a Torah shrine, they eventually adopted this structural proclamation of the importance of text.[37] Hearing the word of God had been and would remain part of worship, yet this structural creation is likely indicative of the practice of reading from scriptural texts as part of the worship process. Whether one was personally literate or not, all would hear in the synagogue not just the *spoken* word of God but also the *written* word of God. (The public reading of scriptural texts as part of worship services is also a practice that manifests the textuality of Christianity, regardless of the literacy of the individuals in the congregation).[38]

Under the Hellenistic influence as experienced by Jews both in Ptolemaic Egypt and in Judea under Ptolemaic control, this movement pressed further forward. Papyrus achieved an apex of availability. The Ptolemies created the great library of Alexandria as part of their push toward literary supremacy.[39] Sacred Jewish texts and Jewish views on textual authority both informed and were informed by these perspectives.[40] We must not oversimplify the issue, though. While Jews, and the ancient world in general, were becoming much more textually oriented, the importance of the spoken word had not disappeared. Oral teachings and traditions continued, and the written and spoken word would jockey for prime position for millennia to come.[41]

ALTERNATIVE WRITING MEDIA

Even though papyrus became generally more accessible during the Hellenistic era, Jewish scribes began to turn to an alternative writing medium. This may have been driven by the sporadic availability of papyrus, which hinged on an ever-changing status as to which great power controlled the Holy Land. When the Ptolemies lost control of the area to the Seleucid Empire, which was often (intermittently from c. 300–80 BC), they may well have cut off the papyrus supply. Whether this is the case or not, the Jews began writing their sacred texts on parchment. Parchment is specially prepared animal skin made suitable for writing. While parchment enjoyed an advantage over papyrus in that animal skins could be obtained anywhere, it was at a disadvantage in that the preparation of parchment was more time con-suming, and the papyrus industry was thousands of years old and held a position of cultural prestige. Still, parchment rolls became somewhat common by the third century BC.[42]

The creation of parchment was made yet more difficult because of Israel's purity laws. While parchment was used for sacred texts, it could only be created by coming into contact with dead animals, which made a person ritually unclean. Hence the tanner, someone absolutely nec-essary for parchment creation, was looked down upon. One example of this view comes from the Talmud, which records, "The world cannot do without a perfume maker and without a tanner. Happy is he whose trade is perfume making, and woe to him who is a tanner."[43] Most texts could be written on parchment derived from the skin of any animal. But because of their special nature, sacred texts were only to be writ-ten on parchment made from clean beasts. Thus, parchment intended for sacred texts could be purchased only from specifically designated, reliable tanners.[44]

As long as sacred texts were written on scrolls of papyrus or parch-ment, the modern notion of a canon was not completely able to gel. Scroll library decisions regarding which texts were sacred could remain somewhat fluid; changes in views of authoritativeness could easily be accommodated by moving a roll from one shelf or room to another. Since each "book" was its own separate scroll, the idea of putting the books in a certain order had no meaning. Scrolls were stacked in jars or on shelves, sometimes labeled and sometimes not. As Latter-day Saints, we are aware of a rare exception to the use of scrolls: the brass plates. However, variations between the books of the brass plates and the Old Testament (such as the books of Zenock and Zenos), and the variations between readings of texts that the two hold in common, as well as the same set of variations in the Dead Sea Scrolls, clearly indicate that there was neither a set canon nor a standard text. Additionally, New Testament writers made reference to texts that they apparently considered authoritative but which did not make it into the canon (see Jude 1:9–16; Hebrews 11:5–27). Undoubtedly there was some consensus on which texts were authoritative, but these were not yet fully fixed. Scroll collections do not lend themselves to the creation of a Bible. Another technological innovation had to come about to foster the worldview that allowed such a collection.

As early as the fourteenth century BC, Mesopotamia and Egypt sporadically used wooden tablets hinged together with cords.[45] These usually consisted of two tablets tied together and treated with wax, thus creating four smooth writing surfaces that could be leafed through and erased with relative ease. Wooden writing tablets were meant only for temporary writing and thus never became a preferred medium for writings intended for perpetuity. As late as AD 50, Pliny the Elder was using waxed wooden tablets as notebooks for ideas, which were then expounded upon and fully written on papyrus rolls. Afterward the notebooks were erased and used again in brainstorming for the next section of his extensive works.[46] But before the end of the first century AD, the idea arose of replacing the wooden tablets with groups of papyrus or parchment sheets bound together in a fashion similar to the wooden tablets.[47] The tradition of sewing together sheets, especially sheets of papyri, gained impetus, and this invention was called the codex. Just before the close of the first century, the codex had become more than a tablet but was not yet a book. While the technology necessary for making books soon followed, cultural concepts regarding the scroll as the proper place for writing serious works yielded less quickly.

When examining Greek literary texts, the use of the codex seems to have shifted toward the end of the third century AD. In the mid-third century, only about 4.5 percent of known Greek, non-Christian texts were written on a codex; the rest were on papyrus scrolls. However, by the end of the third century, 18.5 percent were on codices, and one hundred years later, 73.5 percent were.[48] Christians, however, adopted the codex much more quickly. Of the eleven Christian documents which seem to be from the second century AD, all are in codex form.[49] While there is some doubt as to the exact dating of some of these papyri, and the numbers are not always this one-sided in regard to Christian texts, Christians clearly preferred and adopted the codex long before the rest of society.[50] A number of reasons for this have been put forth.[51] These arguments need not derail us here; for our current purposes, all we need to understand is that from Christianity's early stages, its adherents used the codex for their sacred texts. Eventually the parchment codex would become the standard textual format.

CHRISTIANITY AND THE CANON

We should also understand that early Christians looked to written texts as their source of authority. This was not necessarily a forgone conclusion. The backdrop of Christianity was both the Greco-Roman world and Judaism. Greco-Roman religions are largely nontextual.[52] Indeed, while the Greek and Roman literati demonstrated a great affinity for and ability with texts, they also expressed ambivalence toward them. Ironically, the record we have of their textual reservations is preserved in texts, such as when Plato wrote, "No man of intelligence will venture to express his philosophical views in language, especially not in language that is unchangeable, which is true of that which is set down in written characters."[53] Moreover, Christianity sprang from a society dominated by the Pharisees, a group which had been shifting emphasis back toward oral authority.[54] However, Jewish society concomitantly placed a great deal of emphasis on memorizing and reciting sacred texts.[55]

We can turn to the New Testament text itself for evidence regarding early Christianity's degree of textuality. John the Beloved conveys a mixed message regarding textualization. He begins his Gospel by noting that the Word was not a text but Christ Himself (see John 1:1–14). He closes his book by saying, "And there are also many other things which Jesus did, the which, if they should be written every one, I suppose that even the world itself could not contain the books that should be written" (John 21:25). Here John implies that no written text could suffice in comparison with that which the Word did and which those who were with Him were able to teach. In short, while John had just written a text, he closed it by indicating that the text is a poor substitute for all that he really could tell were he not so restricted by the medium of written communication. This is reminiscent of Moroni's reservations as he finished the Book of Mormon text (see Ether 12:23). Yet not only does John write a sacred document, but texts are an integral part of his great Revelation. Here he was given a book (scroll) by an angel and was commanded to eat it (see Revelation 10:2–10) and to write his revelation in a book (scroll), which he clearly regarded as sacral (see Revelation 22:18–20). He also saw the "book [scroll] of life" (Revelation 3:5)[56] and viewed holy books being opened and read (see Revelation 5:1–9). Non-apostolic early Christian writers also displayed some misgivings about the written word, such as when Papias notes that he preferred to learn from those who had learned from the Apostles themselves, "for I did not think that information from books would help me as much as the word of a living, surviving voice."[57]

Other writers conveyed more uniformly positive views of textuality. Luke begins his Gospel by informing Theophilus that his intention in committing the events of the Savior's life to writing was to create a more authoritative and certain account (see Luke 1:1–4). Paul extols the virtues of knowing the scriptures (see 2 Timothy 3:15–16). The Savior Himself refers to the "book of Moses" (Mark 12:26) and announces His messiahship by reading from the "book of the prophet Esaias [Isaiah]" (Luke 4:17). Scriptural books and writings were often referred to by New Testament authors, indicating a high degree of reliance upon texts. Interestingly, Paul, while imprisoned in Rome, calls for parchment tablets/codex to be brought to him (see 2 Timothy 4:13).[58] Perhaps it was Paul's proclivity for the codex that spurred early Christians to adopt it as the primary medium for written materials.

Whatever the cause, clearly the Christians turned to the codex as they compiled sacred texts. Whereas even long scrolls could only contain one large text—the great Isaiah scroll is about twenty-eight feet long—codices could be expanded to hold a number of texts.

Undoubtedly the idea of choosing some texts as sacred and authoritative had been in place long before this time. However, during the early Christian era, Jewish debates centered on exactly which books were sacred.[59] Additionally, different canonical traditions were developing in Judea than in the diaspora, most notably in Alexandria.[60] As mentioned above, as long as sacred texts were written on scrolls, it was much easier to change ideas as to which texts had achieved authoritative status, and there was no concept of a correct order (other than dividing the texts into the genres of Law, Prophets, and Writings). The codex allowed Christians to carry their sacred texts in one convenient place. The portability and ensuing availability of scriptures was revolutionized by the codex. The incredibly rapid spread of Christian literature attests to the textuality of Christianity.[61] Unquestionably, a cycle of causation took place as Christian textuality affected its adoption of the codex, while simultaneously the use of the codex raised Christian textuality to new heights. The very concept of scripture was greatly affected by the codex; if one is to put sacred texts in one convenient place, one must choose which texts should be included and the order in which they would be arranged. The medium of the codex has a greater ability to freeze the form of sacred texts.[62] In the codex we see the culmination of the process of textualization that would result in the concept of creating the Bible.

Much debate has been spawned regarding the process by which the Savior's teachings came to their textual home. While the only record we have of Jesus' writing was in the dirt (see John 8:6), we have numerous accounts of His teaching orally. Much has been made of this, with some reaching the conclusion that few of the sayings attributed to Jesus in the Bible were actually His, because He focused on oral teachings and His words were not written down as He spoke them.[63] To argue this would be to ignore the developed ability to hear, memorize, and pass on sayings of respected teachers that was part of Jewish culture at the time,[64] as well as to be blind to the developing tendency to carry and use small notebooks (probably waxed wood) by many in the working class that were part of the Savior's listeners.[65] It should be noted that Jews at the time were a more broadly literate society than most.[66] We must admit that we do not know the exact process of how the Savior's words arrived in the textual form we now have. At the same time, we can readily affirm that He pronounced divine teachings and that He did so in an age when respect was concurrently given to the spoken word and written texts. A cultural willingness to freeze the sacred in textual form existed in his day, and the technical ability to easily create written texts was also present. These two facts would combine, shortly after the Savior's life, within the Christian community to lead to the adoption of recording the teachings of Christ and His Apostles in codex form. This form would demand a defined set of texts and a specified order to those texts. Hence we find both the written and spoken teachings of the Lord and His chosen representatives eventually arriving in the Christian canon we revere today.

NOTES

1. Neil Postman, *Amusing Ourselves to Death: Public Discourse in the Age of Show Business* (New York: Penguin, 1985), 31–34.

2. See Klaas A. D. Smelik, *Writings from Ancient Israel: A Handbook of Historical and Religious Documents* (Louisville, KY: Westminster John Knox, 1991), 2.

3. William M. Schniedewind, *How the Bible Became a Book: The Textualization of Ancient Israel* (New York: Cambridge University Press, 2004), 2, 10–14.

4. See J. D. Hawkins, "The Origin and Dissemination of Writing in Western Asia," in *The Origins of Civilization,* ed. P. R. S. Moorey (Oxford: Clarendon, 1979), 131. See also Antonio Loprieno, *Ancient Egyptian: A Linguistic Introduction* (New York: Cambridge University Press, 1995), 12–13.

5. See Denise Schmandt-Besserat, "From Tokens to Tablets," *Visible Language* 15 (1981): 321, 324–25.

6. Schmandt-Besserat, "From Tokens to Tablets," 322–23.

7. John Huehnergard, *A Grammar of Akkadian,* volume 45 of the Harvard Semitic Studies Series (Atlanta: Scholars Press, 1997), xxii.

8. J. A. Black and W. J. Tait, "Archives and Libraries in the Ancient Near East," in *Civilizations of the Ancient Near East,* ed. Jack M. Sasson (Peabody, MA: Hendrickson, 1995), 2201.

9. James Henry Breasted, *Ancient Records of Egypt* (Urbana and Chicago: University of Illinois Press, 1906), 87–206.

10. See Black and Tait, "Archives and Libraries," 2201; see also Bridget Leach and John Tait, "Papyrus," in *The Oxford Encyclopedia of Ancient Egypt,* ed. Donald Redford (Oxford: Oxford University Press, 2001), 3:23.

11. See Dorit Symington, "Late Bronze Age Writing-Boards and Their Uses: Textual Evidence from Anatolia and Syria," *Anatolian Studies* 41 (1991): 111–12, 116–19.

12. For example, the Cairo Linen, CG 25975. For the text, see Edward Wente, trans., "Letters from Ancient Egypt," *Writings from the Ancient World* (Atlanta: Scholars Press, 1990), 211.

13. See Black and Tait, "Archives and Libraries," 2200.

14. John A. Tvedtnes, *The Most Correct Book* (Salt Lake City: Cornerstone, 1999), 26–27.

15. In Egyptian the number of signs commonly employed ranged from about 750 to a few thousand, depending upon the time period. See Loprieno, *Ancient Egyptian,* 12. Cuneiform writing employed from around 800 to 1,500 signs, depending on the time and place. See Henri-Jean Martin, *The History and Power of Writing,* trans. Lydia G. Cochrane (Chicago and London: University of Chicago Press, 1988), 10–11.

16. See Frederick James Mabie, "Ancient Near Eastern Scribes and the Mark(s) They Left" (PhD diss., University of California at Los Angeles, 2004), 346, 355, 375; see also Appendix A, "The Ancient Near Eastern Scribe."

17. P. Anastasi V, 8:1–9. A printed translation of the entire text is available in Adolf Erman, ed., *The Ancient Egyptians: A Sourcebook of Their Writings* (New York: Harper and Row, 1966), 189.

18. Mabie, "Ancient Near Eastern Scribes," 340.

19. See Loprieno, *Ancient Egyptian,* 11. For the date being pushed even earlier, see Steven Feldman, "Not as Simple as A–B–C," *Biblical Archaeology Review* 26, no. 1 (2000): 12.

20. Jack Goody has written about the importance of this concept (see Jack Goody, *The Domestication of the Savage Mind* [Cambridge: Cambridge University Press, 1977]; Jack Goody, *The Logic of Writing and the Organization of Society* [Cambridge: Cambridge University Press, 1986]; and Jack Goody, *The Power of the Written Tradition* [Washington DC: Smithsonian Institution, 2000]). His critics have pointed out, validly, that he overemphasized the dichotomy between orality and textuality (see, for example, Deborah Tannen, ed., *Spoken and Written Language: Exploring Orality and Literacy* [Norwood, NJ: Ablex, 1982]). While these critics understand that oral tradition and well-developed literature can coexist, they miss the point that these are two polarized centers of authority, and that a societal mindset had to turn to one or the other as the primary source of authority. It should also be noted that one can go too far in making the case for orality at the expense of textuality, as in Susan Niditch, *Oral World and Written Word* (Louisville, KY: Westminster John Knox, 1996).

21. For a good explanation of the difference between orally oriented cultures vis-à-vis textually oriented, see Postman, *Amusing Ourselves to Death,* 16–27.

22. See Francis Brown, S. R. Driver, and Charles A. Briggs, eds., *A Hebrew and English Lexicon of the Old Testament* (London: Oxford University Press, 1906), 894–97.

23. Schniedewind, *How the Bible Became a Book*, 48–49.

24. William M. Schniedewind, *Society and the Promise to David: The Reception History of 2 Samuel 7:1–17* (New York: Oxford University Press, 1999), 51–58.

25. See David Jamieson-Drake, *Scribes and Schools in Monarchic Judah: A Socio-Archeological Approach* (Sheffield: Almond, 1991), 79–80.

26. Schniedewind, *How the Bible Became a Book*, 64.

27. As Latter-day Saints, we know that these books went through a revision/redaction process. This is why Joseph Smith would say that he believed the Bible "as it came from the pen of the original writers" (Andrew F. Ehat and Lyndon W. Cook, eds., *The Words of Joseph Smith: The Contemporary Accounts of the Nauvoo Discourses of the Prophet Joseph* [Provo, UT: Religious Studies Center, Brigham Young University, 1980], 256). Of course, many of those who collected and redacted the sacred texts had good intentions (see 2 Nephi 29:4–5). The salient point is that Latter-day Saints have reason to believe that the books of the Bible went through a revision process at some point, no matter how early they were written. This revision process was probably part of a larger movement of collecting and preserving texts, an element of the textualization we are discussing.

28. See Dana M. Pike, "Seals and Sealing Among Ancient and Latter-day Israelites," in *Thy People Shall Be My People and Thy God My God: The 22nd Annual Sidney B. Sperry Symposium on the Old Testament,* ed. Paul Y. Hoskisson (Salt Lake City: Deseret Book, 1994), 101–10.

29. See Schniedewind, *How the Bible Became a Book*, 98, 104.

30. Schniedewind, *How the Bible Became a Book*, 100.

31. See H. Torczyner, *Lachish I. The Lachish Letters* (Oxford: Oxford University Press, 1938).

32. William M. Schniedewind, "Sociolinguistic Reflections on the Letter of a 'Literate' Soldier (Lachish 3)," *Zeitschrift für Althebraistik* 13 (2000): 157–67, especially 162–63.

33. See also William M. Schniedewind, "Orality and Literacy in Ancient Israel," *Religious Studies Review* 26, no. 4 (October 2000): 327–32.

34. *The Origins and Diversity of Axial Age Civilizations,* ed. S. N. Eisenstadt (New York: State University of New York Press, 1986). On the rise of literacy and the increased use of writing in the Greek world, see William Harris, *Ancient Literacy* (Cambridge, MA: Harvard University Press, 1989), 65–70, 90–95.

35. Antonio Loprieno, "Le Pharaon reconstruit. La figure du roi dans la littérature égyptienne au Ier millénaire avant J.C." *Bulletin de la société Française d'égyptologie* 142 (June 1998): 8, 14–16, 23–24.

36. Peter R. Ackroyd, *Exile and Restoration: A Study of Hebrew Thought of the Sixth Century* B.C. (Philadelphia: Westminster, 1968), 7–8. See also Schniedewind, *How the Bible Became a Book*, 140.

37. See Schniedewind, *How the Bible Became a Book*, 198.

38. Harry Y. Gamble, *Books and Readers in the Early Church: A History of Early Christian Texts* (New Haven: Yale University Press, 1995), 8.

39. See Alan B. Lloyd, "The Ptolemaic Period," in *The Oxford History of Ancient Egypt,* ed. Ian Shaw (Oxford: Oxford University Press, 2000), 404–6.

40. See, for example, Joseph Meleze Modrzejewski, *The Jews of Egypt from Rameses II to Emperor Hadrian* (Princeton: Princeton University Press, 1995), 99–106.

41. Even today the television competes with the Internet and newspapers, and we both hear and read church talks, while many alternate between reading the scriptures and listening to them on tape, CD, or in MP3 format.

42. J. B. Poole and R. Reed, "The Preparation of Leather and Parchment by the Dead Sea Scrolls Community," *Technology and Culture* 3, no. 1 (Winter 1962): 14.

43. *Tractate Kiddushin* in *The Babylonian Talmud in Selection,* trans. and ed. Leo Auerbach (New York: Bell, 1944), 204.

44. Poole and Reed, "The Preparation of Leather and Parchment," 17.

45. Black and Tait, "Archives and Libraries," 2199.

46. Colin H. Roberts and T. C. Skeat, *The Birth of the Codex* (London: Oxford University Press, 1983), 12.

47. There is not a full agreement as to how the first codices were originally assembled. See Roberts and Skeat, *The Birth of the Codex,* 26–29; Millard, *Reading and Writing in the Time of Jesus* (New York: Sheffield Academic Press, 2000), 68; and Gamble, *Books and Readers in the Early Church,* 53–54.

48. Roberts and Skeat, *The Birth of the Codex,* 37.

49. Roberts and Skeat, *The Birth of the Codex,* 40.

50. See Gamble, *Books and Readers in the Early Church,* 54.

51. For a summary of many of these ideas, see Millard, *Reading and Writing in the Time of Jesus,* 74–76; and Gamble, *Books and Readers in the Early Church,* 54–64.

52. Gamble, *Books and Readers in the Early Church,* 18.

53. Plato, *Seventh Letter.*

54. See Schniedewind, *How the Bible Became a Book,* 204–6.

55. Gamble, *Books and Readers in the Early Church,* 19.

56. My gratitude to Frank Judd for help with the Greek text in these passages.

57. Papias, as quoted in Paul L. Maier, *Eusebius—The Church History: A New Translation with Commentary* (Grand Rapids, MI: Kregel, 1999), 127.

58. While the KJV translates only "parchment," the term *membranae* generally refers to parchment in a codex form. There is not complete agreement whether this would refer to a few tablets or an early form of the codex. Roberts and Skeat, *The Birth of the Codex,* 63, translate it as "codex," as does Gamble, *Books and Readers in the Early Church,* 52–53.

59. Lawrence H. Schiffman, *Reclaiming the Dead Sea Scrolls* (Philadelphia and Jerusalem: Jewish Publication Society, 1994), 162.

60. Schniedewind, *How the Bible Became a Book,* 196.

61. Gamble, *Books and Readers in the Early Church,* 82.

62. Some have used the idea of a non-frozen canon to argue that early Israel did not exist, such as in Philip Davies, *Scribes and Schools: The Canonization of the Hebrew Scriptures* (Louisville: Westminster John Knox, 1988). This connection is untenable. Concomitantly, we should not allow our distaste for this particular argument to cause us to reject the idea of a non-frozen canon altogether.

63. For example, Werner Kelber, *The Oral and the Written Gospel* (Philadelphia: Fortress, 1983).

64. See Harald Riesenfeld, *The Gospel Tradition and its Beginnings: A Study in the Limits of "Formgeschichte"* (London: Mowbray, 1957); and Birger Gerhardsson, *Memory and Manuscript: Oral Tradition and Written Transmission in Rabbinic Judaism and Early Christianity,* volume 22 of Acta Seminarii Neotestamentici Upsalinensis (Lund: C.W.K. Gleerup, 1964); and Millard, *Reading and Writing in the Time of Jesus,* 188.

65. Millard, *Reading and Writing in the Time of Jesus,* 176–82, 204, 210, 223, 225–28; and Gamble, *Books and Readers in the Early Church,* 23–24.

66. Gamble, *Books and Readers in the Early Church,* 18–20, 29.

4

JEWS AND GREEKS: THE BROADER CONTEXT FOR WRITING THE NEW TESTAMENT

Jennifer C. Lane

When Paul wrote his epistles, he adapted his subject matter to the Saints' earlier beliefs and challenges from their peers. He described this broader context and his message this way: "The Jews require a sign, and the Greeks seek after wisdom: but we preach Christ crucified, unto the Jews a stumblingblock, and unto the Greeks foolishness" (1 Corinthians 1:22–23). Understanding the broader philosophical and religious setting for the writing of the New Testament allows us to make more sense out of the topics Paul and other writers chose to address. In examining the key assumptions Jews and Greeks may have had about the doctrines of Christ, we can better understand New Testament writing, modern-day resistance to the gospel, and the essence of the gospel itself.

This broader context helps us understand the people to whom the Gospels and epistles would have been written. In appreciating their concerns and background, we can better understand the message of the New Testament. The witness of Christ found in these writings came to

Jennifer C. Lane is an assistant professor of religion at Brigham Young University–Hawaii.

people who had various worldviews that created challenges to their acceptance of the gospel. The assumptions that the Jews and Greeks held can explain how the testimony of Christ can be seen as "foolishness" to those who have different beliefs about reality. Recognizing the differences in their basic premises also explains that a witness of Christ will not come with "enticing words of man's wisdom" but only "in demonstration of the Spirit and of power" (1 Corinthians 2:4). In examining the broader intellectual and religious worldviews that create the context for the New Testament, I will look first at the Greeks and then at the Jews. Clearly the scope of this project is vast, but learning some simple points about basic beliefs can provide a valuable entry point into a foreign world. For each of the worldviews indicated by the terms "Greeks" and "Jews," I will give an overview of their beliefs and how those beliefs caused them problems in understanding the gospel message.

"THE GREEKS SEEK AFTER WISDOM"

When people think of a Greek or Roman worldview, some immediately think of Greek and Roman religion and deities such as the Greek gods Zeus and Hera and their Roman counterparts, Jupiter and Juno. The worship of traditional Greek and Roman deities continued through the first century AD. Many additional Near Eastern deities were even adopted during the Hellenistic and Roman periods. But it is significant that Paul emphasized *philosophia,* or the love of wisdom, when trying to characterize the challenge Gentiles faced in accepting the gospel of Jesus Christ. It was the philosophical assumptions developed in this pursuit of wisdom, rather than the belief in different gods, that created barriers to the gospel for the educated.

An analogy from my days as a missionary in France might be helpful. Before I left, many people said to me: "You'll be going to a Catholic country; I'm sure that will be challenging." My experience, however, was much the same as Paul's. It was not the traditional religion that was primarily the barrier. By the late twentieth century, most people in France had their worldview shaped by naturalism, not Catholicism. In other words, most were atheists, not Catholics. Most people's concerns about the gospel message were driven by the basic assumptions of the

Enlightenment, such as "there is no God" and "religion is a manipulative tool." Of course, there were many people who were devoutly Catholic, but most educated people equated being religious with being ignorant, simple, or superstitious.

For hundreds of years in the Greek tradition, there had been growing philosophical resistance to the assumptions about Deity that were part of the traditional stories about the gods. In the Hellenized Roman world, traditional religion still had a very important place, but many of those who were educated wanted to see themselves as being religious but not superstitious. Superstitious, uneducated people saw the gods as fickle and dealing arbitrarily with people.[1] There was also a tradition within philosophy going back even before Plato and Aristotle that can be seen as a form of monotheism.[2] Because of this philosophical movement, the traditional idea of gods taking physical form and being involved in change and passions began to seem distasteful and ludicrous to the more educated.

During the first century AD, there was no one uniform philosophical system. Instead there were several important schools of thought in the Hellenistic world that functioned much as religious worldviews, including Epicureanism, Stoicism, and Middle Platonism.[3] This period, however, was characterized by many shared attitudes; "in fact post Hellenistic philosophy . . . from 100 B.C. onwards was marked more and more by a tendency towards syncretism or fusion of the various schools."[4] While differences existed between the schools, certain general assumptions about reality were common. Many of these general attitudes stemmed from influential Athenian philosophers several hundred years earlier. During the first century AD, the basic assumptions of Plato and Aristotle were widely shared and perpetuated in Middle Platonism.[5]

Educated people shared philosophical assumptions about reality. Because of these views, the message of Christ's Atonement would have been difficult to believe. Paul noted that "the Jews require a sign, and the Greeks seek after wisdom." In contrast, he said that as Christians, "we preach Christ crucified." This declaration of the crucified and risen Lord was, according to Paul, "unto the Greeks foolishness" (1 Corinthians 1:22–23). There were some general attitudes about reality that would have made the gospel message sound foolish to those who shared the worldview of Greek philosophy. The two most significant areas were the prejudice against divine embodiment and Resurrection as seen in Platonic dualism and the prejudice against divine changeability or suffering that can be seen in Aristotle's "Unmoved Mover."

It has been suggested that "the belief in the resurrection of the body" was "possibly the strangest Christian tenet to pagan ears."[6] The prejudice against divine embodiment and Resurrection stemmed from attitudes toward the body that are known as Platonic dualism. In Plato's writings, the soul was seen as radically different from the body, and embodiment could be characterized as a prison. These attitudes are clearly articulated in Plato's Socratic dialogue *Phaedo,* in which he portrays Socrates' discussion before his death. I will first show how these ideas about the body are seen in Plato's writing and then illustrate how this belief created a context for the New Testament.

Plato portrays the ideal human as "entirely concerned with the soul and not with the body. . . . He would like, as far as he can, to be quit of the body and turn to the soul."[7] The body is seen as diminishing the soul's capacity because "the body introduces a turmoil and confusion and fear into the course of speculation, and hinders us from seeing the truth; and all experience shows that if we would have pure knowledge of anything we must be quit of the body, and the soul in herself must behold all things in themselves: then, I suppose, that we shall attain that which we desire, and of which we say that we are lovers, and that is wisdom."[8]

Hope for human beings was in being rid of the body after this life when "the foolishness of the body will be cleared away and we shall be pure and hold converse with other pure souls, and know of ourselves the clear light everywhere; and this is surely the light of truth. For no impure thing is allowed to approach the pure."[9] The body was seen as part of what made the soul impure. Thus, "what is purification but the separation of the soul from the body, . . . the release of the soul from the chains of the body?"[10] The general prejudice against the idea of Resurrection in the Greek world was so widespread and influential, even among the Jews, that "many Diaspora Jews rejected this form of post-mortal hope and espoused a Hellenistic hope in the immortality of the soul."[11]

The influence of the worldview of Platonic dualism in shaping the broader context for the New Testament can be seen in New Testament writings that reaffirm Christ's bodily incarnation, suffering, and Resurrection. A pointed example is found in 1 John 4:2–3: "Hereby know ye the Spirit of God: every spirit that confesseth that Jesus Christ is come in the flesh is of God: and every spirit that confesseth not that Jesus Christ is come in the flesh is not of God: and this is that spirit of antichrist, whereof ye have heard that it should come; and even now already is it in the world." The forcefulness of this clarification highlights the strength of the challenge of docetism, or the view that Christ, being divine, could not have had a physical body.[12]

Additional evidence for Platonic dualism in shaping the context for the New Testament can be found in the writings of Celsus, a Platonist arguing against Christian belief around AD 177–80. Sharing the basic premise of educated people, he maintained that "the soul is God's work, but the nature of the body is different."[13] Since the body was antithetical to God's nature, the idea of the incarnation and the Resurrection were against reason.[14] Celsus spoke against the incarnation, saying that God would not "thrust his own spirit into such foul pollution."[15] Likewise, the idea of Christ's Resurrection seemed foolish: "Jesus could not have risen with his body; for God would not have received back the spirit which he gave after it had been defiled by the nature of the body."[16] The basic assumptions of the educated within the Greek world made the declaration of the crucified and risen Christ seem as foolishness. It is important to remember that this perception grew out of widely shared assumptions about reality. As one scholar concluded, "Pagan disgust at Christian preaching of resurrection of the body is propelled by a set of convictions about God as reason, and spirit, and by an attitude towards the body as inferior matter. Resurrection is just one more of the more dramatic and disdainful examples of Christian credulity, ignorance, arrogance, and mistaken understandings of God and nature."[17]

In addition to the prejudice against divine embodiment and Resurrection, there was also a built-in bias against the idea of divine changeability or suffering. In Book 12 (Lambda) of the *Metaphysics,* Aristotle explains the nature of the Supreme Being, his "Unmoved Mover." This ultimate God is both unmovable and the source of all other movement. He says, "The first principle or primary being is not movable either in itself or accidentally, but produces the primary eternal and single movement."[18]

These deep-seated assumptions about the nature of God go back to the pre-Socratic philosophers. Parmenides, living in the fifth century BC, laid the groundwork for this belief, stating that "being is ungenerated and imperishable, whole, unique, immovable and complete."[19] Even before Aristotle's influential development of the Unmoved Mover, Plato upheld the idea of divine impassibility (God's inability to suffer or feel pain).[20] In fact, in the *Phaedo,* where Plato develops the idea of the body as a prison, he also emphasizes the ideal quality of changelessness: "Absolute equality, absolute beauty, any absolute existence, true being—do they ever admit of any change whatsoever? Or does each absolute essence, since it is uniform and exists by itself, remain the same and never in any way admit of any change?"[21] For Plato, "the realm of the soul is the pure, everlasting, immortal, and changeless."[22]

During the first century AD, Middle Platonists focused on the implications of God being unchangeable and unmovable.[23] The wide esteem in which being unmovable was held in the philosophical world can also be seen in Stoicism. For the Stoics, *apatheia,* or passionlessness, was the highest human virtue. They believed that "since the human soul is a part of the Divine Reason or God, . . . the principle goal of an individual is the pursuit of virtue. . . . The virtuous individual is one who has attained inner discipline by controlling all emotions and passions and, if possible, eradicating them completely."[24]

These views about the divine being unmovable or impassible can be seen in the shock of Celsus, the anti-Christian Platonist, at the implications of the incarnation and suffering of Christ. He shares the views of the educated in saying that "God is good and beautiful and happy, and exists in the most beautiful state. If then He comes down to men, He must undergo change, a change from good to bad, from beautiful to shameful, from happiness to misfortune, and from what is best to what is most wicked. Who would choose a change like this? It is the nature only of a mortal being to undergo change and remoulding, whereas it is the nature of an immortal being to remain the same without alteration. Accordingly, God could not be capable of undergoing this change."[25] The idea that Jesus, being God, could "serve as a slave and be sick and die" seems to him as "wicked and impious."[26] Thus, he rejects Old Testament messianic prophecy as foolish: "It would be impossible to believe in the predictions that He should suffer and do these things."[27]

The idea of God being capable of any kind of change was an affront to basic assumptions of educated people of this era. This reservation was related to the concerns about Christ's embodiment and Resurrection. How could a divine being undergo this kind of change? The sharp reaction to this doctrine can be seen when Paul taught in Athens. His teaching seemed to be well received, but "when they heard of the resurrection of the dead, some mocked" (Acts 17:32). It was precisely to avoid being mocked that some early Christians taught the idea of a spiritual resurrection. Orthodox Christianity did maintain a belief in the resurrection of the body, yet because Christian apologists moved toward characterizing God as impassible, this became part of the creeds. Of course, the Christians had to reconcile Christ's suffering and death with their belief in the impassibility of God, which was a source of debate and division.[28]

"THE JEWS REQUIRE A SIGN"

While the phrase "seeking after wisdom" characterizes Greek philosophy of the Hellenistic-Roman era, the Jewish worldview can be summed up in the phrase "the Jews require a sign." It is true that *sign* has also been translated in other versions of the Bible as "miraculous signs"[29] or "miracles."[30] However, the basic meaning of the Greek word *sēmeion* is "the sign or distinguishing mark by which someth[ing] is known," which could also be rendered as token or indication.[31] This meaning of *sign* more clearly describes the focus of intertestamental Judaism. In saying that "the Jews require a sign," Paul is describing the Jews' focus on outward performances that indicate faithfulness to God.

Just as there were various ways of being a philosopher in the first century, there were also various ways of being a Jew. Different groups, comprising "sectarian" or intertestamental Judaism, had all developed in response to the Hellenistic context of their world. These groups included the Pharisees, Sadducees, and Essenes. While they had competing visions for the true form of Israelite religion in the Second Temple period, they also shared some beliefs. This is not to suggest that there was a standard form of Judaism at this time but that each of these forms of Judaism was drawing upon the Torah as establishing what God had commanded. These commandments were not limited to "signs" or outward performances; however, obedience to certain commandments was generally seen as required to be pleasing unto God.

All of these groups of Jews, even though taking different approaches, sought to keep the faith in an alien world. Most Jews, however, were not allied with any of these groups. The general population was known as the 'am ha-'aretz, or "people of the land." Their level of understanding and commitment to the outward signs of obedience to God's law found in the Torah included circumcision, Sabbath observance, and participation in other rituals such as temple festivals. Some scholars today describe them as "liv[ing] faithfully according to the Law" and being generally observant.[32] The Pharisees and other groups saw these "people of the land" as unreligious, ritually impure, and little different from Gentiles.[33] Other groups, such as the Dead Sea Scrolls sect or Qumran Community, viewed most Jews, including the Pharisees, as failing to live up to the demands of the Torah and as being in apostasy.[34] As we will see, however, all of these groups adhered to outward signs as a measure of their faithfulness, a practice which directly affected their perception of the preaching of the Christian gospel.

Paul observed that "the Jews require a sign, and the Greeks seek after wisdom." In contrast, he said Christians "preach Christ crucified." Believing that Christ is the source of hope and confidence before God was, according to Paul, "unto the Jews a stumblingblock" (1 Corinthians 1:22–23). Examining the general attitudes about reality shared by the Jews helps us understand why the gospel message would have been a stumbling block to them.

First, the key shared concept for the Jews was that God chose Israel as His covenant people and gave the Israelites His law. The five books of Moses, known as the Torah, had a very important role in establishing the expectations for Jewish life, providing a shared sense of God's requirements and relationship with His covenant people. Jews did not agree uniformly about what constituted God's revelation. Some groups, such as the Sadducees, may not have accepted the Prophets and Writings that now are included in the Hebrew Bible.[35] Other Jews had a broader sense of revelations and covenants, as is seen in the pseudepigraphical writings and the Dead Sea Scrolls.[36] In addition, the Pharisees believed in a divinely given oral tradition known in the New Testament as the "tradition of the elders."[37] For all these groups, the Torah provided a collective foundation for God's covenant expectations and promises.

Expectations include circumcision, food purity laws, Sabbath observance, and temple festivals. New Testament scholars debate whether Judaism saw this obedience to the law as a way to gain merit through works or whether adherence to these "works of the law" simply functioned as a way to stay within the election of Israel.[38] Other lines of scholarship emphasize the alternate voices within Judaism that saw the people as a whole as not living up to the covenant requirements.[39] Most scholars, however, would agree that all these forms of Judaism saw themselves as having God's law and being His people, although there was internal debate as to who was living up to what they were given.

The general expectations regarding the biblical requirements of circumcision and food purity can be seen in the beliefs of those who criticized their contemporaries for their perceived laxness in obedience. As was mentioned before, some of the sects of this era had stricter standards than the less educated, who were, according to Calvin Roetzel, "not as scrupulous as others in observing some commandments (especially the laws of purity), and they were ignorant of much of the content of the Torah and shunned its study."[40] Thus, the common people "were doubtless shunned and ridiculed by those who were scrupulous about the laws of purity, observing the tithe and the study of the Torah, namely the Pharisees, Sadducees, and Essenes."[41]

Those who sought to raise the standard for holiness in intertestamental Judaism focused on the observance of the law of Moses, what we might call "requiring a sign." No longer having prophets, the Jews drew upon what they had in scripture as standards and resources to keep themselves separate from the encroachment of Hellenization.[42] An example of this desire to "raise the bar" in efforts to live a holy life can be seen in concerns about circumcision.

The pseudepigraphical book *Jubilees,* dated to the second century BC, states that Israel was not living up to the conditions of the covenantal promise by not properly performing circumcision: "They will not circumcise their sons according to all of this law because some of the flesh of their circumcision they will leave in the circumcision of their sons. And all of the sons of Beliar will leave their sons without circumcising just as they were born. And great wrath from the Lord will be upon the sons of Israel because they have left his covenant and turned aside from his words."[43] The writers of *Jubilees* saw the Jews of their day as being in "an epidemic of malpractice."[44] Their failures to keep the law were understood as neglecting to circumcise altogether, as not being careful to circumcise on the eighth day, or as circumcising in a way that would cut away "less flesh than was normal—a style apparently adopted and preferred during the Hellenistic period in order to help conceal the marks of circumcision."[45] The "works of the law," or the signs of the covenant, were constantly being challenged by the cultural context in which Jews lived.

We can appreciate the importance of circumcision as a sign of the covenant when we realize its place within God's relationship with Abraham: "And God said unto Abraham, Thou shalt keep my covenant therefore, thou, and thy seed after thee in their generations. This is my covenant, which ye shall keep, between me and you and thy seed after thee; every man child among you shall be circumcised. And ye shall circumcise the flesh of your foreskin; and it shall be a token of the covenant betwixt me and you" (Genesis 17:9–11). Paul's writings make it clear that the Jews' emphasis on the signs of the covenant was a very important part of the context for the writing of the New Testament.

Circumcision and other signs of the covenant were major issues that Paul had to address. He taught the Saints at Corinth: "Is any man called being circumcised? let him not become uncircumcised. Is any called in uncircumcision? let him not be circumcised. Circumcision is nothing, and uncircumcision is nothing, but the keeping of the commandments of God" (1 Corinthians 7:18–19). His message was that their whole understanding of how to please God had to be revised: "If ye be circumcised, Christ shall profit you nothing. For I testify again to every man that is circumcised, that he is a debtor to do the whole law" (Galatians 5:2–3). Thus, to many Jews, the message of "Christ crucified" became a stumbling block because it meant that the signs of the covenant were no longer required.

Accepting the gospel message of salvation through the Atonement of Christ required accepting that older requirements could be superseded. Jews did not need to deny that God had given the law of Moses, but the new and challenging message was that the law had been fulfilled in Christ. The questions Paul was asked about the need to circumcise and keep food purity regulations shows the Jews' struggles with the new law. In Acts and the epistles, we can see widespread concern with circumcision and food-purity as signs of the covenant (see Acts 10; 15; 21; Romans 14; 1 Corinthians 8). These Jewish beliefs were an important part of the broader context for the writing of the New Testament. Thus, these issues are essential in understanding the Apostles' efforts to strengthen and clarify the faith of early Church members.

"BUT WE PREACH CHRIST CRUCIFIED"

As we reflect on how important the worldviews of the Greeks and the Jews were in shaping the way they viewed the gospel of Christ, we can appreciate how the broader context of the New Testament sharpened the focus on testifying of Christ. In this contemporary context, the message of the cross of Christ was either foolishness or a stumblingblock. For many Greeks, the logical conclusion of their assumptions was that God could not and would not take on a mortal body, suffer, and then be resurrected. For many Jews, the logical conclusion of their assumptions was that God had already declared the terms of salvation through the Torah and that there was no need for any further revelation. Paul and other New Testament authors could not through logic persuade either Greeks or Jews of the truthfulness of the gospel, because their audience was starting with completely different ideas about the nature and revelation of God. Instead, as Paul explains, the testimony of Christ's Atonement had to be given and received "not with enticing words of man's wisdom, but in demonstration of the Spirit and of power" (1 Corinthians 2:4).

Given these basic prejudices working against him, Paul had to stand his ground and focus on the essentials. He commented, "For I determined not to know any thing among you, save Jesus Christ, and him crucified" (1 Corinthians 2:2). Everything else was peripheral, and every audience needed to understand the message of the Atonement of Christ.

In our day, barriers in teaching how to receive the blessings of Christ's Atonement through His restored Church are similar to earlier ones faced by Paul and other New Testament writers. Like the challenge of the Greeks, some concerns grow out of philosophical reservations. Like the difficulty for the Jews, some hesitations grow out of religious traditions. In the contemporary world, the philosophical reservations are primarily those of naturalism. This worldview developed along with the ability of science to explain natural phenomena without needing to refer to divine causation. Starting in the Scientific Revolution of the seventeenth century and being developed during the Enlightenment of the eighteenth century, basic premises about reality began to be accepted among the educated. With time these have gradually become widely available and influential. These assumptions describe a reality that operates in entirely naturalistic or materialist terms. In this worldview, there are no miracles and thus no resurrection or vicarious atonement.

Those who do not share all the assumptions of naturalism hold on to many different religious traditions. Many share a faith that God acts in history and works miracles in the lives of believers. With many other religious people worldwide, we believe that there is meaning and purpose to life. The specifics of the nature of God, our relationship to Him, and what He requires of us are not, however, uniformly shared. Whether we are talking about non-Christian religious traditions such as Judaism, Islam, Hinduism, Buddhism, or various forms of Christianity, there are great challenges in presenting the message of the gospel. Like the Jews of Paul's time, people within each of these traditions will have reservations about the message of the Restoration based on their own tradition. The message of the restored gospel can be a stumbling block given the assumptions they are starting with. Genuinely religious people may have felt divine influence in their lives, and they will already have assumptions about what God requires based on what they were taught in their own traditions. Unlike the challenge of the philosophically minded, it is not a lack of faith in revelation that can be a stumblingblock to the believers. Instead, it is the idea that revelation continues.

As Latter-day Saints living in a world much like the world of the New Testament, we can learn from how Paul responded to the broader context in which he found himself in his efforts to build the kingdom of God. While both Jew and Gentile had barriers to accepting the message of the gospel, Paul was undaunted and focused. Like him, we too can declare: "For I determined not to know any thing among you, save Jesus Christ, and him crucified" (1 Corinthians 1:2). From the broader context of the writing of the New Testament, we can learn the importance of keeping our focus on the essential message of the gospel. All testifies of the Atonement—modern-day prophets, additional scripture, priesthood restored, temple ordinances, work for the dead, the importance of families, and the hope they can be together forever. Each aspect of our witness to the world stems from the power of the Atonement of Jesus Christ.

Rather than trying to preach the gospel in the "wisdom of words" (1 Corinthians 1:17), we can know there is another path, the one taught by Paul and reemphasized in our day. The witness of Christ is given and received "not with enticing words of man's wisdom, but in demonstration of the Spirit and of power" (1 Corinthians 2:4). Just as in Paul's day, Church members today come from many backgrounds. They had many different assumptions about reality before they joined the Church. But the Holy Ghost's testimony of the divinity of Christ and this work was enough to overcome whatever philosophical or religious reservations they may have held previously. This is the only sure foundation for us in living the gospel and sharing the gospel. As Paul taught, "My speech and my preaching was not with enticing words of man's wisdom, but in demonstration of the Spirit and of power: That your

faith should not stand in the wisdom of men, but in the power of God"
(1 Corinthians 2:4−5).

NOTES

1. These attitudes can be seen in *On Superstition,* usually attributed to Greek
philosopher Plutarch (AD 50−120). See Robert Wilken, *The Christians as the Romans
Saw Them* (New Haven, CT: Yale University Press, 1984), 60−62.

2. Many people will refer to this line of thought as monarchy, in the sense that
the existence of a Supreme Being did not necessarily mean that there were no
other gods. These questions are developed in Frede. He notes that "the Platonists,
the Peripatetics, and the Stoics do not just believe in one highest god, they believe
in something which they must take to be unique even as a god. For they call it
'God' or even '*the* God,' as if in some crucial way it was the only thing which
deserved to be called 'god'" (Michael Frede, "Monotheism and Pagan Philosophy
in Later Antiquity," in *Pagan Monotheism in Late Antiquity,* ed. Polymnia Athanassiadi
and Michael Frede [Oxford: Clarendon, 1999], 43).

3. Middle Platonism is a development of Platonic thought from its original
articulation several centuries earlier. I should also note here that I will not fully
address all the philosophies of this era in any depth. In particular, the perspective
of the Epicureans had a number of distinctive views that are beyond the scope of
this chapter.

4. He continues, "Mutual influence must never be underestimated"
(G. Watson, "The Problem of the Unchanging in Greek Philosophy," *Neue
Zeitschrift für systematische Theologie und Religionsphilosophie* 27 [1985]: 63).

5. "The most significant contribution of the movement was to bring together
and equate the supreme Divine Mind of Aristotle and the Platonic world of Forms
and Ideas" (Antonia Tripolitis, *Religions of the Hellenistic-Roman Age* [Grand Rapids,
MI: Eerdmans, 2002], 41).

6. Claudia Setzer, "'Talking Their Way into Empire': Jews, Christians, and
Pagans Debate Resurrection of the Body," in *Ancient Judaism in Its Hellenistic Context,*
ed. Carol Bakhos, volume 95 of Supplements to the Journal for the Study of
Judaism (Leiden: E. J. Brill, 2005), 155.

7. Plato, *Phaedo,* in *The Republic and Other Works,* trans. B. Jowett (New York:
Anchor, 1973), 496.

8. Plato, *Phaedo,* 498.

9. Plato, *Phaedo,* 498−99.

10. Plato, *Phaedo,* 499.

11. A. J. M. Wedderburn, *Baptism and Resurrection: Studies in Pauline Theology against
Its Graeco-Roman Background* (Tübingen: J. C. B. Mohr, 1987), 183.

12. For a brief introduction to docetism, see Stuart G. Hall, "Docetism," in *The
Oxford Companion to Christian Thought,* ed. Adrian Hastings, Alistair Mason, and Hugh
Pyper (Oxford: Oxford University Press, 2000), 173.

13. Origen, *Contra Celsum,* 4.58, trans. Henry Chadwick (Cambridge: Cambridge University Press, 1965), 232.

14. On the preposterous nature of Christian doctrine, Celsus comments, "But, indeed, neither can God do what is shameful nor does He desire what is contrary to nature" (Origen, *Contra Celsum,* 5.14 [Chadwick, 274–75]).

15. Origen, *Contra Celsum,* 6.73 (Chadwick, 386).

16. Origen, *Contra Celsum,* 6.72 (Chadwick, 386).

17. Setzer, "Talking Their Way," 173.

18. Aristotle, *Metaphysics: Book XII,* part 8, trans. W. D. Ross (Raleigh, NC: Alex Catalogue, 2000), 129.

19. Parmenides, *Fragment 8,* cited in Watson, "The Problem of the Unchanging," 57.

20. Joseph M. Hallman, *The Descent of God: Divine Suffering in History and Theology* (Minneapolis, MN: Fortress, 1991), 1–2.

21. Plato, *Phaedo,* in *Plato,* trans. Harold N. Fowler (Cambridge, MA: Harvard University Press, 1914), 273–75.

22. Hallman, *Descent of God,* 3. Emphasis on the immutable divine is also found in the *Republic.*

23. This can be seen particularly in the need to develop the idea of intermediary beings between the unchanging Supreme Being and the changeable world (see Watson, "The Problem of the Unchanging," 63–65). These assumptions about God's unchanging nature grow even stronger in the era of Neoplatonism with the writings of Plotinus (AD 204–70). It is this line of thinking that had such a profound impact on Church Fathers, such as Augustine, and the development of the creeds (see Watson, "The Problem of the Unchanging," 65–66).

24. Tripolitis, *Religions of the Hellenistic-Roman Age,* 38.

25. Origen, *Contra Celsum,* 4.14 (Chadwick, 192–93).

26. Origen, *Contra Celsum,* 7.14 (Chadwick, 406).

27. Origen, *Contra Celsum,* 7.15 (Chadwick, 406).

28. This effort to resolve questions of Christology can be seen in Origen's response to Celsus. See *Contra Celsum,* 7.16–17 (Chadwick, 407–9). For an introduction to the doctrine of the impassibility of God in early Christianity, see Joseph M. Hallman, "Impassibility," in *Encyclopedia of Early Christianity,* ed. Everett Ferguson, 2d ed. (New York: Garland, 1997), 566–67.

29. 1 Corinthians 1:22; New International Version.

30. 1 Corinthians 1:22; Jerusalem Bible.

31. Walter Bauer, William F. Arndt, and F. Wilbur Gingrich, *A Greek-English Lexicon of the New Testament and Other Early Christian Literature,* 2d ed. (Chicago: University of Chicago Press, 1979), s.v. "*sēmeion.*"

32. Mark A. Elliott, *The Survivors of Israel: A Reconsideration of the Theology of Pre-Christian Judaism* (Grand Rapids, MI: Eerdmans, 2000), 54. This is E. P. Sanders's widely influential assessment. It is discussed by Elliott (53–55).

33. On the *'am ha-'aretz* seen as being like Gentiles in the rabbinic tradition, see Calvin J. Roeztel, *The World That Shaped the New Testament,* rev. ed. (Louisville, KY: Westminster John Knox, 2002), 60. Sanders maintains that the Pharisees, unlike

the Essenes, neither defined themselves as true Israel nor saw the "people of the land" as not being part of Israel (E. P. Sanders, *Paul and Palestinian Judaism: A Comparison of Patterns of Religion* [Philadelphia: Fortress, 1977], 156–57). See the debate in Elliott, *The Survivors of Israel,* 52–56.

34. Elliott, *The Survivors of Israel,* 108–13.

35. The question is addressed in W. J. Moulder, "Sadduccees," in *International Standard Bible Encyclopedia,* ed. Geoffrey W. Bromiley (Grand Rapids, MI: Eerdmans, 1988), 4:279.

36. See Elliott, *The Survivors of Israel,* 119–43, 254–58.

37. While much is debated about the Pharisees, "what does seem certain—because it is the only thing upon which our otherwise irreconcilable sources agree—is that the Pharisees placed a great premium on something called 'ancestral tradition.'" All sources consistently assent to the Pharisees' focus on "ancestral tradition" that the rabbis would later call the oral law (Martin S. Jafee, *Early Judaism* [Upper Saddle River, NJ: Prentice Hall, 1997], 79).

38. This idea of obedience as staying within the covenant rather than earning God's favor is referred to by E. P. Sanders as "covenantal nomism." In this debate, Seyoon Kim, in *Paul and the New Perspective: Second Thoughts on the Origin of Paul's Gospel* (Grand Rapids, MI: Eerdmans, 2002), defends a more traditional Protestant understanding against the "New Perspective" approach of E. P. Sanders and James D. G. Dunn. Dunn argues "that by 'works of the law' Paul intended his readers to think about *particular observances of the law like circumcision and the food laws*" (*Jesus, Paul and the Law* [London: SPCK, 1990], 191, emphasis in original).

39. See Elliott's discussion of their view of apostasy in Israel (*The Survivors of Israel,* 108–13).

40. Roetzel, *The World That Shaped the New Testament,* 60.

41. Roetzel, *The World That Shaped the New Testament,* 60.

42. Elliott observes: "As is well known, establishing *religious authority* was one of the dominating concerns of Second Temple Judaism. This involved defining, or redefining, *who* or *what* was to provide the authoritative standard or rule for conduct and belief for members of God's people at a time when the established offices and instruments of religious authority were breaking down" (Elliot, *The Survivors of Israel,* 119). He discusses changes in the intertestamental period (119–21).

43. *Jubilees,* 15.33–34; James H. Charlesworth, ed., *The Old Testament Pseudepigrapha* (New York: Doubleday, 1985), 2:87.

44. Elliott, *The Survivors of Israel,* 398.

45. Elliott, *The Survivors of Israel,* 398.

5

PRINCIPLES OF NEW TESTAMENT TEXTUAL CRITICISM

Carl W. Griffin and Frank F. Judd Jr.

Most Latter-day Saints would sympathize with the primary goal of New Testament textual criticism: to reconstruct the original text of the New Testament.[1] Both Latter-day Saints and textual critics believe that the Greek text of the New Testament we have today does not faithfully reproduce the original text at all points. The New Testament has not always been transmitted accurately. As scribes in antiquity copied documents, often under difficult conditions, errors of eye and mind inevitably occurred. The damage of these accidental errors was compounded when ambitious scribes undertook to improve upon the exemplar from which they copied, either to correct perceived errors of spelling and grammar or to improve style and content. The result is that no two complete manuscripts of any book from antiquity are exactly alike.[2] This would not be a problem were it not for the fact that thousands of New Testament manuscripts (or fragments of manuscripts) have survived from antiquity, displaying a wide variety of divergent readings.

Carl W. Griffin is a research scholar at the Neal A. Maxwell Institute for Religious Scholarship, Brigham Young University.

Frank F. Judd Jr. is an assistant professor of ancient scripture at Brigham Young University.

Even scribes who took particular care committed errors. The Masoretes, a group of Jewish scribes, for example, took every pain to ensure the uniformity of their work, even down to counting the letters contained in the books of the Old Testament which they copied. Yet even they were prone to common errors.[3] Usually the variation is slight, at least by lay standards, but a text to the textual critic is like a ledger to the accountant—no variation from an absolute norm is acceptable. For an accountant, the books must balance. For the textual critic, the text must be that which the original authors penned, neither jot nor tittle varying. The task of the textual critic is to discover and remove as many transmissional errors as possible. Latter-day Saint scholars can readily agree with and promote such an effort, finding it has the potential to better our understanding of the sacred text.

New Testament textual criticism is unfortunately a technical discipline that nonspecialists may find difficult to negotiate. Accordingly, this chapter will describe and illustrate the suppositions and methodologies of the field with a Latter-day Saint audience in mind.

THE PRACTICE OF TEXTUAL CRITICISM

The work of textual criticism involves several steps. First, the scholar must analyze and describe all the surviving manuscripts of a given work. This involves not only cataloging and dating the manuscripts but also comparing their texts to determine if they agree with one another in content—in wording, spelling, punctuation, and other scribal characteristics—and noting all variations between them. This process of comparison is called *collation*. When collation is complete, the real job of the textual critic begins. All the variations, or *variant readings*, are examined to determine which most likely represent the original readings; that is, those the original document possessed. While a variant reading may be anything from a difference in spelling to the presence or absence of an entire paragraph, normally the term refers to a variant word or phrase.

When scholars first began to produce scholarly editions of classical texts in the sixteenth century, they used very rudimentary methods. They would often have access to only two or three manuscripts of a work for study. When an obvious corruption was encountered, it was usually corrected by *conjectural emendation*. That is, the scholar simply changed the corrupted reading to how he thought it originally read.[4] Eventually, more than two or three manuscripts became available for comparison at a time, and scholars began to formulate rules for determining which of the variant readings in the manuscripts of a work were most likely original. These rules became the "canons" of textual criticism. As this methodology developed, scholars moved away from conjectural emendation toward selecting the most plausible original reading from among the *existing* variant readings. Thus, scholars have relied chiefly on selection to solve textual problems in determining the original text of the Greek New Testament.[5]

This process of selection is very complex. How does a textual critic determine which of these variant readings is the original reading? It is done as any good detective would do it—on the basis of evidence. Textual critics since the late nineteenth century often distinguish between *external* and *internal evidence* for variant readings. External evidence concerns manuscripts, and internal evidence concerns individual variant readings. These two bodies of evidence work together.

Scholars sometimes call this approach *reasoned eclecticism,* and it is broadly employed.[6] Most scholars today believe that both external and internal evidence must be weighed together because the evidence of either category alone is rarely conclusive. This would seem reasonable. But the method is eclectic because, from instance to instance, critics give more weight to one or the other form of evidence according to the nature of the textual difficulty and the available evidence.

As a way to illustrate these principles of modern New Testament textual criticism, we will examine a phrase used by Paul in a farewell speech addressed to church leaders assembled at Miletus. The King James Version (KJV) of Acts 20:28 reports Paul as saying, "Take heed therefore unto yourselves, and to all the flock, over the which the Holy Ghost hath made you overseers, to feed *the church of God,* which he hath purchased with his own blood" (emphasis added).[7] "The church of God" is one particular phrase for which many variant readings exist in ancient manuscripts. Each variant reading answers differently the (hypothetical) question, to whom does the church belong? Various manuscripts read:

1. "the church of God" (*tēn ekklēsian tou theou*)
2. "the church of the Lord" (*tēn ekklēsian tou kyriou*)
3. "the church of the Lord and God" (*tēn ekklēsian tou kyriou kai [tou] theou*)
4. "the church of God and the Lord" (*tēn ekklēsian theou kai kyriou*)
5. "the church of the Lord God" (*tēn ekklēsian kyriou theou*)
6. "the church of Christ" (*tēn ekklēsian Christou*)
7. "the church of Jesus Christ" (*tēn ekklēsian Iēsou Christou*)

We will use reasoned eclecticism to examine the external and internal evidence associated with these variant readings in order that we may answer a fundamental question of textual criticism: Which reading best explains the origin of all other readings?

EXTERNAL EVIDENCE

When weighing the external evidence for a reading, one asks, How many manuscripts contain this reading? When were they written? How were they distributed geographically? Do they all come from a certain region or from several different regions? What are the scribal characteristics of the various manuscripts? For example, were the scribes sloppy and nonprofessional or neat and professional? Which manuscripts, in general, regularly contain good readings? Are all the manuscripts that contain the reading related textually (or *genealogically*)?

The *genealogical method* of textual criticism is important when considering external evidence. It employs a rather complex process of elimination for determining how the many manuscripts and readings relate to each other and which variants are most likely original. Unfortunately, because of the vast number of manuscripts of the New Testament, the genealogical method of comparing and eliminating readings quickly becomes impossibly complex. As a result, scholars have simplified the manuscript tradition by dividing all manuscripts of the New Testament into manuscript *families,* or *text types,* according to the distinctive readings they share.[8] When genealogical analysis is applied to a text type, its relative value can be determined. If a text type contains a larger number of manuscripts that more frequently display readings likely to be original, that text type is considered superior on the whole and is assumed to stand closest to the original documents. There is a bit of circularity in this argument. However, when a manuscript (or a text type) is determined to have more superior readings when the choice between variant readings is fairly obvious, then the readings in that manuscript (or text type) carry greater weight when the selection is not so obvious.

The Alexandrian text type, according to a majority of scholars, most often represents the original text.[9] Modern Greek New Testaments and translations are normally based on the Alexandrian text type. Its chief witnesses—the earliest and most complete manuscripts containing this text type—are two Greek manuscripts, distinctively magnificent in appearance, called Sinaiticus and Vaticanus, usually referred to by the letters Aleph (Hebrew) and B.[10] In general, the Alexandrian text type contains shorter readings than any of the other text types.

A second text type is the Western, whose defining characteristic has been described as "a love of paraphrase."[11] This text type often contains readings which exhibit various kinds of secondary scribal improvements such as additions, omissions, and substitutions.[12] Consequently, the Western text type stands far from the original. A third text type is the Caesarean, which often contains a mixture of Western and Alexandrian readings as well as harmonizations and paraphrases found in Western readings.[13] A fourth is the Byzantine (or Syrian), which often combines the readings of the Western, Caesarean, and Alexandrian into a single text. The Byzantine text type is characteristically smooth and full, removing ambiguous constructions, introducing numerous interpolations, conflating readings from two of the traditions (so that nothing would be omitted), and harmonizing the synoptic Gospels in several places to remove conflicts between them.[14] The Byzantine text type first appeared in the fourth century and is found in the vast majority of Greek manuscripts. Both a printed edition known as the Textus Receptus[15] as well as the King James Version often contain readings from the Byzantine text type.

Let us return to our example from Acts 20:28. External considerations would probably rule out two of the readings and cast doubt on three others. Readings 6 and 7 ("of Christ," "of Jesus Christ") are found in some "versions"[16] (early translations) but not in a single Greek manuscript. Readings 3, 4, and 5 ("of the Lord and God," "of God and the Lord," "of the Lord God") are found in Greek manuscripts of the

Byzantine text type, and none date earlier than the ninth century AD. Reading 4 ("of God and the Lord") is found in a single fifteenth-century Greek "minuscule."[17] That leaves readings 1 and 2 ("of God," "of the Lord") in first place. Both are attested in early, independent manuscripts of the Alexandrian text type. Thus, the external evidence is equally good for readings 1 and 2, while the evidence for the other readings strongly suggests they are not original.

INTERNAL EVIDENCE

Internal evidence is divided into two subcategories: those of intrinsic probability and those of transcriptional probability. Here the considerations become much more complex. When considering *intrinsic probability,* we ask such questions as, Does this reading complement the author's vocabulary and style? Does it fit his thought and theology? Does it fit the immediate context and the reasoning of its thought unit? The answers to these questions are necessarily more subjectively grounded than the external considerations.

Setting aside, for the moment, readings 3, 4, and 5 ("of the Lord and God," "of God and the Lord," "of the Lord God"), let us consider the intrinsic probability of 1 and 2. Reading 2, "the church of the Lord," does not appear elsewhere in the New Testament, which counts against its originality, though it appears seven times in the Septuagint,[18] referring to the assembly of God. Its appearance in the Septuagint could favor its originality in Acts 20:28, since the language of the Greek Old Testament often influenced that of the New Testament. Reading 1, "the church of God," appears numerous times in the Epistles of Paul (at least eight occurrences), though not once in Luke or elsewhere in Acts.[19] These evidences, however, are essentially inconclusive.

With respect to context, one might suppose at first blush that the phrase "the church of the Lord" would fit the context better than "the church of God," for immediately following it we read, "which he hath purchased with his own blood." Would Luke have written that God (the Father) purchased the church with his own blood? Probably not. Unfortunately, the Greek of this text does not allow us to solve the problem so easily. This same line could also be translated "the church of God, which he hath redeemed through the blood of his Own" (*dia tou haimatos tou idiou*), meaning "through the blood of his own [son, Jesus Christ]." This makes either reading possible on the grounds of intrinsic probability.

Perhaps a consideration of *transcriptional probability* would help. Here we begin to explore textual changes effected by scribes. We must ask ourselves: If I were a scribe, what mistakes, common or extraordinary, might I make if I were copying this work? What infelicity of grammar or style might I be tempted to improve upon? Would I have any theological motivation to alter an original reading? With readings 1 and 2 ("of God," "of the Lord"), it would take a very slight error indeed to exchange one word for the other, since "God" and "Lord" were similarly abbreviated in Greek manuscripts: $\overline{\Theta Y}$ and $\overline{KY}$.[20] Note that we are dealing with the change of just one letter.

When considered together with the external evidence, readings 3, 4, and 5 ("of the Lord and God," "of God and the Lord," "of the Lord God") appear to be conflations, or combinations, of 1 and 2, which means the scribes of those texts probably copied from two (or more) different manuscripts, one of which attested reading 1 and the other reading 2. Possibly they felt it was better to include them both rather than risk omitting the reading that might be the original. This is one of the reasons why textual critics have adopted the maxim *brevior lectio potior,* "the shorter reading is better" (although universal applicability of this rule is questionable). Thus, again we are left with readings 1 and 2 as the most likely candidates.

We have already noted that Luke, if reading 1 is original to him, may have meant to say that "the church of God" was "redeemed through the blood of his Own." Actually, he may have written, "the church of God, which he hath redeemed through the blood of his own Son," because the Greek word for "son" (genitive *huiou*) would have had the same last three letters as the phrase "his own" (genitive *tou idiou*). If such were the case, the eye of an early scribe might have accidentally skipped from the ending of one word to that of the next, obliterating this explicit reference to the Son from all manuscripts copied thereafter! This type of scribal mistake "is called *parablepsis* (a looking by the side) and is facilitated by *homoeoteleuton* (a similar ending of lines)."[21]

Admitting these possibilities, are there any motivations which would cause a scribe to change "of God" (1) to "of the Lord" (2) or vice versa? A scribe who interpreted reading 1 to mean that God the Father redeemed the church with His own blood may have changed it to the more theologically sensible reading 2, which was in any event defensible due to its scriptural use in the Septuagint. On the other hand, if 2 were the original reading, what would prompt a scribe to change it, the theologically acceptable reading, into the theologically problematic reading 1? From this type of circumstance, textual critics have derived the maxim *difficilior lectio potior*, "the more difficult reading is better," thus favoring 1, though as with our other maxim, one must be cautious in its application. The overall evidence thus far would seem to favor reading 1 "the church of God."

A further theological motive may have prompted a scribe to change 1, the idea of redemption through the blood of God (the Father), to 2, the idea of redemption through the blood of His Son.[22] At the turn of the fourth century AD, a movement arose called Arianism, named after its chief author, Arius. Arius and his followers held that Christ was created by the Father, and therefore, though Christ was the Creator of all within the material cosmos, He was nevertheless Himself a creature as well. As a creation of the Uncreated, the Son was inferior to the Father. The Arians were opposed by the orthodox, who held that Christ was begotten, not made (or created), and therefore equal to and one with the Father in every respect.[23] One could imagine that a scribe with Arian leanings might have changed the strong wording of 1 ("the church of God"), which could be seen to emphasize the oneness of God the Father and God the Son, to 2 ("the church of the Lord"), which did not imply any particular theological stance with respect to the Godhead. Because of a belief in the oneness of God the Father and the Lord Jesus Christ, an orthodox scribe would have no real cause to exchange 2 for 1, since the theological overtones of both readings would have been perfectly acceptable.[24] Thus, transcriptional probability, like most all other evidence, favors reading here "the church of God," and this would seem to be the original text. This is also the text that stands in the King James Version of the Bible.

The example of Acts 20:28 teaches us much about the limits of textual criticism. A lack of critical information often prevents the New

Testament textual critic from reaching definite conclusions. Regarding the two textual maxims mentioned above ("the shorter reading is better" and "the more difficult reading is better"), there are numerous exceptions to both of these rules. Textual critics have found that certain general guidelines aid in determining correct readings but that each case is unique. What scholars now regard as a correct reading may change tomorrow in the light of new documentary evidence or further analysis of evidence now available. A. E. Housman, the English poet and textual critic, once observed: "A textual critic engaged upon his business is not at all like Newton investigating the motions of the planets: he is much more like a dog hunting for fleas. If a dog hunted for fleas on mathematical principles, basing his researches on statistics of area and population, he would never catch a flea except by accident. They require to be treated as individuals; and every problem which presents itself to the textual critic must be regarded as possibly unique."[25]

Thus, in spite of its advances, the conclusions of textual criticism regarding many readings will always remain tentative because, for all its methodology, textual criticism is more art than science.[26]

CONCLUSION

The debates and uncertainties raised by textual critics might cause concern to those who regard the Bible as scripture. Approximately 5,700 Greek manuscripts of the New Testament are extant,[27] many times that number of manuscripts for early versions in other languages, and there are innumerable citations of the New Testament in the writings of the Church Fathers, much of which could be said to disagree textually. One study has concluded that "it would be difficult to find a sentence, even part of a sentence, for which the rendering is consistent in every single manuscript."[28] But lest one begin to worry about the foundations of the Bible, it should be noted that of the estimated three hundred thousand New Testament textual variants (no one has actually been able to count them all),[29] only a small fraction of these are significant, either in translating the text or for the doctrine they express. Westcott and Hort suggested that "the amount of what can in any sense be called substantial variation . . . can hardly form more than a

thousandth part of the entire text."[30] And of these substantial variations, only a small percentage of that thousandth part involves readings
of doctrinal import to Latter-day Saints.[31] Textual critics would consider the variant in the above example a rather significant one, and a
thorny one to deal with. But, to most Latter-day Saints, the doctrinal
difference between the various attested readings of Acts 20:28 is very
slight.

This being the case, then, is textual criticism really that significant
for Latter-day Saints? Does it illuminate the scriptures, destroy faith in
them, or neither? It does seem like a lot of fuss over details of little
practical consequence. Latter-day Saints have long understood that the
Bible contains errors, but as Elder Joseph B. Wirthlin taught: "The fragmentary nature of the biblical record and the errors in it, resulting from
multiple transcriptions, translations, and interpretations, do not diminish our belief in it as the word of God 'as far as it is translated correctly.'
We read and study the Bible, we teach and preach from it, and we strive
to live according to the eternal truths it contains. We love this collection
of holy writ."[32]

Nephi foresaw the removal of "plain and precious" truths from the
Bible (see 1 Nephi 13:20–29), but it is unlikely that textual criticism
will restore them.[33] Manuscript variants can at times be substantial, and
at times very illuminating, but none would appear to preserve lost plain
and precious truths.

This is not to say that textual criticism holds no significance at all
for Latter-day Saints.[34] All means, both spiritual and intellectual,
whereby we may better understand the Bible are worthy of our attention, even if all are not of equal importance and value. President
Brigham Young explained:

> Take the Bible just as it reads; and if it be translated incor-
> rectly, and there is a scholar on the earth who professes to be a
> Christian, and he can translate it any better than King James's
> translators did it, he is under obligation to do so, or the curse is
> upon him. If I understood Greek and Hebrew as some may
> profess to do, and I knew the Bible was not correctly translated,
> I should feel myself bound by the law of justice to the

inhabitants of the earth to translate that which is incorrect and give it just as it was spoken anciently. Is that proper? Yes, I would be under obligation to do it.[35]

President Young's statement concerning the translation of the Bible may have broader application. We know that when the Prophet Joseph Smith used the word "translation," he also had the concept of transmission in mind. Robert J. Matthews concluded: "Joseph Smith also stated that the Bible had not been preserved in its original purity: 'We believe the Bible to be the word of God as far as it is translated correctly' (A of F 8). The word *translated* as it is used here must be understood to include the idea of *transmission*. That is, error has occurred not only in the translation from one language to another, but also in the transcription of the text from manuscript to manuscript, even in the same language."[36]

Thus, what Brigham Young taught concerning errors in the *translation* of the Bible can also be applied to errors in its *transmission*. If there are passages in the Bible that have been transmitted to us incorrectly, and if we have the resources to determine the original readings "better than King James's translators did it, [we are] under obligation to do so."

NOTES

1. In older works, textual criticism is sometimes called "lower criticism," and the various branches of literary criticism are termed "higher criticism." By the designation "lower criticism," the fundamental task of establishing the text itself was emphasized, as opposed to the "higher" task of literary analysis that is performed secondarily. These terms are generally avoided today because they imply a qualitative difference between the two tasks, are not sufficiently precise, and the term "lower," especially when coupled with the term "criticism," carries pejorative connotations.

2. On the transmission of ancient texts, see L. D. Reynolds and N. G. Wilson, *Scribes and Scholars: A Guide to the Transmission of Greek and Latin Literature*, 3d ed. (Oxford: Clarendon, 1991). On the types of scribal errors, see Bruce M. Metzger and Bart D. Ehrman, *The Text of the New Testament*, 4th ed. (New York: Oxford University Press, 2005), 250–71. For a recent popular introduction to New Testament textual criticism, see Bart D. Ehrman, *Misquoting Jesus: The Story Behind Who Changed the Bible and Why* (New York: HarperSanFrancisco, 2005).

3. For examples, see J. Weingreen, *Introduction to the Critical Study of the Text of the Hebrew Bible* (New York: Oxford University Press, 1982), 21–23, and throughout. The differences between Jewish and Christian scribes were considerable, the typical early Christian scribe being nonprofessional, more error prone, and seemingly less reticent to emend the text. Even the work of professional scribes in the Greco-Roman world was typically laden with errors (see Harry Y. Gamble, *Books and Readers in the Early Church* [New Haven, CT: Yale University Press, 1995], 83–93).

4. While modern manuscript discoveries and editorial methods have rendered the majority of early emendations highly improbable, some remain quite viable, or at least intriguing. For example, in 1574 J. Camerarius suggested that in John 19:29 the sponge soaked with vinegar was placed on a javelin (*hyssos*) and raised up to Jesus rather than on a hyssop stalk (*hyssopos*), since hyssop is a small shrub that would hardly have served that purpose. Camerarius's proposed emendation was later discovered in a Greek manuscript (476), and it has been accepted as original by several scholars and the editors of the New English Bible (see Raymond E. Brown, *The Gospel According to John* [New York: Doubleday, 1970], 2:909–10).

5. Erasmus compiled the first printed edition of the Greek New Testament in 1515. Several other editions followed during the sixteenth century, including that of the great reformer Theodore Beza, which was used extensively by King James's translators. For a brief overview of these first printed editions of the Greek New Testament, see Ehrman, *Misquoting Jesus*, 75–83.

6. For an overview of reasoned eclecticism, see Michael W. Holmes, "Reasoned Eclecticism in New Testament Textual Criticism," in *The Text of the New Testament in Contemporary Research*, ed. Bart D. Ehrman and Michael W. Holmes (Grand Rapids, MI: Eerdmans, 1995), 336–60.

7. For the following analysis of Acts 20:28, we rely heavily on the work of Metzger and Ehrman, *Text of the New Testament*, 331–33, and B. F. Westcott and F. J. A. Hort, *The New Testament in the Original Greek*, vol. 2 (Introduction and Appendix), 2d ed. (New York: Harper and Brothers, 1896; reprint, Peabody, MA: Hendrickson, 1988), (Appendix), 98–100.

8. B. F. Westcott and F. J. A. Hort, two Cambridge scholars in the late nineteenth century, adapted the genealogical method and proposed four basic text types. On Westcott and Hort and the development of text types, see Metzger and Ehrman, *Text of the New Testament*, 174–82, 305–13.

9. Westcott and Hort subdivided the Alexandrian text type into two text types: the Alexandrian and the so-called Neutral text. They felt that the Alexandrian text, though corrupt, stood closer to the original, and its changes "have usually more to do with language than matter" (see Westcott and Hort, *New Testament in the Original Greek*, [Introduction], 130–32). They also felt that the Neutral text had somehow escaped corruption and most faithfully represented the original text. Many scholars now feel that Westcott and Hort's Alexandrian and Neutral texts are not "distinct" text types but, rather, "represent perhaps slightly differing degrees of fidelity to the same text" (see J. Harold Greenlee, *Introduction to New Testament Criticism*, 2d ed. [Peabody, MA: Hendrickson, 1995], 81–82).

10. Most uncial manuscripts (that is, Greek manuscripts written in all capital letters) are given a proper name, like Sinaiticus, and a siglum (a scribal abbreviation), like *aleph* (the first letter of the Hebrew alphabet), by which they are designated in the margins of Greek New Testaments and scholarly works. For the names, sigla, and descriptions of the most important uncials, see Metzger and Ehrman, *Text of the New Testament,* 62–86.

11. Westcott and Hort, *New Testament in the Original Greek,* (Introduction), 122.

12. See Metzger and Ehrman, *Text of the New Testament,* 307–10; Greenlee, *Introduction to New Testament Criticism,* 82–85.

13. See Metzger and Ehrman, *Text of the New Testament,* 310–12; Greenlee, *Introduction to New Testament Criticism,* 85–86.

14. See Metzger and Ehrman, *Text of the New Testament,* 306–10; Greenlee, *Introduction to New Testament Criticism,* 86–87.

15. In 1649 the brothers Bonaventure published an edition of the Greek New Testament that became known as "the received text" (*textus receptus*) from an advertising blurb printed in the front of their edition: "Therefore you [the reader] have the *text* now *received* by all, in which we give nothing altered or corrupted" (*Textum ergo habes, nunc ab omnibus receptum: in quo nihil immutatum aut corruptum damus*) (see Metzger and Ehrman, *Text of the New Testament,* 152n36). Although it and the other early editions differed little from the initial edition of Erasmus, which was based on late manuscripts and was rather hastily done, the Textus Receptus came to be viewed the same way as the King James Version, which was based on its type of text—as sacrosanct and inviolable. Those who did publish texts that varied from the Textus Receptus were either attacked or ignored.

16. What scholars call the "versions" of the New Testament are early translations (Latin *versiones*) of the New Testament into other languages from the original Greek. These include the early translations into Latin, Syriac, Coptic, and numerous other languages. Most introductions to textual criticism include a solid review of the versions and their importance, for example, Metzger and Ehrman, *Text of the New Testament,* 94–134, and Kurt Aland and Barbara Aland, *The Text of the New Testament,* 2d ed., trans. Erroll F. Rhodes (Grand Rapids, MI: Eerdmans, 1989), 185–221. For the fullest treatment in English, see Bruce M. Metzger, *The Early Versions of the New Testament* (Oxford: Clarendon, 1977).

17. A "minuscule" is a Greek manuscript written in lower-case, or minuscule, script (from Latin *minusculus,* "rather little"). This practice was broadly adopted in the late eighth century because minuscule script was faster to write and allowed more text to be crammed onto a precious piece of parchment. Until this time, Greek writing was typically all capitals. The older script is called "majuscule," or "uncial" (Latin *uncus,* "rounded"), and the older manuscripts written in this hand are often called "uncials." On the rise of minuscule script, see Reynolds and Wilson, *Scribes and Scholars,* 59–61.

18. The Septuagint (Latin *septuaginta,* seventy), or LXX (the Roman numeral 70), is a translation of the Old Testament into Greek and was used among hellenized Jews and early Christians in antiquity. According to the famous letter of Ps.-Aristeas, the Pentateuch (or first five books) of the Septuagint was translated

during the reign of Ptolemy II (285–247 BC) by seventy scholars (hence the name), though "unofficial" versions of the Greek Old Testament surely must have been current among Greek-speaking Jews somewhat earlier than this. For an overview, see Karen H. Jobes and Moisés Silva, *Invitation to the Septuagint* (Grand Rapids, MI: Baker, 2000), 29–44.

19. Luke was the author of both the Gospel and Acts, which are two parts of a single work addressed to "Theophilus" (see Luke 1:3; Acts 1:1).

20. $\overline{\Theta Y}$ = ΘΕΟΥ (*theou*) = "of God"; $\overline{KY}$ = KYRIOY (*kyriou*) = "of [the] Lord."

21. Metzger and Ehrman, *Text of the New Testament*, 253.

22. On the method of placing variant readings within the historical circumstances of the early Church, see Bart D. Ehrman, "The Text as Window: New Testament Manuscripts and the Social History of Early Christianity," in *Text of the New Testament*, 361–79.

23. A brief overview of Arianism may be found in Frank L. Cross and Elizabeth A. Livingstone, eds., *The Oxford Dictionary of the Christian Church*, 3d ed. (New York: Oxford University Press, 1997), 99–100.

24. However, see the discussion of this verse and the critical principle espoused here in F. H. A. Scrivener, *A Plain Introduction to the Criticism of the New Testament*, 4th ed. rev., ed. Edward Miller (London: George Bell & Sons, 1894), 2:251–52. For other possible examples of scribal changes related to the Arian controversy, see Bart D. Ehrman, *The Orthodox Corruption of Scripture: The Effect of Early Christological Controversies on the Text of the New Testament* (New York: Oxford University Press, 1993), 92–95.

25. A. E. Housman, "The Application of Thought to Textual Criticism," in *The Name and Nature of Poetry and Other Selected Prose*, ed. John Carter (New York: New Amsterdam, 1989), 132–33.

26. Metzger and Ehrman similarly concluded, "To teach another how to become a textual critic is like teaching another how to become a poet. The fundamental principles and criteria can be set forth and certain processes described, but the appropriate application of these in individual cases rests upon the student's own sagacity and insight" (Metzger and Ehrman, *Text of the New Testament*, 305).

27. This estimate is from Metzger and Ehrman, *Text of the New Testament*, 52.

28. Léon Vaganay, *An Introduction to New Testament Textual Criticism*, 2d ed. rev., ed. Christian-Bernard Amphoux, trans. Jenny Heimerdinger (London: Cambridge University Press, 1991), 2.

29. This estimate is from Ehrman, *Misquoting Jesus*, 89.

30. Westcott and Hort, *New Testament in the Original Greek*, (Introduction), 2; see also Vaganay, *An Introduction to New Testament Textual Criticism*, 3.

31. On this, see Robert L. Millet, "Lessons from the Joseph Smith Translation," in *Selected Writings of Robert L. Millet* (Salt Lake City: Deseret Book, 2000), 124–25; and Richard Lloyd Anderson, "The Testimony of Luke," in *Studies in Scripture, Vol. 5: The Gospels*, ed. Kent P. Jackson and Robert L. Millet (Salt Lake City: Deseret Book, 1986), 103.

32. Joseph B. Wirthlin, "Christians in Belief and Action," in *Ensign,* November 1996, 71. Note also the conclusion of Brigham Young: "I think it is translated just as correctly as the scholars could get it, although it is not correct in a great many instances. But it is no matter about that. Read it and observe it and it will not hurt any person in the world" (Brigham Young, *Journal of Discourses* [London: Latter-day Saints' Book Depot, 1854–86], 14:227).

33. Scholars do not generally question the basic textual integrity of the New Testament. There are no obvious holes from which text has been excised, though one can only guess at what apostolic and inspired writings might have been included in the New Testament but were lost in the early Christian era before the compilation of the canon was completed (see, for example, 1 Corinthians 5:9 and Colossians 4:16). Richard Lloyd Anderson has suggested that the greatest loss of plain and precious truths came about not through textual changes to the Bible, but rather there was an effective loss of truth through the false interpretation of the true doctrines the Bible contains. See Richard Lloyd Anderson, "The Restoration of the Sacrament, Part 1: Loss and Christian Reformations," in *Ensign,* January 1992, 40.

34. J. Reuben Clark, who was a member of the First Presidency, thought it sufficiently important to author a five-hundred-page book on the subject (see J. Reuben Clark Jr., *Why the King James Version* [Salt Lake City: Deseret Book, 1956]).

35. Young, *Journal of Discourses,* 14:226–27.

36. Robert J. Matthews, "The Bible and Its Role in the Restoration," in *Ensign,* July 1979, 41. Matthews observed elsewhere: "Joseph Smith often used the words 'translated' and 'translation,' not in the narrow sense alone of rendering a text from one language into another, but in the wider senses of 'transmission,' having reference to *copying, editing, adding to, taking from, rephrasing, and interpreting.* This is substantially beyond the usual meaning of 'translation'" (Robert J. Matthews, "Joseph Smith Translation of the Bible (JST)," in *Encyclopedia of Mormonism,* ed. Daniel H. Ludlow [New York: Macmillan, 1992], 2:764; emphasis added).

6

NEW TESTAMENT MANUSCRIPTS, TEXTUAL FAMILIES, AND VARIANTS

Carol F. Ellertson

M any years ago in Dublin, Ireland, I went to the Trinity College Library to see the Book of Kells. Arguably the most famous illuminated vellum Latin manuscript of the New Testament, it dates to the eighth century AD. On that same trip, I visited the British Library in London, where I viewed some of the earliest uncials (Greek parchment manuscripts written with stylized capital letters) of the New Testament, dating to the fourth and fifth centuries, and later the Chester Beatty Museum in Dublin to see its collection of biblical papyri dating to AD 200–250 (papyri discovered in Egypt and acquired by Beatty in 1931). An even earlier text of the New Testament is a small bit of papyrus containing a few verses from John's Gospel dating to about AD 125 that resides in the John Rylands Museum in Manchester, England. Found in 1920 in Egypt, it shows that John's Gospel was circulating at a very early date far from Ephesus, its traditional place of origin.

Which of these New Testament texts is more accurate? The one dated AD 700, AD 350, AD 200, or AD 125? Is an earlier dated text

Carol F. Ellertson is a part-time instructor of ancient scripture at Brigham Young University.

always better than a later one? A text from the book of Romans in the Beatty Collection is a case in point: one of the oldest papyrus texts, it dates to AD 200 but has a large percentage of variations when compared with other papyri of that time period.[1] How do we know if the biblical texts we are reading have been copied accurately?

The Prophet Joseph Smith said, "We believe the Bible to be the word of God as far as it is translated correctly" (Article of Faith 8). Joseph learned from Moroni's quotation of biblical books that the King James Version is not the only acceptable translation (see Joseph Smith—History 1:36). The proliferation of New Testament manuscripts and families of texts since the beginning of the second century AD illustrates the Prophet's need to qualify our acceptance of the Bible as it has come down to us today. What follows is an overview of the various textual families of the New Testament, an explanation of the major theories concerning the causes of textual variants, and examples of each. It will support Joseph Smith's vision of needing a more accurate translation and transmission of the Bible in order to more clearly understand the doctrine of the Lord's covenants with the house of Israel.

THE NEED FOR A CLEAR TRANSLATION

Soon (probably within a century) after the word of God flowed from the mouths and pens of the Apostles and leaders in New Testament times, plain and precious truths concerning Christ and His covenants with the house of Israel were removed. Joseph Smith referred to textual corruption when he stated, "From sundry revelations which had been received, it was apparent that many important points touching the salvation of men, had been taken from the Bible, or lost before it was compiled."[2] He further stated, "I believe the Bible, as it ought to be, as it came from the pen of the original writers."[3]

This textual corruption occurred in two ways. The first happened early and intentionally, resulting in the loss of whole doctrines and entire books (see 1 Nephi 13:26–29).[4] A second type of textual corruption occurred generally after the time when plain and precious truths were removed. Well-meaning scribes made inadvertent errors or believed they were improving the text by clarifying passages that appeared unclear, so that small errors built up over decades and centuries until there were hundreds of variants from one manuscript to another.

When Moroni visited Joseph Smith three times during the night of September 21, 1823, he quoted several passages of scripture to illustrate the nature of the mission that lay before the young prophet, as well as some of the biblical prophecies that were about to be fulfilled. Joseph noticed that Moroni quoted some passages differently than they appeared in his King James Version of the Bible (see Joseph Smith—History 1:36–39). This may be the first time Joseph was introduced to the idea that the Bible was not transmitted accurately but that through "the gift and power of God" the truth could be recovered (see Book of Mormon Title Page; Omni 1:20; Mosiah 8:13; 28:13–16). It is noteworthy that at the time when Joseph Smith received new sacred texts, the field of modern biblical textual criticism was just emerging. The eighteenth and nineteenth centuries saw a growing uneasiness with the accuracy of the Greek texts behind the widely used King James Bible. Textual criticism arose when scholars began to realize that the many Greek manuscripts of the New Testament did not agree in thousands of instances. Around this time, German scholars developed critical methods of editing classical Greek texts that spilled over into biblical textual criticism.[5] The concepts of collating (comparing and noting variants) and grouping ancient texts into families were applied to the many Greek biblical manuscripts that were coming to light.[6]

FIVE GROUPS OF MANUSCRIPTS

There are today over 5,700 extant manuscripts of the Greek New Testament. These manuscripts are normally divided into four basic groups: papyri, uncials, minuscules, and lectionaries. Papyrus was a writing material derived from a reed plant and was in use as early as the third millennium BC until well into the first millennium AD.[7] Great quantities of papyri, including biblical papyri, have been preserved in the sands of Egypt. Two of the most important collections of New Testament papyrus manuscripts are those acquired by Chester Beatty of London in 1930–31 and Martin Bodmer of Geneva in 1955. Two significant early papyri manuscripts are P[66] from the Bodmer collection, which contains a major portion of the Gospel of John and is dated sometime before AD 200, and P[45] from Beatty's library, which has portions of all the Gospels and Acts and is dated to the third century. As papyrus became more difficult to obtain, parchment (scraped and prepared animal skin) eventually replaced papyrus around the fourth century for most biblical manuscripts. As a classification of New Testament manuscripts, "uncial" (from "inch-high" letters) refers to parchment texts (similar to papyri with no letter spacing and minimal punctuation). Uncials were written in a formal and careful literary hand using capital letters that were sometimes more rounded than ordinary Greek capitals. This script (also known as "majuscule") was used in biblical texts from the second to the ninth century AD, after which the cursive or "running" hand, known as "minuscule" (small-lettered), became dominant because of its convenience and economy in writing.[8] Most biblical Greek texts are minuscules of which there are about 2,800. Of these, only a very small number contain the complete New Testament. The smaller yet elegant minuscule script was introduced in the ninth century and continued to be used while texts were copied by hand.[9]

After the minuscules, of all the categories of Greek New Testament manuscript evidence, the lectionaries are the least studied because they preserve only cyclical readings, not running text. Numbering about 2,400 manuscripts, lectionaries are church service books containing readings, or "lections," from the Bible for each day of the church year. They were extremely important to the churches, which could get along without a continuous Bible manuscript for study but definitely needed a lectionary for reading during church services.[10]

Though not included in the manuscript evidence, another important source for studying the text of the New Testament is the large body of quotations of the New Testament preserved in the writings of early Christians. Metzger and Ehrman conclude that if all the other Greek manuscripts were lost, almost the entire New Testament could be reconstructed from the writings of the Church Fathers.[11] (The term *Church Fathers* refers to the prominent early Christian writers in the first few centuries after the Apostles.) These quotations help place specific readings and types of texts in definite places and times. Two key factors in assessing these quotes are, first, establishing the best text of the writings of the Church Father himself and, second, determining whether the particular Church Father is paraphrasing a passage, possibly from memory, or quoting verbatim from a manuscript. If a Church Father paraphrased a passage, he would be more likely to introduce elements that were not part of the original text. For example, Irenaeus (about AD 140–202) cites John 1:18 in three different forms:

1. "No man has seen God at any time, the only begotten God . . ."
2. "No man has seen God at any time; except the only begotten Son . . ."
3. "No man has seen God at any time, except the only begotten Son of God . . ."[12]

This verse will be discussed below, but one can see that Irenaeus' quotations appear to complicate the issue.

MAJOR UNCIALS

Before discussing the major Greek textual families, I will highlight some prominent members of these families. Along with the Beatty and Bodmer papyrus collections, some early uncial texts have exerted the most influence on changes made to modern Bibles. In all, there are approximately 310 uncials. Five important ones are Sinaiticus, Alexandrinus, Vaticanus, Ephraemi Rescriptus, and Bezae.[13] These five have enjoyed a prestigious niche in the history of textual criticism. They are quite early and less fragmentary than other manuscripts. Codex Sinaiticus, dated to the fourth century, was discovered in the monastery of St. Catherine at Mount Sinai by Constantin von Tischendorf in 1844 and published in 1862. Tischendorf persuaded the monks of St. Catherine to present the manuscript to the protector of the Greek Church, the czar of Russia, for nine thousand rubles.[14] Years later, in 1933, after the Bolshevik Revolution, the Russians were in need of cash and sold the codex for half a million dollars to the British government. It is now on display in the British Library in London. Because of its importance, it has been assigned the first letter of the Hebrew alphabet, aleph, or 01.[15]

Codex Alexandrinus, known as "A" or 02, dates from the middle of the fifth century. Sir Thomas Roe (English ambassador to the Ottoman court) first mentioned it in a 1624 letter to the earl of Arundel, stating that he had received "an autographall bible intire" as a gift for the king of England. Cyril Lucar, patriarch at Constantinople, brought the manuscripts with him from Alexandria (thus the name Alexandrinus), where he was previously patriarch. He gave it to Roe in recompense for his help in struggles against the Latin Church.[16] This was the first of the great uncials to be made available to scholars.

Dating to the middle of the fourth century, Codex Vaticanus is one of the most valuable manuscripts of the Greek Bible. As the name indicates, it is in the Vatican Library at Rome, where it arrived sometime prior to 1475 (when it was first mentioned in a library catalog). It is designated as "B" or 03 and was not made available to scholars until 1889. Some scholars have suggested that the two oldest parchment manuscripts, Vaticanus and Sinaiticus, were originally part of a collection of fifty that were copied according to Constantine's edict in the fourth century AD.[17]

Codex Ephraemi Rescriptus is what is known as a palimpsest (Greek, "rescraped"), a manuscript that has been erased by scraping and washing and then written over. Originally a complete Old and New Testament from the fifth century, it was erased in the twelfth century and used to copy the sermons of Ephraem, a Syrian church father. After the fall of Constantinople in 1453, an émigré scholar brought the codex to Florence, after which Catherine de' Medici brought it to France as part of her dowry. It was considered unreadable until Tischenforf deciphered nearly the entire manuscript in 1843. It is designated as "C" or 04 and currently resides in the National Library in Paris.[18]

Codex Bezae (also known as Cantabrigiensis) differs significantly from the other four uncials. Presented to Cambridge University by the Protestant scholar Theodore Beza in 1581, it has both Latin and Greek texts. The Gospels are in a different order (Matthew, John, Luke, Mark), and it contains only the Gospels and Acts. Known as "D" or 05, it has been variously dated from the fourth to the sixth century. This manuscript has a remarkable number of variations and was so far removed from the accepted standard Byzantine text that it has been corrected by scribes many times over the centuries. For example, it is the only known Greek text to substitute Luke's version of Jesus' genealogy with a form of Matthew's genealogy in reverse order (beginning with "Joseph, husband of Mary," instead of Abraham).[19]

The early uncials have directly influenced scholarly assessment of New Testament variants. Though these uncials existed prior to the advent of the King James Version, they did not come to light nor were they studied seriously by scholars until the nineteenth century. With the availability of the uncials, along with the gathering of minuscule manuscripts and the discovery of ancient papyri in the twentieth century, the textual evidence for the Bible has increased significantly since the King James translators produced their new version in 1611.

TEXTUAL FAMILIES

For the past few centuries, scholars have catalogued and categorized the papyri and uncials along with the rest of this large group of manuscripts. Since J. A. Bengal first divided New Testament witnesses into three families in 1725,[20] scholars have continued to refine a number of criteria for evaluating manuscripts.[21] Today, there are occasional proposals for regrouping and redefining the families of the extant Greek manuscripts.[22] Currently, however, New Testament textual critics generally agree that there are three main text types or "families" of texts, with the possibility of a fourth. The main families are Byzantine, Alexandrian, Western, and possibly Caesarean.

The majority of Greek manuscripts, both uncials and miniscules (in other words, the Majority Text) are from the Byzantine textual family. This is the text type from which the Textus Receptus was developed. *Textus receptus* means the "received text," or the text that has been accepted universally as authoritative since about 1624. It was essentially that published by the Christian theologians Erasmus, Stephanus, and Beza. The Textus Receptus was the source for most early English versions of the New Testament. These, in turn, influenced the compilers and translators of the Authorized or King James Version. Codex Alexandrinus and Codex Ephraemi contain mixed readings and are often considered typical examples of the Byzantine family The Byzantine text type was used by the Orthodox Church in the Byzantine Empire and originated later than other families. It was widespread during the medieval Christian period, and subsequently manuscripts from this text type were used as the source for the first printed editions of the Greek New Testament. The Byzantine text type is usually regarded as far removed from the original autographs (manuscripts penned by the authors or their scribes) and probably derived from other text types. It is characterized by the replacement of difficult language with easier terms. For example, Matthew 6:1 says, "Take heed lest you do your alms [Greek, "righteousness" or acts of religious devotion] before men." The Byzantine text replaces "righteousness" with "alms." Another characteristic of the Byzantine text type is harmonization and conflation of variant readings. To *harmonize* is to eliminate contradictions within a text by scribal insertion. *Conflation* occurs when different readings of the same passage are combined. For example, in Matthew 8:26, the Alexandrian textual family has "Do not enter the village," and the Western family has "Do not speak to anyone in the village." The Byzantine text type has "Do not enter and do not speak to anyone in the village."

Because of these characteristics, most scholars have long considered the Byzantine text type less accurate and of lower quality than the earlier Alexandrian family. A few scholars have taken a new look at this family and have found justification for some of its readings, which they feel appear older and more original than previously thought.[23] Most scholars, however, are still persuaded that the Byzantine text type often contains a corrupted text.[24]

The Alexandrian textual family is usually considered the oldest and most faithful in preserving the original text of the New Testament. Both Codex Sinaiticus and Codex Vaticanus, along with some significant papyri (Bodmer's P[66] and P[75]), contain this text type. The Alexandrian text type is characterized by brevity and austerity and is a probable source for later texts. For example, this text type concludes the Gospel of Mark at 16:8 and omits the story of the adulterous woman in John 8, both of which lack early manuscript support. This does not mean that the omitted passages are untrue but that they may have been placed in these particular chapters after the Gospels were originally written.[25]

Though some scholars dispute the existence of a distinct Western textual family, most do not.[26] The Western family is often found in manuscripts that contain both the Greek and the Latin New Testament. The term *Western* is a bit of a misnomer because members of the

Western text type have been found in the Christian East. This family is represented by Codex Bezae (its most important example) and Codex Claromontanus[27] (in Paul's letters), as well as many minuscules and the writings of most of the Syriac Church Fathers. These text types are characterized by extensive paraphrase which results in addition, omission, substitution, and "improvement" of the text. For example, in Luke 23:53, the Western text adds "twenty men could not move the stone." Luke 22:19–20 omits the reference to "the cup after supper" and the reference to Christ's sweat as "great drops of blood" (Luke 22:44) and does not have the prayer on the cross, "Father, forgive them . . ." (Luke 23:34).[28] Some scholars see evidence that the Western family eventually combined with a distinct eastern or "Caesarean" text, and together they evolved into the Byzantine family.[29] The so-called Caesarean text employs mild paraphrase and strives for a certain elegance of expression. It is not as extreme as the Western and so is thought to fall between the Alexandrian and Western text types. However, no typical examples of the Caesarean type exist, and most descriptions of this text type are conjectural.[30]

Each of these text families has characteristic variant readings by which it is identified. The earliest biblical manuscripts will sometimes contain evidence of more than one textual family from book to book even within one manuscript. There are enough patterns and consistencies among these variations, especially in later manuscripts, that confirm the existence of these families.

The fact that one text type is attested in thousands of manuscripts does not necessarily mean that the family is more original or accurate. Quantity does not equal quality.[31] Conversely, because a manuscript is dated early and is rare does not automatically mean it is closest to the original (see the discussion of John 1:18 below). Scholars follow certain criteria as they judge individual variants. For example, scholars give more weight to the shorter reading (*lectio brevior*) among variants since scribes tend to add rather than delete.[32] In addition, scholars give more weight to the more problematic reading (*lectio difficilior*) among variants because copyists tend to simplify difficult readings.[33] Scholars also give more weight to those variants which are in higher quality manuscripts, have wide geographical distribution, or appear in more than one textual family.[34]

THE CAUSES OF VARIANT READINGS

How have these variant readings emerged in thousands of manuscripts? There are two categories of variant readings: intentional and unintentional. Scribes introduced intentional changes when they attempted to improve either the grammar or problematic readings of the text.[35] Sometimes scribes harmonized one Gospel with another, or they attempted to clarify a doctrine by adding words or phrases.[36] Scribes introduced unintentional changes when they failed to distinguish between letters of similar appearance, or when they erred in their attempt to write out a passage from memory.[37] Some scribes failed to hear correctly when transcribing a text that was dictated to them.[38] These thousands of variants not only resulted from but also contributed to even more doctrinal confusion in the early Christian church. One aspect of the apostasy occurred early on as the loss of whole books and the corruption of passages of scripture contributed to the loss of doctrinal purity.[39] During the late first and early second century, some early Christian leaders abandoned the original gospel covenant as they battled over who would control the infant church.[40] Today, textual variants can also cause battles over the specific meaning of important passages in the New Testament. The various methods of textual criticism usually involve tracing the transmission of extant manuscripts to the earliest stages. Textual critics also rely on internal criteria such as scribal habits, as well as the author's style, vocabulary, and theology, to determine which variant best suits the passage. All these criteria assist the textual critic to determine which passages are most likely original.[41]

TEXTUAL VARIANTS

One of the prominent textual variants in New Testament manuscripts is 1 John 5:7–8, known as the Johannine Comma. The verses read, "For there are three that bear record *in heaven, the Father, the Word, and the Holy Ghost: and these three are one. And there are three that bear witness in earth,* the Spirit, and the water, and the blood: and these three agree in one." The italicized words are lacking in all early Greek manuscripts before the sixteenth century. Without the added phrase, the verses originally read, "For there are three that bear record, the Spirit, and the water, and the blood; and these three agree in one." Many early English translations, including the King James, include this spurious phrase. In other words, a passage discussing Christ's Atonement and being born again by the spirit, water, and blood was altered to include a comparison of these three elements to the Trinity. This addition originated as a marginal note added to certain Latin manuscripts during the fourth century, which was eventually incorporated into the Vulgate manuscripts. Erasmus, who resisted including the variant in his Greek New Testament because he found it in no early Greek manuscripts, was persuaded to include it in his third edition in 1522. Most of Erasmus's work was later incorporated into the Textus Receptus, which was essentially the source for the King James Version.[42]

Another interesting textual variant is Luke 23:34, "Father, forgive them; for they know not what they do." These words of Christ as He hung on the cross are absent from the earliest Greek witness, P[75] (about AD 200). They are also missing from Vaticanus and Bezae and are crossed out in Sinaiticus. It is possible that the prayer was left out of some early manuscripts because some Christians felt Jesus was referring to the Jews who participated in the Crucifixion and could not believe that He would implore God on their behalf. It is also possible that, like the true story of the woman taken in adultery, this true response of the Savior was added later. Although scholars disagree about whether Jesus was referring to the Roman soldiers or the Jews,[43] the Joseph Smith Translation of the Bible clearly states that Jesus was pleading for forgiveness on behalf of the Roman soldiers (see JST, Luke 23:34).

John 5:3–4 contains another apparent scribal insertion, which describes the tradition of an angel who stirred the waters at the Pool of Bethesda. The verses read, "In these lay a great multitude of impotent folk, of blind, halt, withered, *waiting for the moving of the water. For an angel went down at a certain season into the pool, and troubled the water: whosoever then first after the troubling of the water stepped in was made whole of whatsoever disease he had.*" The italicized passage is missing in the earliest Greek papyri (P[66] and P[75]) as well as Sinaiticus, Vaticanus, Ephraemi, and Bezae. Since it is clear that these words are not original, they are not included in modern English translations.[44] The italicized words were originally a marginal note, and scribes eventually incorporated them into later manuscripts and then the Textus Receptus.

Another variant in John 1:18 reads, "No man hath seen God at any time; the only begotten Son, which is in the bosom of the Father, he hath declared him." The early and best manuscripts (P^{66}, P^{75}, Sinaiticus, Vaticanus, Ephraemi) have "the only begotten God" instead of "the only begotten Son" (Alexandrinus; later correctors of Sinaiticus and Ephraemi and many later Byzantine manuscripts). Despite the early manuscript support for "the only Begotten God," Bart Ehrman feels that "the only begotten Son" is the original reading but was changed from "Son" to "God" by Alexandrian scribes who wanted to emphasize Jesus' divinity against the beliefs of some Gnostics, centered in Alexandria, who thought that He was merely human and adopted as God's Son.[45]

CONCLUSION

There are tens of thousands of New Testament variants. Scholars continue to discuss and debate the evidence for variants of all kinds. The field of textual criticism continues to evolve as scholars generate fresh theories and abandon previously established conclusions. Since 1966 the United Bible Societies have published four editions of the Greek New Testament designed for translators and students. The primary changes have been with the "critical apparatus" which continually updates the textual evidence for variant readings. This brief survey of New Testament manuscripts, families of texts, and textual variants has demonstrated that the King James Version contains some errors.

The Prophet Joseph Smith knew that the King James Version was not perfect yet revered its inspired words. He stated that we as a church "believe the Bible to be the word of God as far as it is translated correctly" (Article of Faith 8). On one occasion, when he was referring to Malachi 4:5–6, the Prophet taught that he could have "rendered a plainer translation" but that the translation was "sufficiently plain" (D&C 128:18). Thus, although the King James Version contains inaccuracies, it still teaches the truth of the gospel. Thankfully, the Joseph

Smith Translation, modern revelation, and teachings of the prophets and Apostles have clarified many of the issues in the New Testament. For Latter-day Saints, a careful study of early manuscripts and textual variants accompanied by responsible scholarship and the Spirit of the Lord may bear fruit. Perhaps Latter-day Saint scholars can discover additional insights from a study of the critical text of the Greek New Testament and modern English translations, in addition to the King James, which are based upon better manuscripts. As we identify scribal and translation errors, we can gain a better understanding of our Lord and Savior, Jesus Christ, and His earliest followers while they established the infant church in the meridian of time.

NOTES

1. Frederic Kenyon, *Our Bible and the Ancient Manuscripts*, rev. A. W. Adams (New York: Harper and Brothers, 1958), 188–89.

2. Joseph Smith, *Teachings of the Prophet Joseph Smith,* comp. Joseph Fielding Smith (Salt Lake City: Deseret Book, 1976), 9–10.

3. Andrew F. Ehat and Lyndon W. Cook, eds., *The Words of Joseph Smith: The Contemporary Accounts of the Nauvoo Discourses of the Prophet Joseph* (Provo, UT: Religious Studies Center, Brigham Young University, 1980), 256.

4. See Bible Dictionary, "Lost Books," 725; John Gee, "The Corruption of Scripture in Early Christianity," in *Early Christians in Disarray,* ed. Noel B. Reynolds (Provo, UT: Foundation for Ancient Research and Mormon Studies, 2005), 163–204; Bart D. Ehrman, *The Orthodox Corruption of Scripture* (New York: Oxford University Press, 1993).

5. According to Bruce M. Metzger and Bart D. Ehrman, three German scholars—Friedrich Wolf (1759–1824), Immanuel Bekker (1785–1871), and Karl Lachmann (1793–1851)—were the first to prepare critical editions of Greek texts and to introduce the concept of textual families (see Bruce M. Metzger and Bart D. Ehrman, *The Text of the New Testament: Its Transmission, Corruption, and Restoration,* 4th ed. [New York: Oxford University Press, 2005], 206).

6. Bart D. Ehrman, *Misquoting Jesus: The Story Behind Who Changed the Bible and Why* (New York: HarperSanFrancisco, 2005), 71–125; Metzger and Ehrman, *Text of the New Testament,* 206–9.

7. John C. Trever, "Papyrus," in *Interpreter's Dictionary of the Bible,* ed. G. Buttrick (Nashville: Abingdon, 1962), 3:649.

8. Eldon J. Epp, "Uncials," in *Anchor Bible Dictionary,* ed. David Noel Freedman (New York: Doubleday, 1992), 6:418.

9. Jack Finegan, *Encountering New Testament Manuscripts* (Grand Rapids, MI: Eerdmans, 1974), 31–32; Metzger and Ehrman, *Text of the New Testament,* 20.

10. Klaus Junack, "Lectionaries," in *Anchor Bible Dictionary,* 4:271.

11. Metzger and Ehrman, *Text of the New Testament,* 126–27.

12. See *Against Heresies,* 4.20.11; 4.20.6; 3.11.6, in Finegan, *Encountering New Testament Manuscripts,* 167–68.

13. Some other important Greek manuscripts include Codex Claromontanus (D^P or 06) of the sixth century and Codex Washingtonensis (I or 016) from the fifth century, which both contain portions of the Pauline Epistles.

14. Later accounts of Tischendorf's transaction with the monks have attempted to discredit the agreement once the true value of the manuscript continued to come to light (see James Bentley, *Secrets of Mount Sinai: The Story of the World's Oldest Bible* [New York: Doubleday, 1986], 106–15).

15. The Trustees of the British Museum, *The Codex Sinaiticus and the Codex Alexandrinus* (Oxford: University Press, 1963), 5–8.

16. British Museum, *The Codex Sinaiticus and the Codex Alexandrinus,* 30–31.

17. Constantine wished to provide copies of the scripture for new churches to be built in Constantinople, so he requested that Eusebius produce without delay "fifty copies of the sacred Scriptures . . . to be written on fine parchment." Other scholars refute this account by noting that the text of Vaticanus and Sinaiticus is a different type than the one usually employed by Eusebius. They point to Egypt as the place of origin for Vaticanus (see Metzger and Ehrman, *Text of the New Testament,* 15–16).

18. Kurt Aland and Barbara Aland, *The Text of the New Testament: An Introduction to the Critical Editions and to the Theory and Practice of Modern Textual Criticism,* trans. Erroll F. Rhodes (Grand Rapids, MI: Eerdmans, 1987), 109.

19. Metzger and Ehrman, *Text of the New Testament,* 70–73.

20. Ehrman, *Misquoting Jesus,* 71–125; Metzger and Ehrman, *Text of the New Testament,* 159.

21. For a discussion of the theories of J. Griesbach, B. F. Wescott, F. J. A. Hort, H. F. von Soden, H. Leitzmann, F. G. Kenyon, and B. H. Streeter, see Metzger and Ehrman, *Text of the New Testament,* 165–94; J. Harold Greenlee, *Introduction to New Testament Textual Criticism,* 2d ed. (Grand Rapids, MI: Eerdmans, 1967), 81–88; Finegan, *Encountering New Testament Manuscripts,* 61–73; Eldon J. Epp and Gordon D. Fee, *Studies in the Theory and Method of New Testament Textual Criticism* (Grand Rapids, MI: Eerdmans, 1993), 274–97; Epp, "Textual Criticism," in Freedman, *Anchor Bible Dictionary,* 6:427–33.

22. See, for example, Aland and Aland, *Text of the New Testament,* 317–37; Eldon J. Epp, "Decision Points in New Testament Textual Criticism," 37–39, "The Significance of the Papyri For Determining the Nature of the New Testament Text in the Second Century: A Dynamic View of Textual Transmission," in Epp and Fee, *Studies in the Theory and Method,* 274–97.

23. Epp, "Textual Criticism," 6:422.

24. See Daniel B. Wallace, "The Majority Text Theory," in *The Text of the New Testament in Contemporary Research,* ed. Bart D. Ehrman and M. W. Holmes (Grand Rapids, MI: Eerdmans, 1995), 297–320.

25. Metzger and Ehrman, *Text of the New Testament,* 316–27.

26. Aland and Aland, *Text of the New Testament,* 54–55.

27. Epp, "Textual Criticism," 6:421.

28. D. Ewert, *A General Introduction to the Bible: From Ancient Tablets to Modern Translations* (Grand Rapids, MI: Zondervan, 1983), 160.

29. Metzger and Ehrman, *Text of the New Testament,* 307–10; Greenlee, *Introduction to New Testament Textual Criticism,* 81–88.

30. Metzger and Ehrman, *Text of the New Testament,* 310–11; Greenlee, *Introduction to New Testament Textual Criticism,* 89–90.

31. For example, most Byzantine and Alexandrian manuscripts have the voice of the Father at Jesus' baptism saying, "Thou art my beloved Son, in whom I am well pleased" (Mark 1:11; Luke 3:23). But one early manuscript, Codex Bezae of the Western text type, says, "Thou art my beloved Son, today I have begotten you."

32. In Romans 8:1, early manuscripts (Sinaiticus, Vaticanus, Bezae) do not include the ending phrase, "who walk not after the flesh, but after the Spirit," which was a marginal explanatory note probably taken from verse 4. This phrase eventually was incorporated into the text in later manuscripts and remains in the English KJV and NIV.

33. Mark 1:2 was originally "As it is written in Isaiah the prophet" (in Alexandrian, Western, and Caesarean witnesses) but was changed in later Byzantine manuscripts to "As it is written in the prophets," because the quote that follows in verses 2–3 is a composite of Isaiah and Malachi.

34. Epp, "Textual Criticism," 6:431.

35. In words of the angel chorus in Luke 2:14, the addition of one Greek letter (sigma) at the end of the noun *eudokia* (goodwill) changes the case of the noun to "of goodwill" (*eudokias*). The phrase becomes "peace to men of goodwill." This variant is in the oldest witnesses of the Alexandrian and Western texts. The meaning becomes one in which peace at Christ's birth comes not to everyone but only to those of goodwill.

36. In Luke 11:2–4, a majority of manuscripts have changed a shorter version of the Lord's Prayer to the longer version in Matthew 6:9–13.

37. 1 Timothy 3:16 reads: "*God* was manifested in the flesh," while the preferred reading according to the best manuscripts is "*Who* was manifested in the flesh." The abbreviation of the word "God" (which was often used in religious texts) in Greek looks like the pronoun *who*.

38. In Revelation 1:5, "and washed us from our sins," the late manuscripts have the Greek word *lousanti* (washed), while the early texts (Sinaiticus, Alexandrinus, Ephraemi) have *lusanti* (loosed), which could have been pronounced the same and confused if the scribes were copying from oral dictation (see Ewert, *General Introduction to the Bible,* 152–55).

39. See Colossians 4:16, which refers to an "epistle from Laodicea" that is lost to us.

40. For example, see Diatrophes versus John in 3 John 9–10; see also Reynolds, "What Went Wrong for the Early Christians?"; "The Decline of Covenant in Early Christian Thought"; "New Testament Evidences and Prophecies of Apostasy in

the First-Century Church," in Reynolds, *Early Christians in Disarray,* 1–28; 295–324; 355–70.

41. Epp, "Textual Criticism," 6:432.

42. Metzger and Ehrman, *Text of the New Testament,* 146. Ehrman, *Misquoting Jesus,* 80–82.

43. Bentley, *Secrets of Mount Sinai,* 134; Ehrman, *Misquoting Jesus,* 191–93.

44. Bruce M. Metzger, *Textual Commentary on the Greek New Testament,* 2d ed. (Stuttgart: United Bible Societies, 1975), 209.

45. Metzger, *Textual Commentary,* 198; Ehrman, *Misquoting Jesus,* 161–62; *Theological Dictionary of the New Testament,* ed. G. Kittel (Grand Rapids, MI: Eerdmans, 1967), 4:740 ff.14; Epp, "Gnosticism," in Freedman, *Anchor Bible Dictionary,* 2:1035–39.

7

FIRST-CENTURY SOURCES ON THE LIFE OF JESUS

Thomas A. Wayment

Any discussion of the documents that were used as source materials when the authors of the New Testament wrote, whether it be the Gospels, Acts, or Epistles, must necessarily begin with the earliest sources and work forward through history. Some later authors such as Matthew and Luke evidently used earlier written sources when writing. And even though these authors borrowed from and referred to the earlier sources available to them, they also introduced new materials into their accounts that had apparently not been recorded elsewhere. No doubt, the earliest sources would seem to have the greatest historical value, whereas later sources would appear to have been susceptible to corruption and alteration for a longer duration of time. However, if a writer introduced new materials into earlier sources at a later stage, we are not required to dismiss the historical value of those additions simply because they were added later. Rather, these later materials and additions may have the same claim to historical accuracy that the earlier sources did when they were composed (see 3 Nephi 23:7–13).

Thomas A. Wayment is an associate professor of ancient scripture at Brigham Young University.

This approach to the study of the New Testament texts can yield important results for how we read and understand the Gospels, Acts, and Epistles. If, for example, an author used an earlier source without abbreviating or altering it, then we can suppose that the author accepted that text as a legitimate source. If, however, the author used an earlier source and altered it in any significant way, then we should consider the possibility that the new author felt hesitant to use that source in the form in which he received it. In practice, it is probable that the authors of the Gospels of Matthew and Luke relied on the Gospel of Mark when they wrote their respective accounts, and at times they were obliged to change their source while at other times they left it largely intact. Similarly, Paul and other early letter writers had to rely on earlier sources, some of which were written and others of which were transmitted orally.

Dating from the period shortly after the Jerusalem conference (AD 49), Paul's letters stand alone as the earliest surviving Christian writings. Contemporary with Paul's later epistles that were written about AD 60 is the Gospel of Mark, which was probably composed during the First Jewish Revolt against Rome (AD 66–73). Other writings, such as James and 1–2 Peter, may have been written AD 50–70, but the majority of them show very little interest in relating biographical information about Jesus and His ministry. With few exceptions, these same epistles preserve very few traces of the sources available to them or the sources they used when writing.[1] On the other hand, the letters of Paul and the Gospels both preserve to a lesser or greater extent some details of Jesus' life and therefore would have made use of similar sources when writing. Thus, the life of Jesus not only provides the focus for the text of the Gospels and some of the information found in Paul's letters, but it also provides a link to earlier sources that appear to have been very similar.

PAUL'S SOURCES

That Paul did not know of Jesus while the Savior taught in Galilee and Judea is obvious from his surviving letters. Moreover, Paul does not appear to relate any information about the life of Jesus that he may have come across in anti-Christian sources during his period as a persecutor.

In fact, in his epistle to the Galatians, he clarifies that his knowledge of the gospel came to him through "the revelation of Jesus Christ," whereas his earthly understanding of Jesus' life was gained through personal interviews with Peter and James the brother of Jesus (see Galatians 1:11–12, 17–19). Fortunately, Paul clearly differentiated between his sources in Galatians. He relied on oral traditions that were passed on to him through two of the men who knew Jesus best, and he received instructions directly from the Lord.

Paul's choice of Peter and James is also telling because it shows that after his conversion to the gospel he had a desire to gain more historical information about Jesus of Nazareth. He sought that information from Jesus' closest disciple and follower from the beginning, and from a sibling of Jesus who could relate very personal details about Him. Additionally, Paul relied on oral traditions because there were probably no written records to consult at that early date (c. AD 34).[2] According to Paul, the most authoritative sources of information in the decade after Jesus' death were the eyewitnesses of the ministry. Furthermore, Paul makes it clear that before his conversion there were churches in Judea who believed in Christ who, interestingly, would also have required some access to the traditions about Jesus' life (see Galatians 1:22–23; 1 Thessalonians 2:14).

Recently, advocates of the theory that Christianity began as a series of fractured communities that were brought together through the suppression of divergent forms of faith have championed the idea that the writings of Paul preserve only a single view among many thriving and competing forms of Christianity in the first century and that each relied on a different textual tradition. Therefore, the sources used by Paul would represent only a fraction of the sources available to early Christian communities.[3] However, this hypothesis begins to crumble when we realize that Paul, our earliest Christian author, is not aware of such divergent forms of the faith. Instead, Paul denounced "false brethren" (Galatians 2:4), the "dissimulation" of Peter and Barnabas (Galatians 2:13), fellow Christians whom he refers to as "dogs" (Philippians 3:2), and "false apostles, deceitful workers" (2 Corinthians 11:13). But nowhere does Paul denounce Christians who worship a human Jesus, a semi-divine Jesus, or a form of Christianity that entirely removes Jesus from the faith.[4] Paul does denounce those who preach "another Jesus" and bring with them "another gospel," but these false brethren are not advocating a human Jesus (2 Corinthians 11:4). Instead, he denounces those who try to corrupt "the simplicity that is in Christ," which should be understood as a corruption of the doctrine and not the nature of Christ (2 Corinthians 11:3).

Another indication of the content of the sources that Paul used when writing is preserved in his sporadic references to details from the life of Jesus. For example, he taught that Jesus was crucified on a cross (see 1 Corinthians 1:23; Philippians 2:8), that He was betrayed on the night He administered the sacrament to the disciples (see 1 Corinthians 11:23–26), that He was resurrected after three days (see 1 Corinthians 15:4), that some Jews were involved in taking His life under the governor Pontius Pilate (see 1 Thessalonians 2:14–15; 1 Timothy 6:13), and that Jesus was crucified at the time of the Passover celebration (see 1 Corinthians 5:7).[5]

Mistakenly, some may assume that these details represent all that Paul knew concerning Jesus. To those who had gathered together to follow Jesus, however, such passing references invoke a more profound understanding than such a cursory reference might suggest.[6] As examples, superficial references such as "the King Follett Discourse" or "I am going like a lamb to the slaughter" invoke not only deep feelings and emotions but also words and biographical details from the life of the Prophet Joseph Smith. The Savior's life was deeply sacred to the first generation of Christians, and although they may not have had written records in the first two decades after His death, when they met together they discussed those details that had been taught to them by the eyewitness generation. Paul needed only to remind them of what they had discussed when he was with them!

SOURCES USED BY THE EVANGELISTS

Perhaps the most explicit mention of earlier sources in the New Testament is found in Luke's prologue to his Gospel: "Forasmuch as *many have taken in hand to set forth in order a declaration of those things which are most surely believed among us,* even as they delivered them unto us, which from the beginning were eyewitnesses, and ministers of the word"

(Luke 1:1–2; emphasis added). Luke knew of "many" who wrote, and perhaps retold orally, the stories of Jesus' life before his time. He also reports that these writings conform to the traditions passed on by the "eyewitnesses, and ministers of the word." To mention such a detail explicitly betrays Luke's uneasiness that he himself was not an eyewitness to the events that he was about to report from Jesus' lifetime. He wanted his audience to know that his account would be in accordance with the established eyewitness tradition and the many who had also written on the subject.

Inserted into this disclaimer is a subtle hint providing the reason why Luke felt it necessary to write another account of the life of Jesus. He reports further, "It seemed good to me also, having had perfect understanding of all things from the very first, *to write unto thee in order, most excellent Theophilus*" (Luke 1:3; emphasis added). What Luke implies is that he has a more accurate (*akríbos*) understanding and therefore intends to present the story anew "in order" (*kathexes*). Although he left the specific implications of his claim unstated, he certainly meant to indicate that (1) his account would conform with the eyewitness tradition and (2) he planned on making some changes to the order of events presented in the accounts that predated his own retelling.

For centuries Luke's sources have remained hidden. But beginning in the eighteenth century, scholars began to realize that a genetic literary relationship existed between Luke's Gospel and the Gospel of Mark.[7] When compared side by side, the wording of these two Gospels is markedly similar in many instances. In other instances, there is a wide divergence in both the sequence and wording. Unfortunately, recognition of the fact that these two Evangelists (Mark and Luke) borrowed from one another does little to explain the direction of borrowing. It is possible that Luke borrowed from Mark or that Mark borrowed from Luke, although Luke's declaration that he used sources would predispose us to think that he borrowed from Mark. The following example may further clarify the direction and nature of borrowing between the two sources.

"And they were exceedingly afraid and said to one another, 'What kind of man is this that even the wind and sea *obeys* him?'" (Mark 4:41; author's translation; emphasis added).

"And he said to them, 'Where is your faith?' But they were afraid and amazed, saying one to another, 'What kind of man is this that he commands and even the winds and water *obey* him?" (Luke 8:25; author's translation; emphasis added).

Mark's account of the story uses a plural subject (wind and sea) but a third-person singular verb (obeys), which is grammatically incorrect but nonetheless preserves the sense of the passage. Luke, on the other hand, transmits the story in nearly verbatim language but corrects the third-person singular conjugation of the verb to a plural (obey), thus preserving both the sense and grammar of the passage.[8]

Two points are evident in the above example. First, Luke corrected Mark's wording or the wording of Mark's source. That Mark borrowed from Luke and then corrupted his grammar and syntax would be a difficult position to maintain. Perhaps in a single instance this type of corruption would be possible, but Luke's consistent correction of Mark's grammar is clear evidence that Luke is later.[9] Second, Luke almost certainly borrowed from Mark rather than a source used by Mark because of the verbatim language between the two Gospels.[10] In some instances, as in the example provided above, the verbatim material suggests direct borrowing. But in other instances, the degree of verbatim overlap is less significant and may therefore result from access to a common written or oral source. The tendency in scholarship today has been to posit that if Luke used Mark as a source in some instances, then he likely used him in all instances of parallel material, even when there is very little verbatim overlap in language.

If Mark provided source material to Luke when the latter composed his Gospel, then a significant percentage of his material can be traced back to its original source. However, Luke also preserves a substantial amount of material in common with the Gospel of Matthew. Like the material he borrowed from Mark, some of the material Luke has in common with Matthew is also preserved in markedly similar language. Thus, we may logically conclude either that Luke used Matthew or vice versa or that they shared a common earlier source. Perhaps the following example will provide a clue concerning how these two Gospels are related textually:

No man can serve two masters: for either he will hate the one, and love the other; or else he will hold to the one, and despise the other. Ye cannot serve God and mammon. (Matthew 6:24)

No servant can serve two masters: for either he will hate the one, and love the other; or else he will hold to the one, and despise the other. Ye cannot serve God and mammon. (Luke 16:13)

In this example, there is only a single difference in wording and order for the entire twenty-seven-word phrase in Greek. Such direct overlap is consistent with direct textual borrowing, either from a similar source or one from the other.

Traditionally, the answer to this question has been to suggest a hypothetical document to which both Matthew and Luke had access. Sometimes called Q, an abbreviation of the German word *Quelle* (source), this hypothetical document became the subject of intense scrutiny and interest in the twentieth century.[11] Today, scholars are more critical of the hypothesis and any definitive conclusions that can be drawn from it; however, it remains the most accepted way to make reference to the verbatim material shared by Matthew and Luke.[12] Hypothetical sources are in reality rather useless for reconstructing the history of Christianity, because they can be made to say almost anything, their content cannot be verified, and all results based on such documents will always remain tentative.

Reference to an earlier source does not explain why Luke has the word "servant" in his account and Matthew does not. Many scholars have proposed that Luke consistently preserved the wording of Q more accurately while Matthew often abbreviated their common source, both unverifiable suppositions. Another solution to this complex problem is that Matthew used Luke as a source or vice versa, and that there is no prior hypothetical source Q. Both of these propositions are being defended with increasing frequency and vigor.[13] It seems wise to move on to those areas where definitive answers can be reached rather than narrowly focus on a hypothetical source that can never be verified. Therefore, we should remain open to the possibility that there was a primitive, written Gospel source used by both Matthew and Luke from which they drew sparingly and also willingly altered, thus suggesting that they were somewhat hesitant to quote freely from this source.[14] Equally possible is the proposition that one borrowed from the other.

Before settling the issue, it will be important to explore whether there is a genetic literary relationship between the Gospels of Matthew and Mark. Returning to the story of the stilling of the storm, the following example demonstrates that, like the Gospel of Luke, the Gospel of Matthew also used the Gospel of Mark as a source.

"And they were exceedingly afraid and said to one another, 'What kind of man is this that even the wind and sea *obeys* him?'" (Mark 4:41; author's translation, emphasis added).

"The men were amazed, saying, 'What kind of man is this that the winds and the sea *obey* him?'" (Matthew 8:27; author's translation, emphasis added).

Similar to the parallel between the Gospels of Mark and Luke, the parallel with Matthew also shows that Mark's incorrect grammar has been corrected but that the sense has again been preserved. Matthew also contains the verb "to be amazed," replacing the idea that the disciples were "afraid." The negative connotations of the disciples being afraid of Jesus are obvious, but the disciples can be respectfully amazed without any negative implications. Again, it appears that the Gospel of Matthew used the Gospel of Mark for some of its material. When seen together, it appears that the logical conclusion would be that Mark wrote first, that Matthew borrowed from Mark, and that Luke borrowed from both, as is evident in his cumbersome phrase "the disciples were afraid (from Mark) and amazed (from Matthew)." This conclusion may, however, give a false sense of security because it implies that the direction of borrowing between the three Gospels will be consistently obvious and in the same direction as the above example. Unfortunately, this is one of the most obvious and clear examples in the Gospels.

To summarize what we know today, it is quite certain that, after Paul, Mark is the earliest existing source on the life of Jesus. Subsequent to him, the authors of the Gospels of Matthew and Luke used the Gospel of Mark in many instances. Not only did they respect the

Gospel of Mark as a source for information concerning the life of Jesus, they also preserved intact most of his language. However, they often felt it necessary to reorder the sequence of events and to correct the grammar of the Gospel of Mark. Additionally, both the author of the Gospel of Matthew and that of the Gospel of Luke had access to other materials that they used when composing their accounts. These sources are difficult to trace, but hints still remain. Like Paul, these authors were strongly influenced by the written and oral traditions about Jesus, and each felt comfortable that his information was not only significant enough to warrant the writing of another Gospel but also valid enough to warrant a reordering of earlier accounts of the life of Jesus.

THE SOURCES OF THE GOSPEL OF JOHN

It is unfortunate that in a discussion of the sources used by the Evangelists there is no means of authenticating the sources used by the Gospel of John, or whether it was written early or late. Generally, any dating of the fourth Gospel relies on presuppositions about its doctrines or structure. And there is a weak scholarly consensus today that the Gospel of John should be dismissed as a historical source.[15] Three important points might be marshaled in support of an early dating for the Gospel and its accuracy as a historical source for information on the life of Jesus. First, the author associates himself with the eyewitness tradition of John the Beloved, and although he does not explicitly mention that he is John the Beloved, a later author added a final epilogue making the connection more obvious (see John 21:24).[16] Our impression of the credibility of this author is therefore at least a personal affirmation of the earliness or lateness of this Gospel and/or the traditions it contains. Second, unlike the other Gospel authors, the author of the fourth Gospel implies that he was the unnamed disciple of John the Baptist who followed Jesus early on, thus making him the earliest follower of Jesus to write a Gospel (see John 1:35–40). This suggestion might be a subtle hint left by the author to establish the authority of his work. Third, the author is definitely not in a discussion with the Synoptic Gospels (Matthew, Mark, and Luke), nor does he correct them in any way, as both Matthew and Luke do to the Gospel of Mark. The author relies on extensive and independent information about

Jesus, both historical narrative and the words of Jesus. Whether the
date of the fourth Gospel can be ascertained or not, there is no
historically compelling reason to dismiss the association that John the
Beloved wrote the Gospel of John from a personal eyewitness perspective. Some evidence remains that a later editor may have introduced at
least minor changes (see John 21:24–25), but that does not compromise
the integrity of the core of the Gospel.

OTHER SOURCES ON THE LIFE OF JESUS

References outside the New Testament preserve some limited
information about Jesus that is independent of the Gospels and Paul
(Josephus, Tacitus, and Suetonius). Josephus, a Jewish author and military leader who later became a Roman sympathizer, chronicled many
events from the first two centuries. Although he is patently pro-Roman
in his work *War,* his later work *Antiquities* shows signs of his continued
affection for his people, the Jews. Two of these sources—Tacitus and
Suetonius—were written after the turn of the first century but report
information from the mid-first century AD. Therefore, these sources
preserve the earliest historical biographical information about Jesus
outside the New Testament.

Josephus wrote: "Now, there was about this time Jesus, a wise man,
if it be lawful to call him a man, for he was a doer of wonderful works—
a teacher of such men as receive the truth with pleasure. He drew over
to him both many of the Jews, and many of the Gentiles. He was [the]
Christ; and when Pilate, at the suggestion of the principal men amongst
us, had condemned him to the cross, those that loved him at the first
did not forsake him, for he appeared to them alive again the third day, as
the divine prophets had foretold these and ten thousand other wonderful things concerning him; and the tribe of Christians, so named
from him, are not extinct at this day."[17]

Farther, "Festus was now dead, and Albinus was but upon the road;
so he assembled the sanhedrin of judges, and brought before them the
brother of Jesus, who was called Christ."[18]

Tacitus wrote: "Therefore, to scotch the rumour, Nero substituted
as culprits, and punished with the utmost refinements of cruelty, a class
of men, loathed for their vices, whom the crowd styled Christians.

Christus, the founder of the name, had undergone the death penalty in the reign of Tiberius, by sentence of the procurator Pontius Pilatus."[19]

And Suetonius recorded: "Since the Jews constantly made disturbances at the instigation of Chrestus, he expelled them from Rome."[20]

Although these sources amount to little more than historical recognition that Jesus lived and had followers in the first century, they are some of the earliest sources on the life of Jesus.

OTHER POTENTIAL FIRST-CENTURY SOURCES

Attempts to date other noncanonical writings as early as the Gospels in the New Testament have proven to be problematic. The most common suggestion is that the document entitled the Gospel of Thomas dates to the latter half of the first century. Its contents are clearly influenced by a deviant form of Christianity and are largely independent from the writings in the New Testament. This independence has led many to suppose that it is as early or earlier than the Gospel of Mark.[21] The fallacy of this conclusion is that independence does not require it to be early or late but only separate from the canonical writings. Independence may equally be an argument for corruption and lateness. Therefore, the majority of scholars today are hesitant to use it as a historical source for information about Jesus of Nazareth.[22]

CONCLUSION

Remarkably, the letters of Paul and the four Gospels together remain the earliest sources for information about Jesus. Informed by oral traditions and perhaps some earlier written sources, Paul and the Evangelists provide us with their understanding of Jesus beginning around AD 50 and stretching forward into the next three or four decades. Assuming that what they wrote represents what was passed on to them in the two decades after the death of Jesus, we are very close to having sources that date from the life of Jesus. No other collection of sources can make an equal claim to authenticity or originality. That is not to say that the four Gospels or the letters of Paul have not suffered corruption but only that they are our earliest sources.

Moreover, it is likely that both the Gospel of Matthew and the Gospel of Luke used the Gospel of Mark as a historically reliable source.

They carefully corrected both his grammar and ordering of events, thus implying that they had access to what they felt were more accurate sources, but they maintained in most instances the wording of Jesus' teachings as Mark reported them. That Matthew and Luke relied on other sources shows that there was authoritative information about Jesus in the first century that was of similar value to the Gospel of Mark. They used these sources, whether written or oral, to rewrite Mark in a positive way. Sometime during this process, the Gospel of John also presented an account of the life of Jesus from an eyewitness standpoint, perhaps the only author in the New Testament to do so. The date when he wrote cannot be confirmed, but we have good historical reasons for trusting his information. Finally, first-century references to Jesus outside the New Testament provide some historical perspective.

All other "gospels" and accounts of the life of Jesus outside the New Testament date from the second century or later. That does not always indicate that someone writing in the second century would not have had access to reliable historical information about Jesus, but they were certainly written after the close of the New Testament record.

NOTES

1. The exception to this would be the direct borrowing that took place between the epistles of Jude and 2 Peter. Although we are uncertain of the direction of borrowing, it appears that the epistle of 2 Peter borrowed from the epistle of Jude. The reason for suspecting that 2 Peter used Jude as source is that Jude presents the material in a single sustained sermon whereas 2 Peter breaks up the material with commentary. For example, see 2 Peter 2:10–11/Jude 1:8–9 and 2 Peter 2:12–13/Jude 1:10–12.

2. The conversion of Paul most likely dates to the second year after the Resurrection (see Rainer Riesner, *Paul's Early Period: Chronology, Mission Strategy, Theology,* trans. Doug Stott [Grand Rapids, MI: Eerdmans, 1998], 59–74; Thomas A. Wayment, "The Birth and Death Dates of Jesus Christ," in *The Life and Teachings of Jesus Christ: From Bethlehem through the Sermon on the Mount,* ed. Richard Neitzel Holzapfel and Thomas A. Wayment [Salt Lake City: Deseret Book, 2005], 383–94).

3. The two most notable advocates are John Dominic Crossan, *The Birth of Christianity* (San Francisco: Harper Collins, 1998), and Bart D. Ehrman, *Lost*

Christianities: The Battles for Scripture and the Faiths We Never Knew (New York: Oxford University Press, 2003).

4. Larry W. Hurtado, *Lord Jesus Christ: Devotion to Jesus in Earliest Christianity* (Grand Rapids, MI: Eerdmans, 2003), 136.

5. Richard Neitzel Holzapfel, "Early Accounts of the Story," in *From the Last Supper through the Resurrection,* ed. Richard Neitzel Holzapfel and Thomas A. Wayment (Salt Lake City: Deseret Book, 2003), 401–21.

6. James D. G. Dunn, *Christianity in the Making: Jesus Remembered* (Grand Rapids, MI: Eerdmans, 2003), 173–86.

7. Heinrich J. Holtzmann is generally credited with being the first to propose what would later be termed the Synoptic theory, see *Die synoptischen Evangelien: Ihr Ursprung und geschichtlicher Chrarakter* (Leipzig: Wilhelm Engelmann, 1863). Compare John S. Kloppenborg Verbin, *Excavating Q: The History and Setting of the Sayings Gospel* (Minneapolis: Fortress, 2000), 9–54, who provides the most complete discussion of the Synoptic theory.

8. The verbatim language in the passage is restricted to "one to another, 'What kind of man is this that even the wind/winds . . . obey him.'"

9. Some of the most obvious examples of Luke's corrective tendency when borrowing from Mark can be seen in Mark 5:1–20/Luke 8:26–39; Mark 5:21–43/Luke 8:40–56; Mark 9:14–29/Luke 9:37–43. At times Luke's corrective tendency has been obscured through translation because very few modern translations are willing to preserve the grammatical infelicities of the Gospel of Mark.

10. It is possible that Mark reproduced a source verbatim and therefore Luke's wording may reflect the wording of the Gospel of Mark and his source.

11. The most comprehensive treatments of the subject remain Kloppenborg Verbin, *Excavating Q,* and Robert H. Stein, *The Synoptic Problem: An Introduction* (Grand Rapids, MI: Baker, 1987).

12. Dunn, *Christianity in the Making,* 147–58; Hurtado, *Lord Jesus,* 217–56. For a recent survey of the hypothesis, see Thomas A. Wayment, "A Viewpoint on the Supposedly Lost Gospel Q," in *Religious Educator* 5, no. 3 (2004): 105–15.

13. See Mark Goodacre, *The Case Against Q: Studies in Markan Priority and the Synoptic Problem* (Harrisburg, PA: Trinity, 2002); Martin Hengel, *The Four Gospels and the One Gospel of Jesus Christ* (Harrisburg, PA: Trinity, 2000), 169–207; Michael D. Goulder, "Is Q a Juggernaut?" in *Journal of Biblical Literature* 115, no. 4 (1996): 667–81.

14. I feel that the most compelling examples of borrowing are Matthew 3:7–10/Luke 3:7–9; Matthew 3:12/Luke 3:17; Matthew 6:24/Luke 16:13; Matthew 6:25–33/Luke 12:22–31; Matthew 7:1–5/Luke 6:37–42; Matthew 7:7–11/Luke 11:9–13; Matthew 8:19–22/Luke 9:57–60; Matthew 11:2–11, 16–19/Luke 7:18–19, 22–28, 31–35; Matthew 11:21–27/Luke 10:12–15, 21–22; Matthew 12:39–45/Luke 11:29–32, 24–26; Matthew 13:33/Luke 13:20–21; Matthew 24:45–51/Luke 12:42–46. Others include substantially longer lists. See John S. Kloppenborg Verbin, *Q Parallels: Synopsis, Critical Notes, and Concordance* (Sonoma, CA: Polebridge, 1988).

15. The most ardent proponent to dismiss the Gospel of John as a historical source was Walter Bauer, *Orthodoxy and Heresy in Earliest Christianity,* ed. Robert A.

Kraft and Gerhard Krodel, 2d ed. (Mifflintown, PA: Sigler, 1996). A later, and quite successful, counterattack was launched by C. H. Dodd, *Historical Tradition in the Fourth Gospel* (Cambridge: Cambridge University Press, 1963).

16. That the author of the final two verses is not the same as the author of the entire Gospel is seen in the statement, "*We* know that *his* [i.e. John's] testimony is true" and "there are also many other things which Jesus did, the which, if they should be written every one, *I suppose* that even the world itself could not contain the books that should be written. Amen" (John 21:24–25, emphasis added). The "we" of verse 24 is distinct from the "I" of verse 25 and thus reveals the work of an editor or compiler.

17. Josephus, *Antiquities,* 18.63–64, trans. William Whiston, in *The Works of Josephus* (Peabody, MA: Hendrickson, 1987). This reference may have been massaged by a Christian scribe who was sensitive to Josephus's wording. Many scholars have suggested that the following phrases were added by a well-meaning Christian scribe, "If it be lawful to call him a man, for he was a doer of wonderful works. . . . He was [the] Christ." Josephus' second quotation is universally recognized as original.

18. Josephus, *Antiquities,* 20.200, trans. Whiston, *The Works of Josephus.*

19. Tacitus, *The Annals of Tacitus,* 15.44, in *Tacitus: Annals XIII–XVI,* trans. John Jackson, Loeb Classical Library (Cambridge, MA: Harvard University Press, 1991).

20. Suetonius, "The Deified Claudius," 25.4, trans. J. C. Rolfe, *Suetonius, The Lives of the Caesars,* 2 vols. (Cambridge, MA: Harvard University Press, 1970).

21. See, for example, Stephen J. Patterson, *The Gospel of Thomas and Jesus* (Sonoma, CA: Polebridge, 1993), 110.

22. Dunn, *Christianity in the Making,* 161–67.

8

WHO REALLY WROTE THE GOSPELS? A STUDY OF TRADITIONAL AUTHORSHIP

Frank F. Judd Jr.

For some, the question of who wrote the books of the New Testament is really no question at all. There are those who would say that all one has to do is look at the title of the book. But the issue of authorship is not that simple. As early as the third century AD, the Christian theologian Origen of Alexandria expressed his doubts concerning the Pauline authorship of Hebrews, while his student Dionysius, bishop of Alexandria, challenged the Johannine authorship of the book of Revelation.[1] Debates concerning the authorship of various books of the Bible continued through the centuries. In the late seventeenth century, the French priest Richard Simon asserted that the titles of the four Gospels were not placed there by the Gospel writers themselves but were added much later.[2]

Even though skepticism of traditional authorship has persisted to the present, this particular issue has been more of an academic exercise than a pivotal issue for many Latter-day Saints and other Christians, who have often accepted traditional authorship without question. The

---

Frank F. Judd Jr. is an assistant professor of ancient scripture at Brigham Young University.

Prophet Joseph Smith, however, understood that the process of writing, transcribing, and compiling the books of the Bible was quite complex. He taught, "From sundry revelations which had been received, it was apparent that many important points touching the salvation of man, had been taken from the Bible, or lost before it was compiled."[3] This chapter will examine the evidence for traditional authorship of the Gospels in light of latter-day scripture and modern revelation.

THE WRITING OF THE GOSPELS

What was the process by which the Gospel accounts were written? Because of the belief in revelation, Latter-day Saints might suppose that each Gospel writer received an extended revelation concerning the ministry of Jesus Christ, which he then simply wrote down from beginning to end. This is certainly possible. It is true that the brother of Jared, Nephi, and John the Revelator received lengthy visions of the history of the world, which they were then instructed to write down (see Ether 3:22–27; 1 Nephi 14:20–28; Revelation 1:11; 21:5). But God has often followed another model for historical or biographical sacred writings. This is most clearly illustrated in the Book of Mormon.

God could have simply given the prophet Mormon a lengthy revelation concerning the history of the Nephites, which Mormon could have subsequently written down. But instead, Mormon, who was not an eyewitness to the events that happened before his time, relied on written source material for compiling his narrative. For example, Mormon stated concerning his use of the records that were in his possession: "After I had made an abridgment from the [large] plates of Nephi, . . . I searched among the records which had been delivered into my hands, and I found these [small] plates. . . . [The] remainder of my record I shall take from the [large] plates of Nephi. . . . But behold, I shall take these [small] plates, which contain these prophesyings and revelations, and put them with the remainder of my record" (Words of Mormon 1:3, 5–6). This is not to say, of course, that the use of previously written sources precludes revelation. Inspiration is essential in order to appropriately select material from those written sources. After explaining the sources he used, Mormon added, "And now I, Mormon, proceed to finish out my record, which I take from the [large] plates of

Nephi; and *I make it according to the knowledge and the understanding which God has given me*" (Words of Mormon 1:9, emphasis added).[4]

Concerning the use of previously written material for the writing of scripture, Elder Bruce R. McConkie explained: "Our understanding of the prophetic word will be greatly expanded if we know how one prophet quotes another, usually without acknowledging his source. . . . Once the Lord has revealed his doctrine in precise language to a chosen prophet, there is no reason why he should inspire another prophet to choose the same words in presenting the same doctrine on a subsequent occasion. It is much easier and simpler to quote that which has already been given."[5] For example, when the resurrected Savior appeared to the Nephites, He decided to teach them many things that had already been taught by Isaiah, Micah, and Malachi.[6] Rather than summarize those teachings in His own words, Jesus quoted directly from the writings of those previous prophets.[7]

How does this apply to the writing of the Gospels? Both Matthew and John were Apostles and eyewitnesses of the mortal ministry of Jesus Christ.[8] But not all of the Gospel writers witnessed the mortal ministry of Jesus themselves. Papias, an early Christian from the second century, preserved the following information concerning Mark: "Mark became Peter's interpreter and wrote down accurately, but not in order, all that he [Peter] remembered of the things said and done by the Lord. *For he [Mark] had not heard the Lord or been one of his followers; but later, as I said, a follower of Peter.* Peter used to teach as the occasion demanded, without giving systematic arrangement to the Lord's sayings."[9] If this tradition is accurate, Mark did not actually witness the events he included in his Gospel but rather wrote down the things he heard Peter teach about the Savior's ministry.

Luke is the only writer to tell us within his Gospel explicitly about his compilation process:

> "Forasmuch as many have taken in hand to set forth in order a declaration of those things which are most surely believed among us, even as they delivered them unto us, which from the beginning were eyewitnesses, and ministers of the word; it seemed good to me also, having had perfect

understanding of all things from the very first, to write unto
thee in order, most excellent Theophilus, that thou mightest
know the certainty of those things, wherein thou hast been
instructed" (Luke 1:1–4).

Luke said that "many" before him had written down (that is, "taken
in hand to set forth," verse 1) accounts of the life and teachings of the
Savior (that is, "those things which are most surely believed among us,"
verse 1) but that it seemed like a good idea to him to write an account
that was better and more orderly (that is, "in order," verse 3). In other
words, Luke knew of previously written Gospel accounts and used them
as he compiled his own Gospel. It is interesting to note that Papias said
Mark's Gospel was accurate, but not "in order." It is possible that Luke
was referring to the Gospel of Mark, among other early written
accounts.

Elder McConkie taught the following concerning Luke's sources:

> Many of the early [Christian] saints recorded their testi-
> monies or gospels, bearing eyewitness accounts of the divinity
> of our Lord and of his ministry among men, just as many with
> personal knowledge of Joseph Smith and his work of restora-
> tion have written journals, letters, and histories delineating
> what took place in the ushering in of this dispensation. *Luke had
> access to many of these ancient gospels.* It may be also, as some scholars
> speculate, that of the four gospels now in the New Testament,
> *Mark was written first; that Matthew and Luke had before them Mark's
> account* when they recorded their testimonies.[10]

But Luke did not claim to have personally witnessed the events he
narrated in his Gospel. The King James Version reads: "even as they
delivered them unto us, which from the beginning were eyewitnesses,
and ministers of the word" (Luke 1:2). Because the KJV English of this
verse reads somewhat ambiguously, some may assume that Luke claimed
that others ("they") gave written and oral information about the Savior
to those, including himself ("us"),[11] who were among the actual "eyewitnesses" of the ministry of Jesus Christ. But that is not what Luke
actually said, nor would it make sense for Luke to solicit information

about the life of the Savior from others—nonwitnesses—if Luke himself was an eyewitness. The English relative clause "which from the beginning were eyewitnesses, and ministers of the word" is a participial phrase in the Greek text that can only refer to the subject of the verb "delivered."[12] A more accurate way to translate this would be, "Even as they, who from the beginning were eyewitnesses and ministers of the word, delivered them unto us."[13] Thus, Luke is not claiming to be an eyewitness of the Lord's ministry, but he is saying that he received his information from eyewitnesses.[14] These eyewitness sources seem to include both written and oral accounts.[15]

Early Christian tradition from the second century also preserved the following concerning Luke: "This physician Luke, after Christ's ascension, since Paul had taken him with him as a companion of his travels, composed it in his own name according to his thinking. Yet *neither did he himself see the Lord in the flesh.*"[16] Once again, if these traditions are accurate, neither Mark nor Luke personally witnessed the events they wrote in their Gospels, but both received information from eyewitnesses.

The fact that an author was an eyewitness, however, would not preclude that person from utilizing previously written sources. Take the Gospel of John, for example. A comparison of John 1 with Doctrine and Covenants 93 suggests that the initial part of chapter 1 of John's Gospel actually came from the writings of John the Baptist.[17] The language of Doctrine and Covenants 93:6–18 is very similar to that found in John 1:1–18. Concerning the source of that information, we are told: "John saw and bore record of the fulness of my glory, and the fulness of John's record is hereafter to be revealed" (D&C 93:6). Which John is this referring to? The revelation continues: "I, John, bear record, and lo, the heavens were opened, and the Holy Ghost descended upon him [Jesus] in the form of a dove, and sat upon him, and there came a voice out of heaven saying: This is my beloved Son" (D&C 93:15). According to the Gospel of John, which never refers to John the Beloved by his name, it was John the Baptist who bore record at the baptism of the Savior: "And John bare record, saying, I saw the Spirit descending from heaven like a dove, and it abode upon him. And I knew him not: but he that sent me to baptize with water, the same said unto me, Upon whom thou shalt see the Spirit descending, and remaining on him, the same is he which baptizeth with the Holy Ghost. And I saw, and bare record that this is the Son of God" (John 1:32–34). Thus, John the Baptist also made a written record, a portion of which was used in the Gospel of John.[18] We have been assured "that if you are faithful you shall receive the fulness of the record of John" (D&C 93:18).

Evidence also suggests that the Gospel of Matthew, although attributed to an eyewitness, utilized previously written sources. This is plausible because the Apostle Matthew only had a firsthand knowledge of the Savior's life after his own conversion. For example, Matthew was not an eyewitness to the birth and first years of the Savior. As the Gospel of Matthew begins narrating the birth of the Lord, it says, "Now the birth of Jesus Christ was on this wise" (Matthew 1:18). The Joseph Smith Translation, however, adds: "Now, *as it is written,* the birth of Jesus Christ was on this wise" (JST, Matthew 2:1, emphasis added).[19] Thus, even though Matthew was an eyewitness, he used previously written sources for parts of his Gospel.[20] Robert L. Millet observed, "For Latter-day Saints, it is not difficult to believe that God could reveal the very same words to Matthew and Luke that he inspired Mark to record. . . . At the same time, it would not be out of harmony with principles of truth for one Gospel writer to utilize the writings of another."[21] As we can see, rather than dictating to the Gospel writers the details of the ministry of the Savior, God seems to have followed the same pattern used in writing the Book of Mormon: the inspired use of previously written material.

COMPILATION OF THE GOSPELS

The canon of the New Testament did not develop in a day. The process of compilation took centuries. The books that eventually became part of the New Testament canon originally existed singly and separately. For example, when Paul wrote his epistle to the Galatians, the Galatian Christians did not instantaneously possess all of Paul's other letters. Over time, early Christian congregations shared and copied documents they collected. Thus, each congregation started out with one or two documents and eventually obtained more and more. Early stages of this process can be seen in the New Testament itself.

Paul encouraged the Saints at Colossae: "And when this epistle is read among you, cause that it be read also in the church of the Laodiceans; and that ye likewise read the epistle from Laodicea" (Colossians 4:16). Paul did not explicitly direct them to make copies of the other documents. We know, however, that copies were indeed being made, or else the documents would not have survived over the centuries.

The implications of this process are important for our understanding of the authorship of the Gospels. Early Christian congregations may have originally possessed only one Gospel account. As such, there was no pressing need to differentiate one Gospel from another. Whichever Gospel they possessed was not the Gospel according to so-and-so, but rather it was for them simply *the* Gospel. For example, the *Didache,* an early Christian document written in the first part of the second century, quoted from and referred to what we know as the Gospel of Matthew in the following way: "Nor should you pray like the hypocrites, but as the Lord commanded *in his gospel.*"[22] This document then quotes from what we know as Matthew 6:9–13. Another early Christian author, Justin Martyr, living in the middle of the second century, quoted from and referred to what we know as the Gospel of Mark in a similar way: "We learn from the *Memoirs* of the apostles that he changed the name of one of the apostles to *Peter* (besides having changed the names of the two brothers, the sons of Zebedee to that of Boanerges, which means 'sons of thunder')."[23] This reference is specifically from what we know as Mark 3:16–17.

The above references suggest that the Gospels may have originally been anonymous. Thus, it is entirely possible, as some scholars had suggested centuries earlier, that the title of each of the Gospels was added after the fact.[24] It is important to note, however, that this premise does *not* necessarily imply that traditional authorship is inaccurate. It only means that early Christians who originally possessed one Gospel seem to have either been unaware of or unconcerned about the identity of the author of their Gospel account. It also may mean that the authors of these Gospels were not really concerned about taking credit for their work. These Gospels were testimonies about the Savior; they were not about the authors.[25] Even Luke, who is the only Gospel writer to say anything about himself, does not refer to himself by name (see Luke

1:1–3; Acts 1:1–2). All the Gospel accounts, even Matthew and John, are written in the third person and not in the first person.[26]

Not until early Christian congregations obtained more than one Gospel account did the need arise to differentiate them. During the second century, traditional authorship became more well known and established. The earliest references to each Gospel by name are from the second century.[27] Irenaeus, a Christian bishop living around AD 180, is the earliest surviving source to make this distinction, naming all four Gospels together. His poetic description states: "There cannot be either more or fewer gospels than there are. . . . The one according to John . . . tells of his primal, powerful, and glorious generation from the Father. . . . That according to Luke . . . begins with the priest Zechariah sacrificing incense to God. . . . Matthew tells of his human generation. . . . But Mark began from the prophetic Spirit coming to men from on high. . . . Four forms of the Gospel; four forms of the activity of the Lord."[28] Thus, sometime before or during the middle of the second century, Christian congregations began to acquire additional Gospel accounts and tried to ascertain who wrote them. As Christians searched for answers, they ascribed the Gospels to Matthew the tax collector, Mark the missionary companion of Peter, Luke the missionary companion of Paul, and John the fisherman.

THE AUTHORS OF THE GOSPELS

Who really wrote each of our four Gospels? The answer to this question is more complex than it may appear to some. An example from Latter-day Saint Church history may help illustrate the issue. When Latter-day Saints refer to the *Lectures on Faith*, they often say that those lectures were authored by the Prophet Joseph Smith. Careful research, however, has revealed that this attribution is not precisely accurate. There seems to have been multiple authors involved in the writing of the *Lectures on Faith*. Larry E. Dahl explained:

> [We have] some historical evidence of Joseph Smith's participation in their preparation, and acknowledge two recent authorship studies which conclude that others, particularly Sidney Rigdon, were also involved. . . . Both studies conclude

that Sidney Rigdon was heavily involved, and that Joseph Smith was probably the author of Lecture 2. The differences [in word-print studies] suggest that Joseph Smith had less to do with Lectures 3, 4, and 6 . . . and that William W. Phelps and/or Parley P. Pratt could have had at least some editorial influence on Lecture 5. . . . What then can we conclude about authorship of the Lectures on Faith? *It is clear that several of the brethren participated in writing them. It is also clear that Joseph Smith and perhaps others prepared them for publication after they were written.*[29]

Thus, although Joseph Smith was involved with the publication of the *Lectures on Faith,* other early Latter-day Saint leaders did most of the writing.[30] This conclusion does not denigrate the *Lectures on Faith.* It only means that other individuals, in addition to the Prophet Joseph Smith, were involved in the production of those lectures.

The issue of who wrote a book of the Bible is no less complex. For example, one might ask who really wrote the epistle to the Romans in the New Testament. Most people would probably say that Paul wrote it. But Paul was not the person who actually took a writing instrument to a sheet of papyrus and wrote the epistle from beginning to end. Rather, Paul used the services of a scribe, to whom he dictated the contents of the letter: "I Tertius, who wrote this epistle, salute you in the Lord" (Romans 16:22).[31] Even though Paul often referred to the letters that he "wrote," it would be more accurate to say that he dictated at least some of them to a scribe who wrote them down. For example, in his letter to the Galatians, Paul said: "Now the things which I write unto you, behold, before God, I lie not" (Galatians 1:20). Later in the same letter, however, we learn that the only part of the letter that Paul actually wrote with his own hand was the closing. "Ye see how large a letter I have written unto you with mine own hand" (Galatians 6:11). A more accurate translation of that verse is "Ye see with what large letters I have written unto you with mine own hand."[32] After the dictated message was written down by a scribe, Paul himself wrote the concluding remarks with very large handwriting, different from the scribe's handwriting. According to 2 Thessalonians, this is the way Paul composed all of his letters: "The salutation of Paul with mine own hand, which is the token in every epistle: so I write" (2 Thessalonians 3:18).

Thus, the answer to the question of who really wrote a document of the Bible depends upon whether the credit is given to the person who actually wrote down (or compiled and edited) the information or to the person who was the original source of the information.[33] Let us apply this perspective to each of the four Gospels. Who is the author of the Gospel of Mark? Recall that according to early Christian tradition, Mark was a missionary companion of the Apostle Peter and wrote down those things that Peter taught him about the life of the Savior.[34] In this particular case, the scribe rather than the source of the information received credit for the Gospel. Thus, this Gospel might have been called the Gospel of Peter, but it is traditionally called the Gospel of Mark.

Who is the author of the Gospel of Luke? Recall that Luke said that he himself was not an eyewitness but that the information contained in his Gospel came from eyewitnesses.[35] Recall also that it is possible that one of those sources could have been the Gospel of Mark, with Peter as the unacknowledged eyewitness.[36] Here we have a situation similar to the Gospel of Mark. In this case again, the scribe, rather than the source of the information, received the credit for the Gospel. Thus, we have the Gospel of Luke rather than the Gospel according to whoever was the source of Luke's information.

Who is the author of the Gospel of John? We know that John was an Apostle and therefore an eyewitness to much of the Savior's ministry (see Matthew 4:20–22; John 20:2–8). As we have seen, this fact did not preclude the use of previously written sources for his Gospel account—in this case, a portion of the writings of John the Baptist (see John 1:1–18; compare D&C 93:6–18). But interestingly, even though this Gospel is traditionally attributed to an eyewitness, it was not written in the first person but rather in the third person. Let us review the previous examples. Rather than personally write out a complete Gospel by hand, Peter taught Mark about the life of the Savior, and Mark wrote it down. Rather than sit down and write out a long letter by hand, Paul dictated to Tertius the letter to the Romans, and Tertius wrote it down. It is possible that the same is true of John and his Gospel.[37]

Toward the end of John's Gospel, Jesus reminded Peter that John would not die but rather live until the Second Coming (see John 21:23; compare D&C 7:1–3). Immediately following that conversation, it says, "This is the disciple which testifieth of these things, and wrote these things: and *we* know that his testimony is true" (John 21:24; emphasis added). In what way did John write these things? In light of what we saw with Paul and his use of scribes, we should investigate further. One can understand the identity of John as the one who testified of the things in this Gospel, but who is "we"? Whoever "we" refers to, they differentiated themselves from John, or "him." It is possible that this anonymous "we" refers to faithful early Christians—functioning like Mark and Luke—who compiled (or edited or revised) and actually wrote down the Gospel account in its present form.[38] This "we" passage is similar to what is found in the Book of Mormon, when Mormon added editorial comments such as "and thus we see."[39]

Another passage illustrates this idea. After narrating the Crucifixion of the Savior, the Gospel of John states, "And he that saw it bare record, and his record is true: and he knoweth that he saith true, that ye might believe" (John 19:35). There may be some who conclude that this was John's way of making a veiled reference to himself in the third person.[40] In light of our discussion of John 21:24, however, it may be more likely that this is another parenthetical comment by the editors of John's Gospel.[41] If so, they received their information about the Crucifixion from the eyewitness John, who testified of the truthfulness of his recollections—to which these anonymous editors added their own testimony in this verse. Thus, the statement in John 21:24 that John "wrote these things" may mean the same thing that Paul means when he said he wrote his epistles: John gave information to scribes, similar to the way Peter gave information to Mark.[42]

By comparison, then, just as Mark compiled and wrote down the recollections of Peter, so also these anonymous Christians possibly compiled and wrote down the recollections of John. Just as Luke used oral recollections as well as previously written eyewitness accounts for the writing of his Gospel, so also these anonymous compilers may have used oral recollections and previously written eyewitness accounts. For the Gospel of John, these sources included the testimony of John the

Beloved and the writings of John the Baptist. Just as Church leaders today use clerks and secretaries to take notes, compile information, and write letters, it is possible that John used faithful Christians to assist him in the work of the kingdom.[43] Just as scribes like Tertius, not Paul himself, actually wrote down what they heard from the Apostles, so also the anonymous "we" in John's Gospel may have written down and then testified of what they heard from John. Unlike the Gospel of Mark, however, it is not the scribe or the compiler who received the credit for authoring the Gospel of John. Instead, the apostolic eyewitness and source of the information received the credit. Thus, we have the Gospel of John, rather than the Gospel according to whoever wrote down John's recollections.

Who was the author of the Gospel of Matthew? Unfortunately, there is less evidence available for answering this question than for the other Gospels. We can, however, make a few observations. First, even though the Gospel of Matthew is attributed to an eyewitness, it is also written in the third person rather than in the first person.[44] In light of our discussion of the other three Gospels, this may suggest the possibility of a similar use of scribes. Second, though this Gospel is attributed to an eyewitness, it used previously written material (compare Matthew 1:18 with JST, Matthew 2:1). It is also possible that the Gospel of Matthew, like the Gospel of Luke, also used the Gospel of Mark as one of its sources. Recall the conclusion of Elder McConkie: "It may be also, as some scholars speculate, that of the four gospels now in the New Testament, Mark was written first; that Matthew and Luke had before them Mark's account when they recorded their testimonies."[45] Lastly, Matthew's Gospel may also be like the Gospel of John in that the eyewitness, not the scribe who may have compiled the sources, received credit for authoring the Gospel.

CONCLUSION

Latter-day Saints love the Bible and revere it as "the word of God as far as it is translated correctly" (Article of Faith 8). Elder Joseph B. Wirthlin explained: "The fragmentary nature of the biblical record and the errors in it, resulting from multiple transcriptions, translations, and interpretations, do not diminish our belief in it as the word of God 'as far as it is translated correctly.' We read and study the Bible, we teach and preach from it, and we strive to live according to the eternal truths it contains. We love this collection of holy writ."[46]

Thus, even though there have been problems with translation and transmission of the Bible, Latter-day Saints still believe that the Bible is an inspired document. Elder Neal A. Maxwell taught that "inaccuracy of some translating must not, however, diminish our appreciation for the powerful *testimony* and ample *historicity* of the New Testament. . . . These pages are a treasure trove testifying of Jesus."[47]

Latter-day Saints should feel the same way about the issue of authorship of books of the Bible. We believe traditional authorship as far as it has been handed down to us correctly. We also understand that the issue of who wrote a biblical book is not as important as the truth that the book contains. Concerning this, President J. Reuben Clark concluded:

> I am not really concerned, and no man of faith should be, about the exact authorship of the books of the Bible. More than one Prophet may well have written parts of books now collected under one heading. I do not know. There may have been 'ghost writers' in those days, as now. The Lord gave Aaron to Moses in an equivalent capacity, and spoke to Israel through Moses by the mouth of Aaron. He may have done the same in other cases. If so, what of it?[48]

Thus, the issue of authorship of books of the Bible should not affect the way we feel about the inspiration of those books. Mark's and Luke's Gospels are inspired, even if they used oral or previously written sources and even if the scribes rather than the apostolic sources received the credit for writing them. John's and Matthew's Gospels are inspired, even if these Apostles only personally witnessed some of the events included in these Gospels and even if they utilized other early Christians to compile, edit, and write down these recollections. Each New Testament Gospel testifies of the same gospel that the resurrected Savior declared to the Nephites: "And this is the gospel which I have given unto you—that I came into the world to do will of my Father, because my Father sent me. And my Father sent me that I might be lifted up upon the cross; and after that I had been lifted up upon the cross, that I might draw all men unto me" (3 Nephi 27:13–14).

NOTES

1. See Werner Georg Kümmel, *The New Testament: The History of the Investigation of Its Problems,* trans. S. McLean Gilmour and Howard C. Kee (New York: Abingdon, 1972), 15–18.

2. Kümmel, *The New Testament,* 43–46.

3. Joseph Smith, *History of the Church of Jesus Christ of Latter-day Saints,* ed. B. H. Roberts, 2d ed. rev. (Salt Lake City: Deseret Book, 1957), 1:245.

4. Note the conclusion of Ezra Taft Benson: "Under the inspiration of God, who sees all things from the beginning, he [Mormon] abridged centuries of records, choosing the stories, speeches, and events that would be most helpful to us" (*A Witness and a Warning* [Salt Lake City: Deseret Book, 1988], 19).

5. Bruce R. McConkie, "The Doctrinal Restoration," in *The Joseph Smith Translation: The Restoration of Plain and Precious Things,* ed. Monte S. Nyman and Robert L. Millet (Provo, UT: Religious Studies Center, Brigham Young University, 1985), 17–18.

6. He also quoted his own words that eventually would be recorded in the Gospel of Matthew. Compare Matthew 5–7 with 3 Nephi 12–14.

7. When the Savior quoted from Isaiah (see 3 Nephi 22) and from Malachi (see 3 Nephi 24–25), He identified the sources from which He was quoting (see 3 Nephi 23:1; 24:1). When He quoted from Micah (see 3 Nephi 21:12–21), however, there is no indication that He identified the source.

8. According to Matthew's Gospel, Matthew was a tax collector when he became a disciple: "And as Jesus passed forth from thence, he saw a man, named Matthew, sitting at the receipt of custom: and he saith unto him, Follow me. And he arose, and followed him" (Matthew 9:9). Matthew's Gospel also informs us that John was a fisherman when he started following the Lord: "And going on from thence, he [Jesus] saw other two brethren, James the son of Zebedee, and John his brother, in a ship with Zebedee their father, mending their nets; and he called them. And they immediately left the ship and their father, and followed him" (Matthew 4:21–22).

9. Papias, quoted in Eusebius, *History of the Church,* 3.39.15–16, emphasis added. Compare also the following preserved by Eusebius: "When, by the Spirit, Peter had publicly proclaimed the Gospel in Rome, his many hearers urged Mark, as one who had followed him for years and remembered what was said, to put it all in writing. This he did and gave copies to all who asked. When Peter learned of it, he neither objected nor promoted it" (*History of the Church,* 6.14.6–7). English translations are from Paul L. Maier, *Eusebius: The Church History* (Grand Rapids, MI: Kregel, 1999), 129–30, 218.

10. Bruce R. McConkie, *Doctrinal New Testament Commentary,* 3 vols. (Salt Lake City: Bookcraft, 1965–73), 1:69, emphasis added.

11. Luke's plural reference to "us" may indicate that he was not working alone when compiling this information.

12. The phrase "which from the beginning were eyewitnesses and ministers" (*hoi ap' arches autoptai kai hyperetai genomenoi*) is in the nominative case and must be the subject of "they delivered" (*paredosan*). It cannot somehow modify the dative indirect object "us" (*hemin*) (see I. Howard Marshall, *The Gospel of Luke: A Commentary on the Greek Text* [Grand Rapids, MI: Eerdmans, 1978], 41–42).

13. See François Bovon, *Luke 1* (Minneapolis: Fortress, 2002), 21, and Joseph A. Fitzmyer, *The Gospel According to Luke* (New York: Doubleday, 1981), 1:294–96.

14. Luke also said that he "had perfect understanding of all things from the very first" (Luke 1:3). This statement most likely means that Luke had carefully "researched" all things from the very beginning of Jesus' ministry (see Bovon, *Luke 1,* 21–22; Fitzmyer, *The Gospel According to Luke,* 296–98; and Marshall, *The Gospel of Luke,* 42–43).

15. Luke knew previously *written* accounts ("many have taken in hand to set forth") as well as *oral* accounts ("they delivered them unto us"). The word *delivered* is translated from the Greek verb *paradidomi,* which can mean "to pass on to another what one knows, of oral or written tradition" (Frederick W. Danker, ed., *A Greek-English Lexicon of the New Testament and other Early Christian Literature,* 3d ed. [Chicago: University of Chicago Press, 2000], 762).

16. The Muratorian Canon, emphasis added. English translation is from Harry Y. Gamble, *The New Testament Canon: Its Making and Meaning* (Philadelphia: Fortress, 1985), 93.

17. See Robert L. Millet, "The Formation of the Canonical Gospels," in *Apocryphal Writings and the Latter-day Saints,* ed. C. Wilfred Griggs (Provo, UT: Religious Studies Center, Brigham Young University, 1986), 207–8. It would be natural, of course, for John to quote from John the Baptist. Before John became a disciple of the Savior, he seems to have been a disciple of John the Baptist. It is likely that John the Beloved is the unnamed disciple referred to in John 1:35–40. See Robert J. Matthews, *A Burning Light: The Life and Ministry of John the Baptist* (Provo, UT: Brigham Young University Press, 1972), 43–44.

18. Note the conclusion of Bruce R. McConkie: "From latter-day revelation we learn that the material in the forepart of the gospel of John (the Apostle, Revelator, and Beloved Disciple) was written originally by John the Baptist. By revelation the Lord restored to Joseph Smith part of what John the Baptist had written and promised to reveal the balance when men became sufficiently faithful to warrant receiving it" (McConkie, *Doctrinal New Testament Commentary,* 1:70–71, parentheses in original). See also Stephen E. Robinson and H. Dean Garrett, *A Commentary on the Doctrine and Covenants* (Salt Lake City: Deseret Book, 2000–5), 3:178–79.

19. See Scott H. Faulring, Kent P. Jackson, and Robert J. Matthews, eds., *Joseph Smith's New Translation of the Bible: Original Manuscripts* (Provo, UT: Religious Studies Center, Brigham Young University, 2004), 160, 236. For a convenient collection of

the JST changes in the New Testament, see Thomas A. Wayment, ed., *The Complete Joseph Smith Translation of the New Testament* (Salt Lake City: Deseret Book, 2005).

20. See Millet, "The Formation of the Canonical Gospels," 205.

21. Robert L. Millet, "The Testimony of Matthew," in *Studies in Scripture, Vol. 5: The Gospels,* ed. Kent P. Jackson and Robert L. Millet (Salt Lake City: Deseret Book, 1986), 50.

22. *Didache,* 8.1–3, emphasis added. English translation from *The Apostolic Fathers,* trans. Bart D. Ehrman, Loeb Classical Library (Cambridge, MA: Harvard University Press, 2003), 1:429.

23. Justin Martyr, *Dialogue with Trypho,* 106.3; italics are in the English translation, from *St. Justin Martyr: Dialogue with Trypho,* trans. Thomas B. Falls (Washington DC: Catholic University of America, 2003), 159.

24. Kümmel, *The New Testament,* 43–46.

25. The JST designates the Gospel of Matthew and the Gospel of John as "testimonies," rather than as "Gospels" (see Faulring, Jackson, and Matthews, *Joseph Smith's New Translation of the Bible,* 235, 442). See also Millet, "The Formation of the Canonical Gospels," 211.

26. Compare sections of the book of Acts which are written in the first person: Acts 16:10–16; 20:6–15; 21:1–17; 27:1–37; 28:10–16. There are different ways to explain the first-person accounts in Acts. Maybe Luke was an eyewitness for those sections. Or maybe Luke was using eyewitness accounts (travel diaries). It is also possible that Luke was an eyewitness for some sections and used eyewitness accounts for others. Unfortunately, Luke does not give us enough information to determine the answer.

27. See Luke Timothy Johnson, *The Writings of the New Testament: An Interpretation,* 2d ed. (Minneapolis: Fortress, 1999), 159, 187, 213–15, 525–27. The earliest extant copies of the Gospels date to the second century and contain the traditional titles. A study of the earliest manuscripts, therefore, does not answer the question of when these attributions were first included as titles of the Gospels (see Philip W. Comfort and David P. Barrett, eds., *The Text of the Earliest New Testament Greek Manuscripts* [Wheaton, IL: Tyndale House, 2001], 54).

28. Irenaeus, *Against Heresies,* 3.11.8. English translation is from Robert M. Grant, *Irenaeus of Lyons* (London: Routledge, 1997), 131–32.

29. Larry E. Dahl, "Authorship and History of the Lectures on Faith," in *The Lectures on Faith in Historical Perspective,* ed. Larry E. Dahl and Charles D. Tate Jr. (Provo, UT: Religious Studies Center, Brigham Young University, 1990), 7–8, 10, emphasis added.

30. For a recent study that concludes that Sidney Rigdon was the "principal author" of the *Lectures on Faith,* see Noel B. Reynolds, "The Case for Sidney Rigdon as Author of the Lectures on Faith," *Journal of Mormon History* 31, no. 3 (Fall 2005): 1–41, esp. 35. On this conclusion, see also Noel B. Reynolds, "The Authorship Debate Concerning *Lectures on Faith:* Exhumation and Reburial," in *The Disciple as Witness: Essays on Latter-day Saint History and Doctrine in Honor of Richard Lloyd Anderson,* ed. Stephen D. Ricks, Donald W. Parry, and Andrew H. Hedges (Provo, UT: Foundation for Ancient Research and Mormon Studies, 2000), 355–82.

31. The Apostle Peter also used the service of a scribe when composing his letters. See 1 Peter 5:12: "By Silvanus, a faithful brother unto you." For more on Paul's use of scribes, see E. Randolph Richards, *Paul and First-Century Letter Writing: Secretaries, Composition, and Collection* (Downers Grove, IL: InterVarsity, 2004); and Jerome Murphy-O'Connor, *Paul the Letter-Writer: His World, His Options, His Skills* (Collegeville, MN: The Liturgical Press, 1995).

32. See F. F. Bruce, *Commentary on Galatians* (Grand Rapids, MI: Eerdmans, 1982), 267–68, and J. Louis Martyn, *Galatians* (New York: Doubleday, 1997), 560.

33. Consider also the example of Paul's other letters. Paul often seems to have been a coauthor with other early Christian leaders such as Sosthenes (1 Corinthians 1:1), Timothy (2 Corinthians 1:1; Philippians 1:1; Colossians 1:1; 1 Thessalonians 1:1; 2 Thessalonians 1:1; Philemon 1:1), and Silvanus (1 Thessalonians 1:1; 2 Thessalonians 1:1). In each of these cases, however, Paul still received sole credit in the titles for these epistles. On Paul and his coauthors, see Richards, *Paul and First-Century Letter Writing*, 33–36, and Murphy-O'Connor, *Paul the Letter-Writer*, 16–19.

34. Papias, quoted in Eusebius, *History of the Church*, 3.39.15–16 and 6.14.6–7.

35. See Luke 1:1–3; see also the Muratorian Canon list mentioned above.

36. See McConkie, *Doctrinal New Testament Commentary*, 1:69.

37. Robert L. Millet observed: "There should be no doubt among Latter-day Saints that the canonical Gospels were compiled and composed and organized and written under the spirit of revelation. At the same time, we do not remove any of the importance or spiritual significance from these inspired authors by acknowledging Matthew, Mark, Luke, and John as divinely directed *editors* as well as creative authors" ("The Formation of the Canonical Gospels," 208, emphasis in original).

38. Stephen Robinson and Dean Garrett concluded that in John 21:24, "the pronoun 'we' identifies John's editors" (Robinson and Garrett, *A Commentary on the Doctrine and Covenants*, 3:179). Compare also John 1:14: "The Word was made flesh and dwelt among *us*, (and *we* beheld his glory, the glory as of the only begotten of the father,) full of grace and truth" (emphasis added; parentheses in KJV), and John 1:16: "And of his fullness have all *we* received, and grace for grace" (emphasis added).

39. For example, Alma 24:19, 27, 30; 28:13–14; 30:60; 46:8; Helaman 3:27–28; 6:34–36, 40; 12:1. Unlike this anonymous "we" in the Gospel of John, sometimes Mormon and Moroni identified themselves by name (see Words of Mormon 1:1, 9, 3 Nephi 5:8–20; Ether 12:6, 29).

40. According to this Gospel, John was at the feet of Jesus during at least some of the Crucifixion. From the cross, "when Jesus therefore saw his mother, and the disciple standing by, whom he loved, he saith unto his mother, Woman, behold thy son! Then saith he to the disciple, Behold thy mother! And from that hour that disciple took her unto his own home" (John 19:26–27).

41. Compare Mormon's very similar testimony concerning his use of previously written material and his own eyewitness recollections: "I do make my record from the accounts which have been given by those who were before me, until the

commencement of my day; And then I do make a record of the things which I have seen with mine own eyes. *And I know the record which I make to be a just and a true record*" (3 Nephi 5:16–18, emphasis added).

42. Or it may mean that the anonymous "we" had access to some earlier drafts written by John and used them (as well as the writings of John the Baptist) to compile John's Gospel.

43. According to Metzger and Ehrman, the use of professional scribes (as opposed to lay Christians) for the reproduction of New Testament manuscripts did not become normal practice until the fourth century (see Bruce M. Metzger and Bart D. Ehrman, *The Text of the New Testament: Its Transmission, Corruption, and Restoration,* 4th ed. [New York: Oxford University Press, 2005], 24–25).

44. It is interesting to note that the Gospel of Matthew even narrates Matthew's own call in the third person, not the first person (see Matthew 9:9). It is possible, according to Elder Alexander B. Morrison, that the author of the Gospel of Matthew was not the Matthew (that is, tax collector, Apostle, eyewitness) mentioned in Matthew 9:9. See Alexander B. Morrison, "Plain and Precious Things," in this volume. The possibility that the author of this Gospel may have been an early Christian who was not an eyewitness to the ministry of Jesus could help explain the use of the third person rather than the first person.

45. McConkie, *Doctrinal New Testament Commentary,* 1:69. Note also the conclusion of S. Kent Brown: "It has become increasingly plain to many scholars that the least complex and most convincing solution to the Synoptic Problem holds that Mark was not only the earliest Gospel written but also served as one of the sources for both Matthew and Luke" (S. Kent Brown, "The Testimony of Mark," in *Studies in Scripture, Vol. 5: The Gospels,* ed. Kent P. Jackson and Robert L. Millet [Salt Lake City: Deseret Book, 1986], 65).

46. Joseph B. Wirthlin, "Christians in Belief and Action," *Ensign,* November 1996, 71.

47. Neal A. Maxwell, "The New Testament—A Matchless Portrait of the Savior," *Ensign,* December 1986, 20, emphasis in original.

48. J. Reuben Clark Jr., *On the Way to Immortality and Eternal Life* (Salt Lake City: Deseret Book, 1950), 209–10. Compare also: "Notwithstanding the corruptions themselves, the Good Old Book stands as a record of God's dealings with and commandments and promises to his children, in their days of righteousness and in their generations of sin. It still, though corrupted, points out the way of righteousness to the man of faith seeking to serve God. It contains some of God's counsel to his children" (Clark, *On the Way to Immortality and Eternal Life,* 210).

9

MATTHEW AS AN EDITOR OF THE LIFE AND TEACHINGS OF JESUS

Gaye Strathearn

The Gospel According to Matthew, or, as the Joseph Smith Translation notes, the Testimony of St. Matthew, is the first of the four Gospels in our New Testament.[1] This Gospel was very influential among early Christians.[2] Tertullian, one of the early Church Fathers (c. AD 155–230), described Matthew as the "most faithful chronicler of the Gospel."[3] In this dispensation, the Prophet Joseph often used the first Gospel in his sermons.[4] Although modern scholars have debated the authorship of this Gospel, ancient Christian writings are unanimous in ascribing it to the tax collector named Matthew in Matthew 9:9.[5]

The purpose of this chapter is to examine the role of Matthew as an editor of Jesus' acts and teachings. In other words, modern readers can learn much from this Gospel by examining *what* Matthew chose to include and *how* he chose to write it. This concept is not unfamiliar to Latter-day Saints. The Book of Mormon shows clear evidence that both Mormon and Moroni actively edited the texts that they had before them and inserted their voices into them. On a number of occasions,

Gaye Strathearn is an assistant professor of ancient scripture at Brigham Young University.

Mormon lamented that he could not include even "a hundredth part of the proceedings of [his] people" in his record (Helaman 3:14; see also Words of Mormon 1:5; 3 Nephi 5:8; 26:6). He had to make choices about what to include and what to leave out. We also know that Mormon inserted the Words of Mormon to bridge the gap between the small and large plates of Nephi, and Moroni inserted his commentary into the writings of Ether. Elder Gene R. Cook has taught that readers can gain significant insights when they look for editorial phrases such as "and thus we see" that alert the reader to the reason why the editor included particular passages.[6]

As we approach Matthew's Gospel from this editorial perspective, we should note that while it is true that, as one of the Apostles, Matthew would have been present at many of the events during Jesus' ministry, it is also clear that he used a number of oral and written sources to compile his Gospel. In many respects, Matthew was in a similar position to that of Mormon and Moroni, collecting and editing material in order to create a specific message about Jesus Christ for his audience.[7] Part of that message, however, can be lost to the reader if he or she is not aware of the editorial nuances of the text. Before we can recognize Matthew's editorial hand, however, we must first briefly discuss both his audience and the sources he used.

MATTHEW'S AUDIENCE

Although we may never be able to identify a specific congregation in a specific city as Matthew's intended audience, there are clues from both external and internal evidence that help us to draw some broad conclusions. Eusebius, using an unnamed source, says that Matthew wrote his Gospel to the Hebrews at a time when he had decided to expand his missionary work.[8] Internal evidence from the Gospel itself seems to confirm that the intended audience was Jewish.[9] Matthew went to great lengths to show that Jesus was the fulfillment of Old Testament prophecy (see Matthew 1:22–23; 2:15, 17–18; 4:14–15; 8:17; 12:17–18; 21:4–5; 27:35). Matthew also began his work with a genealogy that links Jesus with the royal Davidic line and with Abraham, the father of the covenant (see Matthew 1:1–17), and he portrayed Jesus as the new Moses, who came out of Egypt (see Matthew 2:13–23) and gave a new law on a mountain (see Matthew 5:1).

In the text, three characteristics of Matthew's editorial hand suggest that his audience was in tension with, or had recently split with, the synagogue. In Matthew's editorial passages the synagogue is always referred to as "their" synagogue (Matthew 4:23; 9:35; 12:9; 13:54) or "your" synagogue (Matthew 23:34).[10] Thus the synagogue stood in some tension with the church. Matthew is the only Gospel author to include Jesus' sayings where He referred to the "church" (*ekklēsia;* Matthew 16:18; 18:17). Additionally, Matthew referred to "their scribes" (*grammateis auton;* Matthew 7:29), whereas Mark just said "the scribes" (*hoi grammateis;* Mark 1:22). All of these Matthean characteristics point to an "us" and "them" situation for Matthew's audience. Some scholars have argued that this situation reflects a time during the Jamnian period (AD 70–100) when Judaism was seeking to redefine itself after the destruction of the temple.[11] Rifts within Judaism, however, were not exclusive to this time period and may reflect a much earlier period.[12]

Matthew, therefore, would have chosen sayings and deeds of Jesus that would have had meaning for a Jewish audience. This is a very different scenario from the ones faced by Mark and Luke, where the internal evidence suggests they were intended primarily for Gentile audiences.

MATTHEW'S SOURCES

There is internal evidence in the text to suggest that Matthew relied, at least in part, on written sources to write his Gospel. For example, we know that he relied heavily upon texts from the Old Testament. He often used the Greek word *gegraptai* ("it is written") to introduce his scriptural quotations indicating that, on these occasions, he was not relying on oral versions.[13] It is clear that Matthew knew both the Hebrew and Greek versions of Old Testament texts.[14] However, it is also possible that Matthew did not have access to written accounts of some of the Minor Prophets. In Matthew 21:16 he recorded Jesus' quotation of Micah 2:25 but, unlike most of his scripture citations, did not identify the source of the quote. Again, in Matthew 27:9 he quoted Zechariah 11:13, but attributed it to Jeremiah.[15] In these cases, he may have relied upon oral versions of the prophecies. The Joseph Smith Translation also indicates that Matthew used a written source for his account of Jesus' birth: "Now, *as it is written,* the birth of Jesus Christ was on this wise" (JST, Matthew 1:18, emphasis added). Unfortunately, we no longer have access to that original source.

Modern scholarship also identifies two other major sources for Matthew's Gospel: the Gospel of Mark and a written source of Jesus' sayings. We must consider each of these briefly if we are to recognize Matthew's editorial work in his Gospel.

Many early Christians considered that Matthew's was the first written Gospel.[16] This belief undoubtedly influenced the Gospel's position in our present canon. Modern scholars, however, have debated the question of Matthean priority. Many now believe that Mark was the first written Gospel and that Matthew used it as a source for his own Gospel.[17] While there are some difficulties with this position,[18] there are two arguments that are compelling for me and for most scholars. First, even though Papias says that Mark was not particularly interested in writing the sayings and events in chronological order,[19] Matthew and Luke tend to follow Markan order. In Matthew's case, this is particularly evident in chapters 14–28, although even in the earlier chapters we can discern its influence.[20] It is true that Markan priority is only one way of explaining this phenomenon. The more telling characteristic is that when Matthew disagrees with Mark's chronology, the difference can be understood to be the result of Matthean editorial tendencies.[21] In part, the differences in Markan chronology in Matthew 4–13 can be attributed to Matthew's penchant for collecting materials into thematic blocks (see the collections of miracle stories in Matthew 8–9 and of the parables in Matthew 13). Second, in at least twelve verses, Matthew appears to change Mark's rare or difficult word or phrase and renders it with more common terminology.[22] It is difficult to acknowledge Matthean priority over Mark in these cases, because we would then have to explain why Mark would want to obscure the message for his readers.

A second source that many scholars see behind Matthew's Gospel is a hypothetical document known as Q (from the German word *Quelle,* meaning "source").[23] It is hypothetical because no copy of it has ever been found. Nevertheless, scholars have identified a number of places where Matthew and Luke shared material that is not found in Mark. They noted that much of this material consisted of the sayings of Jesus. For example, one passage found in Matthew and Luke, but not in Mark, is John the Baptist's tongue-lashing against the Pharisees and Sadducees in Matthew or the multitude in Luke. "O generation of vipers, who hath warned you to flee from the wrath to come? Bring forth therefore fruits meet for repentance: and think not to say within yourselves, We have Abraham to our father: for I say unto you, that God is able of these stones to raise up children to Abraham" (Matthew 3:7–9; see also Luke 3:7–8). In both Matthew and Luke, the Greek in these passages is almost exactly the same and suggests to scholars that they borrowed from a written, rather than an oral, source.

The question in scholars' minds, once they identified this phenomenon of shared sayings in Matthew and Luke, was whether early Christians would have been interested in just the sayings of Jesus without a corresponding narrative context. Frankly, there was no evidence for this view until the discovery of the Nag Hammadi Library in Egypt in 1945. Among the codices, scholars found a text known as the Gospel of Thomas that included 114 purported sayings by Jesus without any narrative. This text showed that the hypothetical genre of Q was indeed a reality for some Christians.[24] While I do not accept all of the assumptions that Q scholarship has developed,[25] I do find the basic concept of a written source of Jesus' sayings compelling and helpful in identifying Matthew's editorial work, particularly in chapters 4–11, where the sayings shared by Matthew and Luke are most prevalent.[26]

In highlighting these sources, I am not suggesting that they were the only sources Matthew drew upon. One New Testament scholar has recently reminded us: "Scholars of the twenty-first century must take more seriously than their twentieth-century predecessors the fact that first-century Israel was an oral culture and the probability that the Jesus tradition was processed in oral form through the first two generations of Christians (and beyond), prior to, including Q, and alongside the written Gospels."[27] Matthew undoubtedly tapped into this oral culture as well. Nevertheless, it is with the written texts that we can most easily discern his editorial hand.

MATTHEW AS EDITOR

Matthew did not just collect Jesus' teachings and stories; he edited them as he fashioned his Gospel.[28] Just as Mormon and Moroni included phrases such as "And thus we see," Matthew also includes a number of techniques that help readers to identify his editorial hand. Recognizing these techniques will help us to appreciate the specific emphases of Jesus' ministry that Matthew felt were most important for his audience.

Matthew's five discourses of Jesus. First, we have already noted that Matthew wrote to a Jewish audience and that he portrayed Jesus as the new Moses. Within Matthew's Gospel, we find him delineating five major discourses by the Savior: the Sermon on the Mount (Matthew 5–7), the Apostolic Commission (Matthew 10), the Kingdom of God discourse (Matthew 13), the Church Administration discourse (Matthew 18), and the Eschatological discourse (Matthew 24–25). We know that Matthew intended his readers to see these as distinct but related discourses by the way that he concluded each of them. At the end of each of the first four discourses, he added, "And it came to pass, when Jesus had ended these" sayings, teachings, or parables (*kai egeneto hote etelesen ho Iēsous;* Matthew 7:28; see also Matthew 11:1; 13:53; 19:1). At the conclusion of the last discourse, he added, "And it came to pass, when Jesus had finished *all* these sayings" (emphasis added; *kai egeneto hote etelesen ho Iēsous pantas tous logous toutous;* Matthew 26:1). B. W. Bacon has argued that in doing so, Matthew's intent was to create for his readers a Christian Pentateuch (that is, the five books of Moses) to once again emphasize that Jesus was the new Moses.[29]

Matthew's literary use of bookends. Second, Matthew uses "bookends" around his Gospel as a whole and around important sections within his Gospel. Just as the function of bookends is to keep books together, so scriptural bookends help us to identify the parts of the Gospel that Matthew wanted his audience to read as a single unit. This is important because our current chapter divisions often divide passages that Matthew intended to be read as a single unit.

An important thematic bookend encapsulates the entire Gospel. We have noted already that Matthew intended his Gospel to be read by a predominantly Jewish audience. This point serves as an important point of demarcation from the other synoptic Gospels. The importance of the Jewish mission for Matthew is highlighted in two of his editorial inclusions. Matthew is the only Gospel writer to include Jesus' instruction to the Apostles that they were to "go not into the way of the Gentiles, and into any city of the Samaritans enter ye not: but go rather to the lost sheep of the house of Israel" (Matthew 10:5–6). Furthermore, unlike Mark, in the story of the healing of the Canaanite woman's daughter, Matthew includes Jesus' statement, "I am not sent but unto the lost sheep of the house of Israel" (Matthew 15:24).

While acknowledging the importance of the Jewish mission, it is significant that Matthew frames his Gospel within a gentile context. The first two chapters emphasize the importance of Gentiles in the establishment of Jesus' ministry. Matthew's genealogy differs from the one found in Luke. We have noted that Matthew begins with Abraham, the father of the covenant, but Genesis makes it clear that through this covenant all nations, not just the Israelites, would be blessed (see Genesis 12:3; 18:18).[30] In addition, Matthew includes four Gentile women in Jesus' genealogy, highlighting the importance of Gentiles in the coming forth of the Messiah. Tamar and Rahab were Canaanites, and Ruth was a Moabite. Matthew does not mention Bathsheba by name, but only as the wife of Uriah. Why would Matthew not identify Bathsheba by name? The scriptures are silent on her ethnic background; therefore it served Matthew's purposes to identify her instead by her relationship to Uriah, who was known to be a Hittite (see 2 Samuel 11:3). As one scholar has noted, Matthew's genealogy, therefore, "contains a universalistic overtone: it is indicated in a hidden way that the son of David, the Messiah of Israel, brings salvation for the Gentiles."[31] This universalistic tone is further strengthened in chapter 2, where the Wise Men seek out and worship the Christ child as "King of the Jews" when the representatives of Judaism fail to do so.[32]

The corresponding bookend that is unique to Matthew's Gospel is Jesus' commission to the disciples before His Ascension. "Go ye therefore, and teach all nations, baptizing them in the name of the Father, and of the Son, and of the Holy Ghost: teaching them to observe all things whatsoever I have commanded you: and, lo, I am with you alway, even unto the end of the world" (Matthew 28:19–20).[33] This passage is in stark contrast to Jesus' command to the Apostles to go to "the lost sheep of the house of Israel" (Matthew 10:6).

Yet Matthew has prepared his readers for the shift in missionary emphasis with his accounts of the healings of the centurion's servant and the Canaanite woman's children. The story of the centurion may have come from Q because Luke also includes the story, and it is not found in Mark. Matthew does not include Luke's description of the centurion as one who "loveth our nation" and who "built us a synagogue" (Luke 7:5). Both Matthew and Luke record Jesus' declaration that in the centurion He found faith that had not been manifested in Israel (see Matthew 8:10; Luke 7:9). But only Matthew includes Jesus' statement, "Many shall come from the east and west, and shall sit down with Abraham, and Isaac, and Jacob, in the kingdom of heaven. But the children of the kingdom shall be cast out into outer darkness: there shall be weeping and gnashing of teeth" (Matthew 8:11–12). Luke records this statement in a different setting (see Luke 13:28–29). Thus, Matthew emphasizes that at times Gentiles have more faith than the covenant people and will participate in the eschatological feast when many of the house of Israel will miss out. The story of the healing of the Canaanite woman's daughter also shows evidence of Matthean editing. Mark also includes the story (see Mark 7:24–30), but only Matthew records the woman's plea that Jesus "have mercy on me, O Lord, thou Son of David" (Matthew 15:22) and Jesus' declaration "O woman, great is thy faith" (Matthew 15:28). Both the centurion and the Canaanite woman address Jesus with the title "Lord" (*kurios*), the title used by disciples and other supplicants.[34]

What benefit would this aspect of Matthew's editorial work be for his audience? One explanation may lie with the experiences of Matthew's intended audience. We know from Acts and the Pauline Epistles that the expansion of missionary work to include the Gentiles was a difficult transition for the early Church, and that there were members who resisted it. We recall Eusebius' statement that Matthew wrote this Gospel when he was about to begin preaching to others besides the Hebrews, that is, Gentiles. Therefore, he may have written to try and convince his readers of the importance of the gentile mission. If this conclusion is accurate, then once again we are reminded of the possibility of an early date for this Gospel.

We find another example of Matthew's use of bookends in Matthew 4:23 and 9:35. Here the bookends are textual, rather than thematic. Matthew 4:23 reads, "And Jesus went about all Galilee, teaching in their synagogues, and preaching the gospel of the kingdom, and healing all manner of sickness and all manner of disease among the people." The passage in chapter 9 is almost identical except that it has "Jesus went about all the cities and villages" instead of "all Galilee," and the critical Greek text (contrary to the King James Version) does not have "among the people."[35] Matthew uses these parallel verses to prompt the reader to recognize that all of the material between them belongs to the same literary unit. This is one example of where chapter breaks in our modern New Testament interrupt the author's flow of ideas. Therefore, Matthew expected that his readers would recognize that the Sermon on the Mount in chapters 5–7 should be read in conjunction with the collection of miracles in chapters 8 and 9. Thus, Matthew wants his readers to see that Jesus is the Messiah in both word (the Sermon on the Mount) and deed (His miracles).

Matthew's use of "the coming one." The last major aspect of Matthew's editorial practice noted here is found in Matthew 3–11. As can be readily seen, these chapters include the emphasis of Jesus as the Messiah in word and deed that we have just discussed. In this section, Matthew merges that concept with two important passages dealing with John the Baptist and his disciples. The baptism of John plays an important role in each of the four Gospels, although only Matthew and Luke record that he sent his disciples to Jesus, saying, "Art thou he that should come, or do we look for another?" (Matthew 11:3; see also Luke 7:20). This passage may stem from Q because it is not found in either Mark or John. Matthew, in distinction from Luke, links this passage with his description of John's baptism in Matthew 3. The link is not readily discernable in the King James Version but is recognizable in the Greek with the catch phrase *ho erchomenos* ("the coming one").

The account of John the Baptist's activities in the Judaean wilderness plays a prominent part in Matthew's Gospel. His calls for repentance attract many Pharisees and Sadducees to attend one of his baptisms. As noted above, John identifies them as a "generation of vipers" (Matthew 3:7). He prophesies that "the axe is laid unto the root of the trees" and promises them that "every tree which bringeth not forth good fruit is hewn down, and cast into the fire" (verse 10). Then John declares, "I indeed baptize you with water unto repentance: but the coming one [who is] after me is mightier than I, whose shoes I am not worthy to bear: he shall baptize with the Holy Ghost, and with fire" (verse 11, my translation). In contrast to Matthew, Mark (1:7) and Luke (3:16) do not use *ho erchomenos* in their accounts.[36] Matthew makes no explicit mention here of the identity of "the coming one," although he implies that it refers to Jesus by following the prophecy with the description of His baptism.

The next mention of John the Baptist in Matthew's Gospel is found in chapter 11. By this time John was in prison and sent his disciples to Jesus to inquire if He was "the coming one" (*ho erchomenos;* verse 3). Immediately the reader is reminded of Matthew's account of John's earlier prophecy to the Pharisees and Sadducees. Jesus did not answer them directly. Instead, He told them to "go and shew John again those things which ye do hear and see: the blind receive their sight, and the lame walk, the lepers are cleansed, and the deaf hear, the dead are raised up, and the poor have the gospel preached to them" (Matthew 11:4–5).[37] Jesus' response is significant for a number of reasons. First, it portrayed the coming one in a different light than John's expectation in Matthew 3:10, where he was an axe who would hew down any tree that did not bring forth good fruit. In Matthew 11, Jesus was the coming one who, unlike the expectation in chapter 3, would heal and preach. This was not a common messianic expectation in Jesus' day.[38]

This portrayal of a healing and preaching Messiah influenced the Matthean order in chapters 4–9. It is here that, in chiastic format, we find the evidence for Jesus being the expected coming one. The evidence that Jesus taught the gospel to the poor is the Sermon on the Mount, where the opening line is "Blessed are the poor" (Matthew 5:3). Prior to Matthew 11, the opening beatitude is the only verse that uses the word "poor" (*ptōchoi*).³⁹ Likewise, Matthew provided evidence that Jesus performed healings in Matthew 8–9, where there is at least one example of every miracle that is mentioned in Matthew 11:5. The only difficulty is finding an example of the deaf hearing, but this is a difficulty only in the English text, not the Greek. The Greek word for "deaf" in Matthew 11:5 is the plural of *kōphos,* the same word used to describe the demoniac who is dumb (*kōphos;* see Matthew 9:32–33).⁴⁰ Matthew therefore arranged the material in chapters 5–9 to provide evidence for his readers that Jesus was indeed the coming one.

CONCLUSION

Matthew's Gospel is a powerful testimony of Jesus as the Christ. It was never intended that this work be a biography of Jesus' mortal life from birth to resurrection. Instead, as the Joseph Smith Translation notes in the title, he was bearing his testimony to his readers. In that testimony, Matthew drew on Jesus' teachings and experiences from his own memories as well as from other sources. His editorial work has helped readers throughout the ages to see Jesus as the new Moses who gave a new law to His people, as the Messiah of both word and deed, and as the Coming One who preached and healed. Through his work, we are able to gain a greater appreciation of the magnitude and depth of Christ's ministry. Thus, it is no wonder that this Gospel was a frequent part of the Prophet Joseph's sermons. As one New Testament scholar has noted, "The Gospel of Matthew is a book intended to be read as a whole and not in parts or pericopes. It is intended to be read not just once but several times."⁴¹ The Prophet Joseph taught, "He who reads it [the Bible] oftenest will like it best."⁴² This has certainly been my experience with Matthew's Gospel.

NOTES

1. For all Joseph Smith Translation quotes, see Scott H. Faulring, Kent P. Jackson, and Robert J. Matthews, eds., *Joseph Smith's New Translation of the Bible: Original Manuscripts* (Provo, UT: Religious Studies Center, Brigham Young University, 2004).

2. It seems to have been referred to by Peter (2 Peter 1:16–18) and James (James 1:13; 2:13; 3:5–6, 18; 4:8, 11; 5:12), although they may be using a similar

source. It is quoted in the writings of Ignatius (*To the Ephesians*, 14.2; *To the Smyrnaeans*, 1.1; 6.1; *To Polycarp*, 2.2), and the *Didache* (1.4; 3.7; 7.1; 8.2; 9.5; 13.2). It was the only book of scripture used by the Ebionites (Irenaeus, *Against Heresies*, 1.26.2), and the Valentinians, Marcionites, and Basilidians also taught from it (Clement, *Stromata*, 7.17).

3. *On the Flesh of Christ*, in *The Ante-Nicene Fathers: Translations of the Writings of the Fathers down to A.D. 325*, ed. Alexander Roberts and James Donaldson (Grand Rapids, MI: Eerdmans, 1980), 3:540.

4. Joseph's use of Matthew is seen in a survey of the scripture index in *Scriptural Teachings of the Prophet Joseph Smith*, comp. Joseph Fielding Smith, annot. Richard C. Galbraith (Salt Lake City: Deseret Book, 1993), 462–67. In this index there are 545 references to Matthew; 96 references to Mark, 233 references to Luke, and 274 references to John.

5. For examples of the issues of authorship, see Ulrich Luz, *Matthew 1–7: A Continental Commentary*, trans. Wilhelm C. Linss (Minneapolis: Fortress, 1989), 93–95; John Nolland, *The Gospel of Matthew: A Commentary on the Greek Text* (Grand Rapids, MI: Eerdmans, 2005), 2–4; R. T. France, *Matthew, Evangelist and Teacher* (Downers Grove, IL: InterVarsity, 1989), 50–80. The unanimity among ancient authors is significant because at times they did question the authorship of texts (see Eusebius, *History of the Church*, 3.3.1–5; 6.14.1–3).

6. Gene R. Cook, *Searching the Scriptures: Bringing Power to Your Personal and Family Study* (Salt Lake City: Deseret Book, 1997), 81–82.

7. James D. G. Dunn writes, "Not every [early Christian] church knew or thought it necessary to know all there was to know about Jesus; and that the Evangelists were probably at least in some measure selective in their use of the Jesus tradition" (*Jesus Remembered, Christianity in the Making* [Grand Rapids, MI: Eerdmans, 2003], 1:161).

8. See Eusebius, *History of the Church*, 3.24.6.

9. Eusebius preserves a famous statement from Papias, which states: "Matthew collected the oracles in the Hebrew language, and each interpreted them as best he could" (*History of the Church*, 3.39.16). Although many have interpreted this statement as referring to Matthew's Gospel, there are major difficulties with doing so because it was written in Greek not Hebrew. The phrase "in the Hebrew language" may mean "in Jewish forms of expression" (see Graham N. Stanton, *A Gospel for a New People: Studies in Matthew* [Louisville, KY: Westminster John Knox, 1992], 116).

10. In Matthew 4:23, Matthew may be using the Markan phrase "their synagogues" (Mark 1:39) but, unlike Mark, Matthew repeats it in 9:35. In the other instances, Matthew has added the pronoun to the Markan passages (see Matthew 12:9; 13:54). There is no Markan parallel for Matthew 23:34.

11. W. D. Davies, *The Setting of the Sermon on the Mount* (Atlanta: Scholars Press, 1989), 256–315; Stanton, *A Gospel for a New People*, 113–45.

12. Nolland, *The Gospel of Matthew*, 15–16.

13. He uses the phrase ten times; see Matthew 2:5; 4:4, 6, 7, 10; 11:10; 21:13; 26:24, 31; 27:37. See also Matthew 26:56, "That the scriptures of the prophets might be fulfilled," where "scriptures" is a translation of *graphai*, "writings." In

addition, the Joseph Smith Translation adds the phrase "as the prophets have writ-ten" to Matthew 1:16; see also additions to 2:4; 5:27, 31, 33. Matthew also intro-duces formula quotations with variations of phrases such as "To fulfil what was spoken by the prophet" (*hina plērōthē to rhēthen . . . dia tou prophetou;* Matthew 1:22; 2:15, 17, 23; 4:14; 8:17; 12:17; 13:14, 35; 21:4; 27:9), and "It was said by them of old time" (*errethē tois archaiois;* Matthew 5:21, 27). While the idea of a written text may be implied with these phrases, they are not specific and so I have not included them in this discussion.

14. For a discussion of the issues, see W. D. Davies and Dale C. Allison Jr., *Matthew,* The International Critical Commentary (Edinburgh: T&T Clark, 1998), 1:32–57; and Nolland, *The Gospel of Matthew,* 29–33.

15. See Luz, *Matthew 1–7,* 157.

16. One possible exception is Tertullian, where he indicates that "John and Matthew first instil faith into us" while "Luke and Mark renew it afterwards" (*Against Marcion,* 4:2; see also chapter 5). Tertullian's intent, however, seems to differentiate John and Matthew from Luke and Mark rather than to make a state-ment about the priority of John over Matthew (see Origen, *Commentary on Matthew,* in Eusebius, *History of the Church,* 6.25.4; cf. Irenaeus, *Against Heresies,* 3.1.1–2; Tertullian, *Against Marcion,* 4.2).

17. For two Latter-day Saint views on Markan priority, see Bruce R. McConkie, *Doctrinal New Testament Commentary* (Salt Lake City: Bookcraft, 1979), 1:69; S. Kent Brown, "The Testimony of Mark," in *Studies in Scripture, Volume Five: The Gospels,* ed. Kent P. Jackson and Robert L. Millet (Salt Lake City: Deseret Book, 1986), 65.

18. See William R. Farmer, *Jesus and the Gospel: Tradition, Scripture, and Canon* (Philadelphia: Fortress, 1982).

19. See Eusebius, *History of the Church,* 3.39.15.

20. Scholars have long noted the "editorial fatigue," in the latter half of Matthew (Robert H. Gundry, *Matthew: A Commentary on His Literary and Theological Art* [Grand Rapids, MI: Eerdmans, 1982], 10). Markan order can still be detected fre-quently in Matthew 4–12. "Where Markan order is changed by Matthew, he can be shown to have been inspired by his sources" (Stanton, *A Gospel For a New People,* 31). For more detailed examinations of this phenomenon in Matthew 8–9, see C. M. Tuckett, "Arguments from Order: Definition and Evaluation," in *Synoptic Studies: The Ampleforth Conferences of 1982 and 1983* (Sheffield: JSOT, 1984), 207–11, James M. Robinson, "The Matthean Trajectory from Q to Mark," in *Ancient and Modern Perspectives on the Bible and Culture: Essays in Honor of Hans Dieter Betz,* ed. Adela Yarbro Collins (Atlanta: Scholars Press, 1998), 125, and Linden Eric Youngquist, "Matthew and Q" (unpublished dissertation, Claremont Graduate University, 2003).

21. Tuckett, "Arguments From Order," 207.

22. For a list of the verses in Greek, see Davies and Allison, *Matthew,* 105–6.

23. James M. Robinson, Paul Hoffman, and John S. Kloppenborg, eds., *The Critical Edition of Q* (Minneapolis: Fortress, 2000).

24. The copy of the Gospel of Thomas found at Nag Hammadi was in Coptic and dates from the fourth century AD, but the original was probably a much

earlier document. The Oxyrhynchus papyri seem to represent an earlier Greek version of the text. Greek paleographic evidence dates these fragments to before AD 200.

25. For an excellent Latter-day Saint review of the assumptions of Q scholarship, see Thomas A. Wayment, "A Viewpoint of the Supposedly Lost Gospel Q," *Religious Educator* 5, no. 3 (2004): 105–15.

26. Q scholars have postulated a Q community and divided Q into three redactional layers (see John S. Kloppenborg, *The Formation of Q: Trajectories in Ancient Wisdom Collections* [Philadelphia: Fortress, 1987]). In particular, I do not agree with statements such as the following: "Q puts us in touch with the earlier history of the Jesus movements, and their recollections of Jesus are altogether different. The first followers of Jesus did not know about or imagine any of the dramatic events upon which the narrative gospels hinge. These include the baptism of Jesus; his conflict with the Jewish authorities and their plot to kill him; Jesus' instruction to the disciples; Jesus' transfiguration, march to Jerusalem, last supper, trial, and crucifixion as king of the Jews; and finally, his resurrection from the dead and the stories of an empty tomb. All of these events must and can be accounted for as mythmaking in the Jesus movements, with a little help from the martyrology of the Christ, in the period after the Roman-Jewish war" (Burton L. Mack, *The Lost Gospel: The Book of Christian Origins* [San Francisco: HarperSanFrancisco, 1993], 247). The weaknesses that I see in this position are three-fold: (1) We cannot be certain that our constructed version of Q contains all of the sayings of Jesus; (2) The genre of Q as a sayings source would necessarily preclude a description of many of the "events" of Jesus such as the baptism, transfiguration, and resurrection; and (3) I question why a hypothetical text should be given precedence over texts that have survived from antiquity.

27. Dunn, *Jesus Remembered*, 161.

28. Modern scholars use the term "Redaction Criticism" to describe the process of looking for signs of editorial emphases and insertions into a scriptural text. While I recognize the value of this technique, I consider myself to be a minimalist. Many scholars argue that Matthew (and other scriptural authors) created stories and events and inserted them into the text. As a result, they question the historical veracity of many parts of the scriptural texts. One biblical scholar, however, has argued, "So often scholarship assumes that if something *could* have been made up by early Christians, then it *must* have been made up by early Christians. But that is to show undue skepticism. Early Christian tradents . . . operated with a sense of integrity and responsibility which is often not adequately reckoned with" (Nolland, *The Gospel of Matthew*, 13). As a minimalist redaction critic, therefore, I recognize that Matthew has reworked the order of events and retold the stories of Jesus in a way that would better emphasize and teach doctrines that were important for his audience without having to create fictional events or sayings.

29. B. W. Bacon, *Studies in Matthew* (New York: Holt, 1930).

30. This point was not lost on Paul in Galatians 3.

31. Luz, *Matthew 1–7*, 110.

32.   Elder Bruce R. McConkie suggests that the Wise Men were probably diaspora Jews (see *The Mortal Messiah: From Bethlehem to Calvary,* 4 vols. [Salt Lake City: Bookcraft, 1979–81], 1:358). This may be the case, but for Matthew, they were Gentiles. In Matthew's Gospel only Gentiles use the phrase "King of the Jews" (see Matthew 27:11, 29, 37). In contrast, the scribes and elders called Him mockingly "King of Israel" (see Matthew 27:42).

33.   Luke records a similar statement, but he places it in Acts 1 rather than at the conclusion of his Gospel.

34.   Ulrich Luz, *Matthew 8–20,* trans. James E. Crouch, ed. Helmut Koester (Minneapolis: Fortress, 2001), 339.

35.   The phrase "among the people" is a scribal addition in Codex Sinaiticus (‭א‬*), and in Codex Ephraemi it is added by a third scribal hand (C^{3}). It then becomes a part of the text in manuscripts during the eighth century and beyond: Codices Basiliensis (E), Boreelianus (F), Wolfii A (G), Regius (L), and Koridethi (Θ), etc.

36.   In Mark and Luke we have the articular use of the substantive comparative adjective *ischuros* as the subject of the conjugated definite verb *erchomai* (*erchetai* [*de*] *ho ischuroteros mou*), while Matthew uses the nominal substantive attributive participle of *erchomai* with the present indicative of the verb *eimi* (*ho de . . . erchomenos ischuroteros mou estin*). John's account, like Matthew's, uses *ho erchomenos,* but like Mark's, does not include the story of John's disciples coming to Jesus.

37.   This passage is not found in Mark but is included in Luke 7:22, which may suggest that it comes from Q. Luke, however, includes the following verse between the disciples' question and Jesus' answer: "And in that same hour he cured many of their infirmities and plagues, and of evil spirits; and unto many that were blind he gave their sight" (Luke 7:21). This verse acts as proof for the response Jesus gives. Matthew does not include this verse because, as we shall see, he uses chapters 8 and 9 as proof of Jesus' response.

38.   One possible exception is a messianic fragment from the Dead Sea Scrolls (4Q521) that describes God, through His Messiah, giving sight to the blind, raising the dead, and preaching to the poor.

39.   We do not know how the early Christians identified the Sermon on the Mount, but the modern title was not used until the fourth century AD, when Augustine coined it (see *Reply to Faustus the Manichaean,* 5.3). One practice that was used in antiquity was to identify a text by a word or phrase from the opening line. For example, Akkadian documents refer to the Babylonian Creation story as the Enuma Elish ("When on high"), and the Hebrew titles for the books of the Torah all come from the opening words of the text.

40.   "The blind receive their sight" = Matthew 9:27–31; "the lame walk" = Matthew 9:1–8; "the lepers are cleansed" = Matthew 8:2–4; "the deaf hear" = Matthew 9:32–33; "the dead are raised up" = Matthew 9:18–19, 23–26. There is a lot more editorial work going on in these chapters than I have mentioned. For a more detailed discussion, see Ulrich Luz, "Die Wundergeschichten von Mt 8–9," in *Tradition and Interpretation in the New Testament,* ed. Gerald F. Hawthorne and Otto

Betz (Grand Rapids, MI: Eerdmans, 1987), 149–65, and Youngquist, "Matthew and Q," 107–15.

41. Ulrich Luz, *Studies in Matthew,* trans. Rosemary Selle (Grand Rapids, MI: Eerdmans, 2005), 3.

42. Joseph Smith, *Teachings of the Prophet Joseph Smith,* comp. Joseph Fielding Smith (Salt Lake City: Deseret Book, 1976), 56.

10

ADDING AND TAKING AWAY "WITHOUT A CAUSE" IN MATTHEW 5:22

Daniel K Judd and Allen W. Stoddard

The book of Revelation ends with the following words of warning familiar to many Latter-day Saints: "For I testify unto every man that heareth the words of the prophecy of this book, if any man shall add unto these things, God shall add unto him the plagues that are written in this book: and if any man shall take away from the words of the book of this prophecy, God shall take away his part out of the book of life, and out of the holy city, and from the things which are written in this book" (Revelation 22:18–19). Latter-day Saint familiarity with these verses comes, in many cases, from confrontations with those who use this biblical text to challenge the legitimacy of the Book of Mormon or other latter-day scripture. Some individuals reject the idea of adding any new scripture to the canon.[1]

Many traditional New Testament scholars have the same point of view as latter-day prophets, apostles, and scholars who teach that the warning in the book of Revelation and a similar text found in the Old Testament (see Deuteronomy 4:2–3) are warnings against corrupting

Daniel K Judd is a professor of ancient scripture at Brigham Young University.
Allen W. Stoddard is a senior at Brigham Young University majoring in English and Asian Studies.

the contents of the *individual* books of scripture and not against adding *additional* books of authorized scripture.[2] These conclusions are supported by the sixty-one books of scripture following the warning in Deuteronomy and scholars' belief that the epistles of John were written and added to the New Testament after the book of Revelation.[3] There is, however, ample evidence that the Savior's warning in Revelation 22:18–19 has not been heeded and that both the Old and New Testaments have undergone textual corruption.

In the Book of Mormon, the prophet Nephi stated, "Many plain and precious things . . . have been taken out of the book [Bible], which were plain unto the understanding of the children of men" (1 Nephi 13:29). Nephi also explained that "because of these things which are taken away out of the gospel of the Lamb, an exceedingly great many do *stumble,* yea, insomuch that Satan hath great power over them" (1 Nephi 13:29, emphasis added). While there are countless examples of biblical texts that have not been "translated [or transmitted] correctly" (Article of Faith 8), this study aims to describe in some detail the textual and theological corruption of the teachings of Jesus concerning anger in Matthew 5:22. This study will also briefly discuss the implications of the textual changes and the inspired translation, correction, and understanding of latter-day prophets, seers, and revelators.[4]

TEXTUAL CHANGES THROUGH TRANSLATION AND TRANSMISSION

The Prophet Joseph Smith taught, "I believe the Bible as it read when it came from the pen of the original writers."[5] But he also declared, "From sundry revelations which had been received, it was apparent that many important points touching the salvation of men, had been taken from the Bible, or lost before it was compiled."[6] Many ancient and modern clergyman and scholars have come to similar conclusions. Writing as early as the third century AD, Christian theologian Origen recorded, "The differences among the [New Testament] manuscripts have become great, either through the negligence of some copyists or through the perverse audacity of others; they either neglect to check over what they have transcribed, or, in the process of checking, they make additions or deletions as they please."[7] Nearly a century later, Jerome wrote of the copyists who "write down not what they find but what they think is the meaning; and while they attempt to rectify the errors of others, they merely expose their own."[8]

One New Testament scholar, after acknowledging and discussing the many "mistakes" in biblical translation and transmission, concludes that "scribes occasionally altered the words of their sacred texts to make them more patently orthodox and to prevent their misuse by Christians who espoused aberrant views."[9] Elder Jeffrey R. Holland noted that because of "a misreading (and surely, in some cases, a mistranslation) of the Bible," "some in the contemporary world suffer from a distressing misconception of [God]."[10]

As the Prophet Joseph Smith and others have stated, plain and precious writings and teachings of the Savior and His servants were modified both by those who made simple mistakes in copying, translating, and transmitting the text, and by others who did so intentionally. While there are many examples of innocent mistakes in both the Old and New Testaments, there are also examples of similar unintentional errors in the Book of Mormon. Alma 32:30 provides one classic example of what translators call "parablepsis."[11]

ALMA 32:30–31 (ORIGINAL MANUSCRIPT)[12]	ALMA 32:30–31 (1830 EDITION)
But behold, as the seed swelleth, and sprouteth, and beginneth to grow, then you must needs say that the seed is good; for behold it swelleth, and sprouteth, and beginneth to grow. *And now, behold, will not this strengthen your faith? Yea, it will strengthen your faith: for ye will say I know that this is a good seed; for behold it sprouteth and beginneth to grow.* And now behold . . .	But behold, as the seed swelleth, and sprouteth, and beginneth to grow, and then ye must needs say, That the seed is good; for behold it swelleth, and sprouteth, and beginneth to grow.

And now behold . . . |

A careful comparison of both the Original Manuscript and Printer's Manuscript of Alma 32 with the printed edition published in 1830 reveals that the typesetter omitted thirty-five words from the end of Alma 32:30. This innocent mistake was probably made when the type-setter's eyes moved from the phrase "sprouteth, and beginneth to grow. And now behold" to the similiar phrase later in the verse— inadvertently skipping the words in between. The missing text was restored in the 1981 edition and is found in each subsequent printing. This is an example of a mistake with no apparent harmful conse-quences. And while there have been a number of editorial changes in the Book of Mormon over the years, even those who criticize its authenticity acknowledge that the changes are not of major doctrinal significance.[13] However, many of the errors in the translation, transmis-sion, and editing of the New Testament *are* of significantly greater consequence.

THE TEACHINGS OF JESUS ON ANGER

In the Sermon on the Mount in the King James translation, Jesus provided the following counsel concerning anger: "Ye have heard that it was said by them of old time, Thou shalt not kill; and whosoever shall kill shall be in danger of the judgment: But I say unto you, that whoso-ever is angry with his brother *without a cause* shall be in danger of the judg-ment: and whosoever shall say to his brother, Raca, shall be in danger of the council: but whosoever shall say, Thou fool, shall be in danger of hell fire" (Matthew 5:21–22, emphasis added). The portion of this scripture that has been the subject of controversy and discussion for centuries, and which is the primary focus of this study, is the phrase "without a cause." Some manuscripts and versions of the text in Matthew 5:22 include the phrase "without a cause," and others do not. The inclusion of the phrase implies that anger is justified if one has sufficient cause. The exclusion of "without a cause" eliminates such justification and appears to be an invitation from Jesus to eliminate anger from our lives.

MANUSCRIPT AND EARLY TEXTUAL EVIDENCE

Many scholars in the fifteenth and sixteenth centuries adopted the motto *ad fontes,* which is Latin for "to the source." Instead of relying on commentary, those scholars attempted to identify truth by going directly to the ancient documents. In addition to Classical scholars examining the original writings of philosophers such as Aristotle and Cicero, biblical scholars sought to examine the earliest texts of the Bible. The major problem, however, with attempting to examine the teachings of Jesus on anger by examining the original New Testament documents is that the original documents do not exist (or have not been discovered). All of the 5,735 ancient manuscripts (whole or partial) of the New Testament that have been catalogued are copies of copies.[14] While opinions vary concerning the dates when the New Testament manuscripts were written, many scholars believe that "the earliest known New Testament manuscript" is a papyrus fragment of the Gospel of John, identified by the symbol P^{52}, that has been dated between AD 100 and 150.[15] The earliest surviving manuscript of Matthew 5:22 has been dated as early as AD 125–50.[16] The reference is included on a small fragment designated as the "Barcelona" papyrus and is identified by the symbol P^{67}. The Barcelona text does not include any form of the phrase "without a cause."[17]

Table 1 is a listing of the earliest and most reliable ancient manuscripts and versions of Matthew 5:22.[18] It also indicates whether the phrase (or a form of the phrase) "without cause" is included. It is significant to note the great variance among manuscripts and versions concerning the inclusion or omission of the "without a cause" phrase.

By examining the earliest manuscripts and versions of the New Testament, it is clear that the absence of the phrase "without a cause" represents the earliest reading. The manuscripts which do not contain this phrase are normally of the Alexandrian text type. Although more Byzantine and other text types exist, the Alexandrian text types are considered older and more reliable.[19] Textual evidence shows that the phrase "without a cause" was first added to some New Testament texts by at least the third or fourth century. Because this phrase is referred to by Irenaeus (c. AD 130–202), noted New Testament scholar Bruce Metzger believes the addition may have been even earlier: "Although the reading with ["without a cause"] is widespread from the second century onwards, it is much more likely that the word was added by copyists in order to soften the rigor of the precept, than omitted as

TABLE 1: EARLY MANUSCRIPTS AND VERSIONS
OF MATTHEW 5:22

MANUSCRIPT NAME	INCLUDES "WITHOUT A CAUSE"?
Papyrus 67 [P⁶⁷] "Barcelona" (AD 125–50)	No
Coptic [cop^(sa, meg, bo)] (third–fifth century)	Yes
Old Syriac [syr^(s, c)] (third–fourth century)	Yes
Vaticanus [B] (AD 400)	No
Sinaiticus [ℵ*] (AD 400)	No
Sinaiticus [ℵ²] (after AD 400)	Yes[20]
Old Latin [it^(a,b,c,d,f,h,k,l,q)] (fourth–thirteenth century)	Yes
Vulgate [vg] (fourth–fifth century)	No
Ethiopic [eth^(ms)] (about AD 500)	No
Ethiopic [eth^(TH)] (about AD 500)	Yes
Georgian [geo] (fifth century)	Yes
Armenian [arm] (fifth century)	Yes
Peshitta/Palestinian [syr^(p,pal)] (fifth–sixth century)	Yes
Bezae Canta. [D] (AD 500)	Yes
Washington [W] (AD 500)	Yes
Old Latin [it^(aur)] (AD 700)	No
Byzantine (*Byz* [E S]) (AD 600–800)	Yes
Paris [L] (AD 800)	Yes
Old Church Slavonic [slav] (ninth century)	Yes
St. Gall [△] (AD 900)	Yes
Tbilisi [Θ] (AD 900)	Yes
Greek Lectionaries [*Lect*] (AD 900–1576)	Yes
Family 1,13 [f^(1,13)] (eleventh–fifteenth century)	Yes
Miniscule 1292 [1292] (thirteenth century)	No

unnecessary."[21] While many scholars agree with Professor Metzger, there are those who disagree. Professor David Alan Black, for example, while acknowledging that the shorter text is clearly an early reading, argues that the widespread nature of the longer reading as found in the majority of the Byzantine, Western, and Caesarean texts is a valid argument for the longer reading being original.[22]

PATRISTIC WRITINGS

Jerome, a fourth-century Catholic priest, scholar, and translator of the Latin Vulgate Bible,[23] stated: "In some codices [manuscripts] 'without cause' is added; however in the authentic codices the statement is unqualified and anger is completely forbidden, for if we are commanded to pray for those who persecute us, every occasion for anger is eliminated. 'Without cause' then should be deleted, since the anger of man does not work the justice of God."[24] John Chrysostom, a Catholic bishop and a contemporary of Jerome, provided an alternative perspective on Matthew 5:22: "He who is angry without cause will be guilty, but he who is angry with cause will not be guilty, for without anger, teaching will be ineffective, judgments unstable, crimes unchecked."[25]

Writing shortly after the time of Jerome and Chrysostom, John Cassian added his opinion to the debate concerning the verse: "The words 'without a cause' are superfluous, and were added by those who did not think that anger for just causes was to be banished: since certainly nobody, however unreasonably he is disturbed, would say that he was angry without a cause. Wherefore it appears to have been added by those who did not understand the drift of the Scripture."[26]

Table 2 provides a sampling of the writings of many of the early Christian Fathers and whether they include the phrase "without a cause" in their discussion of Jesus' words in Matthew 5:22.[27]

The disparity between those of ancient date who included "without a cause" in their commentary on Matthew 5:22 and those who did not is representative of the debate that has continued to this day. Whether ancient or modern, those who include the phrase generally argue that anger is acceptable in some circumstances, while those who exclude the phrase believe Jesus was calling for anger to be eliminated from our lives.[28] Consider the contrasting views of two scholars of the

TABLE 2: WRITINGS OF EARLY CHURCH FATHERS
ON MATTHEW 5:22

CHURCH FATHER	INCLUDES "WITHOUT A CAUSE"?
Justin (about AD 165)	No
Irenaeus[lat] (AD 200)	Yes
Tertullian[vid] (after AD 220)	No
Origen (AD 253/254)	No
Cyprian (AD 258)	Yes
Eusebius (AD 339)	Yes
Theodore-Heraclea (AD 355)	No
Hilary (AD 367)	Yes
Lucifer (AD 370/371)	Yes
Basil (AD 379)	Yes
Justin (fourth–fifth century)	Yes
Chromatius (AD 407)	No
Jerome[mss] (AD 419/420)	No
Augustine (AD 430)	Yes
Augustine (AD 430)	No
John Cassian (AD 435)	No
Cyril (AD 444)	Yes
Theodoret (about AD 466)	Yes
Speculum (AD 500)	Yes

twentieth century concerning the teachings of Jesus on the morality of anger. First from New Testament scholar Dale C. Allison Jr.: "Although human experience teaches the dangers of anger, . . . Jesus here [Matthew 5:22] seems to go further. He does not say that one should not be angry for the wrong reason. Nor does he imply that there might be some good reason for being angry with another. He seemingly prohibits the emotion altogether."[29] Compare this view with that of feminist scholar Beverly Wildung Harrison: "All agree that anger is not only a disposition but a relational dynamic and in no way the deadly sin of classical

tradition. Feminist theologies all but unanimously reject the patriar-
chal definition of the Christian life as involving 'sacrifice' of self and
refuse the notion that the self-assertions involved in the expression of
our passions, including anger, are 'wrong.'"[30] This ongoing debate concerning anger and Christ's words in Matthew 5:22 demonstrates that
while statements from patristic authors and contemporary scholars are
indeed valuable, they are not a sufficient measure in determining
whether "without a cause" was original to the words of Jesus in
Matthew 5:22 or a later addition.

ENGLISH VERSIONS OF THE BIBLE

The first complete English translation of the Bible did not exist
until the distinguished scholar and priest John Wycliffe, along with his
associates, produced a translation in 1382. The words of Jesus on anger
in the Wycliffe translation are as follows:

> Ye han herd that it was seid to elde men, Thou schalt not
> slee; and he that sleeth, schal be gilti to doom. But Y seie to you,
> that ech man that is wrooth to his brothir, schal be gilti to
> doom; and he that seith to his brother, Fy! schal be gilti to the
> counseil; but he that seith, Fool, schal be gilti to the fier of helle
> (Wycliffe New Testament, Matthew 5:21–22).[31]

Note that the phrase (or any form of the phrase) "without a cause"
does not appear in the Wycliffe translation. John Wycliffe and those
with whom he associated based their English translation on the Latin
Vulgate, which was the standard scripture of the Roman Catholic
Church. Jerome completed the Vulgate in AD 400 and believed the
phrase in question "should be deleted."[32]

Wycliffe's fourteenth-century English translation was followed in
the sixteenth century by several printed English translations: Tyndale
(1526), Coverdale (1535), Matthew's (1537), Great (1539), Geneva
(1560), and the Bishops' Bible (1568). In 1604, King James I authorized the translation of what is now called the King James Version,
attempting to resolve the controversy over which version of the Bible
should be used by the Church of England. This was completed in 1611.
Table 3 summarizes these English translations relative to the inclusion

TABLE 3: EARLY ENGLISH TRANSLATIONS[33]

BIBLE	INCLUDES "WITHOUT A CAUSE"?
Wycliffe Bibles (1382, 1388)	No
Tyndale Bible (1526)	No
Coverdale Bible (1535)	No
Matthew's Bible (1537)	No
Taverner's Bible (1539)	No
Great Bible (1539)	Yes
Geneva Bible (1560)	Yes
Bishops' Bible (1568)	Yes
Rheims-Douai Bible (1610)	No
King James Bible (1611)	Yes

or exclusion of the phrase "without a cause" or its variants in Matthew 5:22.

The first instance of "without a cause" appearing in an English Bible text is in the Great Bible of 1539 in the form of the word "unadvisedly" (*vnaduysedly*).[34] The Great Bible, Geneva Bible, and Bishops' Bible all include the word "unadvisedly."

Miles Coverdale, the translator of the Great Bible, was the first of the English translators to break with the Wycliffe, Tyndale, and even his own 1535 version, and include the phrase of exception. Thomas Cromwell instructed Coverdale to base his text primarily on Matthew's Bible, the Vulgate, and both Sebastian Münster's and Erasmus's Latin translations.[35] But while Coverdale was the first to include the phrase in the English Bible, because his primary sources for the translation did not include the phrase of exception, it is unclear why he chose to introduce the phrase in question. Like the King James translators that would follow, it may have been that Coverdale was influenced by what at the time was the growing scholarly acceptance of the reading of Matthew 5:22 as found in the Textus Receptus, which contains the phrase.[36]

TABLE 4: LATER ENGLISH TRANSLATIONS

NAME	INCLUDES "WITHOUT A CAUSE" ?	COMMENTS
Alexander Campbell (1832)	Yes	"unjustly"
Noah Webster (1833)	Yes	
Joseph Smith Translation (1833)	No	
Darby Translation (1890)	No	
Young's Literal Translation (1898)	Yes	
American Standard (1901)	No	
New World Translation (1950)	No	
Revised Standard Bible (1952)	No	
New English Bible (1970)	No	footnote a: "some witnesses insert without a good cause"
New American Bible (1971)	No	
New International Version (1978)	No	footnote a: "some manuscripts . . . [include] without cause"
New King James (1979)	Yes	footnote a: "NU-Text omits without a cause"
New Jerusalem Bible (1985)	No	
New Revised Standard Version (1989)	No	footnote a: "other ancient authorities add without cause"
The Message (1993)	No	
New American Standard (1995)	No	
New Living Translation (1996)	No	footnote a: "some manuscripts add with out cause"
English Standard Version (2001)	No	footnote a: "some manuscripts insert without cause"

LATER ENGLISH VERSIONS OF THE BIBLE

From the time of the publication of the King James Bible to the present day, there have been at least 291 English translations of the Bible.[37] Table 4 lists a sampling of those translations and whether they include the phrase "without a cause."[38]

While the majority of the later translations are based on the earlier Greek manuscripts and do not contain the phrase "without a cause," some modern translations retain the phrase. The inclusion or exclusion of the phrase in Matthew 5:22 continues to be a topic of debate.

THE SIGNIFICANCE OF RESTORATION WITNESSES

The long-standing debate concerning the Savior's words in Matthew 5:22 based on manuscripts, patristic Fathers, and Bible translations is indicative of humankind's struggle to discover truth. Latter-day Saints are greatly blessed to have modern prophets, additional scripture, and personal as well as institutional revelation as means of identifying and understanding truth. Elder Dallin H. Oaks of the Quorum of the Twelve Apostles stated: "We rely on prophets and revelation in circumstances where others rely on scholars and scholarship. . . . Latter-day Saints believe that as a source of knowledge, the scriptures are not the ultimate but the penultimate. The ultimate knowledge comes by revelation."[39]

In terms of modern prophets and revelation, both the Joseph Smith Translation of Matthew 5:22 and the Savior's similar sermon in the ancient Americas exclude the phrase "without a cause." They, along with the traditional reading from the King James Version of the Bible, read as follows:

KJV, JST, AND BOOK OF MORMON READINGS

KJV, MATTHEW 5:22	JST, MATTHEW 5:22[40]	3 NEPHI 12:22
But I say unto you, that whosoever is angry with his brother without a cause shall be in danger of the judgment:	But I say unto you, that whosoever is angry with his brother shall be in danger of his judgment . . .	But I say unto you, that whosoever is angry with his brother shall be in danger of his judgment.

While several General Authorities have commented on the text of Matthew 5:22, Elder Lynn G. Robbins of the Seventy gave the most detailed and representative statement on the subject:

> The Lord expects us to make the choice *not* to become angry. Nor can becoming angry be justified. In Matthew 5, verse 22, the Lord says: "But I say unto you, That whosoever is angry with his brother *without a cause* shall be in danger of the judgment" (emphasis added). How interesting that the phrase "without a cause" is not found in the inspired Joseph Smith Translation . . . , nor in the 3 Nephi 12:22 version. When the Lord eliminates the phrase "without a cause," He leaves us without an excuse. "But this is my doctrine, that such things should be done away" (3 Ne. 11:30). We can "do away" with anger, for He has so taught and commanded us.[41]

Latter-day Saint scholars have also commented on the differences in renderings of Matthew 5:22.[42] Professor John W. Welch notes that "the absence of *without a cause* [in latter-day scripture] has important moral, behavioral, psychological, and religious ramifications."[43] In considering the abundance of early manuscripts which have been found since 1830, Professor Welch concludes that while the "high degree of confirmation of the [received Greek texts] speaks generally in favor of the [Book of Mormon's] Sermon at the Temple, . . . one could not have wisely gambled on such confirmations a century and a half ago, before the earliest Greek New Testament manuscripts had been discovered."[44]

Some critics of Joseph Smith and the scriptures of the Restoration have attempted to explain the absence of "without a cause" from the Joseph Smith Translation of the Bible and the Book of Mormon by asserting that the Prophet Joseph borrowed the idea from the writings of protestant reformer John Wesley.[45] While Wesley's commentary on Matthew 5:22—consistent with many of the early Christian Fathers—does state that the inclusion of "without a cause" "is utterly foreign to the whole scope and tenor of our Lord's discourse" and that "we ought not for any cause to be angry,"[46] no evidence suggests that Joseph Smith knew of Wesley's work or referred to it while translating the Book of Mormon or the Bible.

CONCLUSION

This chapter has shown a multitude of conflicting opinions among early texts and manuscripts, Christian Fathers, English Bible translations, and New Testament scholars (ancient and modern), concerning the legitimacy of the phrase "without a cause" in the text of Matthew 5:22. From the evidence presented, the teachings of latter-day scripture, and prophetic direction, we can conclude that the addition of the phrase "without a cause" is evidence of Nephi's prophecy that the New Testament text would be corrupted and that truths would be lost from the New Testament and from the lives of individuals, families, and the world at large.

In addition to prophesying of truths being taken from scripture, the Lord also revealed that these truths would eventually be restored: "And after the Gentiles do stumble exceedingly, because of the most plain and precious parts of the gospel of the Lamb which have been kept back, . . . I will be merciful unto the Gentiles in that day, insomuch that I will bring forth unto them, in mine own power, much of my gospel, which shall be plain and precious, saith the Lamb" (1 Nephi 13:34). The Book of Mormon prophet Nephi recorded that additional scripture would come forth that would testify of the divine truths retained in the Bible and restore those that were taken away: "These last records [Book of Mormon, Doctrine and Covenants, Pearl of Great Price, and the Joseph Smith Translation of the Bible], which thou hast seen among the Gentiles, shall establish the truth of the first [the New Testament], which are of the twelve apostles of the Lamb, and shall make known the plain and precious things which have been taken away from them" (1 Nephi 13:40).

Through modern revelation, we can be confident that in the Sermon on the Mount, Jesus clearly taught the following concerning anger: "Ye have heard that it hath been said by them of old time, that thou shalt not kill; and whosoever shall kill shall be in danger of the judgment of God. But I say unto you, that whosoever is angry with his brother shall be in danger of his judgment; and whosoever shall say to his brother, Raca, or Rabcha, shall be in danger of the council; and whosoever shall say to his brother, Thou fool, shall be in danger of hell fire."⁴⁷ While various texts, patristic Fathers, and scholars throughout time have helped contribute to a better understanding of these teachings, the Prophet Joseph Smith restored and clarified what was originally taught by Jesus concerning anger.⁴⁸ These verses clearly teach that when we are angry, we are "in danger of" losing our intimate associations with our family and friends ("his judgment"), the Church ("the council"), and with God ("hellfire").⁴⁹ It is not surprising that with such important relationships at risk, the adversary of all that is good would attempt to confuse us with respect to the morality of anger by tampering with the text of the New Testament.

NOTES

1. John MacArthur, *The MacArthur New Testament Commentary (Revelation 12–22)* (Chicago: Moody, 2000), 310.

2. Howard W. Hunter, "No Man Shall Add to or Take Away," *Ensign*, May 1981, 64. See also David E. Aune, *Word Biblical Commentary Volume 52C, Revelation 17–22* (Nashville: Thomas Nelson, 1998), 1232; and Stephen E. Robinson, *Are Mormons Christian?* (Salt Lake City: Deseret Book), 47.

3. Stephen L. Harris, *The New Testament: A Student's Introduction*, 5th ed. (Mountain View, CA: Mayfield, 2006), 11.

4. See Daniel K Judd, "A Scriptural Comparison Concerning Anger: 3 Nephi 22 and Matthew 5:22," in *The Book of Mormon and the Message of the Four Gospels*, ed. Ray L. Huntington and Terry B. Ball (Provo, UT: Religious Studies Center, Brigham Young University, 2001), 57–76, for a detailed discussion of the morality of anger.

5. Joseph Smith, *Teachings of the Prophet Joseph Smith*, comp. Joseph Fielding Smith (Salt Lake City: Deseret Book, 1938), 327.

6. Smith, *Teachings of the Prophet Joseph Smith*, 9–10.

7. Origen, *Commentary on Matthew 15:14*, in Bart D. Ehrman, *Misquoting Jesus: The Story Behind Who Changed the Bible and Why* (New York: Harper Collins, 2005), 52.

8. Jerome, *Epistulae*, 71.5, *Ad Lucinum* (J. Migne, *Patrologia Latina*, 22.671; *Corpus Scriptorum Eccleriasticorum Latinorum*, 55, 51), in Bruce M. Metzger and Bart D. Ehrman, *The Text of the New Testament: Its Transmission, Corruption, and Restoration*, 4th ed. (New York: Oxford University Press, 2005), 260n13.

9. Bart D. Ehrman, *The Orthodox Corruption of Scripture: The Effect of Early Christological Controversies on the Text of the New Testament* (New York: Oxford University Press, 1993), xi.

10. Jeffrey R. Holland, "The Grandeur of God," *Ensign*, November 2003, 70.

11. *Parablepsis* is a haplographic error—a mechanical error in writing which occurs by writing only once something that occurs two or more times in the original document. The term *parablepsis* ("looking aside") refers specifically to the omission of one line of text due to confusing the text with another line which has a similar ending (see Glen G. Scorgie, Mark L. Strauss, and Steven M. Voth, *The Challenge of Bible Translation* [Grand Rapids, MI: Zondervan, 2003], 274).

12. Based on Royal Skousen, ed., *The Original Manuscript of the Book of Mormon: Typographical Facsimile of the Extant Text* (Provo, UT: Foundation for Ancient Research and Mormon Studies, 2001), 304.

13. Jerald and Sandra Tanner, *The Changing World of Mormonism* (Chicago: Moody, 1980), 131.

14. Metzger and Ehrman, *The Text of the New Testament,* 50.

15. Philip W. Comfort and David Barrett, *The Complete Text of the Earliest New Testament Manuscripts* (Grand Rapids, MI: Baker, 1999), 13–17.

16. Comfort and Barrett, *The Complete Text,* 35. Carsten Peter Thiede estimates the dating of papyrus 67 at AD 70, in *Rekindling the Word: In Search of Gospel Truth* (Herefordshire, UK: Gracewing Fowler Wright, 1995), 27.

17. Comfort and Barrett, *The Complete Text,* 34, 61. Professor Eric Huntsman of Brigham Young University examined an image of the Barcelona papyrus and provided a second witness that "without a cause" is not found in the text. See also David Allen Black, "Jesus on Anger: The Text of Matthew 5:22a Revisited," *Novum Testamentum* 30, no. 1 (1988): 5n14.

18. Barbara Aland, and others, eds., *The Greek New Testament,* 4th ed. rev. (New York: United Bible Societies, 1993), 13.

19. Ehrman, *Misquoting Jesus,* 224–25n2.

20. The phrase was later added to the original by a second corrector.

21. Bruce M. Metzger, *A Textual Commentary on the Greek New Testament,* 2d ed. (New York: United Bible Societies, 2002), 11.

22. Black, "Jesus on Anger," 5–6.

23. In AD 383, under the direction of Pope Damasus, Jerome began working to "produce a uniform and dependable text of the Latin Scriptures." The confusing diversity among the several Old Latin manuscripts which Jerome had to work with made the production of a reliable, revised Bible text a particularly arduous task (Bruce M. Metzger, *The Bible in Translation: Ancient and English Versions* [Grand Rapids, MI: Baker, 2001], 31–32).

24. Jerome in Thomas Aquinas, *On Evil,* trans. Jean Oesterle (Notre Dame: University of Notre Dame Press, 1995), 371.

25. John Chrysostom in Aquinas, *On Evil,* 373.

26. Philip Schaff and Henry Wace, eds., *Nicene and Post-Nicene Fathers, Second Series, Volume 11, Slpitius Severus, Vincent of Lerins, John Cassian* (Peabody, MA: Hendrickson, 1995), 263.

27. Aland, and others, *The Greek New Testament,* 13.

28. John Cassian summarized the argument in these words: "For the end and aim of patience consists, not in being angry with a good reason, but in not being angry at all" (Schaff and Wace, *Nicene and Post-Nicene Fathers,* 263).

29. Dale C. Allison Jr., *Matthew: A Shorter Commentary* (London: T and T Clark International, 2004), 77.

30. Beverely Wildung Harrison, in Andrew D. Lester, *The Angry Christian: A Theology for Care and Counseling* (Louisville: Westminster John Knox, 2003), 134.

31. Wesley Center for Applied Theology, *Wycliffe Bible,* Northwest Nazarene University; http://wesley.nnu.edu/biblical_studies/wycliffe/ Mat.txt (accessed January 13, 2006); see also *The Wycliffe New Testament 1388,* spelling modernized by W. R. Cooper (London: British Library, 2002), 11.

32. Jerome in Aquinas, *On Evil,* 371.

33. Metzger, *The Bible in Translation,* 56–67. The online collection of English Bibles found at http://collections.chadwyck.com/ was used to determine whether the phrase was included.

34. The 1551 edition of Matthew's Bible (New Testament) is the first English version to include the actual phrase "without a cause."

35. Benson Bobbrick, *Wide as the Waters: The Story of the English Bible and the Revolution it Inspired* (New York: Simon and Schuster, 2001), 149.

36. The King James Version was primarily based on Beza's and Stephanus' editions of what would later be called the Textus Receptus. (William W. Combs, "Erasmus and the Textus Receptus," *Detroit Baptist Seminary Journal,* Spring 1996, 53n86, in reference to Vaganay, *Introduction to New Testament Textual Criticism,* 134. Scrivener [*A Plain Introduction to the Criticism of the New Testament,* 391], citing Wetstein, says that Beza's text differs from that of Stephanus in about 50 places.) Beza's 1598 edition does contain the word *eike,* or "without a cause."

37. Laurence M. Vance, *A Brief History of English Bible Translation,* as referenced in Metzger, *The Bible in Translation,* 186.

38. Sampling of Bibles adapted from Metzger, *The Bible in Translation,* 90–104, 117–62.

39. Dallin H. Oaks, "Scripture Reading and Revelation," remarks given at *BYU Studies* Academy dinner meeting, January 29, 1993, at Provo, Utah; transcript in author's possession.

40. New Testament Manuscript 2, folio 1, page 8; spelling, punctuation, and capitalization standardized (see Scott H. Faulring, Kent P. Jackson, and Robert J. Matthews, eds., *Joseph Smith's New Translation of the Bible: Original Manuscripts* [Provo, UT: Religious Studies Center, Brigham Young University, 2004], 244).

41. Lynn G. Robbins, "Agency and Anger," *Ensign,* May 1998, 80.

42. See Daniel K Judd, "A Scriptural Comparison Concerning Anger," 57–76.

43. John W. Welch, "A Steady Stream of Significant Recognitions," in Donald W. Parry, Daniel C. Peterson, and John W. Welch, eds., *Echoes and Evidences of the Book of Mormon* (Provo, UT: Foundation for Ancient Research and Mormon Studies, 2002), 335.

44. John W. Welch, *The Sermon at the Temple and the Sermon on the Mount* (Salt Lake City: Deseret Book and Foundation for Ancient Research and Mormon Studies, 1990), 146–47.

45. See Ronald V. Huggins, "'Without a Cause' and 'Ships of Tarshish': A Possible Contemporary Source for Two Unexplained Readings from Joseph Smith," *Dialogue* 36, no. 1 (Spring 2003): 157–79.

46. See John Wesley, *Explanatory Notes Upon the New Testament* (Philadelphia: Joseph Crukshank, 1791), 1:29; spelling modernized.

47. New Testament Manuscript 2, folio 1, page 8, spelling, punctuation, and capitalization standardized (see Faulring, Jackson, and Matthews, *Joseph Smith's New Translation*, 244).

48. Also compare the KJV and JST translations of Ephesians 4:26.

49. See Daniel K Judd, *Hard Questions, Prophetic Answers: Doctrinal Perspectives on Difficult Contemporary Issues* (Salt Lake City: Deseret Book, 2004), 79–99, for more on the anger of God.

11

THE BREAD OF LIFE DISCOURSE AS DIALOGUE

Charles Swift

As a jeweler uses different lenses to look at a diamond's facets, we can review the Gospels using a number of techniques. We can look at the materials and sources available to the writers, how much the writings tell us about the Savior and about those for whom the Gospels were written, how interpretations of what was done or said change between when they occurred and when they were recorded, the doctrinal purposes behind what the writers chose to record, and what variations may exist among the different manuscripts.[1] Such "traditional methods of interpretation [are] more concerned with what [lies] behind NT narratives than with their form and their literary, artistic features. Although most of these methods [comprise] meticulous exegesis of NT narrative, none of them [seeks] to answer the question, 'What artistry is there in these NT stories?'"[2] In keeping with this question of artistry, this chapter will explore how the literary structure of a dialogue contributes much to our understanding of the discourse of the Bread of Life in the sixth chapter of John.

Charles Swift is an assistant professor of ancient scripture at Brigham Young University.

John wrote his account of this discourse as a work of doctrinal truth that would bring readers to Christ. However, he also wrote it the way he did for a reason, and the way he wrote it can be studied effectively through a literary lens. Understanding how the literary qualities of his writing affect readers will help us appreciate the truth of what he wrote as well. And, as one scholar has written, studying these literary qualities does not mean that we view the text as fiction: "One can call attention to the gospel's literary features because the author used standard literary conventions in order to make his gospel interesting and lively. In no way does the use of literary criticism suggest that his gospel is 'only' a story; but it is no less than that."[3] Therefore, rather than considering this discourse in a historical sense or in regard to its original language, we will explore what can be seen in the text from a literary perspective.

Noted literary scholar Robert Alter writes about his study of biblical stories:

> I have constantly sought to uncover through my analysis the multifaceted artistry of the biblical narratives themselves. In order to underscore the wider applicability of the approach I have put forth, let me briefly summarize the chief distinctive principles of biblical narrative that have been considered in this study. Reading, of course, is far too complex an activity to be reduced to checklists, but it may be helpful to keep certain features in mind, to ask ourselves certain questions, in order to direct the appropriate close attention on these highly laconic, finely articulated tales. Let me propose that for the purposes of synopsis we group what we have been discussing under four general rubrics: words, actions, dialogue, and narration.[4]

Since much has already been written about how particular words are used in the discourse,[5] a careful consideration of the other three literary elements can give readers of John new and helpful insights. The approach John takes in writing about this discourse (narration), the account of what is actually done by those who are part of the scriptural text (action), and the content of what is said and how the speakers interact with one another verbally (dialogue) are literary elements that help determine how we benefit from reading the text. The way in which the author chose to write his account *of* the discourse shapes the ways readers view the Savior's teachings *in* the discourse.

NARRATION

John is the narrator of the discourse on the Bread of Life. We do not have the Lord's direct account of the experience, nor the crowd's, but we do have John's. He matches well Alter's observations about biblical narrators: "Perhaps the most distinctive feature of the role played by the narrator in the biblical tales is the way in which omniscience and inobtrusiveness are combined. . . . He is all-knowing and also perfectly reliable: at times he may choose to make us wonder but he never misleads us."[6] John knows everything he needs to know in order to give us an accurate, reliable account of the discourse, but he never intrudes into the account by becoming an actor in the scene, nor does he offer commentary in the place of allowing the Lord's words to speak for themselves.

The account of the Savior's Bread of Life teachings is not a sermon; the Lord does not address the gathering as though He were giving a lecture to a group of people expected to sit quietly and listen. Instead, John portrays the teachings in the context of an encounter: it is a dialogue between the Savior and the crowd. Now, of course, such a dialogue is technically impossible. One can have a discussion with a member of a crowd, or even with several different members, but not with the crowd itself. The entire crowd did not say in unison, "Rabbi, when camest thou hither?" (John 6:25) or "What shall we do, that we might work the works of God?" (verse 28). Yet that is precisely how John chooses to write about the discourse. As we can see from the following, the text indicates a discussion between the Lord and the crowd as though the crowd were one person:

> *They* said unto him (v. 25)
> Jesus answered *them* (v. 26)
> Then said *they* unto him (v. 28)
> Jesus answered and said unto *them* (v. 29)
> *They* said therefore unto him (v. 30)

Then Jesus said unto *them* (v. 32)
Then said *they* unto him (v. 34)
And Jesus said unto *them* (v. 35)
And *they* said (v. 42)
Jesus therefore answered and said unto *them* (v. 43)
The Jews therefore strove *among themselves,* saying (v. 52)
Then Jesus said unto *them* (v. 53; emphasis added throughout)

Even when the people in the crowd are speaking among themselves and not to the Lord, John writes as though one person is speaking: "The Jews therefore strove among themselves, saying, How can this man give us his flesh to eat?" (verse 52). Nowhere in the text does John indicate that only one person from the crowd is addressing the Savior, nor does he portray Him as speaking to just one person.

We do not want to make the mistake of thinking there is no significance to this format for the discourse, or that John always had a group speak as though it were one person and had the Lord address the group collectively. We could look at a number of instances in John's Gospel in which this format is not followed, but it would be most relevant to study the other events written of in chapter 6. For example, in this same chapter, once the discourse on the Bread of Life is concluded, the Lord addresses the Twelve as a group, but one person speaks from the group: "Then *said Jesus unto the twelve,* Will ye also go away? Then *Simon Peter answered* him, Lord, to whom shall we go? Thou hast the words of eternal life. And we believe and are sure that thou art that Christ, the Son of the living God. *Jesus answered them,* Have not I chosen you twelve" (verses 67–70, emphasis added). Likewise, in this same chapter, the Savior specifically speaks to Philip and possibly to Andrew (verses 5, 10), though there are other disciples there as well, and Philip and Andrew directly speak to Him (verses 7–8).

By deciding to present the crowd as one person in this discourse with the Savior, John essentially transforms the event into a dialogue between two people. This approach simplifies the account. We readers do not need to be concerned with the crowd as individuals—we do not have to deal with disagreements among them, for example, or with differing personalities. The focus is not on group dynamics but doctrine, not on the wide spectrum of possible questions a group might ask but on the pure answers the Lord offers. Perhaps more importantly, this dialogic approach creates a more personal tone, as if the Lord were talking directly to us. The Lord *is* addressing us, in many ways, and John's text calls upon us to consider how we would respond to what He is saying.

ACTION

John Dominic Crossan writes that "the simplest reading of the text reveals how the predominance of Narrative in 6.1–21 gives way to the predominance of Discourse in 6.22–71."[7] One of the dominant aspects of the Bread of Life discourse is the lack of description of any action. Obviously, something is going on during the discourse other than speaking. People are moving in a variety of ways. The Savior is most likely looking in one direction now, another later. But there is not even a word in John's account that conveys action other than speaking. The Jews "murmured at him" (John 6:41) and "strove among themselves" (John 6:52), but still the verbs refer to speaking.

As we turn to chapter 6 for evidence of narrative action, we see that this lack of action description is unusual for John. We first read about the feeding of the five thousand. In the fifteen verses that constitute the account of the miraculous feeding, only six contain quoted dialogue. In the nine verses that constitute the account of the Savior's walking on water and related verses, one verse contains quoted dialogue. But of the thirty-five verses relating the Bread of Life discourse, thirty-four of them include quoted dialogue. By leaving out action, John places the complete emphasis and the reader's attention on what is being said.

Two passages of the discourse are of particular interest regarding the balance of speaking with action. John writes that the "Jews then murmured at him, because he said, I am the bread which came down from heaven. And they said, Is not this Jesus, the son of Joseph, whose father and mother we know? how is it then that he saith, I came down from heaven?" (John 6:41–42). They do not appear to be addressing Jesus, since they speak of Him in the third person, but rather they are grumbling among themselves about what they are being taught. In the second relevant passage, John writes that the "Jews therefore strove

among themselves, saying, How can this man give us his flesh to eat?"
(John 6:52). In both of these passages, John chooses to write about the
grumbling and arguing as speech rather than as actions. It would probably be more accurate to write, "The Jews argued among themselves,
discussing how it could be possible to eat the flesh of Jesus," because
that most likely portrays what happened more accurately than claiming
that the members of the crowd actually said the same thing. However,
to write it more accurately would be to write about action rather than
speech, to place—even for just a verse—emphasis on what was happen-
ing rather than on what was being said.

DIALOGUE

Alter writes that "everything in the world of biblical narrative ultimately gravitates toward dialogue. . . . As a rule, when a narrative event
in the Bible seems important, the writer will render it mainly through
dialogue, so the transitions from narration to dialogue provide in themselves some implicit measure of what is deemed essential, what is con-
ceived to be ancillary or secondary to the main action."[8] Keeping this
principle in mind, it is significant that John chooses to present the
experience of the Savior's speaking with the crowd as a dialogue. We
might overlook the significance, saying that because the experience was
a discourse, John would have to portray it as such. However, that is
actually not the case. John certainly could have made his account a narrative summary of what was said. While the other two scenes in John
6 are far from unimportant, the author's writing of the Bread of Life
discourse in such a dialogue-intensive way, for such an extended length,
may indicate the level of importance he grants it in the text. For
example, if we compare John's account of the Lord walking on water
(the scene immediately preceding the discourse) with Matthew's
account, we can see how little dialogue John uses in comparison to
Matthew (see Matthew 14:24–33; John 6:16–21).

Alter continues his discussion of biblical dialogue by explaining that
since "the very occurrence of extended dialogue should signal the need
for special attentiveness as we read, there is a set of more specific questions we might ask ourselves about the way the dialogue emerges and
develops." He offers five basic questions to consider in studying biblical

dialogue: (1) Is this "the first reported speech" for either of the speakers? (2) If so, "why did the writer choose this particular narrative juncture" for the speaker to "reveal himself through speech"? (3) How does the kind of speech "delineate" the speaker and "his relation to the other party to the dialogue"? (4) When do the speakers "ostensibly answer one another without truly responding to what the other person said"? (5) And when does "the dialogue break off sharply, withholding from us the rejoinder we might have expected from one of the two speakers"?[9]

First reported speech? This is obviously not the first reported speech for the Savior in the book of John, but it is the first reported of any significant length for the crowd. The only other occurrence of the crowd speaking is John 6:14: "Then those men, when they had seen the miracle that Jesus did, said, This is of a truth that prophet that should come into the world." It is interesting that the only words John offers us from the crowd before the discourse will be ultimately refuted by their unwillingness to accept the Lord as the Bread of Life.

Why this narrative juncture? Once again, we need to be careful not to answer with the easiest response: "Because that's what happened." While it is true that the Lord actually gave the Bread of Life discourse at this particular moment in history, John did not have to use this opportunity to "reveal" the Lord "through speech." If we were to ask why the Lord chose to speak on the Bread of Life at this specific point, one of the reasons would be that it was such a powerful teaching opportunity considering the miraculous experience the crowd had shared the day before. They had just partaken of bread provided for them in a miraculous manner; now it was time for them to partake of the Bread of Life. However, the question of dialogue does not ask why the Lord chose to speak at that moment but rather why the author would choose to give the account in the form of speech.

One result of the author's use of speech at this specific time in the story—this "particular narrative juncture"—is the effect of the discourse on the reader. As mentioned earlier, the text becomes more than an account of a historical event—it is a dialogue between our Savior and us. As we read the first sections of John 6, we witness two remarkable miracles: the feeding of the five thousand and His walking on the water.

But as we read the discourse, the author asks us to confront ourselves with the same questions the members of the crowd must ask of themselves. Are we disciples of Christ because of what we think we may gain from the discipleship? Are we seeking miracles, or are we seeking Christ? Are we like the crowd, willing to follow Christ at a safe distance and only when we stand to gain much with little required of us? Or are we willing not only to follow Him but also to allow Him to become a part of us so that we may have life in ourselves? In John 6, "the feeding of the five thousand, coupled with the discourse on Jesus as the heaven-sent bread who gives true life, again points to the unifying theme that Jesus brings life to all who come to share in his feast. This is the heart of both the message and story of the gospel."[10]

Kind of speech? While others have written of the discourse in terms of such elements as imagery,[11] we are concerned here with the way in which the speech delineates the speaker and his relation to the other party. It is clear from the discourse that Jesus and the crowd have a particular relationship: Master Teacher to reluctant students. The great majority of the discourse is the words of the Savior, while the crowd says relatively little. Jesus speaks of doctrine, teaching who He really is and what people need to do in order to be saved, while the crowd, for the most part, asks questions. The crowd asks five questions, but, with one possible exception, the questions do not reflect a yearning to know and live the truth. One question asks when He arrived at the location, one for a sign, and two are more statements of complaint than sincere questions. Only one might be considered an honest question from someone wanting to learn—"What shall we do, that we might work the works of God?" (verse 28)—and, as we shall discuss later, the sincerity of that question is open to interpretation. Despite the apparent stubborn attitude of the crowd, the Lord's tone is never harsh or defensive. He maintains a consistent tone of a teacher throughout the discourse, patiently explaining to His students what they need to know.

Answering without responding? Withholding rejoinders? The Bread of Life discourse is full of instances in which a question is asked but not directly responded to and when anticipated speech is not given.[12] The first question the crowd asks, "Rabbi, when camest thou hither?" (verse 25), is not even acknowledged in the Savior's answer. He does not say anything about when He came but instead challenges them about their purpose for coming themselves. "Verily, verily, I say unto you, Ye seek me, not because ye saw the miracles, but because ye did eat of the loaves, and were filled" (verse 26). The Prophet Joseph Smith's translation of that verse is even more revealing about what the Lord knows of His audience: " . . . *not because ye desire to keep my sayings,* neither because ye saw the miracles" (verse 26, emphasis added). He then teaches the crowd that they should be less concerned with working for "the meat [i.e., food] which perisheth, but for that meat which endureth unto everlasting life, which the Son of man shall give unto you: for him hath God the Father sealed" (verse 27). Masterfully, the Savior teaches the gathering by using the setting to help them understand the difference between what they are looking for and what they *should* be looking for. Their stomachs may hunger for food—as Elder Jeffrey R. Holland writes, they have "flocked to Him expecting a free lunch"[13]—but it is their spirits that should be hungering for the meat of eternal life. He wastes no time answering their unimportant question about when He got there but immediately instructs them, using symbolic language, about what they really need to know—what they should really be asking about.

The crowd's answer is interesting and somewhat unanticipated. We might expect them to ask something such as "What is this food that endures unto everlasting life?" or "Who is this Son of man?" or "How can the Son of man give us this food that leads to everlasting life?" Instead, they say to Him, "What shall we do, that we might work the works of God?" (John 6:28). Whether we understand the crowd to be sincere, earnestly wanting to know what they need to do in order to do the works of God, or we think they are still focused on how they can get more food without effort, they do not seem to understand the significance of what Jesus has just said. Perhaps this is an instance in which "the symbolic function of Jesus' actions and discourse is not understood," giving "rise to one of the features most characteristic of the gospel, namely, the repeated misunderstandings on the part of the characters who encounter Jesus."[14] And, according to R. Alan Culpepper, these misunderstandings have a pattern to them: "These misunderstandings may be characterized in general terms by the following elements: (1) Jesus makes a statement which is ambiguous, metaphorical, or contains a double-entendre; (2) his dialogue partner responds either in terms of the literal meaning of Jesus' statement or by a question or protest which shows that he or she has missed the higher meaning of Jesus' words; (3) in most instances an explanation is then offered by Jesus or (less frequently) the narrator."[15]

As we shall see, repeatedly throughout this dialogue the crowd appears to not understand what they are being told. Often it may be that they do not want to understand.

Jesus tells them that "the work of God" is to "believe on him whom he hath sent" (verse 29). This is another example of the speaker saying something that we do not expect. The Lord's "rejoinder" has little to do with work but is instead centered on belief. His reply is not about what the crowd of people has to *do*, but in whom they must *believe*. The crowd's reply reveals that they are still interested in what they experienced the previous night with the miraculous feeding—they want bread without effort. "What sign shewest thou then," they say, "that we may see, and believe thee? what dost thou work? Our fathers did eat manna in the desert; as it is written, He gave them bread from heaven to eat" (verses 30–31). They still do not understand what the Lord is trying to teach them, but it appears their ignorance is a product of their stomachs. They are trying to manipulate the conversation back to the food they want, even trying to tempt Jesus to prove God has sent Him by giving them free bread to eat. The crowd's request is not unlike that of Satan in the wilderness when he said to the Lord, "If thou be the Son of God, command that these stones be made bread" (Matthew 4:3). Similarly, the Lord's answer to the crowd of disciples reminds us of His answer to the tempter in the wilderness: "It is written, Man shall not live by bread alone, but by every word that proceedeth out of the mouth of God" (Matthew 4:4). The Lord offers the crowd and Satan the same thing: when they seek physical bread, He instead gives them the word of God.

After the Savior explains that the "true bread from heaven" comes from the Father and "giveth life unto the world" (John 6:32–33), the crowd responds in such a way that we readers may hopefully infer that they are converted: "Lord, evermore give us this bread" (verse 34). Perhaps they are finally not asking for tangible, common bread but instead for the gift of eternal life through Christ. However, it is probable that they are still thinking of the manna they have asked about and assume that the "true bread from heaven" will feed them literally as the manna had fed their ancestors. In either case, the Lord's lengthy answer teaches the crowd about who He actually is. "I am the bread of life," He says, "he that cometh to me shall never hunger; and he that believeth on me shall never thirst. . . . For I came down from heaven, not to do mine own will, but the will of him that sent me. And this is the Father's will which hath sent me, that of all which he hath given me I should lose nothing, but should raise it up again at the last day. And this is the will of him that sent me, that every one which seeth the Son, and believeth on him, may have everlasting life: and I will raise him up at the last day" (verses 35, 38–40).

John reports that these Jews, who just moments previous were pleading with the Lord to give them the bread of which He spoke, now murmur among themselves about how He could say He came down from heaven when they knew Him and knew of His earthly parents (see verses 41–42). "They ask the question which becomes typical of earthly, literal, superficial understanding: 'how?'"[16] The crowd is answering without truly responding. They do not respond to the Savior's teaching by accepting or rejecting Him as the Bread of Life, but they grumble among themselves, casting doubt on His claims. We readers are left to ask if the crowd is earnestly trying to grasp what Jesus is teaching or is purposefully closing minds and hearts to His message in a vain attempt to continue living their lives in ways that merely please themselves.

In another lengthy response, Jesus tells the crowd not to murmur and continues His discourse on the Bread of Life. This is another example of speech that does not actually answer the crowd's question in that "Jesus never answers the question about his origins on a human plane; . . . but on a theological plane."[17] The Lord speaks of Himself in symbolic language: "I am the living bread which came down from heaven: if any man eat of this bread, he shall live for ever: and the bread that I will give is my flesh, which I will give for the life of the world" (verse 51). Again, the crowd does not respond directly to the Savior but argues among itself, saying, "How can this man give us his flesh to eat?" (verse 52).

Once again the members of the crowd misunderstand what Jesus is teaching. We benefit from their misunderstanding, because they "provide an opportunity to explain the meaning of Jesus' words and develop significant themes further. They are more, however, and their effect on the reader is greater than if the meaning had merely been stated plainly from the beginning."[18] There is also a "cumulative affect" of how the Lord responds to these misunderstandings, teaching us how to better come unto Him:

> With each misunderstanding, Jesus corrects the blatant miscomprehension on the part of the character in the story. By reading the gospel from beginning to end, the reader has the benefit not only of Jesus' correcting and explanatory words each time, but also of the cumulative affect of those various correctives. Thus with each subsequent misunderstanding, the reader learns that to hear Jesus aright one must ask about the deeper meaning that his words hold. For the true significance of what he says and offers is to be found not in some thing, but in his very presence among them. In short, the Johannine misunderstandings teach the reader how to read the gospel, for they show the reader what mistakes not to make if Jesus is to be understood correctly.[19]

Jesus does not answer the crowd's question but continues to speak metaphorically. "Verily, verily, I say unto you, Except ye eat the flesh of the Son of man, and drink his blood, ye have no life in you. Whoso eateth my flesh, and drinketh my blood, hath eternal life; and I will raise him up at the last day. . . . As the living Father hath sent me, and I live by the Father: so he that eateth me, even he shall live by me. This is that bread which came down from heaven: not as your fathers did eat manna, and are dead: he that eateth of this bread shall live for ever" (verses 53–54, 57–58). He brings the discourse back to its beginning, teaching how what He has to offer is so much more than the manna they sought.

THE DISCOURSE CONCLUDED

It is significant to note what John tells us happens after the discourse is concluded. When Jesus sees that many in the crowd murmur about how He is asking them to do something difficult, He says: "Doth this offend you? What and if ye shall see the Son of man ascend up where he was before? It is the spirit that quickeneth; the flesh profiteth nothing: the words that I speak unto you, they are spirit, and they are life. But there are some of you that believe not. . . . Therefore said I unto you, that no man can come unto me, except it were given unto him of my Father" (verses 61–65). Historically speaking, we do not know what, if anything, the crowd said in response. However, John, as author, abruptly ends his account and discussion of the Bread of Life discourse: "From that time many of his disciples went back, and walked no more with him" (verse 66). This is an example of what Alter referred to as a time when the dialogue is broken off sharply, with anticipated rejoinders withheld. Realistically, it is difficult to imagine that many in the crowd would simply walk away without saying a word, but that is the effect of the account as it is written. It is this description of action, not an account of dialogue, that reveals so much about certain disciples in the crowd.

We can learn as much from the action of the disciples who abandon Him as we do from the discourse itself. As Elder Holland explains: "In that little story is something of the danger of our day. It is that in our contemporary success and sophistication we too may walk away from the vitally crucial bread of eternal life; we may actually *choose* to be spiritually malnourished, willfully indulging in a kind of spiritual anorexia. Like those childish Galileans of old, we may turn up our noses when divine sustenance is placed before us."[20]

The Lord teaches in the discourse on the Bread of Life who He is, what He does for us, and what we need to do to come to Him and have eternal life. But, in our dialogue with the Savior, we cannot afford to misunderstand what He has to say, nor should we walk away.

NOTES

1. These approaches may be called, respectively, form criticism, source criticism, historical criticism, tradition history, redaction criticism, and textual criticism. See Mark W. G. Stibbe, *John as Storyteller: Narrative Criticism and the Fourth Gospel* (Cambridge: Cambridge University Press, 1992), 5.

2. Stibbe, *John as Storyteller*, 5.

3. Marianne Meye Thompson, "John," in *A Complete Literary Guide to the Bible,* ed. Leland Ryken and Tremper Longman III (Grand Rapids, MI: Zondervan, 1993), 409.

4. Robert Alter, *The Art of Biblical Narrative* (New York: Basic Books, 1981), 179. In this foundational book, Alter, as a Jewish scholar, writes of the Hebrew Bible (what we Christians call the Old Testament). However, in the spirit of the "wider applicability" he mentions, I believe the rubrics can pertain to the New Testament as well.

5. "John 6 may well be called 'the Grand Central Station of Johannine critical issues.' In no other place does the same confluence of historical, literary, and theological debates come to the fore as they relate to the Gospel of John. From comparison/contrasts with Synoptic corollaries—to inferences of narrative and discourse sources—to redaction analyses—to christology, semeiology and sacramentology debates—to text disruption and rearrangement theories—to form-critical midrashic analysis—to reader-response approaches (just to mention some of the obvious critical issues), John 6 has time and again provided the *locus argumenti* for scholars wishing to make a definitive contribution to Johannine studies" (Paul N. Anderson, "The *Sitz Im Leben* of the Johannine Bread of Life Discourse and Its Evolving Context," in *Critical Readings of John 6,* ed. R. Alan Culpepper, volume 22 of the Biblical Interpretation series [Leiden: E. J. Brill, 1997], 1).

6. Alter, *Art of Biblical Narrative,* 183–84.

7. John Dominic Crossan, "It Is Written: A Structuralist Analysis of John 6," in *The Gospel of John as Literature: An Anthology of Twentieth-Century Perspectives,* ed. Bruce M. Metzger and Bart D. Ehrman, volume 17 of New Testament Tools and Studies (Leiden: E. J. Brill, 1993), 152.

8. Alter, *Art of Biblical Narrative,* 182.

9. Alter, *Art of Biblical Narrative,* 182–83.

10. Thompson, "John," 414.

11. For a study centered on the words of the discourse (such as symbolism and typology) from an LDS perspective, see Thomas R. Valleta, "John's Testimony of the Bread of Life," in *The Lord of the Gospels: The 1990 Sperry Symposium on the New Testament,* ed. Bruce A. Van Orden and Brent L. Top (Salt Lake City: Deseret Book, 1991), 173–88.

12. For the purposes of keeping continuity in our discussion of the discourse, I will discuss both of these questions together. To discuss them separately would tend to break up the dialogue in a way that would make it difficult to follow the analysis.

13. Jeffrey R. Holland, "He Hath Filled the Hungry with Good Things," *Ensign,* November 1997, 65.

14. Thompson, "John," 418.

15. R. Alan Culpepper, *Anatomy of the Fourth Gospel: A Study in Literary Design* (Philadelphia: Fortress, 1983), 152.

16. Culpepper, *Anatomy of the Fourth Gospel,* 92.

17. Raymond E. Brown, *The Gospel According to John,* volume 29 of the Anchor Bible series (New York: Doubleday, 1966), 277.

18. Culpepper, *Anatomy of the Fourth Gospel,* 152. Culpepper here is referring to the misunderstandings found throughout the book of John, but his observations certainly apply to those particularly within the discourse.

19. Thompson, "John," 418. Thompson, like Culpepper, is referring to the entire book, but her observation is relevant to the discourse as well.

20. Holland, "He Hath Filled the Hungry with Good Things," 65.

12

THE OCCASIONAL NATURE, COMPOSITION, AND STRUCTURE OF PAUL'S LETTERS

Eric D. Huntsman

Even as our beloved brother Paul also according to the wisdom
given unto him hath written unto you; as also in all his epistles, speaking in
them of these things; in which are some things hard to be understood,
which they that are unlearned and unstable wrest,
as they do also the other scriptures,
unto their own destruction.
—2 Peter 3:15–16

The heart of much Catholic and especially Reformation theology, the Pauline epistles frequently prove to be unfamiliar and difficult territory for many Latter-day Saints.[1] Some of Paul's teaching, taken in isolation and out of context, can seem confusing or even to be in contradiction with gospel principles explicated elsewhere in the scriptures generally or even in the rest of the Pauline corpus itself.[2] This is partly because the letters of Paul, by and large, are not treatises of systematic theology, a fact that undercuts the efforts of some to establish extensive

Eric D. Huntsman is an assistant professor of ancient scripture at Brigham Young University.

theological positions based largely upon the Apostle's writings alone.[3] Instead, the letters were written to congregations or individuals in response to specific circumstances or problems and therefore emphasize or apply specific aspects of gospel principles in response to the original situation.

Paul was a prolific and lengthy writer. Whereas the average ancient letter was 87 words long, the literary letters of the Roman authors Cicero and Seneca averaged 295 and 995 words respectively. The average letter of Paul, however, was 2,495 words long![4] Often covering a variety of subjects and addressing each with complex argumentation, his letters can be difficult to follow, especially in translation. However, by considering the original context of the letters and Paul's original reasons for writing them, the types of writing that these letters represent, and how he actually composed and formatted them, the modern student of the Pauline epistles can better interpret the letters and understand both their original and current applications, thereby avoiding "wresting" them improperly.

OCCASIONAL NATURE

Although an occasion, or reason for writing, can be identified for all of the letters of the Pauline corpus, the occasional nature is particularly apparent in some of the earliest of the Apostle's letters, each of which is a response to specific situations in the early branches of the Church.[5] While the principles that these letters teach are abiding and applicable in our age, understanding the original occasion of each letter is especially important for understanding and interpreting it,[6] as can be seen particularly in some of the early letters of Paul such as those written to the Saints in Thessalonica, Galatia, Corinth, and Rome.

Paul, Silvanus (Silas), and Timothy had come to Thessalonica early in the Second Missionary Journey, about AD 50, and had spent only a few weeks in the city, where they had established a largely Gentile congregation. Dated to AD 50 or 51, Paul's two letters to the Thessalonians are generally considered to be the earliest of his preserved writings, and the formal occasion for Paul's writing is his concern for the further instruction of these new Saints.[7] Lacking Paul's later focus on righteousness by faith rather than by the works of the law, much of these letters consist of ethical exhortations as Paul endeavors to teach these new Christians how to live as Saints (see 1 Thessalonians 4:1–12; 5:12–22; 2 Thessalonians 3:6–15).

Nevertheless, considerable portions of both letters to the Thessalonians are devoted to treating the specific topic of the Parousia, or glorious return of Jesus Christ (see 1 Thessalonians 4:13–5:11; 2 Thessalonians 2:1–12), which included the promise that those who were Jesus' at His coming would live with Him forever.[8] While this part of Paul's teaching is best preserved in 1 Thessalonians 4:13–18, this same passage also makes clear that it caused some confusion among the Thessalonians that Paul's letter sought to resolve: because the Thessalonians, and possibly Paul himself, expected the Lord to return soon, they were concerned when the Parousia did not happen immediately and, furthermore, when members of the congregation began to die before Jesus' return. Accordingly, Paul explained in his first letter that "the dead in Christ shall rise first" to be followed by those who were alive at His coming who would be "caught up together with them in the clouds, to meet the Lord in the air" (1 Thessalonians 4:16–17). This preoccupation with Jesus' return, however, seems to have been at the heart of Paul's second letter, where he needed to moderate the enthusiasm of the Thessalonians, noting some of the significant signs that would precede the Parousia (see 2 Thessalonians 2:1–12) and encouraging the Saints with admonitions to work that seem to have been occasioned by the "disorderly walk" (*ataktos peripatountos*) or idle behavior of Saints whose indolence seems to have been the result of an unrealistic expectation of an imminent Second Coming (see 2 Thessalonians 3:6–15).

The letter to the Galatians, conventionally dated AD 54–55 but perhaps composed as early as AD 48 if it were written before the Council of Jerusalem in AD 49, was written in response to a very specific and real problem in the churches spread throughout the southern or northern parts of the Roman province of Galatia. These congregations also consisted largely of Gentile converts, but in Paul's absence a subsequent group of missionaries had disturbed the new converts by teaching them "a different gospel" (see Galatians 1:6–10). Paul's succeeding arguments, especially in Galatians 5:2–12, have suggested that these false teachers had convinced some of the Galatians of the necessity of adopting certain aspects of the Mosaic law—notably circumcision—leading many modern scholars to refer to them as "Judaizers."[9] This context and Paul's efforts to counter this false teaching are necessary to understand properly one of his central points in the letter: "Knowing that a man is *not* justified *by the works of the law,* but by the faith of Jesus Christ, even we have believed in Jesus Christ, that we might be justified by the faith of Christ, and *not by the works of the law: for by the works of the law shall no flesh be justified*" (2:16; emphasis added). On the other hand, Paul may have had a second group of opponents, because his letter later seeks to counter the efforts of those who think that the grace of Christ had made all obedience and law unnecessary. In reaction to the false teaching of these "libertines," a second emphasis is found in a strong ethical section of the letter, where Paul enjoins the Galatians to reject the works of the flesh in favor of the fruits of the Spirit (see 5:16–26).

Paul's first letter to the Corinthians, one of a series of letters of which only two are preserved, was written as a result of problems within one of the largest congregations that he had established. A mixed congregation of converted Jews and Gentiles in the cosmopolitan Roman capital of the province of Achaia (Greece), this branch had been established during Paul's second missionary journey, AD 50–52, when he had stayed there for eighteen months (see Acts 18:7–11). The beneficiaries of thorough gospel instruction, upon Paul's departure the Corinthian Saints developed internal divisions arising from factionalism, pride over special knowledge and gifts, and moral misbehavior arising from doctrinal speculation.[10] Accordingly, Paul devoted considerable portions of his letter to dealing with problems in Corinth such as factions (see 1 Corinthians 1:10–4:21); moral misbehavior, including problems of sex and property (see 5:1–6:20); problems regarding marriage and celibacy (see 7:1–40); Christian freedom and its abuse (see 8:1–11:1); correct and incorrect Christian worship, including the veiling of women (see 11:2–16); abuses of the Lord's Supper (see 11:17–34); misunderstanding and misusing spiritual gifts (see 12:1–14:40); and doctrinal correction regarding the nature of the Resurrection and its application to Christians (see 15:1–58).

Paul's important letter to the Romans is significant both because Paul wrote it to a congregation with which he was not yet familiar and also because of the particular history of the congregation there. He seems to have written it from Corinth in the winter of AD 57–58, when Paul began making plans to visit Rome on his way to Spain and the west after first delivering a collection of money to the poor Saints in Jerusalem (see Romans 15:14–33). Since he knew individual Saints from Rome but had not yet been there himself, the letter was partially intended as a letter of introduction in which he hoped to familiarize the Roman congregation with "his" gospel, perhaps recognizing that his views had been incorrectly represented to the Roman Saints by others (see Romans 3:8).[11] Furthermore, Paul wrote this letter with over a decade of preaching and writing behind him, including the letters to the Thessalonians, Galatians, Corinthians, and perhaps to the Philippians and to Philemon. As a result, in this letter Paul provides a masterful survey of many of the issues he treated in earlier letters to other congregations, producing in the process what is perhaps his most systematic treatment of the issue of justification by faith (see Romans 1:16–8:39).[12]

The background of the Roman church itself influenced both how Paul approached the issue of justification and why he also introduced another topic, God's promises to Israel. Christianity had been brought to Rome by others, presumably Jewish Christians, perhaps as early as the AD 40s or even earlier since Jews from Rome had been among those in Jerusalem at the time of Pentecost (see Acts 2:10). The introduction of Christianity in the capital had apparently led to conflict within the large Jewish community in the city, leading the emperor Claudius to expel all Jews from the city in AD 49.[13] Consequently, in Romans, Paul addresses many of the same issues as he did in Galatians, but here the situation is reversed. In Galatians, Paul addressed a congregation that he had founded but which had subsequently been infiltrated by Judaizers bringing with them old practices of the Mosaic law. In Romans he was addressing a church founded by others and one in which Jewish Christians had been significant but were no longer dominant. As a result, he is less strident and more diplomatic about some of the same principles.

After the death of Claudius in AD 54, Jews and Jewish Christians were allowed to return to Rome, but in the meantime the Church had continued to grow among Gentiles, perhaps resulting in some tension between them and the returning Jewish Christians. The failure of the majority of ethnic Israel to accept Christ and the confusion about what role Jewish Christians should play in the Church led to questions such as whether the Gentiles had superceded the Jews or whether the promises of Israel had passed to the Church, subjects that Paul addresses in his treatise on God's promises to Israel (see Romans 9:1–11:36). Largely misunderstood by sectarian Christianity, Paul's arguments here regarding such issues as God's election of Israel (see 9:1–29), Israel's unbelief (see 9:30–10:5), the availability of salvation to all (see 10:6–21), the fact that Israel's rejection is not final (see 11:1–10), Paul's allegory of the ingrafted branches and the salvation of the Gentiles (see 11:11–24), and the promise that all righteous Israel will be saved *as a group* (see 11:25–32) have a particular importance in the context of the restored gospel.[14]

THE GENRES OF PAUL'S LETTERS

When a specific occasion influenced Paul to write regarding certain topics, he employed the basic letter form common in the Mediterranean world at that time. However, as noted above, Paul's letters were unusually long, and he adapted the standard letter format to meet each occasion. Although the differences in the types of writing found in the gospels, the book of Acts, the book of Revelation, and the various "epistles" or letters in the New Testament are fairly obvious, distinctions in genre also exist among the various letters themselves. Part of this is a result of the fact that New Testament letters vary according to intended audience and how widely the authors expected them to be circulated beyond their original audiences. Paul's letter to Philemon and his family, for instance, reads very much like a personal letter about a particular subject of concern to the sender and recipient—namely how Philemon should treat his slave, Onesimus, who is also Paul's convert. Accordingly, Philemon is termed a "real letter," as opposed to a literary or philosophical exercise intended for wider publication. Paul's other early letters—such as 1–2 Thessalonians, Galatians,

Philippians,[15] 1–2 Corinthians, and Romans—were written to individuals or congregations, but, like Greek philosophical letters, they were considerably longer than an average ancient letter and were meant to teach and exhort. Nevertheless, these are still considered "real letters" because they were written to specific individuals or communities and addressed practical and theological issues relevant to their recipients.

In Ephesians and Colossians, however, there are indications that Paul expected the letters to be circulated among a broader audience. (See Colossians 4:16. Some early manuscripts of Ephesians 1:1 lack "at Ephesus," opening the possibility that the letter was meant for more than just the branch at Ephesus.)[16] This concept of an encyclical, or circular letter, is further developed in 1 Peter and in the other "general epistles." Some scholars, in fact, have tried to reserve the term "epistle" for letters of this type, comparing them to the literary letters of classical authors such as Cicero and Pliny, who, even when they were writing "real letters" to specific individuals, expected their letters to be more widely published and so often wrote with a broader audience in mind.[17] While being familiar with the circumstances that faced Christianity in the first century is still important for understanding the general epistles, as a whole these letters tend to address more than one congregation or were even directed to the entire Church, much like a First Presidency message or letter is today. Ephesians and Colossians, midway between real and circular letters, follow the same general structure of most of Paul's other letters, whereas the general epistles of other authors, although they open and close as letters, are generally shorter and have a less complex structure than a Pauline letter.[18]

The remainder of Paul's letters either fall into different generic categories or combine different types of writing. First Timothy and Titus, commonly called "pastoral epistles," are in effect priesthood handbooks or collections of instructions for the practical organization and regulation of branches of the Church. In them Timothy and Titus are given instructions for the selection and appointment of Church officials, warnings against false teachings, and practical advice on community behavior and belief. While 2 Timothy also addresses some of these issues, it also takes the form of a "testament" or final expression of belief before Paul met his death. Hebrews, which has been closely

associated with Paul in both ancient tradition and Restoration teaching despite being significantly different in style and theme from the
secure Pauline letters, has been identified as a work that "begins like a
treatise, proceeds like a sermon, and closes like an epistle."[19]
Nevertheless, it is not simply a theological treatise but rather has an
apologetic purpose, defending the superiority of Christ and preventing
the readers from lapsing back to the Mosaic system. Furthermore, it is
more of a homily, which is an explication closely connected to scriptural
text, rather than a sermon, which is generally more topical. Only at
Hebrews 13:1–25 does it read like a letter or epistle.

THE MECHANICS OF WRITING
AN ANCIENT LETTER

While the occasion helped determine *what* Paul wrote and to some
extent the *form* the letter took, the realities of ancient letter writing
affected *how* he wrote. Contrary to modern notions of letter writing,
Paul did not sit alone at a desk quietly composing his epistles. Instead,
the composition process was a more lengthy procedure that involved
others at every step.[20] Paul probably stayed with other Christians in his
travels and would have enjoyed little privacy.[21] But more significantly,
his letters frequently included in their opening formula references to
coauthors, who are different from others, such as scribes, who, if mentioned by name, are usually noted in the conclusion.

Examples of coauthors include Silvanus and Timothy in 1–2
Thessalonians; Timothy in 2 Corinthians, Philippians, Colossians, and
Philemon; Sosthenes in 1 Corinthians; and "all the brethren" with Paul in
Galatians. These individuals can be viewed as collaborators in the composition process and may have contributed substantively to much of the
initial material that the scribe, under Paul's direction, later wove into
the final draft.[22] The involvement of Silvanus and Timothy in the
Thessalonian correspondence makes particular sense because they had
been involved with Paul in the initial evangelizing of Thessalonica, and
Timothy was often Paul's messenger to the congregation there, as he was
in the case of other letters where he is listed as coauthor. The nature of
their participation in the formulation of the material used in the letter is
best described by Richards, who notes that Paul worked as leader of a

missionary team, the members of which would have discussed and prayed with him about problems facing the congregations to which they were writing.[23] The case of Sosthenes—who may well be the same individual mentioned in Acts 18:17 as the former ruler of the synagogue, as well as an opponent of Paul, in Corinth—is intriguing. Familiar with both Jewish customs and scripture on the one hand and Greek philosophy and lifestyle in Corinth on the other, he may have been particularly sensitive to the problems facing the congregation there.[24]

The involvement of a secretary or scribe in the actual writing of an ancient letter is more important than modern readers might suspect. Professional writers were used for virtually every letter written in antiquity. For those who were themselves illiterate and needed someone to write for them, a scribe usually took down notes regarding the subjects that concerned the sender and then employed a standard format and used conventional expressions to write the letter. For those who were themselves able to read and perhaps write, scribes were still often used to take down literal dictation—although the skill involved often made this prohibitively expensive—or to take notes from which they wrote a first draft, which the "author" then reviewed, altered, and approved. Two New Testament scribes are identified by name: Tertius in Romans 16:22 and Silvanus in 1 Peter 5:12. In both cases, they seem to have been fellow Christians who were competent in letter writing. In the case of Paul's scribe Tertius, he may have been a professional secretary who was able to take dictation in ancient shorthand and had volunteered his services since Romans has many oratorical features that seem to reflect spoken composition.[25]

Most of Paul's letters, however, were probably not the result of such transcription, which would have taken hours of continuous dictation: by some estimates 1 Thessalonians and Philippians could have been dictated in about two and a half hours, but 1 Corinthians would have required over ten hours, and Romans itself over eleven if an expensive professional not using shorthand were transcribing it.[26] While scribes are not named in any Pauline epistle other than Romans, they can be presumed in the other letters, where their involvement in the actual composition of the letter and the degree to which they were involved in wording of the final draft could vary greatly. Nevertheless, their involvement in the composition process may, in fact, help to explain the differences of style and diction between the different letters of Paul.[27]

Because parchment and especially finer quality papyrus were expensive, scribes may have first taken notes and even written initial drafts on tablets of wood or ivory coated with wax. The scribe then composed, or in the case of a dictated letter, revised the letter and set it down in a neat, professional hand on a good paper, usually papyrus (for a detailed discussion of the involvement of scribes in the writing of an ancient letter, see Lincoln Blumell's chapter in this volume). Letters often went through several drafts before the author reviewed it and then either applied his seal or "signed it" with a postscript at the end. While a postscript could in fact be additional information added after the close of a letter, as is often the case today, in antiquity an "author" more generally used a postscript to guarantee that the contents written by a scribe reflected his thinking. In such a postscript, the author might summarize the contents and then sign his name or affirm the contents in some other fashion.[28] Such postscripts that are actual parts of the preserved text differ from the postbiblical subscriptions that copyists began to add in the fourth century to note assumed facts about a letter but which are often wrong.[29]

Noted examples of postcripts in the Pauline corpus include 1 Corinthians 16:21–24, Galatians 6:11–18, Colossians 4:18, 2 Thessalonians 3:17–18, and Philemon 1:19, where Paul uses his own name and mentions that he is writing this "with mine own hand." Other possible, but unsigned, postscripts include 1 Thessalonians 5:27–28 and Romans 16:21–23.[30] Therefore, regardless of the role of a coauthor or scribe in the composition of a letter, the final product was reviewed and accepted by Paul, who thereby attributed to it apostolic authority. Second Thessalonians 3:17, "The salutation of Paul with mine own hand, which is the token in every epistle: so I write," is a clear example of an authoritative postscript, and it is particularly interesting since the authenticating postscript seems also to have been a device used to prevent forgery by a letter purporting to be from Paul. Apparently this had occurred, because 2 Thessalonians 2:2 suggests that the eschatological fervor that Paul was trying to counter in that letter had been inflamed by such a forgery: "That ye be not soon shaken in mind, or be troubled, neither by spirit, nor by word, *nor by letter as from us,* as that the day of Christ is at hand."[31]

After the postscript was added, the letter was either folded or rolled and then sealed. The entire process of composition, dictation, writing, revision, review, and approval was not only time-consuming but also expensive. The cost of the finished letter included both the cost of the papyrus and secretarial labor and could be quite high. According to some calculations, Romans (979 manuscript lines) would have cost $2,275 in 2004 U.S. dollars, and even short Philemon (44 lines) would have cost $101![32] The letter was then dispatched, sometimes being carried by a friend or associate traveling to the recipient's destination but sometimes just sent with some traveler who was found going to the intended destination. The imperial post carried only official government correspondence, so it was not available to Paul and other New Testament letter writers.

THE STRUCTURE AND FORMAT OF PAUL'S LETTERS

In antiquity, even personal letters were read aloud.[33] Letters to groups, such as Paul's letters to various congregations, were often read to a majority of the recipients (the probable meaning of Colossians 4:16), so most individuals never actually read the letters themselves. As a result, care was given to the way the letter was written, both in its language and its structure, so that it could best be understood, remembered, and repeated to others. Most ancient letters followed a standardized format, one that can often be discerned in other letters of the New Testament, but the length of Paul's letters and the fact they would generally be heard rather then read required additional organization. Briefly analyzing this format and the rhetorical structure of Paul's letters allows a reader to see how Paul used, and in many instances changed, the conventional letter format in order to emphasize certain points.

Ancient letters began with an *opening formula,* identifying the sender (which we saw above could include coauthors) and the recipient (which could be a local congregation, specific members of a branch, or an individual).[34] For example, "Paul, and Silvanus, and Timotheus, unto the church of the Thessalonians which is in God the Father and in the Lord Jesus Christ: Grace be unto you, and peace, from God our Father, and the Lord Jesus Christ" (1 Thessalonians 1:1). While ancient Greek letters consistently included the salutation *chaire*—"be well" or "rejoice"—in the opening formula, here Paul seems to have changed the conventional greeting by substituting *charis,* or "grace," a typically Pauline usage that immediately called to mind the saving work of Jesus Christ. Then, rather than refer to his earthly family or household as a typical letter writer would have done (e.g., "Paul, son of X, of Tarsus . . ."), he identified himself with a new, spiritual household and identified his position to emphasize his authority (e.g., "Paul, a servant or apostle of Jesus Christ" as in 1–2 Corinthians, Galatians, Ephesians, Colossians, 1–2 Timothy, and Titus).[35]

The introductory formula of an ancient letter was routinely followed by either a prayer for health or a *thanksgiving* to the gods. This section of the letter is often considerably extended in Christian letters, particularly the letters of Paul, where it includes expressions of gratitude to the one true God, doxologies or expressions of praise, and even extended prayers.[36] A short example from what is perhaps Paul's earliest extant letter illustrates the thanksgiving section of one of his letters: "We give thanks to God always for you all, making mention of you in our prayers; remembering without ceasing your work of faith, and labour of love, and patience of hope in our Lord Jesus Christ, in the sight of God and our Father; knowing, brethren beloved, your election of God" (1 Thessalonians 1:2–4). These thanksgivings were so standard in Pauline letters that their absence is obvious, as in the letter to the Galatians, where Paul's anger is apparent.[37]

The *body* of a longer letter was frequently structured according to the principles of Classical rhetoric, varying the style depending upon the purpose of the letter, while a shorter letter could be written quite simply. The body of a longer letter of Paul also often contained some of the elements found in the literary letter of a Classical philosopher, such as containing a section of instruction or teaching followed by a section of exhortation. Hence the body of a letter is often divided then into distinct parts, sometimes referred to as "Pauline Indicative" for the section of instructions and "Pauline Imperative" for the section containing admonitions,[38] as can be seen in the body of 1 Thessalonians, in which Paul begins with an indicative section reviewing his relationship to the Thessalonians (2:1–3:13) and follows with an imperative section of exhortations and instructions (4:1–5:22), which includes not only a subdivision of ethical admonitions (4:1–12) but also a further subsection that gives the Saints directions on how they should live given their expectation of the Parousia (4:13–5:11).

This frequent two-fold division into indicative and imperative sections is important because many commentators focus on Paul's doctrinal teaching without sufficiently noting that almost every letter also discussed how the reality of the message of Christ should affect how Saints should *live* as Christians. For instance, the weighty doctrinal section of Romans (1:16–11:36) is followed by a shorter but still significant imperative or hortatory section (12:1–15:13) that includes important discussions of Christian ethics (12:1–13:14) and relations between the strong and the weak (14:1–15:13). Even when indicative and imperative sections alternate or are otherwise spread throughout the body of a letter, the modern reader must always keep in mind that Paul's letters not only teach *doctrine* but also call to *action* and insist that Christians must live according to the highest ethical and moral standards, that their "whole spirit and soul and body be preserved blameless unto the coming of our Lord Jesus Christ" (1 Thessalonians 5:23).[39]

While formal divisions into indicative and imperative sections may have helped a listening audience follow one of Paul's letters, what was even more significant to an ancient audience was his use of rhetorical styles. Dubbed "the art of persuasion," Classical rhetoric involved both the pleasing use of language—which was meant to help it be both understood and remembered—and appropriate use of argumentation. The three modes of argumentation were forensic or judicial, often meant to defend a position; deliberative or hortatory, intended to persuade an audience to make practical decisions; and demonstrative or "epideictic," which sought to inspire, praise, affirm common beliefs, and gain support. According to these divisions, Galatians, meant to defend both Paul's teaching of the gospel and his own authority, is an example of judicial oratory; 1 Corinthians, intended to correct behavior, is an example of deliberative writing; and Romans, which sought to introduce Paul, affirm his doctrine, and gain the support of the Saints in Rome, serves as an example of demonstrative rhetoric.[40] The rhetorical intent of a letter could, in fact, dictate the way Paul organized the body of the letter. For instance, the indicative section of Galatians (1:6–5:1) takes the form of a courtroom speech in which the introduction of Paul's argument that there is no other gospel (see 1:6–10) is followed by a formal *apologia* or "defense" (see 1:11–21) and a series of six proofs demonstrating that one is indeed saved by the faith of Jesus Christ and not by the works of the law (see 3:1–5:1).[41]

The simple *concluding formula* of a Greek or Roman letter is considerably developed in New Testament letters. In place of a simple expression of affection and the occasional wish for strength and health for the recipient, the letters of Paul, for instance, frequently include a final blessing, greetings to various individuals in the community receiving the letter, sometimes the instructions "to greet with a holy kiss," and a final peace wish.[42] Most letters then concluded with a postscript like those discussed above, written and often signed by Paul.

PAUL'S LETTERS, THEN AND NOW

The frequent personal greetings often appended to the end of Paul's letters—such as the list of twenty-six individuals and five groups in Romans 16:3–16—remind us that these were actual letters written to real people in the first century AD. One must try to understand the circumstances in which these individuals and groups found themselves in order to understand what and how Paul was trying to teach them. Nevertheless, Paul's final doxology, or expression of praise, at the end of his letter to the Romans reminds us that his fervent testimony is as vital and true today as it was then: "Now to him that is of power to stablish you according to my gospel, and the preaching of Jesus Christ, according to the revelation of the mystery, which was kept secret since the world began, but now is made manifest, and by the scriptures of the prophets, according to the commandment of the everlasting God, made known to all nations for the obedience of faith: to God only wise, be glory through Jesus Christ for ever. Amen" (Romans 16:25–27).

NOTES

1. See the representative excerpts of Augustine's AD 427 treatise *On Grace and Free Will,* and Martin Luther's 1531 "Lectures on Galatians," in *The Writings of St. Paul,* ed. Wayne A. Meeks (New York: Norton, 1972), 220–50.

2. See Richard L. Anderson, *Understanding Paul* (Salt Lake City: Deseret Book, 1983), 177–83.

3. Morna D. Hooker, *A Preface to Paul* (New York: Oxford University Press, 1980), 8–9, 16–18.

4 E. Randolph Richards, *Paul and First-Century Letter-Writing: Secretaries, Composition, and Collection* (Downers Grove, IL: InterVarsity, 2004), 163–64.

5. Hooker, *Preface to Paul,* 9.

6. Hooker, *Preface to Paul,* 9–11.

7. In this note and subsequent notes, I have given a representative chronological sampling of scholarship from both LDS and non-LDS commentators who consider the occasion of each of the letters briefly discussed here. For 1–2 Thessalonians, see Sidney B. Sperry, *Paul's Life and Letters* (Salt Lake City: Bookcraft, 1955), 94–98; Anderson, *Understanding Paul,* 72–90; Jo Ann H. Seely, "Hope for the 'Children of Light' as the Darkness Descends (1, 2 Thessalonians)," in *Studies in Scripture, Vol. 6: Acts to Revelation,* ed. Robert L. Millet (Salt Lake City: Deseret Book, 1987), 146–50; Charles A. Wanamaker, *The Epistles to the Thessalonians,* New International Greek Testament Commentary (hereafter NIGTC) (Grand Rapids, MI: Eerdmans, 1990), 53–63, 164–90; E. P. Sanders, *Paul* (New York: Oxford University Press, 1991), 26–33; Raymond E. Brown, *Introduction to the New Testament* (New York: Doubleday, 1997), 459–62.

8. Sanders, *Paul,* 21–22.

9. Sperry, *Paul's Life and Letters,* 158–71; F. F. Bruce, *The Epistle to the Galatians,* NIGTC (Grand Rapids, MI: Eerdmans, 1982), 19–32; Anderson, *Understanding Paul,* 152–58; George A. Horton Jr., "Concern, Correction, and Counsel for Converts (Galatians)," in Millet, *Studies in Scripture, Vol. 6,* 83–88; Sanders, *Paul,* 44–64; Brown, *Introduction to the New Testament,* 468–77.

10. Sperry, *Paul's Life and Letters,* 118–37; Anderson, *Understanding Paul,* 95–129; David R. Seely, "'Is Christ Divided?' Unity of the Saints through Charity (1, 2 Corinthians)," in Millet, *Studies in Scripture, Vol. 6,* 57–66; Brown, *Introduction to the New Testament,* 511–35; Anthony C. Thiselton, *The First Epistle to the Corinthians,* NIGTC (Grand Rapids, MI: Eerdmans, 1982), 29–40.

11. Sperry, *Paul's Life and Letters,* 179–200; Anderson, *Understanding Paul,* 172–95; Robert L. Millet, "The Just Shall Live by Faith (Romans)," in Millet, *Studies in Scripture, Vol. 6,* 46; Sanders, *Paul,* 65–76; Joseph A. Fitzmyer, *Romans* (New York: Doubleday, 1993), 25–36; Brown, *Introduction to the New Testament,* 559–75.

12. Brown, *Introduction to the New Testament,* 563, notes that "Romans was in a way a summary of Paul's thought, phrased with an air of finality as he pulled together his ideas before going to Jerusalem where he would have to defend them."

13. See Suetonius, *Claudius,* 25.3, which attributes the expulsion order to riots over one *Chrestus,* the Latin form of a common Greek slave name meaning "useful" or "serviceable" (*Chrestos*), which apparently he had confused with the name *Christos.* Priscilla and Aquila, whom Paul met in Corinth, were Jewish Christian refugees from Rome (see Acts 18:1–3; Romans 16:3–4). Paul himself had relatives who later returned to the city (Andronicus and Junia; see Romans 16:7).

14. Early in the postapostolic period and in the centuries since, many Christians have seen the necessity of accepting Jesus Christ and the failure of Israel to do so as a sign that the Christian Church, as New Israel, had superseded, or taken the place, of ethnic Israel. This view of supersession, sometimes called "replacement theology," saw the Mosaic law and the old covenant of God with His people as being replaced by the new covenant ushered in by Jesus' sacrificial death. In addition to early patristic authors such as Justin Martyr, Tertullian, and Origen, later reformers such as Martin Luther and John Wesley subscribed to some degree of supersessionism. In contrast, for an LDS understanding of Romans 9–11, see Millet, "The Just Shall Live by Faith," 53–54.

15. Although Philippians, as one of the "imprisonment epistles," has been traditionally associated with Paul's (first) Roman imprisonment, c. AD 61–63, this is based largely upon the text's later subscription (see below) as well as to references to "the palace" (Greek *praitorion*, Philippians 1:13) and Saints "of Caesar's household" (Greek *hoi ek tēs kaisaros oikias*, 4:22), both of which terms were not, in fact, limited to Rome itself. Consequently, alternative suggestions include a postulated Ephesian imprisonment, c. AD 54–55, or Paul's detention in Caesarea, c. AD 58–60, both of which would allow for an earlier letter to the Philippians, proposals that are attractive because of Philippians' similarity in style, content, and situation to Galatians and 1 Corinthians (see Brown, *Introduction to the New Testament*, 493–96, and Peter T. O'Brien, *The Epistle to the Philippians*, NIGTC [Grand Rapids, MI: Eerdmans, 1991], 19–26). See Brown, *Introduction to the New Testament*, 507–9, for similar arguments that have been made about the dating of Philemon.

16. Brown, *Introduction to the New Testament*, 600–1, 626–27, 631–33.

17. First proposed by Adolph Deissmann, *Bible Studies* (Edinburgh: Clark, 1901), 3–59, the strict distinction between an actual *letter* and a literary *epistle* has largely been abandoned by New Testament scholarship. Nevertheless, "real letters" and "apparent letters" continue as basic categories, especially if the latter are considered to include circular letters, treatises, homilies, and other kinds of writing that only contain superficial epistolary features (see Jerome Murphy-O'Connor, *Paul the Letter-Writer: His World, His Options, His Skills* [Collegeville, MN: Liturgical Press, 1995], 42–45).

18. 1–2 Peter, 2–3 John, and Jude do not divide the body of the letter into the two usual sections of instruction and admonition. Paul's letters often do. James, although it begins as a letter, continues as a homily based on scriptural references and the teachings of Jesus, employing the diatribe style. Shaped in letter format in its opening and focusing on practical religion, it is somewhat in the tradition of Old Testament wisdom literature. First John does not read like a letter at all but is probably best seen as a theological treatise or a doctrinal homily rather than a letter, although it was sent to a "general" audience and is usually termed an epistle.

19. H. E. Dana, *Jewish Christianity: An Expository Survey of Acts I to XII, James, I and II Peter, Jude and Hebrews* (New Orleans: Bible Institute Memorial, 1937), 201.

20. See Richards, *Paul and First-Century Letter Writing*, 19–31.

21. Richards, *Paul and First-Century Letter Writing*, 36–44.

22. Murphy-O'Connor, *Paul the Letter-Writer,* 16–19; Richards, *Paul and First-Century Letter Writing,* 33–36.

23 Richards, *Paul and First-Century Letter Writing,* 32–33.

24. Murphy-O'Connor, *Paul the Letter-Writer,* 20–24, reviews carefully both 1 Corinthians and considerable commentary on said letter to try to discern what contributions Sosthenes indeed made to the letter. He suggests that the more theologically involved passages, such as 1:18–31 and 2:6–16, may possibly represent Sosthenes' presumably exegetical and philosophical bent, whereas Paul insisted on pragmatic counsel. How the involvement of Sosthenes and his concerns for Corinthian customs might have affected some of the more controversial sections of 1 Corinthians (e.g., the role of women) is unrecoverable.

25. Richards, *Paul and First-Century Letter Writing,* 92.

26. Richards, *Paul and First-Century Letter Writing,* 92.

27. Murphy-O'Connor, *Paul the Letter-Writer,* 8–16, 34–35; Richards, *Paul and First-Century Letter Writing,* 59–93.

28. Murphy-O'Connor, *Paul the Letter-Writer,* 110–13; Brown, *Introduction to the New Testament,* 419; Richards, *Paul and First-Century Letter Writing,* 171–75.

29. For instance, the subscription to 1 Thessalonians reads: "The first epistle unto the Thessalonians was written from Athens." First Thessalonians 3:1–6, taken together with Acts 18:1–5, make it clear that Paul wrote the letter from Corinth, after he had left Athens and when Timothy had come to Corinth with news about the Church in Thessalonica (see Anderson, *Understanding Paul,* 72).

30. Murphy-O'Connor, *Paul the Letter-Writer,* 112–13, and Richards, *Paul and First-Century Letter Writing,* 174–75, differ in their assessments of 2 Corinthians—Murphy-O'Connor seeing 2 Corinthians 1–9 and 10–13 as two different letters (and all of 2 Corinthians 9 as the postscript of the first letter), whereas Richards sees 10–13 as an after-the-fact postscript or addition to the original letter.

31. Sperry, *Paul's Life and Letters,* 102, 104–5, notes, "A careful reading of [2 Thessalonians 2:2] . . . gives the impression that some person might have forged a letter purporting to come from Paul, which gave faulty information to the Thessalonians and caused them to be shaken in mind and considerably troubled. . . . These reports from Macedonia together with accounts of continued persecution, convinced the great missionary that he ought to write the Thessalonian Saints another letter. . . . In this one and some others he writes a greeting toward the end in his own distinctive handwriting, to give a warm personal touch and also to prevent forgery."

32. Richards, *Paul and First-Century Letter Writing,* 169.

33. Richards, *Paul and First-Century Letter Writing,* 202.

34. Murphy-O'Connor, *Paul the Letter-Writer,* 45–55; Brown, *Introduction to the New Testament,* 413–15.

35. Murphy-O'Connor, *Paul the Letter-Writer,* 45–53; Richards, *Paul and First-Century Letter Writing,* 128–29.

36. Murphy-O'Connor, *Paul the Letter-Writer,* 55–59; Richards, *Paul and First-Century Letter Writing,* 129–30.

37. Murphy-O'Connor, *Paul the Letter-Writer,* 60–61.

38. See Brown, *Introduction to the New Testament*, 416n16.

39. Sanders, *Paul*, 22.

40. The classical point of discussion begins with Aristotle, *Ars rhetorica*, 1.3 (§1358b) and includes Quintillian, *Institutio oratorio*, 3.4.12–15. See Brown, *Introduction to the New Testament*, 411–12, for a brief review and this particular application to Paul's letters, as well as the more detailed discussion of Murphy-O'Connor, *Paul the Letter-Writer*, 65–95.

41. Brown, *Introduction to the New Testament*, 412.

42. Murphy-O'Connor, *Paul the Letter-Writer*, 98–110; Brown, *Introduction to the New Testament*, 418–19.

13

SCRIBES AND ANCIENT LETTERS: IMPLICATIONS FOR THE PAULINE EPISTLES

Lincoln H. Blumell

I Tertius, who wrote this epistle, salute you in the Lord.
—Romans 16:22

Of the twenty-seven books that make up the New Testament, thirteen directly bear the name of the Apostle Paul.[1] While Paul is the sender of these letters, and by implication the author, upon close examination it appears that Paul did not actually write some of these epistles. This is not a matter of pseudonymity, where someone else composed certain epistles and fraudulently passed them off as the Apostle's, and does not necessarily imply that it is inappropriate to call Paul the "author" of the thirteen epistles bearing his name. Rather, it has to do with issues directly related to their original writing and composition. With some of Paul's epistles, we can be certain that he did not actually sit down with a *calamus* (reed pen) and *charta* (parchment sheets) or papyrus and write them out. This can be established fairly easily from the reference, cited above, to Romans 16:22. At the end of this letter,

---

Lincoln H. Blumell is a PhD student at the Centre for the Study of Religion at the University of Toronto.

we are informed that it was Tertius, not Paul, who actually wrote the main body of the letter, even though Paul claims at the beginning of the letter that he is the one sending it (see Romans 1:1–7). This suggests that Paul used a scribe, either lay or professional, to pen this letter.[2]

This insight has potentially far-reaching consequences for the way we ought to understand the processes that went into the writing of Romans and likely Paul's other letters. There are a number of possible scenarios for how Paul could have employed scribes given what we know about scribes and how they functioned in letter-writing capacities in antiquity. For example, Paul could have verbally dictated certain letters to a scribe, by either spelling out exactly what he wanted in a given letter or by merely providing the scribe with a general outline to follow. Or he could have provided the scribe with a written rough draft that was to be subsequently polished into a final draft to be sent.

The fact that Paul employed scribes is significant because it could help to resolve some of the tension that currently exists in contemporary scholarship over the "genuine" and "pseudonymous" Pauline epistles. For some time, scholars have been divided over the status of certain of Paul's letters, namely Ephesians, Colossians, 2 Thessalonians, and the Pastorals (1 and 2 Timothy and Titus), with the consensus being that these are not genuinely Pauline. The greater part of scholarship holds that these six letters were likely written sometime after Paul's death by a group of Paul's followers who presumed to write in his name. This assessment is based on a number of factors, such as the letters' distinctive vocabulary and literary style when compared with the seven "genuine" Pauline epistles (Romans, 1 and 2 Corinthians, Galatians, Philippians, 1 Thessalonians, and Philemon). Nevertheless, if scribes were used extensively in the original writing process of Paul's letters—a fact that many still fail to fully acknowledge—then such differences among the Pauline letters do not necessarily imply that they were not authored by Paul. In most cases, an individual scribe could imprint a distinct literary style on any document he or she wrote, which would greatly affect its form, vocabulary, and perhaps even content.

SCRIBES AND LETTER WRITING

Before the age of movable type, printing presses, photocopiers, and word processors, all documents were written by hand. In the

Greco-Roman world, the class of people who were largely responsible for writing and preserving documents were most commonly referred to as "scribes."[3] While their various tasks might often have been menial and tedious, especially if they were merely recopying decrees or tax receipts, their role was vital. They were largely responsible for producing and reproducing much of the written material that existed in ancient society. Scribes were used to copy and recopy certain texts, both literary and bureaucratic, to document registries or transactions, and to do a host of other literary activities, including recording speeches, taking dictation, and making notes. In most cases, the qualifications for a scribe were not extremely rigorous, as a basic education afforded the essential skills of the trade—aural comprehension, reading, and writing.[4]

In antiquity, scribes were an integral component of society and were employed by people from all social strata, from the emperor and wealthy aristocrat right down to the plebeian. Because even in the most ideal circumstances the literacy rate was not more than 10–15 percent of the population (including women and slaves), scribes were used extensively by the lower classes who could not write or read.[5] People would go to the local *agora* (marketplace) and hire a scribe to write such things as a business transaction, a will, a letter, or just about any other personal document they required.[6] Even those in the highest positions of government—an emperor, a senator, or a consul—employed the services of scribes in order to adequately deal with matters of business.[7] It is reported that Julius Caesar frequently employed scribes in his administration because it gave him the ability to "multitask" and deal with the all-pressing business required of him: "We are told that he used to write or read and dictate or listen simultaneously, and to dictate to his secretaries [scribes] four letters at once on his important affairs—or, if otherwise unoccupied, seven letters at once."[8] Despite the hyperbole, it is clear that Caesar regularly, and perhaps somewhat proficiently, employed scribes in the letter-writing process.

Aside from both the government and the illiterate segments of society, who were largely compelled out of necessity to employ scribes, rich aristocrats commonly used them. However, in their case it was not always out of necessity but rather out of simple luxury and convenience because they had the means to do so.[9] Cicero, one of the most

accomplished and prolific writers of ancient Rome, details how he frequently used scribes when making notes, both composing and copying
literature, or when he was too busy to write or was simply too lazy and
not in the mood to pick up the pen.[10] With respect to the employment
of scribes for the specific purpose of letter writing, Cicero is extremely
illuminating, because many of his letters survive and because he periodically informs the addressee of a given letter that a scribe was
employed to write it:[11] "I don't think you ever before read a letter of
mine which I had not written myself"; "The bare fact that my letter is
by the hand of [an amanuensis (scribe)] will show you how busy I am";
"This letter is dictated as I sit in my carriage on my road to the camp."[12]

For letter writing, a scribe could be used in a variety of ways, but
three appear most prominent from the source material: recorder, editor,
or substitute author.[13] At the most basic level, a scribe could simply serve
as a kind of recorder. Either the author would provide the scribe with a
written draft of a letter that was to be recopied in a neat hand or would
dictate the letter verbally to the scribe. In the latter case, the scribe
would be equivalent to a stenographer and would simply write out verbatim the *ipsissima verba* (very words themselves) of the speaker. This
might sometimes mean that the speaker would have to slow down his or
her speech in order for the scribe to accurately follow. Cicero once
reported that when he was writing a letter to his friend Varro, he had
to slow down his speech to the point of dictating "syllable by syllable"
because he was employing an inexperienced scribe to write the letter.[14]
While this slow dictation might ensure that everything in the letter was
written exactly as the author intended, it also was very tedious and
sometimes caused the speaker to lose his train of thought or grow
excessively weary.[15]

However, evidence does exist that some scribes, those who were
very skilled in their trade, could write at the normal speed of speech,
vive voce, through the use of a kind of shorthand. Tachygraphy, shorthand
where symbols were used in place of words, dates from the first century
BC, and by the first century AD it seems to have been more widespread
in society.[16] Nevertheless, it was still quite rare, and scribes possessing
the ability to write shorthand, whether Latin or Greek, were few.

While the skill allowed one to record at the normal speed of speech, it too had its drawbacks as it did not allow the author, speaking orally, enough time to adequately ponder over what he had said.[17] In the cases where a scribe had recorded a dictated letter in shorthand, it would then be the scribe's responsibility to convert the shorthand rough draft into a final polished version that was devoid of symbols and employed normal spelling. Following the conversion, the scribe would present this draft to the author, who would then look it over to make sure that it accurately represented what he had said, or at least thought he said, when he originally dictated the letter. Depending on its length, it might take more than a day to complete the conversion and present it back to the author.

Another role a scribe could play in the writing of a letter was that of editor. However, depending on the skill of the scribe and the relationship between the author and scribe, the editorial responsibilities invested in the scribe might vary substantially. In the writing of the final draft, some scribes were permitted to make only minor changes to the author's rough draft, whether it was a written rough draft presented to the scribe or whether it had been a dictated rough draft from the author.[18] On the other hand, some scribes were given slightly more power over the final draft of a letter, being permitted to tinker with its vocabulary, style, and form. Cicero repeatedly praises his trusted assistant and scribe Tiro because of his ability as a proficient editor—not only did he correct Cicero's mistakes in the final drafts he furnished, but he also provided him with many editorial improvements.[19] Thus, Cicero was delighted when he once found in a letter from Tiro that he had incorrectly used an adverb, because he could now boast that he was correcting his corrector.[20]

The last way in which a scribe could function in the letter-writing process was in the role of substitute author. Here the scribe was given considerable, and in a few rare cases total, control over the final draft of the letter. While the author would inform the scribe of the occasion or purpose of the letter and might possibly give him a general outline to follow, the actual writing of the letter was done by the scribe, and consequently the vocabulary, style, form, and even certain parts of the letter's content would have been solely the scribe's. Yet for all intents and purposes, the letter was still considered to be authentically the sender's, as he was always expected to read over the final draft and ensure that it accurately conveyed what he intended.[21]

With certain types of letters—namely, business or official correspondence—it would have been common for scribes to exercise considerable control over their composition, given that they had a set form, vocabulary, and style. In these cases, the author might do no more than merely inform the scribe of the general purpose of the letter and leave everything else up to the scribe. This kind of procedure is illustrated in Cicero's letter to his brother Quintus, who was on his first Roman government appointment. Here Cicero reveals how Quintus had employed his trusted scribe Statius to check over his outgoing letters: "Statius has told me that they [letters] used to be brought to you [Quintus] already drafted, and that he would read them and inform you if they were inequitable, but that before he joined you letters were dispatched indiscriminately. And so, he said, there are collections of selected letters and these are adversely criticized."[22] Cicero reveals that Quintus had invested various scribes with total power over the composition of certain letters and that before Statius had come along, likely in the role of chief scribe to check for errors or inconsistencies, no one had apparently done this.[23]

In two rare examples from Cicero, we have him giving a scribe complete control over every aspect of the letter, not just its form or style but even its content. In 58 BC, when Cicero was banished from Rome, he wrote to his close friend and confidant Atticus and asked him to compose and send letters in his name to anyone he thought necessary so that he would not be forgotten during his banishment.[24] Ten years later, Cicero repeated the request and asked Atticus to write more letters: "I am so fearfully upset both in mind and body that I have not been able to write many letters; I have only answered those who have written to me. I should like you to write in my name to Basilus and to anyone else you like, even to Servilius, and say whatever you think fit."[25] What makes these examples so noteworthy, and in fact unusual, is that Cicero gives Atticus no guidelines whatsoever for the letters, nor does he intend to look them over before they are sent. It is usual, even when scribes were given considerable or almost total control over the production of a letter, for scribes to be informed of the purpose or occasion of the letter and to have the final draft checked over and approved by the sender. While these last two examples from Cicero are exceptional, they do highlight the potential control that a scribe, or someone acting in the capacity of a scribe, could be given over the production of a letter in another's name.

Before moving on to the scribes in Paul's letters, one other important issue deserves brief treatment. How do we know when a scribe has been employed to write a letter? In certain of Cicero's letters, he directly informs the addressee that he was using a scribe because he was either busy, sick, traveling, or simply not in the mood to pick up the pen and write.[26] In some cases, scribes themselves would directly inform the addressee(s), as is the case with Tertius and Romans, that they were the ones actually writing the letter. This could be done in one of two ways. Periodically scribes would insert a set phrase at the end of a letter or business document to indicate that they had written the document on behalf of an illiterate person.[27] The other way scribes could make their presence known was through scribal remarks within the body of the text. For example, Cicero informs his friend Atticus that if Cicero's scribe Alexis wished to send Atticus greetings, then he really should put them in a letter of his own, instead of continually putting them in Cicero's letters to Atticus.[28]

Another way to determine the presence of a scribe in a letter is a change in handwriting. If the body of the letter was written in one hand and the signature of the author or either the conclusion or the postscript in another hand, then it can be safely assumed that a scribe was employed to write the main body of the text. It was common in letters written by scribes to have the sender sign the letter at the end and even add a few closing remarks or a postscript in his own hand.[29] There are a number of letters preserved in the Greek papyri from Egypt where this is the very case; the main body of the text is written in one hand and the signature at the end is written in a very different one.[30] Likewise, there are also examples of letters preserved among the Greek papyri where multiple letters exist from a single sender but are all written in a different hand, establishing the use of a scribe.[31] However, there is a significant problem with this approach. With most texts from antiquity, we do not possess the autograph editions but only much later copies of the originals, making handwriting analysis impossible. This is certainly the case with all the texts of the New Testament. While Paul's letters were written in the mid-first century, we do not possess any of the auto-graph copies, and the earliest surviving collection we have is the Chester Beatty Papyrus (P^{46}) that dates to about AD 200, which includes at best copies of copies of copies.[32]

Though all of the evidence surveyed in this section has been drawn from the Greco-Roman world, it should not be supposed therefore that Jews living in Judea employed markedly different writing habits or did not use scribes. There is considerable evidence that Jews had been employing scribes in letter-writing processes for some time.

The prophet Jeremiah on multiple occasions employed a scribe by the name of Baruch to compose various letters and oracles as he dic-tated them to him (see Jeremiah 36:4, 32; 45:1). Closer to the time of the New Testament, there is direct evidence in Judea for the employ-ment of scribes in letter writing. The Bar-Kokhba letters that date to the early second century AD, discovered in the famous "Cave of Letters" along the Nahal Hever west of the Dead Sea in the early 1960s, establish this. Of the fifteen surviving letters sent by Bar-Kokhba, no two contain the same handwriting, establishing the use of a scribe, and some even mention the name of the scribe who wrote the letter on Bar-Kokhba's behalf.[33] Consequently, it is likely that Jews living in Judea in the first and subsequent centuries AD employed scribes when writing letters, or perhaps other documents, and like their Greek or Roman counterparts were probably able to go to the local village market and hire out a scribe to do so.[34]

SCRIBAL EVIDENCES IN PAUL'S LETTERS

Though Paul never directly informs his addressees that he was employing a scribe for the writing of any of his letters, six of the thir-teen letters bearing his name clearly indicate that a scribe was used to write a considerable part of the letter. As mentioned earlier, Romans 16:22 demonstrates that a scribe actually wrote that epistle: "I Tertius, who wrote this epistle, salute you in the Lord."[35] Rather surprisingly, it is the scribe, and not Paul, who informs the Romans that he is the one who actually wrote the main body of the letter.[36] What this strongly suggests is that Tertius was a close associate of Paul's, since a hired scribe, one who was simply procured for the sole purpose of penning the letter, would have scarcely taken such liberties. This may also suggest, given the close relationship between Paul and Tertius, that Tertius was not a professional scribe.[37] In all likelihood, given what we generally know about early Christian scribes, Tertius was not a professional but rather a Christian who had the necessary literary skills—he was well educated and could write.[38]

Unfortunately, we are not able to determine precisely in what specific capacity Tertius functioned in writing Romans, whether he merely acted as a recorder or played a more significant role in the composition of the epistle. If he only served as a recorder, then it is very doubtful that he recorded Romans *viva voce,* as Paul dictated it or gave it in a liturgical setting. To do so would have required the expertise of a highly skilled professional scribe, one who was well trained in tachygraphy, and the literary sophistication of Romans strongly suggests against it originally being given as an extemporaneous dictation. Given that Tertius could exercise authority in Romans to introduce himself and greet the Romans, it is likely that he probably had a more significant role in the letter than merely a recorder and was almost certainly invested with some editorial responsibilities.

In none of Paul's other letters do any of his scribes intervene and directly identify themselves. Nevertheless, there is still clear evidence that scribes wrote considerable portions of other letters. In the letter to the Galatians, it is clear that Paul had a scribe write the body of the text while he wrote with his own hand only the last few verses. This can be shown from Galatians 6:11, "See what large letters I make when I am writing in my own hand!" (New Revised Standard Version, hereafter cited as NRSV).[39] This refers to the fact that Paul has now picked up the pen to write the last few verses of the letter. Paul is explaining to the Galatians why a shift in handwriting has occurred, from smaller letters, written by a scribe, to larger letters, written by himself. The Galatian recipients would have noticed the change in handwriting, and Paul here is simply informing them why the change has occurred.

Not much, if anything, can be said concretely about the scribe employed to write the body of the letter to the Galatians. He does not identify himself, nor can it be determined in what capacity he functioned, whether as recorder or editor. However, a possible clue for Paul's employment of a scribe in this epistle might be found in Galatians 4:15. Here Paul seems to imply that he had some sort of eye problem that was bothering him when he visited the Galatians and may still have been troubling him when he wrote his letter to them, preventing him from writing himself. In a similar case, Cicero specifically reports in one of his letters that he was forced to dictate it to a scribe because his eyes were inflamed and he was unable to write.[40] If this is the case, this may also make further sense of Paul's remark that he wrote excessively "large letters."[41]

In four more of Paul's letters, he betrays the definite use of a scribe. At the very end of 1 Corinthians, Paul adds a postscript to the letter and tells the Corinthians that he is now writing in his own hand, clearly indicating the employment of a scribe for the main body of the letter: "I, Paul, write this greeting with my own hand. Let anyone be accursed who has no love for the Lord. Our Lord, come! The grace of the Lord Jesus be with you. My love be with all of you in Christ Jesus" (NRSV, 1 Corinthians 16:21–24).

In verse 21, Paul makes it clear that he is now writing for himself, and the ensuing three verses work well as a postscript since the letter effectively ends in verse 20. In the postscript Paul signs the letter, signifying approval of its content and adding a few last words of exhortation. While it is virtually impossible to determine the exact role of the scribe in 1 Corinthians, it may be possible, given that 1 Corinthians was joint-authored by a certain Sosthenes, that Sosthenes was the one who actually wrote the body of the letter from 1 Corinthians 1:1 to 16:20.

In the letters to the Colossians and to Philemon, it is clear that Paul had employed a scribe to write the body of both epistles. In the very last verse of Colossians, Paul writes with his own hand in order to greet and admonish the Colossian Saints: "I, Paul, write this greeting with my own hand. Remember my chains. Grace be with you" (NRSV, Colossians 4:18). Likewise, in verse 19 of the letter to Philemon, Paul picks up the pen and adds the concluding remarks:

I, Paul, am writing this with my own hand: I will repay it. I
say nothing about your owing me even your own self.

Yes, brother, let me have this benefit from you in the Lord!
Refresh my heart in Christ.

Confident of your obedience, I am writing to you, knowing that you will do even more than I say.

One thing more—prepare a guest room for me, for I am
hoping through your prayers to be restored to you.

Epaphras, my fellow prisoner in Christ Jesus, sends greetings to you,

and so do Mark, Aristarchus, Demas, and Luke, my fellow
workers.

The grace of the Lord Jesus Christ be with your spirit.
(NRSV, Philemon 1:19)

An important similarity exists at this point between Colossians and
Philemon; in both references, Paul makes it clear that he is sending the
letter from prison. This might explain why Paul was employing a
scribe—environmental factors necessitated it.

One other explicit reference exists within Paul's letters that estab-
lishes the use of a scribe; however, this is not as straightforward as the
previous references, as it contains certain difficulties. At the conclusion
of 2 Thessalonians, Paul writes: "I, Paul, write this greeting with my
own hand. This is the mark in every letter of mine; it is the way I write.
The grace of our Lord Jesus Christ be with all of you" (NRSV,
2 Thessalonians 3:17–18).

In verse 17, Paul characteristically points out that he is the one actually writing the postscript, but then he follows up by somewhat enig-
matically reporting that "this is the mark in every letter of mine; it is
the way I write." This last statement is to be understood in light of the
forged letters that were circulating, presumably in Paul's name, that he
warns the Thessalonians about earlier in the letter (2:2). But even in
this context, it is still somewhat unclear exactly what Paul is saying. If
Paul intended it to mean that he always added an explicit autographed
postscript with a subscription to his letters in order to show their
genuine authenticity, then what about the six letters that lack such an

explicit postscript with a subscription? Likewise, if he is simply telling the Thessalonians that all letters written specifically to them contain an explicit postscript, then why does 1 Thessalonians not contain one? Possibly the best way to understand this remark is that Paul may have always written the concluding remarks of each letter with his own hand, but he did not always explicitly point this out.[42] That is, he did not always leave his subscription, or signature, at the end of a letter or directly inform his addressee(s) that he was now picking up the pen to write either the conclusion or postscript. Surely the change in hand-writing in the autograph version would signal to the recipient(s) that Paul was now writing, especially if they were aware of standard episto-lary conventions.[43] If this interpretation of 2 Thessalonians 3:17 is correct, then Paul may well have employed a scribe for all of his letters.

IMPLICATIONS FOR THE PAULINE EPISTLES

While Paul's use of scribes for the composition of various epistles provides an important insight into the ways some or even all of his letters were written, it is more than a point of mere historical interest. As mentioned at the start of this paper, Paul's use of scribes has the potential to resolve much of the tension that exists in contemporary scholarship over the debate surrounding the "genuine" and "pseudony-mous" Pauline epistles. For quite a while it has been argued in certain quarters of scholarship that some of Paul's letters were not actually writ-ten by him but rather by later Christians writing in his name.[44] Central to the argument that certain of Paul's are actually pseudonymous is the claim that these letters are stylistically different and tend to employ a different vocabulary than the seven undisputed letters bearing Paul's name.

On stylistic grounds, the argument most often marshaled against their authenticity has to do with their unique sentence structure. In these letters, sentences tend to be very long, complicated, and are marked with a lot of hypotaxis (the frequent use of subordinate clauses), whereas in the "genuine" letters the sentences tend to be quite short and are very concise and succinct. For example, the letter to the Colossians and the letter to the Ephesians are both marked with a num-ber of long, complicated, hypotactic sentences. The first sentence in the letter to the Colossians, after the introductory formula, covers five verses (see Colossians 1:3–8) and is made up of eighty-three Greek words.[45] In the epistle to the Ephesians, which contains about one hundred sentences in total, nine contain more than fifty words.[46] When these statistics are compared with those of the undisputed letters, a stark difference emerges. In the first four chapters of the epistle to the Romans, roughly commensurate in length to the epistle to the Ephesians, there are 481 sentences and only three longer than fifty words, and in the first four chapters of 1 Corinthians there are 621 sentences and only one longer than fifty words.[47]

The other kind of argument typically marshaled to support the claim that some of Paul's letters are pseudonymous has to do with the allegedly different diction they employ when compared with the "genuine" letters.[48] It is commonly advocated that the use of unusual vocabulary in these letters can demonstrate that Paul did not actually write them because he does not employ such vocabulary in his undisputed letters. In the Pastorals, where some 848 words are employed (excluding proper names), 306 of these words are not found in the remainder of Paul's letters, including 2 Thessalonians, Colossians, and Ephesians, and 175 words do not appear anywhere else in the New Testament.[49] Likewise, it is often pointed out that the epistle to the Ephesians contains an extremely high number of unique words, 116 to be exact, that cannot be found in any other of Paul's undisputed letters.[50]

While such statistical studies are interesting in that they do highlight literary trends and differences among the various Pauline letters, much of the force of such arguments is completely blunted when one recognizes and acknowledges that Paul employed scribes frequently in his letter writing. Rather than assigning pseudonymity to certain letters, it becomes much more likely that the hand of an individual scribe is at play and ultimately responsible for the various literary differences. As this chapter has demonstrated, depending on how a scribe was used in the letter-writing process, he could have greatly affected the consequent style and vocabulary used in the final draft of a letter. Therefore, scholarly attempts to distinguish between "genuine" and "pseudonymous" Pauline letters based on criteria of vocabulary, style, or other statistical data might prove very little about the actual authenticity of certain letters except the kind of Greek preferred by Paul's different scribes. Likewise, the presence of scribes in Paul's letters should also prevent us from reading too much into every linguistic variation in Paul, making it out to be some nuanced theological difference.

CONCLUSION

In six of the thirteen epistles bearing Paul's name, there is explicit evidence that he employed the hand of a scribe to write the main body of the epistle: Romans, 1 Corinthians, Galatians, Colossians, Philemon, and 2 Thessalonians. It is also quite possible, given the evidence in 2 Thessalonians, that Paul employed scribes in the other letters bearing his name and that in these letters he left only an "unsigned postscript."[51] But to undertake an analysis of the possible scribal influences in these other letters where there is not explicit evidence for the use of scribes would unduly extend the scope of this chapter well beyond its present objectives and confines. The primary purpose of this analysis has only been to demonstrate that Paul did in fact use scribes and that their employment could have had a significant impact on the final form of certain epistles affecting their consequent vocabulary, style, and perhaps even content.

In light of how Cicero and others in antiquity employed scribes for the specific purpose of letter writing, a variety of possible scenarios exist for the ways in which Paul could have used his scribes. On one extreme, Paul could have dictated his letters to his scribes very meticulously, making sure that the *ipsissima verba* he spoke were written down carefully. On the other extreme, he could have given his scribes either a written or verbal outline of the main points he wished to express and expected them to flesh it out into the final form of the letter. Assuming that Paul's scribes were close friends and associates, as was the case with Tertius, it might not seem unreasonable that they were given substantial control over the final draft of the letter. But regardless of the capacity in which Tertius or any other of Paul's scribes functioned, Paul was ultimately responsible for the letters written in his name. He checked over the final draft, as can be seen from the presence of either his subscription or postscript at the end of each letter, and made sure that they accurately conveyed what he intended. Therefore, despite Paul's rather extensive use of scribes, for all intents and purposes the letters bearing his name should be regarded as authentic Pauline letters.

NOTES

1. Romans, 1 and 2 Corinthians, Galatians, Ephesians, Philippians, Colossians, 1 and 2 Thessalonians, 1 and 2 Timothy, Titus, and Philemon. In the opening verse of each of these epistles, Paul is referred to as the sender. As for the Epistle to the Hebrews, strictly speaking, it is anonymous as no name, either that of the sender or the author, is given within the body of the work.

2. 1 Peter 5:12, like Romans 16:22, reveals that Peter used a scribe by the name of Silvanus to pen this letter. This is the only other instance besides Romans 16:22 in the New Testament where a scribe is specifically named as the writer of a letter.

3. While the Greek term *grammateus* is most often translated as "scribe," it can mean a number of different things, from a mere copyist of texts to a government official (see Acts 19:35). Latin is more technical with its vocabulary and employs three different words for "scribe," *scriba* (public or official secretary), *librarius* (a private secretary, also *amanuensis*), and *notarius* (a shorthand writer). No specific distinctions will be drawn in this paper between the different Latin terms for "scribe," because all refer to some literary aspect.

4. Plutarch, *Crassus*, 2.6; unless otherwise indicated, all quotations from ancient authors are from the English translation in the Loeb Classical Library. Raffaela Cribiore gives an excellent assessment of the objectives of an ancient education. She specifically states that she is principally interested in investigating the acquisition of writing by beginners and not scribes (Raffaela Cribiore, *Writing, Teachers, and Students in Graeco-Roman Egypt* [Atlanta: Scholars Press, 1996], 28). Nevertheless, this work is still very helpful for the kind of literary skills a scribe would naturally acquire through formal education (see also Kim Haines-Eitzen, *Guardians of Letters: Literacy, Power, and the Transmitters of Early Christian Literature* [Oxford: Oxford University Press, 2000], 53–75). P.Oxy. 724 (AD 155) shows how in some situations someone might take on an apprenticeship as a scribe to improve his or her literary abilities. For papyrological publications, I have followed the standard abbreviations given in J. F. Oates and others, *Checklist of Editions of Greek Papyri and Ostraca*, 2d ed., BASP Supplements, 1 (Missoula, MT: Scholars Press, 1978), and updated editions online at http://scriptorium.lib.duke.edu/papyrus/texts/clist.html.

5. William V. Harris, *Ancient Literacy* (Cambridge, MA: Harvard University Press, 1989). Harris has combined literary, inscriptional, and papyrological evidence from the ancient world with modern anthropological and sociological studies to demonstrate that the necessary preconditions for mass literacy were not present in ancient society, even in the most ideal circumstances in classical Athens. For literacy rates among Jews, see Catherine Hezser, *Jewish Literacy in Roman Palestine* (Tübingen: J. C. B. Mohr [Paul Siebeck], 2001).

6. The evidence for scribes' servicing the illiterate segments of society in this way is most abundant in Egypt, where the papyrological record preserves numerous examples. These texts can be identified because they contain illiteracy formulae that specifically point out that they were written by a scribe for someone who was illiterate (e.g., P.Oxy. 264 [AD 54]).

7. Suetonius, *Vespasian*, 21; *Titus*, 6.

8. Pliny, *Natural History*, 7.91.

9. Roger Bagnall states, "One might almost say that there was a direct correlation between the social standing that guaranteed literacy and the means to avoid writing. But this should not be taken to mean that men of this standing did not do a fair amount of writing all the same" (*Reading Papyri, Writing Ancient History* [London: Routledge, 1995], 25).

10. Cicero, *Letters to Atticus*, 2.23, 5.12, 7.13a, 8.13, 8.15, 12.32.1, 13.32; *Letters to His Friends*, 11.32.2; *Letters to His Brother Quintus*, 2.2, 2.16, 3.3.

11. The following three references to Cicero are taken from Jerome Murphy-O'Connor, *Paul the Letter-Writer: His World, His Options, His Skills* (Collegeville, MN: Liturgical Press, 1995), 6.

12. Cicero, *Letters to Atticus*, 2.23; 4.16.1; 5.17.1.

13. I have adapted and slightly modified the various scribal capacities in the letter-writing process from E. Randolph Richards, *The Secretary in the Letters of Paul*, Wissenschaftliche Untersuchungen zum Neuen Testament, 2. Reihe, vol. 42 (Tübingen: J. C. B. Mohr [Paul Siebeck], 1991), 23–53.

14. Cicero, *Letters to Atticus*, 13.25.3. In this same passage, Cicero claims that his usual scribe, Tiro, "can follow whole sentences."

15. Quintillian, a professor of rhetoric in the late first century AD, sometimes complained that a slow scribe prevented him from attaining full concentration when dictating (*Institutio Oratia*, 10.3.20).

16. Richards, *The Secretary in the Letters of Paul*, 26–43; Murphy-O'Connor, *Paul the Letter-Writer*, 9–11. Some important ancient references to shorthand include Plutarch, *Cato Minor*, 23.3–5; *Caesar*, 7.4–5; Seneca, *Epistles*, 14.208.

17. Quintillian complains that a scribe who is able to write at the speed of speech can sometimes cause the speaker to move along too hastily without giving necessary forethought for what he was saying (*Institutio Oratia*, 10.3.19–20).

18. For a good example of a rough draft of an ancient letter, one that will have to be edited before it is sent, see P.Tebt. 13 (114 BC).

19. Cicero, *Letters to His Friends*, 16.4.3; 16.11.1.

20. Cicero, *Letters to His Friends*, 16.17.1. "But look you here, sir, you who love to be the 'rule' of *my* writings, where did you get such a solecism as '*faithfully* ministering to your health'?"

21. It needs to be emphasized that even when scribes were given much control over the writing of a given letter, it was not the scribe that was considered the real author but rather the sender named in the letter. This was because it was that person's responsibility to read over the final draft. If there were any errors or inaccuracies, the sender was to catch them in the final reading and make sure that

they were corrected because he bore ultimate responsibility for the letter's content.

22. Cicero, *Letters to His Brother Quintus*, 2.8.

23. Thus, one may rightly doubt whether certain routine correspondences from antiquity are in fact directly from the pen of the author.

24. Cicero, *Letters to Atticus*, 3.15.8: "If there is anyone to whom you think a letter ought to be sent in my name, please write one and see that it is sent."

25. Cicero, *Letters to Atticus*, 11.5.

26. Cicero, *Letters to His Friends*, 11.32.2; *Letters to Atticus*, 5.12, 7.13, 8.15, 12.32.1, 13.32; *Letters to His Brother Quintus*, 2.2.1, 2.16, 3.1.

27. P.Oxy. 264 (AD 54). This was done most often in legal documents or business transactions where it was necessary to specify that a scribe was employed. Although the illiteracy formulae hardly appear in private letters, there can be no doubt that scribes were sometimes used in the writing of these letters (see P. Lond. 948, 962, 968, 1122; P.Oxy. 3314). Herbert C. Youtie, "ΥΠΟΓΑΦΕΥΣ: The Social Impact of Illiteracy in Graeco-Roman Egypt," *Zeitschrift für Papyrologie und Epigraphik* 17 (1975): 209, points out that it was "common practice for professional scribes to remain anonymous."

28. Cicero, *Letters to Atticus*, 5.20.

29. Gordon J. Bahr, "The Subscriptions in the Pauline Letters," *Journal of Biblical Literature* 87 (1968): 27–41; Cicero, *Letters to His Friends*, 2.13.3, "The postscript in your own handwriting gave me a twinge of pain. What's this? 'Curio is now defending Caesar'"; *Letters to His Friends*, 8.1.1, where Cicero claims to have received a letter from Pompey where the postscript was in his own hand. P.Oxy. 3314 (fourth century AD) is a private letter written by a scribe but where the concluding remarks are in the hand of someone else, presumably the sender.

30. P.Rainer 215; P. Lond. 897 (AD 84); P. Lond. 1173 (AD 125); B.G.U. 37 (AD 50); S.B. 4639 (AD 209).

31. P. Lond. 948, 962, 968, 1122 are four letters written from a certain Heraclides to Hermonius during the mid-third century AD. Although they are all sent by Heraclides, each one is clearly written by a different hand. P. Amh. 131 and 132 are both letters from a certain Sarapion written during the reign of Hadrian at the beginning the second century AD. The first letter (131), to his wife, is written in a very nice hand, while the second letter (132), written to his son, is in a terrible hand. He likely had a scribe compose the letter to his wife and wrote the letter to his son by himself.

32. There are still other ways to detect the presence of a scribe within a letter, but these criteria are more difficult to gauge and yield less certain conclusions because they are often based on implicit indicators that cannot often yield very definite answers (see Richards, *The Secretary in the Letters of Paul*, 80–97).

33. Yigael Yadin, *Bar-Kokhba: The Rediscovery of the Legendary Hero of the Second Jewish Revolt Against Rome* (New York: Random House, 1971), 124–28. P.Yadin 50 (Aramaic), P.Yadin 54 (Aramaic), P.Yadin 63 (Aramaic), all mention the name of the scribe who wrote on behalf of Bar-Kokhba. Likewise, in other letters from the Nahal Hever area that also date to the early second century, the presence of scribes

can be detected since the writing style of the valediction or subscription at the end of a letter differs markedly from the body of the letter. In P. Yadin 52 (Greek), the valediction is written in a hand that is clearly different from the body of the letter.

34.   Martin Goodman, "Texts, Scribes and Power in Roman Judea," in *Literacy and Power in the Ancient World,* ed. Alan K. Bowman and Greg D. Woolf (Cambridge: Cambridge University Press, 1994), 102, states, "It was assumed in rabbinic texts that scribes (*soferim*) could be found in village markets with blank forms to record loans and sales."

35.   What Tertius exactly meant by the phrase "in the Lord" is somewhat unclear. Did he mean that he was writing as Paul's scribe? While "Lord" or "master" often refers to Christ in Paul's letter, here it seems to suggest Paul. Therefore the verse might best be rendered as "I, Tertius, who write the letter in the service of my master [Paul], greet you." On the other hand, "in the Lord" could mean he sends his greetings literally "in the Lord," which sounds more Pauline (see 1 Corinthians 1:31; 4:17; 7:22, 39; 9:1f; 11:11; 15:58; 16:19; 2 Corinthians 10:17; Ephesians 1:15; 2:21; 4:17; 5:8; 6:1, 10, 21; Phillippians 1:14; 2:19, 24, 29; 3:1; 4:1f, 4, 10; Colossians 3:18; 4:7, 17; 1 Thessalonians 1:1; 3:8; 5:12; 2 Thessalonians 3:4; Philemon 1:16, 20).

36.   It would appear that Tertius ends at 16:24 and that Paul likely wrote 16:25–27 with his own hand.

37.   By professional scribe, I mean one who was specifically trained in the vocation and was paid for his literary services.

38.   Bart D. Ehrman, *Misquoting Jesus: The Story Behind Who Changed the Bible and Why* (New York: HarperSanFrancisco, 2005), 71; Kim Haines-Eitzen, *Guardians of Letters,* 16. Richards, *The Secretary in the Letters of Paul,* 170–73, believes that Tertius could have been a professional scribe who was trained in tachygraphy and that he might have recorded Romans *viva voce.* However, he also notes, "The odds are against such a luxury [professional scribe] for the majority of Paul's letters" (195). In his more recent work, *Paul and First-Century Letter Writing: Secretaries, Composition, and Collection* (Downers Grove, IL: InterVarsity, 2004), 77, 92, Richards still maintains the possibility that Tertius was a professional scribe but also acknowledges that they were rare, expensive, and even criticizes those scholars who argue that certain of Paul's letters were written *viva voce* (30–31, 92). Beyond Tertius's mere literary skills, Paul's choice to employ him as scribe for this particular epistle may also have had something to do with Tertius's relationship to the Romans, especially since at the time of the composition of Romans Paul had not yet been to Rome.

39.   I have deliberately used the New Revised Standard Version rendering of Galatians 6:11 instead of the King James Version because it more accurately reflects the meaning of the Greek. The KJV reads, "Ye see how large a letter I have written unto you with mine own hand," completely missing the real sense of the verse.

40.   Cicero, *Letters to Atticus,* 8.13.1.

41.   Paul's reference to "large letters" might also refer to a sloppy, unprofessional hand.

42. Murphy-O'Connor, *Paul the Letter-Writer,* 112, believes that 1 Thessalonians 5:27–28 is an "unsigned" postscript.

43. Sometimes when a scribe was used for the composition of a letter, the sender would not sign his or her name at the end of a letter but only add a postscript or a few final words of exhortation. This is the case with P.NYU 25, a private Christian letter from the early fourth century, where the final farewell is written in the hand of the sender but unsigned. He writes in his own hand at the end of the letter, "Goodbye, I pray for you often."

44. Considerable ink has been spilt over the authorship of the disputed letters. For a concise and up-to-date analysis of the various arguments, see Bart D. Ehrman, *The New Testament: A Historical Introduction to the Early Christian Writings,* 3d ed. (Oxford: Oxford University Press, 2004), chapter 23, "In the Wake of the Apostle: The Deutro-Pauline and Pastoral Epistles," 372–94.

45. I have not included definite articles in this number. Including definite articles, this sentence would be 102 words long.

46. Ehrman, *The New Testament,* 383.

47. Ehrman, *The New Testament,* 383.

48. For a concise chart laying out the percentages of different vocabulary employed by the various Pauline epistles, see John W. Welch and John F. Hall, *Charting the New Testament* (Provo, UT: Foundation for Ancient Research and Mormon Studies, 2002), chart 11–9.

49. Norman Perrin, *The New Testament, an Introduction: Proclamation and Parenesis, Myth and History* (New York: Harcourt Brace Jovanovich, 1982), 264–65.

50. Ehrman, *The New Testament,* 383.

51. Murphy-O'Connor, *Paul the Letter-Writer,* 112.

14

PAUL'S USE OF
OLD TESTAMENT SCRIPTURE

Jared W. Ludlow

Throughout the New Testament, Jesus, Paul, and others often quoted from Old Testament scripture in their sermons and letters. In fact, quoting from and dialoging with scripture was a significant background source for the writing and compilation of the New Testament. The LDS Bible Dictionary, for example, lists some 342 instances of quotations from the Old Testament found in the New Testament.[1] The most oft-quoted Old Testament books in the New Testament were Deuteronomy (35 instances), Psalms (95), and Isaiah (75).[2] Some instances of quoting existing scriptures were to reinterpret their meaning in a new higher-law setting. One of the most recognizable examples of this technique is from the Sermon on the Mount, when Jesus repeatedly stated: "Ye have heard that it was said by them of old time, . . . [quotation of scripture or tradition], but I say unto you, . . . [reinterpretation or giving the higher law]" (for example, see Matthew 5:21–22, 27–28, 33–34, 38–39, 43–44). In other cases as in Paul's writings, earlier scripture was allegorized to give it an entirely new

---

Jared W. Ludlow is an associate professor of ancient scripture at Brigham Young University.

meaning in a Christian context (see Galatians 4:22–31). Yet another use of quoted scripture was to demonstrate the fulfillment of earlier prophecy. The Apostle Matthew was particularly adept at this strategy in his efforts to convince his readers that their awaited Messiah had arrived (see Matthew 1:22–23; 2:17–18, 23; 27:9). What becomes clear from these varied techniques for using scripture is that the earlier Old Testament scriptures were an important resource from which to draw upon in the creation of what would become new or additional scripture, the New Testament. It also becomes evident that these scriptures were read, recited, and known well enough by the listeners and readers to use as support and authority for their teachings.

But what constituted scripture to the early Christians, and what authority did it hold? How and in what languages were these scriptures recorded and transmitted to the people? How widespread were literacy and education during the New Testament period? Were scriptures primarily read or recited orally? These are a few of the questions that will frame the discussion in this chapter. First, I will give an overview of how and in what languages Old Testament scriptures were transmitted to the early Christians. Then I will focus on Paul's use of the Old Testament among his New Testament writings. For Paul and other New Testament writers, the Old Testament was a prime source of material to draw from that gave authority to their teachings as they dialogued with fellow Jews and Christians about the gospel.

BACKGROUND

Ancient Hebrew was strongly influenced by early Canaanite and Phoenician languages. One of the most significant improvements that simplified these languages was the development of the alphabet. Rather than relying on hundreds or thousands of symbols and characters, as had been the case in ancient Babylon and Egypt, writing could be reduced to the use of a few dozen letters representing sounds. Because of this development, literacy expanded in the region, which naturally affected the formation, transmission, and reception of biblical traditions. Based on the more frequent references to reading and writing in both biblical and other written sources, we can conclude that literacy spread beyond a scribal and socioeconomic elite during the latter part of the first millennium BC.[3] However, some studies show that in the Greco-Roman period, only a small percentage of the population could read and write.[4]

The political history of the kingdom of Judah also affected its linguistic development. Starting with the Assyrians, but continuing with the Babylonians, Persians, Greeks, and Romans, the inhabitants of ancient Judah usually found themselves under the domination of outsiders. One result of this domination was the adoption of the occupiers' language. The Assyrian, Babylonian, and Persian dominions in the eighth–fourth centuries BC spread Aramaic throughout the region and had lasting effects in Judah as Aramaic became the common spoken language of the people (until Arabic replaced it with the rise of Islam in the seventh century AD). Portions of the Old Testament were written in Aramaic (parts of Ezra and Daniel), several Aramaic words show up in the New Testament (*Golgotha; Talitha cumi; Eloi, Eloi, lama sabachthani*), and many of the personal names in the New Testament use the Aramaic word for "son," *bar*, rather than the Hebrew *ben* (Barabbas, Bartholomew, Simon Bar-Jona).

When the Macedonians conquered Judah following Alexander's military exploits in the region, Greek became another dominant language, especially as an instrument of education. Along with the language came a flood of Greek thought and influence. This Greek influence is commonly called Hellenism (from *Hellas*, the Greek word for "Greece"). Although it predated Alexander, Hellenism increased in Judah following his conquest and was prevalent among Jews who lived outside of Judea in the eastern Mediterranean. In fact, Greek became so dominant among these diasporic Jews that a translation of the Hebrew Bible into Greek was required. The translation of the Septuagint (commonly abbreviated LXX) was thus accomplished, and it became the Bible of Hellenized Jewish communities and most early Christians. It included several books of original Greek composition and translations of Hebrew or Aramaic originals that were not found in the Hebrew Bible. These additional books are known today as the Apocrypha. Although they are not accepted as canonical by many modern Christians, they were probably considered authoritative by early Christians.[5]

When Rome took over the former Hellenistic empires, Latin, alongside Greek, came to be found in the eastern Roman Empire. However, Latin never had the same influence that Greek had over the Jews or earliest Christians. The Latin preserved in the New Testament primarily deals with administrative matters, such as coins, military offices, and the charge against Jesus written above His cross (see John 19:20; also written in Hebrew and Greek). It was not until a few centuries later, especially after Christianity became the religion of the Roman Empire, that Latin became dominant within the Christian Church in the West, and the Latin translation of the Bible (Vulgate) became the authoritative text for many Christians.

Today most individual members of the Church have their own copies of the scriptures. But how common was that at the time of the New Testament? Since printing had not been developed by this time, the only means of reproducing texts of scripture was through hand copying. Hand copying required significant resources of materials and labor; hence few individuals had personal copies of scriptural texts in their homes. Most early Christians *heard* the scriptures at public assemblies, particularly in the synagogue or earliest church houses.[6] In fact, most of the reading in the ancient world was done aloud, even individually, so it would have appeared strange to see someone looking at a text but not saying anything.[7]

Because of the lack of printing, it would have also been extremely rare to have extensive collections of all the scriptural texts available. Most of the earliest New Testament writings, for example, existed as copies of letters that had been sent by Apostles to be read in various congregations. The extent of a text's distribution would simply depend on whether a particular area found access to one of these texts and then copied it.[8] Copies of Old Testament texts were available, but again, congregations had to gather and copy these texts in order to make them available for public reading. We do find several references in the New Testament to Jewish sacred books described as "scriptures" or "holy scriptures," but no identification of these texts is given (see Matthew 22:29; John 5:39; Romans 1:2; 2 Timothy 3:15).

A primary use of the Old Testament texts by the earliest Christians was to highlight the fulfillment of the awaited Messiah's coming. According to one scholar, "they had learned from the Old Testament something of the ways of God in redeeming His people, and the promises bound up in the prophets concerning the Coming One who should deliver His people. In Jesus the first Christians had found the reality to which the Old Testament shadows led on. They found themselves living in the age of fulfilment, and looked back to the earlier centuries as those of promise."[9] In so doing, they saw continuity with the covenant people of this ancient record, yet since the Messiah had now arrived, they also saw the need for new scripture to clarify, amplify, and reinterpret.

By examining how Paul used the Old Testament in his teaching and writing, we can likewise see that he highlighted the fulfillment of Old Testament prophecies and expectations. But Paul's use of the Old Testament went beyond simply showing fulfillment; he selected phrases from many contexts to weave into his teachings and lend support to his ideas. Sometimes these quotations were woven seamlessly into the text so that only one very familiar with the Old Testament would have recognized the allusion. More often, however, Paul directly relied on the authority of a prophet, or simply "scripture" itself, by identifying the source of his quotation. Since Paul came from a strongly Jewish-educated background, his knowledge and use of the Old Testament were particularly extensive. One can identify Paul's use of the Old Testament in at least nine different categories: election, faith and works, ministry/Paul's defense, ethical teachings, separation from sin, resurrection, wisdom, collection for the poor, and the gift of tongues. By looking at his use of the Old Testament in these different categories, we can gain a clearer picture of the different purposes for which Paul quoted from the Old Testament.[10]

ELECTION

In many settings, Paul addressed the issue of God's election of a people through covenant. More specifically, he believed that the followers of Christ were now the elect people of God. Paul did not reject the Jews; in fact, he strongly wished for their acceptance of Jesus. But he nevertheless believed they must profess faith in Jesus in order to be among the elect. In order to show God's choice of the Christians as the elect people of God, Paul cited at least twenty-eight Old Testament passages, mostly within his letter to the Romans. The book of Romans was written as a letter of introduction to a congregation Paul was planning to meet for the first time. Unlike Paul's other epistles that addressed random issues, Romans is the closest thing to a summary of Paul's theology. Perhaps because of its context as a carefully crafted defense of his teachings, Paul relied heavily on the Old Testament to support his viewpoints.

As Paul began his debate about election in Romans 9, he used five pairs of scriptures—each pair, except one, from the same Old Testament book—to present his argument. The Old Testament passages were randomly "cut and pasted" from within these books rather than copied as sequential verses. Romans 9 became a mosaic of Old Testament thought that highlights figures and events of the Old Testament as examples and specifically mentions teachings by the prophets Moses, Hosea, and Isaiah. Most of these passages show that God would elect whom He chose, not always who might be perceived as the right choice. Although the firstborn was traditionally seen as the rightful heir, this pattern was frequently suspended in the Old Testament examples Paul cited. Becoming a child of promise or covenant was more important than being an heir after the flesh.

First, Paul gave the example of Abraham's two sons, Ishmael and Isaac, to show that even though Ishmael was chronologically the firstborn, the blessings went to Isaac because of a promise made to Sarah (see Romans 9:7, 9; Genesis 21:12; 18:14). This allegory was carried further in Galatians when Paul talked about these two sons being born of different mothers—Hagar, representing Mount Sinai and the law given there, and Sarah, the mother of us all, representing Jerusalem and freedom (see Galatians 4:27, 30; Isaiah 54:1; Genesis 21:10). In a similar manner, Rebecca was told that Jacob would be elected over his elder brother Esau (see Romans 9:12–13; Genesis 25:23; Malachi 1:2–3). Thus, God will choose whom He will choose (see Romans 9:15, 17; Exodus 33:19; 9:16). He will even call the Gentiles *His* people (see Romans 9:25–26; Hosea 2:23; 1:10). But He will save a remnant from among Israel that will be accepted with the elect if they have faith in Christ (see Romans 9:27, 29; Isaiah 10:22–23; 1:9).

FAITH AND WORKS

Another major issue that Paul addressed, and consequently used some twenty-three Old Testament excerpts to prove, was the question of salvation through faith in Christ or through the works of the law. This argument and the accompanying quotations are found in Romans and Galatians. Particularly in Galatians, Paul seems to be directing his use of the Old Testament towards the Judaizers, who believed that early Christians should still continue to practice the law of Moses, specifically circumcision. Paul tried to show that individuals such as Abraham received promises and blessings from covenants with God even before the law of Moses was given. Therefore, Christians could receive promises and blessings through faith in Christ and covenants with God without practicing the law of Moses. Abraham was the great exemplar of receiving promises and blessings to himself and his seed as a result of faith in God, not works of the law (see Galatians 3:6, 8; 16; Genesis 15:6; 12:3, 7; compare Romans 4:3, 9, 22; and Genesis 15:6 [three times]; also Romans 4:17–18; Genesis 17:5; 15:5). Paul also wrote about how those people who were of the works of the law were under the curse (see Galatians 3:10; Deuteronomy 27:26) and were only justified through faith (see Galatians 3:11–12; see also Romans 1:17; 10:5; Habakkuk 2:4; Leviticus 18:5). Paul next introduced an ironic argument that Christ became a "curse" in order to redeem from "the curse of the law" (see Galatians 3:13; Deuteronomy 21:23).

The argument about faith in Christ versus works of the law in Romans brings out a few additional points. First, the spirit of the law is more essential than the letter of the law. If one has the law, one must *faithfully* observe it; and although sin comes from knowledge of law, God's righteousness by faith on Christ will justify (see Romans 2:24; 3:4, 10–18; 7:7; Isaiah 52:5; Psalm 50:6; 13:1–3; Exodus 20:17). Paul also stated that God will credit righteousness without works (see Romans 4:7–8; Psalm 31:1–2). Paul, then, compared the works of law to a stumblingstone because the Jews did the works of the law rather than accept Christ (see Romans 9:33; 10:11; Isaiah 28:16 [two times]). Finally, he gave a small explanatory section wherein he quoted an Old Testament phrase then gave its meaning as it applied to Christ and the righteousness which came from faith (see Romans 10:6–8; Deuteronomy 9:4; 30:12–14).

MINISTRY/PAUL'S DEFENSE

Another area in which Paul applied Old Testament scripture was in defense of his preaching of the gospel of Christ and of his calling as an Apostle. Since Paul had not been among the original disciples during Jesus' mortal ministry, opponents questioned the source of his authority and particularly his use of the title "Apostle." Although Paul's ultimate argument for his authority derived from his experience with the resurrected Savior near Damascus, he also used the Old Testament to explain the need for sharing the gospel and specifically to clarify his role within that ministry. These passages, about twelve in total, deal with the ministry of the gospel to those who have not accepted it and are found in both letters to the Corinthians and in Romans. In many aspects, these passages can be related to other topics covered elsewhere in this chapter because they show how preaching the gospel will lead one to faith, election, and true wisdom.

In his first letter to the Corinthians, Paul stated that the Saints preach the gospel of Christ crucified, which is foolishness to the unbelievers but the power of God to those being saved. Thus, the wisdom of the world would be frustrated through their preaching (see 1 Corinthians 1:19; Isaiah 29:14). But though their word had great power, the teacher should not boast of himself (see 1 Corinthians 1:31; 2 Corinthians 10:17; Jeremiah 9:23 [two times]). Paul also used an Old Testament citation while stating that he did not receive temporal support from his preaching but sought only spiritual blessings (see 1 Corinthians 9:9; Deuteronomy 25:4).

In 2 Corinthians, Paul utilized a Psalm to present the motivation for preaching: having believed, they must now speak (see 2 Corinthians 4:13; Psalm 116:10). Also, as ministers of God, they preached that now was the time to accept the day of salvation (see 2 Corinthians 6:2; Isaiah 49:8). He closed his argument against those who believed he did not have the power of Christ by stating that two or three witnesses (visits or letters to Corinth) would prove his calling (see 2 Corinthians 13:1; Deuteronomy 19:15).

Within Romans, Paul addressed the tribulations that would come upon those within the ministry who believed in Christ, but he promised that eventually they would conquer all (see Romans 8:36; Psalm 44:22). He also discussed the necessity of preaching the gospel so that others could hear of Christ, accept Him, and be saved by their faith on Him (see Romans 10:15, 16, 18; Isaiah 52:7, 15; 53:1; Psalm 19:4).

ETHICAL TEACHINGS

Paul employed eight Old Testament citations dealing with various ethical teachings, mostly in a section on Christian ethics in Romans 12–14, perhaps to show that although the law of Moses was fulfilled through Christ, basic ethical rules or laws found in Old Testament scripture were still required. One rule he gave, within the context of a discussion on the validity of the law, was the need to love another as oneself and to please and edify others just as Christ sought to help others, not please oneself (see Galatians 5:14; Romans 13:9; 15:3; Leviticus 19:18 [two times]; Psalm 69:9). One prohibition Paul gave was against seeking revenge (see Romans 12:19; Deuteronomy 32:35). He stated that one should do good even to one's enemy (see Romans 12:20; Proverbs 25:21–22). He reiterated some of the Ten Commandments, such as no adultery, murder, stealing, bearing false witness, or coveting (see Romans 13:9; Exodus 20:13–15, 17). He also argued that one should not judge another, because in the end only God will judge (see Romans 14:11; Isaiah 49:18; 45:23).

SEPARATION FROM SIN

A fifth topic, where Paul used seven Old Testament verses to counsel his followers, was his exhortation to the believers to separate themselves from the unbelievers, especially in acts of immorality and idolatry. In general, he admonished them to put away the wicked from among themselves because they were temples of God and would be His children (see 1 Corinthians 5:13; 2 Corinthians 6:16–17; Deuteronomy 17:7; Leviticus 26:12; Isaiah 52:11; 2 Samuel 7:14). Specifically, he warned them to guard against immorality (see 1 Corinthians 6:16; Genesis 2:24) and idolatry (see 1 Corinthians 10:7; Exodus 32:6). Even more specifically, he used Old Testament scripture while addressing the issue of whether it was lawful to eat food sacrificed to idols or sold by unbelievers (see 1 Corinthians 10:26; Psalm 24:1). Thus, because the Old Testament Israelites faced some of the same challenges in trying to separate themselves from sin, Paul could use examples from scripture to encourage Christians to obey likewise.

RESURRECTION

In a discourse on the Resurrection found in 1 Corinthians 15, Paul used five Old Testament texts to put forward his belief in the Resurrection. Although none of the Old Testament passages directly focused on resurrection, they alluded to conquering death and Adam's becoming the first living soul. First, Paul explained that Christ was resurrected so He could eventually subdue all His enemies and rule over everything (see 1 Corinthians 15:27; Psalm 8:6). Then he explained that if there were no resurrection, there would be no need for law or righteous living (see 1 Corinthians 15:32; Isaiah 22:13). He compared resurrection to Adam's becoming a living soul and then a quickened spirit (see 1 Corinthians 15:45; Genesis 2:7). In the end, resurrection will conquer death (see 1 Corinthians 15:54–55; Isaiah 25:8; Hosea 13:14).

WISDOM

In 1 Corinthians, Paul attacked those who felt that man's wisdom was the great power in the universe. He used four Old Testament verses to show that God's wisdom is the greatest and will destroy the wisdom of man. First, he showed that God would reveal things not yet imaginable to man (see 1 Corinthians 2:9; Isaiah 64:3), for who can know the mind of God? (see 1 Corinthians 2:16; Isaiah 40:13). Second, he showed that man's wisdom is really nothing and that God will eventually take the wise in their own craftiness (see 1 Corinthians 3:19–20; Job 5:13; Psalm 94:11).

COLLECTION FOR THE POOR

Paul used Old Testament references in two cases where he addressed the need for the Saints to contribute to a collection for the poor in the

Church. First, he reminded the Saints that there should be greater equal-ity (see 2 Corinthians 8:15; Exodus 16:18), and second, he taught that God would provide for all (see 2 Corinthians 9:9; Psalm 112:9).

THE GIFT OF TONGUES

Finally, Paul used one Old Testament example when treating the matter of the gift of tongues versus prophecy in 1 Corinthians 14. By using a passage from Isaiah, Paul was trying to show that the gift of tongues was for a sign to those who did not believe, whereas prophecy was necessary to edify the believers (see 1 Corinthians 14:21; Isaiah 28:11–12).

CONCLUSION

By paying attention to the many stereotypical *formulae quotationis* scattered throughout the New Testament, such as "as it is written," "for the scripture says," "for [prophet] says," and "according to the law," we begin to see how much the Old Testament was used by the New Testament Apostles in their writing. In this chapter, these formulae show how often the Old Testament was consciously cited by the Apostle Paul to strengthen his arguments and illuminate doctrine. It truly was an important source to lend authority to his teachings and enrich his writings. Because of the abundance of quotations, we can conclude that the Old Testament, particularly the Septuagint version, was familiar to many of Paul's contemporaries and that by quoting it Paul lent authority to his message. The vast number of Old Testament quotations in his letters seems to indicate his early Pharisaic schooling and his desire to defend his beliefs through the Old Testament. In many doctrinal matters, he relied heavily on the Old Testament, which is noteworthy because of his great emphasis on a new covenant with a new elect people and the fulfillment of the law with now a need for faith in Jesus Christ. So despite all these changes within the belief sys-tem, Paul employed Old Testament passages to admonish and teach his followers. Perhaps the reason for the greatest number of quotations coming from Isaiah, Psalms, and the narrative section of Genesis was to avoid sections mostly containing the now-fulfilled Mosaic law.

Occasionally these citations were different from what we have in

Septuagint or Hebrew manuscripts. Some may have been changed by Paul to strengthen his argument or to fit the new situation. For example, in Romans 9:33, Paul quoted Isaiah 28:16 but added the words "stumblingstone and rock of offence," rather than a "precious corner stone." In Paul's teachings, the crucified Messiah became a stumblingstone to belief for many, so perhaps he added these words here to emphasize that fact. But many of the differences between the New Testament and the Septuagint and Hebrew Bible may simply have resulted from each group using different manuscripts, not just the transmission into the New Testament, because there were also differences between the Septuagint and Hebrew versions (such as the Dead Sea Scrolls, Samaritan Pentateuch, Masoretic tradition, and others). As I have shown above, Paul's primary emphasis when using these Old Testament passages was to show that covenant blessings and promises preceded the law of Moses and likewise continued after the fulfillment of the law. Paul also frequently used the Old Testament to demonstrate the election of the Christians, the importance of faith, and the necessity of preaching these messages to those who had not yet accepted them.

From Paul's and others' use of the Old Testament in their teaching, we learn that the fulfillment of the law of Moses did not mean an end to the validity and value of the Old Testament. Perhaps, like Paul encouraged, we also can gain knowledge and hope from the Old Testament (and other scriptures): "For whatsoever things were written aforetime were written for our learning, that we through patience and comfort of the scriptures might have hope" (Romans 15:4).

TABLES OF OLD TESTAMENT CITATIONS

Some 107 explicit citations to the Old Testament appear in Paul's writings.[11] Many of these passages are set off by stereotypical *formulae quotationis* such as "as it is written," "for the scripture says," "for [prophet] says," or "according to the law." By far, the greatest number of Old Testament citations are in Romans, followed by 1 Corinthians, Galatians, and 2 Corinthians. Several of Paul's epistles do not include any explicit Old Testament citations (for example, 1 and 2 Thessalonians, Philippians, and Philemon). The most oft-quoted book of the Old Testament in Paul's writings is Isaiah, followed by Psalms, Genesis, and Deuteronomy. For the most part, these quotations were copied closely from the Septuagint and Hebrew versions of the Old Testament with only minor changes. Sometimes, however, larger differences are found. A detailed analysis of these variations is not possible here, but listed below are the basic, noteworthy discrepancies where one text varies from the other two, or in the last case, where all three differ from one another. Overall, Paul seems to rely most heavily on the Septuagint, but occasionally he seems to be giving his own translation of the Hebrew text.[12]

HEBREW (MASORETIC TRADITION) DIFFERS FROM SEPTUAGINT AND NEW TESTAMENT

CITATION	HEBREW	LXX AND NT
Isa. 40:13; 1 Cor. 2:16	Spirit	Mind
Isa. 49:8; 2 Cor. 6:2	Answer	Listen
Isa. 54:1; Gal. 4:27	"children of the married wife"	"she which hath an husband"
Isa. 42:5; Rom. 2:24	(missing)	"among the Gentiles"
Ps. 50:6; Rom. 3:4	Be pure	Overcome
Ps. 14:1–3; Rom. 3:10–18	(missing)	Verses 13–18; LXX Psalms 13:3b*
Gen. 15:6; Rom. 4:3, 9, 22	(missing)	Abraham "on the Lord"
Isa. 1:9; Rom. 9:29	Survivor	Seed
Isa. 28:16; Rom. 10:11	(missing)	(stumble) "on this"
Joel 3:5; Rom. 10:13	Escape	Be saved
Isa. 53:1; Rom. 10:16	(missing)	Lord
Isa. 65:2; Rom. 10:21	(missing)	Obstinate
Ps. 68:23–24; Rom. 11:9–10	Loins	Back
Isa. 40:13; Rom. 11:34	Spirit	Mind
Isa. 45:23; Rom. 14:11b	"sworn by myself" (missing)	Confess "to God"

*Material found in Rom. 3:13–18 and LXX Ps. 13:3b is found in other places in the Hebrew Bible: Ps. 5:10; 140:4; 10:7; Isa. 59:7–8; and Ps. 36:2.

NEW TESTAMENT DIFFERS FROM
SEPTUAGINT AND HEBREW BIBLE

Citation	NT	LXX and Hebrew
1 Cor. 1:19; Isa. 29:14	Confounded	Hid
1 Cor. 1:31; Jer. 9:23	Paraphrase (glory) "in the Lord"	"thus saith the Lord"
1 Cor. 14:21; Isa. 28:11–12	Another "will not hear"	Stammering "do not want to hear"
2 Cor. 6:16; Lev. 26:12	"I will dwell in them"	(missing)
2 Cor. 6:17; Isa. 52:11	"I will receive you"	"be ye clean that bear the vessels of the Lord"
2 Cor. 6:18; 2 Sam. 7:14	"and daughters"	(missing)
2 Cor. 10:17; Jer. 9:23	"in the Lord"	"in this"
Rom. 9:9; Gen. 18:14	Come	Return
Rom. 9:25; Hosea 2:23	Call "beloved, which was not beloved"	Say "have mercy upon her that had not obtained mercy"
Rom. 9:27; Isa. 10:22–23	(missing)	"with righteousness"
Rom. 9:33; Isa. 28:16	"stumblingstone and a rock of offence"	"precious cornerstone"
Rom. 10:7; Deut. 30:13	"descend into the deep"	"go over the sea"
Rom. 11:8; Deut. 29:3	"spirit of slumber"	"heart to perceive"
Rom. 11:9–10; Ps. 68:23–24	"and a trap"	(missing)

SEPTUAGINT DIFFERS FROM NEW TESTAMENT AND HEBREW BIBLE

CITATION	LXX	NT AND HEBREW
Isa. 64:3 and 1 Cor. 2:9	Plural nouns (missing)	Singular nouns "ear" (to hear)
Job 5:13 and 1 Cor. 3:19	"way of thinking"	"craftiness"
Hab. 2:4 and Gal. 3:11a, Rom. 1:17	"(faith) in me"	(missing)
Job 41:3 and Rom. 11:35	Many differences*	
Deut. 32:35 and Rom. 12:19	"in the day" (of vengeance)	"vengeance is mine"

*Rom. 11:35 "may be a quotation of Job 41:3, but it does not agree with LXX of that verse, being closer to the MT [Hebrew Masoretic text] (who has preceded me that I should repay). But the OT text is uncertain; others think that Paul may be alluding to Job 35:7 or 41:1." From Joseph A. Fitzmyer, *Romans*, volume 33 of the Anchor Bible series (New York: Doubleday, 1993), 635.

ALL THREE VERSIONS DIFFER

CITATION	NT	LXX	HEBREW
1 Cor. 15:54; Isa. 25:8	"in victory"	"strength"	"forever"
1 Cor. 15:55; Hosea 13:14	"victory"	"penalty" or "justice"	"plague"
Rom. 2:24; Isa. 52:5	"through you"	"through all you"	"all the day"
Rom. 10:20; Isa. 65:1		Reverses verbs	Reverses phrases

NOTES

1. See Bible Dictionary, "Quotations," 756–59.
2. The same three Old Testament books were the most quoted among the Dead Sea Scrolls.
3. Michael D. Coogan, "Literacy in Ancient Israel," in *The Oxford Companion to the Bible,* ed. Bruce M. Metzger and Michael D. Coogan (New York: Oxford University Press, 1993), 438.
4. Bart D. Ehrman, *The New Testament: A Historical Introduction to the Early Christian*

Writings, 3d ed. (New York: Oxford University Press, 2004), 54. See also William V. Harris, *Ancient Literacy* (Cambridge: Harvard University Press, 1989), 328–30.

5. See Doctrine and Covenants 91 for a revealed answer as to the reliability of the Apocrypha.

6. An interesting verse that may capture this dual nature of reading and hearing scripture is Revelation 1:3: "Blessed is he that *readeth*, and they that *hear* the words of this prophecy" (emphasis added; see also 2 Maccabees 15:39). The Greek verb used here for reading, *anaginōskō*, can mean "read" or "read aloud" in public.

7. "An excellent New Testament example of this practice [reading aloud] can be found in Acts 8:28–31. Philip *hears* the Ethiopian reading alone in his chariot because he was, obviously, reading aloud. Other reading aloud scenes are . . . [found in] Luke 4:16 and Acts 15:21. The first person from antiquity who is actually reported to have read without sound is St. Ambrose" (Mary Ann Tolbert, *Sowing the Gospel: Mark's World in Literary-Historical Perspective* (Minneapolis: Fortress, 1989), 44n35.

8. In one case, Paul encouraged congregations to swap letters between them (see Colossians 4:16).

9. G. C. D. Howley, "The Authority of the New Testament," in *The International Bible Commentary*, ed. F. F. Bruce (Grand Rapids, MI: Marshall Pickering/Zondervan, 1986), 997.

10. For a more detailed look at the differences between the Septuagint, Hebrew Bible, and New Testament in Paul's quotations of the Old Testament, see the tables on pages 239–41.

11. See chart in M. Silva, "Old Testament in Paul," in *Dictionary of Paul and His Letters: A Compendium of Contemporary Biblical Scholarship*, ed. Gerald F. Hawthorne, Ralph P. Martin, Daniel G. Reid (Downers Grove, IL: InterVarsity, 1993), 631. This does not include allusions where a complete list would be very long. The influence of the Old Testament is dominant in his thought and language.

12. "His dependence on the current Greek translation of his day is clearly established, but there is good reason to think that he was familiar with the original Hebrew and that the latter, in at least some cases, determined how he used the OT [Old Testament]" (Silva, "Old Testament in Paul," 632).

15

AUTHORSHIP OF THE EPISTLE TO THE HEBREWS

Terrence L. Szink

Upon opening the Latter-day Saint edition of the King James Version of the Bible to the book of Hebrews, one reads the title, "The Epistle of Paul the Apostle to the Hebrews." What is the evidence that Paul was in fact the author of the epistle to the Hebrews? This chapter addresses that question by examining the text itself, early Christian traditions, and the statements of modern scholars and Latter-day Saint prophets.

EVIDENCE FROM THE TEXT

The author of Hebrews never identified himself as Paul or as any other person. In every other epistle attributed to him, however, Paul not only identified himself but did so in the first word.[1] In light of this, some have argued that if Paul in fact wrote Hebrews, he would have identified himself as he did in the other epistles. Clement of Alexandria (AD 160–215) explained that Paul did not attach his name to Hebrews because he was not liked or respected among the Jews, so "he wisely did

---

Terrence L. Szink is an assistant professor of ancient scripture at Brigham Young University.

not offend them at the start by adding his name."[2] Clement also argued that since Jesus was sent to the Hebrews and Paul was an Apostle to the Gentiles, Paul did not use his name because of modesty and deference to the Lord.[3] It is not certain, however, that the intended audience for the epistle to the Hebrews was Jewish. Bart Ehrman suggests that based on the content of the epistle, the audience may have been Gentile Christians who were contemplating conversion to Judaism.[4] Furthermore, Romans, an epistle in which Paul did identify himself, was addressed to an audience that was at least partly Jewish. For example, Paul addresses those like himself who had Abraham as their father, "as pertaining to the flesh" (Romans 4:1) and "them that know the law" (Romans 7:1), meaning the law of Moses. If Paul did not hesitate to identify himself in Romans to an audience which was at least partially Jewish, either because of modesty or desire to avoid offence, why would he have done so in Hebrews?

Some scholars have pointed out significant differences between Hebrews and the other epistles of Paul, including diction (vocabulary choice) and themes. These differences were not just noted with the rise of modern biblical criticism; scholars in the early church recognized them. Thus Eusebius (AD 260–339) reported the conclusion of Origen (AD 185–251): "The diction in Hebrews does not have the rough quality the apostle himself admitted having [2 Cor. 11:6], and its syntax is better Greek. The content of the epistle is excellent, however, and not inferior to the authentic writings of the apostle."[5] Many modern scholars agree with Origen's assessment. Regarding diction, Craig Koester notes that the epistle to the Hebrews contains 154 *hapax legomena,* or words that appear only once in a corpus text—a number much higher than in the rest of the Pauline epistles combined. Furthermore, he and others have provided large lists of words that appear in Paul's letters which do not appear in Hebrews, or that conversely are found in Hebrews but not in the other Pauline epistles.[6] For example, Bruce Metzger notes that Paul used the phrase "Christ Jesus" around ninety times, but that phrase does not occur in the text of Hebrews.[7] The fact that the author of Hebrews uses so many *hapax legomena* when compared to the rest of the Pauline epistles and that his vocabulary choices are so different can be used to argue that Paul did not write Hebrews. On the other hand, Eric D. Huntsman has explained that establishing a Pauline vocabulary is a difficult task; there are as many differences in the vocabulary of Romans as there are in Hebrews when compared to the other Pauline epistles.[8]

Eusebius also summarized Clement of Alexandria's opinion regarding these problems: "The epistle to the Hebrews he [Clement] attributes to Paul but says that it was written in Hebrew for Hebrews and then carefully translated by Luke for the Greeks. Therefore the translation has the same style and color as Acts."[9] F. F. Bruce points out one problem with this proposal. Not only are the Old Testament passages quoted in Hebrews all from the Septuagint, a Greek translation of the Old Testament (abbreviated "LXX"), but furthermore "the author argues on the basis of a LXX deviation from the Hebrew text" in at least two passages.[10] This would be equivalent to drawing conclusions about Joseph Smith's translation of the Book of Mormon not on the basis of the English text, but on a Spanish translation of the Book of Mormon and using a passage in which the Spanish differed from the English text. Had Paul originally written the epistle to the Hebrews in Hebrew, it is not likely that he would have made an argument based on a passage in a Greek translation of the text that was different from the original Hebrew. This argues strongly against the possibility of the text of Hebrews being a Greek translation of an original Hebrew text.

It is important in any discussion of diction and writing style to acknowledge that Paul used scribes to help write his epistles. The best evidence that Paul did not personally handwrite his epistles is his special mention of writing the final greeting with his own hand in 2 Thessalonians 3:17. The use of different scribes may have affected vocabulary choices and writing style of the epistles.

Some modern scholars have also pointed out some thematic differences between Hebrews and the other Pauline epistles. For example, Bruce Metzger notes that "Paul mentions the resurrection of Christ many times in his letters; here it is referred to only once."[11] However, this particular thematic difference may not be as strong as Metzger concludes. In addition to the reference to the Resurrection of Christ cited by Metzger (Hebrews 13:20), there are two additional passages which refer to the resurrection in general (Hebrews 6:2 and 11:35). While the number of references to the resurrection in general in Hebrews pales in comparison to the number found in Romans, and there is no extended theological explanation of the resurrection such as is in 1 Corinthians 15, the three references in Hebrews exceed the number found in Galatians (1), Ephesians (2), Philippians (1), Colossians (2), 1 Thessalonians (2), 2 Thessalonians (0); 1 Timothy (0), 2 Timothy (2), Titus (0), and Philemon (0).

Bart Ehrman notes that "the way this author [of Hebrews] understands such critical terms as 'faith' (11:1) differs markedly from what you find in the writings of the apostle [Paul]."[12] Metzger explains this difference: "For Paul it is personal commitment to Christ, who makes the believer one with him; here [in Hebrews] it is confident assurance of God's providential care, which undergirds the Christian's certainty of spiritual realities."[13] L. David Hurst, examining the ideas of faith in Hebrews and the other epistles, concluded that the differences are not as great as some scholars claim.

> In both Paul and Hebrews there seems to be a similar intermingling of terms and ideas connected with the notion of faith. A certain overlapping may be found in other NT writers. But at least Hebrews and Paul are closer at this point than has been generally acknowledged. Many have attempted to "pin down" Paul and *Auctor* to one particular idea of faith and then contrast them. Such a method ignores that any given situation will inevitably bring to the fore certain nuances of an idea, nuances which, when given the same situation in Paul's letters, appear there as well. Nowhere in the two writers' treatment of faith does there appear to be enough closeness to indicate literary borrowing; but at least it can be said that the two writers reflect a similar, if not the same, intellectual milieu.[14]

For Latter-day Saints, these two ideas of faith are two sides of the same coin, and certainly not exclusive of one another. Thus our "personal commitment to Christ" brings with it a "confident assurance of God's providential care."[15]

Perhaps too much is made of these thematic differences. Certainly authors need not always write on the same topics. In 1 Corinthians

11:23–34, for example, Paul wrote of the sacrament of the Lord's Supper. In no other place does he mention this important doctrine. Should we conclude that 1 Corinthians was not written by the same person who wrote 2 Corinthians or Romans, or any of the other epistles because they do not mention the sacrament? If such conclusions should not be made regarding 1 Corinthians, care should be taken to not draw similar conclusions about Hebrews based on thematic differences.

Those who argue against Pauline authorship often cite another passage: "How shall we escape, if we neglect so great salvation; which at the first began to be spoken by the Lord, and was confirmed unto us by them that heard him" (Hebrews 2:3). Here the writer claimed that he had learned from others who had heard Jesus directly. In other epistles Paul adamantly claims that he had received the gospel directly from Jesus Christ, through revelation and not from any other person. In the epistle to the Galatians, he wrote, "But I certify you, brethren, that the gospel which was preached of me is not after man. For I neither received it of man, neither was I taught it, but by the revelation of Jesus Christ" (Galatians 1:11–12; see Ephesians 3:3). Homer Kent responds, "This would not appear conclusive, however, for all will readily admit that Paul had not been an eyewitness of the miracles or of the preaching of Jesus, and thus had not the confirming testimony of others for these things. The statement does not speak of initial impartation of the message but of confirmation."[16] Sidney Sperry adds that the "statements (Hebrews 2:3 and 13:7) simply exhibit a natural deference to those who were acquainted with and associated with the Savior during His ministry."[17]

On the other hand, some items in the epistle may support Pauline authorship. Variations of the phrase "grace be with you all" conclude Hebrews and all of Paul's epistles but are not found in any other New Testament epistle. The reference to Paul's close associate Timothy in Hebrews 13:23 could be used to support Paul's authorship. However, Timothy was a common name at the time of the composition of Hebrews, and there is no way to know if the Timothy mentioned is the one who worked with Paul.[18] Some have concluded that the reference to the author's "bonds" in 10:34 and 13:3, along with the salutation from "they of Italy" (Hebrews 13:24), would make sense if Paul were writing while imprisoned in Rome. But again, these details may fit other authors as well. There are other similarities.[19] Other scholars have noted that there are "fifteen impressive convergences," that show "a large amount of common ground to exist between Paul and Hebrews."[20]

Modern non-LDS scholars are almost unanimous in rejecting Pauline authorship: Bart Ehrman explains that "modern scholars . . . are unified in recognizing that" Paul did not write Hebrews.[21] Raymond Brown writes: "The evidence against Paul's writing Heb is overwhelming."[22] After examining some of the evidence already cited, R. McLean Wilson concludes: "From this brief survey some conclusions may immediately be drawn: first, whoever the author was, he certainly was not Paul."[23] Even the introduction to the epistle to the Hebrews in the relatively conservative New International Version Study Bible states that "since the Reformation it has been widely recognized that Paul could not have been the writer."[24] Those few who have continued to maintain Pauline authorship for Hebrews are, certainly, a small minority.[25]

EARLY TRADITIONS

The early Christian traditions about the authorship of Hebrews can be divided geographically into east and west. This section will briefly survey some of the opinions expressed in the early church regarding Paul and the epistle to the Hebrews.[26] The evidence will show that there has been no unanimous opinion regarding authorship. Some scholars have suggested that early Christians based their acceptance of Pauline authorship and canonicity of Hebrews on whether or not they agreed with the doctrines contained in it.[27]

East. Generally the Eastern Church, with its theological center in Alexandria, accepted Pauline authorship earlier than the church in the west, centered in Rome.[28] The earliest Christian writer to mention the issue was Clement of Alexandria, who argued that the stylistic differences are because Paul wrote in Hebrew and Luke translated those words into Greek.

The Chester Beatty Papyrus (P[46]) from Egypt is the oldest-known preserved text of the Pauline epistles and dates to approximately AD 200.[29] Generally, in canonical lists, the epistles of Paul are arranged roughly by size.[30] P[46] reflects the Alexandrian tradition by placing

Hebrews immediately following Romans, exactly where one would expect it if Paul had written it.

Eusebius believed that Paul was the author of Hebrews but acknowledged that this opinion was not universal.[31] However, not all in the East were in agreement. As noted above, the stylistic differences influenced Origen, Clement's student, to such a degree that he finally concluded: "Who wrote the epistle only God knows. Traditions reaching us claim it was either Clement, Bishop of Rome, or Luke, who wrote the Gospel and the Acts."[32]

West. The earliest reference to Hebrews could be in 1 Clement, an early letter (c. AD 96) traditionally ascribed to Clement, the third bishop of Rome, and addressed to the Christians in Corinth.[33] Many scholars have noted similarities between 1 Clement and a series of passages in Hebrews. Koester, for example has concluded that "1 Clement drew elements from several parts of Hebrews."[34] The probability that 1 Clement knew and used Hebrews indicates, at the very least, that the author of 1 Clement considered Hebrews to be authoritative, yet it would not decisively prove Pauline authorship.[35] For example, because of the similarities between 1 Clement and Hebrews, Origen reports the suggestion that Clement of Rome and not Paul was the author of Hebrews.[36]

Most early church writers in the west did not accept Pauline authorship.[37] Tertullian (AD 160–225) felt that Barnabas had written Hebrews.[38] Eusebius reported that Gaius, a priest at Rome, "mentions only thirteen epistles of the holy apostle [Paul], not including that to the Hebrews with the rest, for even to this day some at Rome do not consider it the apostle's."[39] Although Eusebius believed that Paul was the author of Hebrews, he acknowledged that this opinion was not generally held in the West: "Paul was obviously the author of the fourteen letters, but some dispute the epistle to the Hebrews in view of the Roman church's denial that it is the work of Paul."[40]

Indeed, the Muratorian Fragment (c. AD 170–90), which contains a list of books considered canonical by the Western church at that time, does not mention Hebrews.[41] Other western writers knew of an epistle to the Hebrews, whoever they thought was the author, so it is likely that the author of the Muratorian Fragment also knew of the existence of

Hebrews. Had the author of the Muratorian Fragment considered Paul the author, it is likely that he would have included it in his canon based on Paul's apostleship.

F. F. Bruce suggests that Athanasius of Alexandria (AD 300–373) may have influenced how the Western church viewed Hebrews during his stay at Rome after his exile in AD 340: "It is probable that he persuaded the Roman Christians to fall into line with their eastern brethren in admitting the canonicity, if not the Pauline authorship, of Hebrews."[42] Koester notes that the prestige of Hebrews increased as western theologians used it to fight the ideas of Arianism. As a result, ultimately Pauline authorship gained more acceptance in the West.[43]

Jerome (AD 342–420), who produced the Latin Vulgate, wrote concerning Hebrews: "We must admit that the epistle written to the Hebrews is regarded as Paul's, not only by the churches of the east, but by all church writers who have from the beginning written in Greek." Yet he also recognized that others attributed it to Barnabas or Clement.[44]

Augustine (AD 354–430) seems to have undergone a change in his opinion regarding Pauline authorship. A. Souter, citing the work of O. Rottmanner, explains: "In his earliest writings (down to 406) [Augustine] cites the Epistle as Paul's; in the middle period he wavers between Pauline authorship and anonymity; in his old age (409–30) he refers to it always as anonymous."[45]

As noted above, the Chester Beatty Papyrus (P[46]), an eastern manuscript, places Hebrews immediately following Romans, while the Muratorian Fragment, a western manuscript, does not include it. Later, as western Christians more generally accepted Hebrews they included it in their canon, although they placed it in a variety of positions.[46] The current canon places Hebrews after Philemon, based on the western tradition, and may reflect an attempt to separate it from the Pauline epistles of which there was no question of authorship. On the other hand, the late date at which Hebrews was generally accepted as authoritative may be the reason for its placement after Philemon.[47]

This brief survey of early Christian traditions surrounding the authorship of the epistle to the Hebrews illustrates the diversity of opinion expressed on the subject. Certainly it is difficult to conclude decisively that Paul wrote Hebrews solely by citing early Christian traditions.

EVIDENCE FROM JOSEPH SMITH

The Prophet Joseph Smith never made any direct statement regarding the complex issue of the authorship of Hebrews. He did, however, quote passages of scripture from the epistle to the Hebrews and attribute them to Paul. For example, he attributed a passage from Hebrews 6:17: "Paul said to his Hebrew brethren that God b[e]ing more abundantly willing to show unto the heirs of his promises the immutability of his council [']confirmed it by an oath.'"[48] I feel that this type of statement, however, is not by itself sufficiently strong to definitively answer the question. In my view, Joseph was simply following the view of Pauline authorship as he read it in the title, "The Epistle of Paul the Apostle to the Hebrews," rather than making an overt statement about the authorship of Hebrews. On one occasion, Willard Richards recorded the Prophet saying, "St Paul exhorts us to make our Calling & Election shure."[49] We know, however, that these teachings appear in 2 Peter 1:10 and not in any of Paul's writings. Certainly no one should use this statement as evidence that Joseph Smith considered Paul the author of 2 Peter. Thus the phrase "Paul said," followed by a quote from Hebrews, does not necessarily mean that the Prophet was weighing in on the question of the authorship of Hebrews.

There is another example of someone who referred to Paul as the author of Hebrews and yet did not believe that he wrote it. Koester has pointed out that Origen, who, as we have seen, did not believe that Paul wrote Hebrews, "commonly referred to Paul as the author."[50] Thus, the fact that a writer or speaker casually mentions Paul when quoting Hebrews does not necessarily imply that he or she believes that Paul actually wrote it.

A number of Latter-day Saint General Authorities, scholars, and writers, in citing passages from Hebrews, attribute them to "the writer of Hebrews" rather than to "Paul." For example, the First Presidency, under the direction of President Joseph F. Smith, in the document "The Father and The Son: A Doctrinal Exposition by The First Presidency and the Twelve," taught, "The writer of the Epistle to the Hebrews affirms the status of Jesus Christ."[51] Significantly, this statement appears between quotes from Colossians and Romans in which Paul is explicitly identified as the author. Other leaders of the Church have used the phrase "the writer of Hebrews" when citing passages from Hebrews, including Hugh B. Brown,[52] James E. Talmage,[53] Charles W. Penrose,[54] Milton R. Hunter,[55] B. H. Roberts,[56] Thomas S. Monson,[57] Howard W. Hunter,[58] John H. Vandenberg,[59] and Spencer W. Kimball.[60] Interestingly, the phrase "the writer of . . ." is not commonly used when referring to passages from any other epistle.[61] It is important to note that just because writers or speakers use this phrase does not necessarily mean that they reject Pauline authorship. For example, Joseph Fielding Smith, who on occasion used the phrase "the writer of the epistle to the Hebrews,"[62] also referred to Paul when citing Hebrews.[63]

The Joseph Smith Translation of the Bible sheds little light on this issue. In New Testament Manuscript 2 of the JST, the Prophet renders the title of Hebrews, "The Epistle to the Hebrews,"[64] rather than "The Epistle of Paul, the Apostle, to the Hebrews," which is the title in the 1828 Phinney edition of the King James Bible which Joseph used to produce his translation. But in the JST manuscripts, none of the titles of the epistles of Paul contain his name. Thus, Romans is titled "The Epistle to the Romans," rather than "The Epistle of Paul, the Apostle, to the Romans."

The strongest evidence that Joseph Smith thought Paul wrote Hebrews is found in his discussion of Hebrews 11:4. The verse reads, "By faith Abel offered unto God a more excellent sacrifice than Cain, by which he obtained witness that he was righteous, God testifying of his gifts: and by it he being dead yet speaketh" (Hebrews 11:4). Joseph does not merely attribute a passage from Hebrews to Paul, but he explains exactly how Paul acquired this particular piece of knowledge that would appear in Hebrews.

> How doth ye yet speak? Why he magnified the Priesthood which was confired upon him and died a righteous man, and therefore has become an angel of God by receiving his body from the dead, therefore holding still the keys of his dispensation and was *sent down from heaven unto Paul* to minister consoling

words & to *commit unto him a knowledge* of the mysteries of Godliness and if this was not the case I would ask how did Paul know so much about Abel and why should he talk about his speaking after he was dead. How that he spoke after he was dead must be, by being sent down out of heaven, to administer.[65]

The Prophet said that Paul knew this specific bit of information because Abel appeared to him and instructed him, showing Joseph's belief that at least one specific idea expressed in Hebrews, the knowledge of Abel's sacrifice, came from Paul.

How can we fit together the ideas that a specific bit of information expressed in Hebrews came from Paul, with the rather strong indications discussed above that Paul was not the author of Hebrews? Eric Huntsman has concluded: "Another resolution to the question of who wrote Hebrews may lie in the ancient idea of authorship, which was somewhat different than either the modern conception or expectation. In the Classical world, the *auctor* was the originator of a work or the person whose authority or ideas lay behind it."[66] Thus, while someone associated with Paul and familiar with his ideas may have been responsible for the vocabulary, organization, and the writing of Hebrews, Paul may ultimately have been the source of the ideas (certainly at least one idea) expressed in Hebrews.[67] This is very much in line with what Origen believed anciently: "If I were to venture my own opinion, I would say that the thoughts are the apostle's but the style and construction reflect someone who recalled the apostle's teachings and interpreted them. If any church, then, regards this epistle as Paul's, it should be commended, since men of old had good reason to hand it down as his."[68]

APOSTLESHIP, AUTHORITY, AND AUTHORSHIP

How important is the issue of authorship and the authority of the text? As noted above, some scholars have suggested that early Christians based their view of Pauline authorship of Hebrews on whether or not they agreed with the doctrines it contained. This demonstrates the importance of apostolic authorship to early Christians. Early Christians attributed two of the Gospels to the Apostles Matthew and John, even though the texts themselves do not mention who wrote them. They attributed the other two gospels to Luke and Mark, whom they traditionally associated with the Apostles Paul and Peter, respectively.[69]

Thus, apostolic authorship was certainly an important element in the canonization process. As members of The Church of Jesus Christ of Latter-day Saints, we rightly tend to give more credence to the writings of Apostles. If a text is not written by an Apostle, does that lessen the value of any truths it might contain? Modern revelation teaches, "And whatsoever they shall speak when moved upon by the Holy Ghost shall be scripture, shall be the will of the Lord, shall be the mind of the Lord, shall be the word of the Lord, shall be the voice of the Lord, and the power of God unto salvation" (D&C 68:4). The critical issue is not necessarily who said or wrote it, but whether the speaker or writer was inspired by the Holy Ghost and spoke or wrote the truth. The value of a text is not entirely dependent on authorship. President J. Reuben Clark explained: "I am not really concerned, and no man of faith should be, about the exact authorship of the books of the Bible. More than one Prophet may well have written parts of books now collected under one heading. I do not know. There may have been 'ghost writers' in those days, as now. The Lord gave Aaron to Moses in an equivalent capacity, and spoke to Israel through Moses by the mouth of Aaron. He may have done the same in other cases. If so, what of it?"[70] Applying President Clark's statement to Hebrews, this epistle would not be diminished if some other inspired Christian other than Paul, such as Barnabas, Apollos, or Luke, wrote it. As R. McLean Wilson has written, "Even if it was not written by Paul, it remains an important document in its own right, both as coming from the earliest days of Christianity and as the work of an author of great skill and capacity."[71]

Thus, the importance of the doctrine and truth contained in Hebrews outweighs any questions regarding its authorship. This idea is not new. Jerome, writing in AD 414 in an epistle to Dardanus, said, "It is of no great moment who the author is, since it is the work of a churchman and receives recognition day by day in the public reading of the churches."[72]

Even Elder Bruce R. McConkie, who strongly believed that Paul was the author of Hebrews, nevertheless felt that the doctrine and ideas expressed in it were ultimately more important than the issue of authorship. After strongly affirming that Paul was the author, he wrote: "However, the principles set forth in the Epistle are more important than the personage who recorded them; an understanding of the doctrines taught is of greater worth than a knowledge of their earthly authorship."[73]

This study has demonstrated that (1) at the very least, according to Joseph Smith one specific idea in the epistle to the Hebrews came from Paul; (2) the differences in vocabulary, style, and organization from Paul's other epistles do not preclude him from being the *auctor*; (3) even some General Authorities have used language that suggests their uncertainty about the authorship of Hebrews; and (4) the fact that modern prophets have often quoted and continue to teach the ideas expressed in Hebrews is ample support that the author was inspired by the Holy Ghost, and therefore the book is scripture, the "will of the Lord, the mind of the Lord, the word of the Lord, the voice of the Lord, and the power of God unto salvation" (D&C 68:4).

NOTES

1. Paul's authorship of some of these epistles has been questioned by many modern scholars. Second Thessalonians, Colossians, Ephesians, and the pastoral epistles of 1 and 2 Timothy and Titus are most often mentioned in this regard. The authorship of these epistles is beyond the scope of this chapter. See Bart Ehrman, *The New Testament: A Historical Introduction to the Early Christian Writings*, 3d ed. rev. (New York: Oxford Univeristy Press, 2004), 376–93; and Lincoln H. Blumell, "Ancient Letters and Scribes: Implications for the Composition of the Pauline Epistles," in this volume.

2. Eusebius, *History of the Church*, 6.14, in *Eusebius: The Church History*, trans. Paul L. Maier (Grand Rapids, MI: Kregel, 1999). All Eusebius quotations are from Maier's translation.

3. Eusebius, *History of the Church*, 6.14.

4. Ehrman, *The New Testament*, 411–12.

5. Eusebius, *History of the Church*, 6.25.

6. Craig R. Koester, *Hebrews*, volume 36 in the Anchor Bible Series (Garden City, NY: Doubleday, 2001), 43n. Koester lists thirty-two terms as well as eight "rhetorical formulas" that appear in the other Pauline epistles but are not found in Hebrews.

7. Bruce M. Metzger, *The New Testament: Its Background, Growth, and Content*, 3d ed. (Nashville: Abingdon, 2003), 284.

8. Richard Neitzel Holzapfel, Eric D. Huntsman, and Thomas A. Wayment, *Jesus Christ and the World of the New Testament: An Illustrated Reference for Latter-day Saints* (Salt Lake City: Deseret Book, forthcoming).

9. Eusebius, *History of the Church*, 6.14.

10. F. F. Bruce, *The Epistle to the Hebrews* (Grand Rapids, MI: Eerdmans, 1990), 15n. The two passages are Hebrews 10:5, which quotes Psalm 40:6, and Hebrews 9:15–20.

11. Metzger, *The New Testament*, 284. See also Raymond E. Brown, *An Introduction to the New Testament* (New York: Doubleday, 1997), 694. Resurrection is referred to in Paul's epistles in Romans 1:4; 4:24–25; 6:4–5, 9; 7:4; 8:11; 10:9; 14:9; 1 Corinthians 6:14; 15; 2 Corinthians 1:9; 4:14; 5:14; Galatians 1:1; Ephesians 1:20; 5:14; Philippians 3:10–11; Colossians 1:18; 2:12–13; 1 Thessalonians 1:10; 4:16; 2 Timothy 2:8, 18. It is mentioned twice in Hebrews 6:2 and 11:35 and referred to in 13:20.

12. Ehrman, *The New Testament*, 411.

13. Metzger, *The New Testament*, 284.

14. L. David Hurst, *The Epistle to the Hebrews: Its Background of Thought* (Cambridge: Cambridge University Press, 1990), 124.

15. For an explanation of Latter-day Saint understanding of faith and grace, see Stephen E. Robinson, *Believing Christ* (Salt Lake City: Deseret Book, 1992), 85–104.

16. Homer A. Kent, *The Epistle to the Hebrews: A Commentary* (Grand Rapids, MI: Baker, 1972), 50.

17. Sidney B. Sperry, *Paul's Life and Letters* (Salt Lake City: Bookcraft, 1955), 271–72.

18. Raymond F. Collins offers several reasons why he believes the Timothy of Hebrews 13:23 was not Paul's friend and colleague (see Raymond F. Collins, *Letters That Paul Did Not Write*, in Good News Studies [Wilmington, DE: Michael Glazier, 1988], 20).

19. Brown, *Introduction to the New Testament*, 694n.

20. Hurst, *Epistle to the Hebrews*, 108.

21. Ehrman, *The New Testament*, 411.

22. Brown, *Introduction to the New Testament*, 694.

23. R. McLean Wilson, *Hebrews*, in New Century Bible Commentary (Grand Rapids, MI: Eerdmans, 1987), 3.

24. Kenneth Barker, ed., *The NIV Study Bible*, 10th ed. (Grand Rapids, MI: Zondervan, 1995), 1856.

25. For example, Homer A. Kent mentions three contemporary scholars who still view Paul as the author of Hebrews (see *Epistle to the Hebrews*, 18n).

26. For a more extensive survey of the opinions regarding authorship, see Koester, *Hebrews*, 19–46.

27. Koester, for example, explains, "Theological controversies in the forth and fifth centuries concluded several centuries of uncertainty about the status of Hebrews and led to the broad acceptance of Hebrews as canonical Scripture" (*Hebrews*, 19). Wilson writes, "The reservations of the Western Fathers are

probably based not only on grounds of authorship, but also on reasons of doctrine" (*Hebrews,* 4).

28. See Harold W. Attridge, *The Epistle to the Hebrews,* in Hermeneia—A Critical and Historical Commentary on the Bible (Philadelphia: Fortress, 1989), 2n.

29. For a description of this manuscript, see Bruce M. Metzgar and Bart D. Ehrman, *The Text of the New Testament: Its Transmission, Corruption, and Restoration,* 4th ed. (New York: Oxford University Press, 2005), 54–55.

30. Attridge writes, "Placement (of Hebrews) indicates the judgements about the authorship and genre of the work which were current in the Eastern church, or more specifically in Alexandria, by the middle of the second century" (*Epistle to the Hebrews,* 1). Bruce adds, "A Pauline codex of the same date [as that of P[46]] emanating from Rome would not have included Hebrews (the Roman church did not recognize Hebrews as Pauline until the fourth century)" (F. F. Bruce, *The Canon of Scripture* [Downers Grove, IL: InterVarsity, 1988], 130–31).

31. Eusebius, *History of the Church,* 3.3.

32. Origen, in Eusebius, *History of the Church,* 6.25.

33. For a translation of this text, see Bart D. Ehrman, *Lost Scripture: Books That Did Not Make It into the New Testament* (New York: Oxford University Press, 2003), 331–33.

34. See Koester, *Hebrews,* 22; Richard L. Anderson, *Understanding Paul* (Salt Lake City: Deseret Book, 1983), 197–98; The passage in 1 Clement is 36.1–5, which is similar to Hebrews 1:1–14; 2:17–18; 4:14–16.

35. On the other hand, Richard Anderson believes that 1 Clement's use of Hebrews is proof of Pauline authorship. He notes that all other quotations in the epistle come from letters attributed to Apostles and that at the time of the composition of 1 Clement, no other Apostle had been considered as the author of Hebrews. Therefore, according to Anderson, Hebrews must have been written by Paul (see *Understanding Paul,* 97).

36. Eusebius, *History of the Church,* 6.25.

37. Koester writes, "Western readers disputed the Pauline authorship of Hebrews and its authoritative status more vigorously than those in the east" (*Hebrews,* 23).

38. Tertullian, *De Pudicitia,* 20, in *Ancient Christian Writers,* trans. William P. Le Saint (New York: Newman, 1959), 115.

39. Eusebius, *History of the Church,* 6.20.

40. Eusebius, *History of the Church,* 3.3.

41. Bruce, *Canon of Scripture,* 165; for a translation of this text, see Bart D. Ehrman, *Lost Scripture,* 311–12.

42. Bruce, *Canon of Scripture,* 221.

43. Koester, *Hebrews,* 26. Arianism, named for Arius (AD 256–336), is a doctrine in which Christ the Son was understood as being created by God the Father and therefore not co-eternal with Him. The Council of Nicea (AD 325) condemned Arianism and formulated the Necean Creed, which advanced the doctrine of the trinity. See Dennis E. Groh, "Arius, Arianism," in *The Anchor Bible Dictionary,* ed. David Noel Freedman (New York: Doubleday, 1992).

44. Jerome, *Epistulae*, 129.7, in Koester, *Hebrews*, 27.

45. O. Rottmanner, in Alexander Souter, *Study of Ambrosiaster* (Cambridge: Cambridge University Press, 1905), 196n; see also Wilson, *Hebrews*, 3.

46. See William H. P. Hatch, "The Position of Hebrews in the Canon of the New Testament," *Harvard Theological Review* 29, no. 2 (April 1936): 133–51, for a complete study of the placement of Hebrews within the New Testament.

47. Hatch writes, "When the epistle was officially recognized it was appended to the end of the Pauline corpus" ("The Position of Hebrews," 144).

48. Dean C. Jessee, *Personal Writings of Joseph Smith*, rev. ed. (Salt Lake City: Deseret Book: 2002), 323.

49. Andrew F. Ehat and Lyndon W. Cook, *The Words of Joseph Smith: The Contemporary Accounts of the Nauvoo Discourses of the Prophet Joseph* (Provo, UT: Religious Studies Center, Brigham Young University, 1980), 4.

50. Koester, *Hebrews*, 21.

51. James E. Talmage, *The Articles of Faith* (Salt Lake City: Deseret Book, 1986), 472.

52. Hugh B. Brown, in Conference Report, April 1959, 110; Conference Report, October 1969, 105.

53. James E. Talmage, *Jesus the Christ* (Salt Lake City: Deseret Book, 1983), 127; *The Vitality of Mormonism* (Boston: Gorham Press, 1919), 356; Conference Report, October 1918, 59–60.

54. Charles W. Penrose, "Rays of Living Light," in *Handbook of the Restoration: A Selection of Gospel Themes Discussed by Various Authors* (Independence, MO: Zion's Printing and Publishing, 1944), 164.

55. Milton R. Hunter, *The Gospel through the Ages* (Salt Lake City: Stevens and Wallis, 1945), 78.

56. B. H. Roberts, *Contributor* 10, no. 12 (October 1889): 451–52.

57. Thomas S. Monson, *An Invitation to Exaltation* (Salt Lake City: Deseret Book, 1997), 3.

58. Howard W. Hunter, in Conference Report, April 1970, 8; "Faith: The First Step," in *Faith* (Salt Lake City: Deseret Book, 1983), 35.

59. John H. Vandenberg, in *BYU Speeches of the Year*, January 7, 1964, 8.

60. Spencer W. Kimball, *Faith Precedes the Miracle* (Salt Lake City: Deseret Book, 1972), 249.

61. I have used the WordCruncher search engine to examine the use of the phrase "writer of the book of Hebrews" in general conference talks from 1950 to 1970. It appears five times, while no other epistle is referred to using this phrase.

62. Joseph Fielding Smith, "The Martyrs," *Improvement Era*, June, 1944, 6; *The Progress of Man* (Salt Lake City: Deseret Book, 1964), 236–37; *The Restoration of All Things* (Salt Lake City: Deseret News, 1945), 186.

63. Joseph Fielding Smith, *Answers to Gospel Questions* (Salt Lake City: Deseret Book, 1992), 1:188; 4:91.

64. Scott H. Faulring, Kent P. Jackson, and Robert J. Matthews, eds., *Joseph Smith's New Translation of the Bible: Original Manuscripts* (Provo, UT: Religious Studies Center, Brigham Young University, 2004), 535.

65. Ehat and Cook, *The Words of Joseph Smith*, 40, emphasis added.

66. Holzapfel, Huntsman, and Wayment, *Jesus Christ and the World of the New Testament*.

67. Hurst, after comparing the theology of Hebrews and that of Paul, writes: "This evidence leads us to draw the following three conclusions: (1) The differences rule out Hebrews as 'deutero-Pauline' in the sense of literary borrowing by a Pauline disciple. (2) The similarities indicate an interaction with the same ideas normally identified with Paul himself, and rule out the view of Ménégoz and others that *Auctor* could *not* at some point have been a disciple of Paul. (3) If it is recognized that there is a sense in which the apostolic tradition grew in a way in which Paul and his associates may have had a significant part, there may be a basis for claiming Pauline influence in the epistle without recourse to the literary solution. Taken in this highly qualified sense, then, the phrase 'deutero-Pauline' might be suitable for Hebrews" (*Epistle to the Hebrews*, 124).

68. Eusebius, *History of the Church*, 6.25.

69. See Bruce, *Canon of Scripture*, 161; 124–25.

70. J. Reuben Clark, *On the Way to Immortality and Eternal Life* (Salt Lake City: Deseret Book, 1950), 210.

71. Wilson, *Hebrews*, 4.

72. Jerome, *Epistle*, 129.3, in Bruce, *Canon of Scripture*, 227.

73. Bruce R. McConkie, *Doctrinal New Testament Commentary* (Salt Lake City: Bookcraft, 1973), 3:133.

16

THE EARLIEST "NEW TESTAMENT"

Richard D. Draper

One of the ironies of ecclesiastical history is that the New Testament as a whole is one of the primary legacies of the early Christian Church, yet there is virtually no information on who brought it together, precisely when, or even how. The development of this wonderful book was totally separate from the theological debates of the third- and fourth-century councils and therefore did not receive the documentation those councils' debates and decisions did. As one scholar observed, "Nothing is more amazing in the annals of the Christian Church than the absence of detailed accounts of so significant a process."[1]

From a Latter-day Saint perspective, the lack of such accounts is not all that amazing. We have the Pearl of Great Price as an example in our own history. One might expect that, given the fact that the book became one of the standard works, the Church would possess a detailed record of its development. As a matter of fact, information on its creation and compilation is rather sparse. We know who originally

---

Richard D. Draper is a professor of ancient scripture at Brigham Young University.

created it and why, and some of the process, but not a lot else. Further, after its initial publication in England, and in spite of the fact that it contained material many recognized as significant, inspired, and authoritative, it made little impact for over two decades. Eventually, those at the highest levels of the Church became aware of it, saw its importance, and in 1880 canonized it. However, accounts of the discussions leading up to the work's presentation for canon are rather thin.[2]

What we learn from the Pearl of Great Price in our own history is that people were doing their best to preserve and disseminate materials that they felt were important and holy. It was not the process that was significant to them but the material itself. As a result, they left scanty records of the editorial process. This same condition seems to have applied during the time that early Christians copied, collected, organized, and eventually brought the New Testament documents into the Christian canon. "The history of its formation," Bruce Metzger writes, "is the history, not of a series of sporadic events, but of a long, continuous process. It was a task, not only of collection, but also of sifting and rejecting. Instead of being the result of a deliberate decree by an individual or a council near the beginning of the Christian era, the collection of New Testament books took place gradually over many years by the pressure of various kinds."[3]

Metzger's words best apply to the final form of the canon, but such a scenario does not work for those documents that to me are the core writings. This chapter, in fact, takes exception to the idea that these documents were gathered gradually over many decades.[4] Instead, it will show that around the turn of the first century, a significant segment of the disparate Christian groups, one which I will refer to as the proto-orthodox, had a collection of writings which they held sacred and used in their scattered congregations from Rome to Egypt. Further, this paper will show that the documents that composed this core highly influenced the final compilation of what we call the New Testament today.

A real benefit for the later church was that because they were collected early, these documents were protected against the most flagrant abuses and thus preserved accurate accounts for later generations.[5]

THE EARLIEST RECORDS

In the year Jesus died not a single document that would eventually make up the New Testament existed. Indeed, there was no written standard for the Church outside the Old Testament. It is very likely, as many scholars believe, that Jesus wrote neither book nor letter. But did he expect His disciples to do likewise? Nothing in the Bible suggests that He did, but an interesting statement in Joseph Smith—Matthew opens the door to the possibility. There the Lord predicts the fulfill-ment of the prophecy of Daniel concerning the desolation of abomi-nation. He then instructs the Saints that when this sign is given, they "shall stand in the holy place; whoso *readeth* let him understand. Then let them who are in Judea flee" (Joseph Smith—Matthew 1:12–13, emphasis added). The Lord's instructions may be based on the com-mon practice at the time where, during worship services, one read and the congregation listened. The Lord's words suggest He assumed that one of those who were with Him that day would preserve the warning in written form so that the next generation of leaders could read it to their congregations and all would know how to respond to the sign.[6]

This suggestion does not preclude the possibility that the early Christians passed on the Lord's teachings orally (an opinion held by many scholars). From evidence clear to Latter-day Saints, however, it seems likely that there were some records even from the earliest period, especially if the Book of Mormon provides a model. It shows that the people were expected to pass along the Lord's teachings both orally and in written form. This condition resulted from instructions given by none other than the Lord Himself. In instructing the people, He said, "Blessed are ye if ye shall give heed unto the *words* of these twelve," which words would include His doctrine and teachings (3 Nephi 12:1, emphasis added). He went on to say, "Blessed are they who shall believe in your *words* because that ye shall testify that ye have seen me" (3 Nephi 12:2, emphasis added), suggesting that much would be passed on through word of mouth. After giving His major sermon, He admonished His hearers that "whoso remembereth these sayings of mine and doeth them, him will I raise up at the last day" (3 Nephi 15:1). These words suggest the Lord expected His hearers to remember and pass on His teachings—that is, to create an oral tradition.

The record also, however, shows that He had additional expectations. He commanded His leaders to "write these sayings after I am gone" (3 Nephi 16:4). He explained, at least in part, why it was important: a time would come, according to "the will of the Father," when "they [His words] shall go forth unto the Gentiles" (3 Nephi 23:4). He explained further that the disciples must "write the things which ye have seen and heard, save it be those which are forbidden. . . . For behold, out of the books which have been written, and which shall be written, shall this people be judged, for by them shall their works be known unto men" (3 Nephi 27:23–25). The Church leaders were faithful to their charge, and therefore Mormon could report that "the plates of Nephi do contain the more part of the things which he [Jesus] taught the people" (3 Nephi 26:7).

It is clear that the Lord took great pains to see that the Nephites recorded His words, in part so His teachings could go forth unto the latter-day Gentiles and also form the basis of judgment. It seems reasonable that He would have taken the same pains with the words He shared with His Jewish followers. After all, they too would take His word to the Gentiles.

Admittedly, there is little evidence that written records existed among the early Christians before the sixth decade, but there is some.[7] Eusebius reported that Mark recorded and disseminated Peter's memoirs not long after the latter's death.[8] At the beginning of his Gospel, Luke, writing about that time, notes he used preexisting written source material (see Acts 1:1–2). Though some believe these may have been little more than lists of quotes attributed to Jesus,[9] the documentary evidence suggests that the Christians had more than a mere collection of sayings. It appears that they had access to full and descriptive accounts, and these documents made up the bulk of their sacred material.[10]

THE COLLECTION OF CORE MATERIALS

Recently, some scholars have rejected the idea that the documents in the modern Bible came together slowly. David Trobish maintains that an edition of the Bible, not simply a collection of documents, existed before the mid-second century that exactly matched the books in the modern Bible. He uses the text-critical method as the basis of his work. As appealing as I find his view, it seems overstated because historical sources do not bear out his full position. On the other hand, those same sources do suggest that collections of documents existed very early. That is not to say that each collection was exactly the same as every other. In fact, it is likely that they were not. Some congregations had materials others did not have access to, and some included materials that other congregations rejected. The point is, however, that though the collections may have differed in the details, the core material was the same.[11]

The core consisted of materials written during the first century AD. To establish what documents formed the core that the proto-orthodox church gathered and disseminated, this chapter examines the scriptures included in the preserved noncanonical materials produced between roughly AD 80 and 140.[12] Those who produced these writings are known collectively as the Apostolic Fathers. The quotes they used and paraphrases they made reveal which writings were available to them. It is of note that these seem to have been in place by the time the last of the Apostles, John, left the scene and therefore witness that the Christians had a basic Christian Bible in place before the apostolic era ended.

A NOTE ON PROCEDURE

Before turning to the Apostolic Fathers to determine which books formed the core and in what geographical areas they appeared, a note of procedure seems in order.

The Apostolic Fathers quoted materials that would make up both the Old and New Testaments. How they used the Old Testament provides a window on how to detect New Testament inferences in their writings when they give no attribution. For example, we can suppose that those writers who were careful in quoting an Old Testament passage would do so with the New Testament, thus making the pieces they used easy to identify. Conversely, those who used Old Testament material in a less accurate way would do so with the New Testament as well, thus making it more difficult to detect the source of their teachings.[13] It is apparent that most of these early Christian writers relied greatly on their memories and therefore seldom produced exact quotes of the passages they cited or used.

Only rarely do the writers actually name the piece they are quoting or paraphrasing. They often signal a quote with a phrase like, "As it is written," "According to the Lord," or "It has been said," and so forth. More often, however, they simply work the material into their arguments without any attribution whatsoever. Since Matthew, Mark, and Luke share many stories and sayings, determining which Gospel an author had in mind presents difficulties. Fortunately, in many instances there are sufficient differences in the original accounts to make a determination or, at worst, an educated guess as to the source.

For the purposes of this study, a passage must fall into one of four categories in order to be identified as a New Testament piece. First, there is the actual quote, in which the material is introduced by a *formula citandi* (words such as "The Lord said," or "It has been written"). The next category is the paraphrase, where it is obvious where the material came from due to the use of identical or near identical phrases. Next is similarity of thought, where only a word or two are identical, but the thought is the same. Finally, there is the allusion, which has no words in common, but we can postulate the source of the idea.[14]

In our analysis, however, we cannot assume that the Apostolic Fathers quoted from every piece in their collections. For example, none of the Apostolic Fathers quote from Paul's epistle to Philemon,[15] yet it is found on the earliest lists of authentic books. Thus, silence does not prove a work's absence, only that it contained nothing useful for the Apostolic Fathers' current debates or admonitions. Even so, this chapter does not list unused works, like Philemon, as part of the core documents.

THE CORE THAT FORMED THE EARLIEST COLLECTIONS

Fortunately, there are enough secure references in these early writings to establish the core materials. Looking at the locations where the writers lived gives a view of how widespread the collections were.[16] We have writings from Rome, Asia Minor, Syria, and Egypt. Thus, the writings represent a large area surrounding the Mediterranean Sea, covering the area where early Christians congregated and collected sacred writings.

Most theologians and students of the Bible agree that the writings of Paul were the earliest written materials and that certain congregations collected and disseminated them. Debate still flourishes over when the Gospels were written, but most agree that the Gospels of Matthew, Mark, and Luke were written well before the end of the first century, while John's was written toward the end.[17] By AD 125, the Gospel writings seem to have formed a collection of their own, which early Christians added to the Pauline collection, thus providing the proto-orthodox group with a kind of standard work which was widely recognized and used. But do the writings of the Apostolic Fathers bear out this model?

Though the following is painted with a rather broad brush, so to speak, the ancient literature allows us to make the following conclusions.

First, the four Gospels were all known. With the exception of Clement of Rome and Polycarp, all the early writers use them.

Second, there is good evidence that the documents formed a single collection very early. Ignatius, bishop in Syrian Antioch, writing about AD 115, referred in his works to "the Gospel" as an authoritative document. Since his writing shows that he knew of more than one such document, it seems that the phrase "the Gospel" referred to the fourfold collection. His words, with those of others, imply that Christians viewed Matthew, Mark, Luke, and John as a single Gospel having four parts, and that this Gospel was compiled around the turn of the century.[18]

Third, the book of Acts is well attested. It may have been that Acts was separated from Luke's Gospel when the Gospels were made into a collection. With the possible exception of Barnabas and Papias, all the early writings show the authors were familiar with Acts and considered it authoritative.[19]

Fourth, of the epistles of Paul, all are well certified with the exception of 2 Timothy, Titus, and Philemon. Hebrews, often separated from Paul, is cited as well (though only by Clement, Ignatius, Barnabas, and the Shepherd of Hermas). Even so, the extant references show this work was known in Rome, Syria, and Egypt.

Finally, of the general epistles, only 1 Peter, 1 John, and Jude are referenced. The book of Revelation is poorly attested this early.

Taken all together, the writings of the Apostolic Fathers suggest that widely separated Christian congregations held similar collections of writings.[20] From Egypt to Rome, the proto-orthodox churches were using a set of holy materials that consisted of the four Gospels and the epistles of Paul, except perhaps for 2 Timothy, Titus, and Philemon. They also had at least 1 John and 1 Peter. This is not to say that the other works that eventually made their way into the New Testament were unknown. It only shows that the Apostolic Fathers did not use them in their extant writings. Thus, some collections may have actually approached the content of the modern New Testament.

It is likely, as noted above, that no one congregation had a collection of scriptures exactly like another's.[21] Some of the collections that have survived, albeit not before the fourth century, include noncanonical works like the Shepherd of Hermas, the Didache, and 1 Clement, while others do not.[22] The core documents, however, seem to have held a place in the major collections of the early second century, whatever else those collections may have contained.

It is also likely that the collections did not stay stagnant as the Church moved through the second century. Documents continued to surface and circulate. Many of these found their way into collections but more easily into those of congregations that did not follow the path of the proto-orthodox. Before the end of the second century, a large number of documents competed with the core material as authentic and deserving of credit. Many of these were rejected out of hand by the emerging orthodox community, while others found some acceptance. Eventually, some of the latter became what we now call the New Testament Apocrypha.[23]

IMPETUS TO MAKE A CANON

By the third century, the emerging orthodox congregations felt the need for a standard collection of scripture, a canon. To serve their purposes, they determined that the work had to be unalterable; once it was formed, nothing could be added and nothing taken away. It would act as the foundation for belief, practice, and faith forevermore, thus guarding the church from all the false writings and their negative influence.

It is of note that those who gathered and disseminated the original core documents had different motivation than those who were working for a canon. Devout persons developed the early collections from a desire to preserve the words and acts of the Lord. Those who sought to establish the canon of scripture, on the other hand, sought to produce a document they could use to prove they were the true Christians.[24] It is neither an accident nor coincidence that some of the leaders of the emerging orthodox church threw their energy into hardening a canon *after* Marcion published his personal, highly edited, and tilted version of the scriptures about the middle of the second century. His work seems to have galvanized them into working toward a sacred text according to their standards.[25] Widespread acceptance of their canon would validate their right to rule God's kingdom on earth and to declare His truth.

FIVE CRITERIA FOR CANONIZATION

Over time, they settled upon five interrelated criteria that a document must meet to enter their canon. The major criterion was whether the piece conformed to the "rule of faith." In other words, for these later leaders, the first and foremost point of judgment was the work's content.[26] This fact suggests that, contrary to a number of scholars who insist on a late development of christology and soteriology, the nascent church had a concrete view of who Jesus was and what He did. The core documents preserved this view and formed the foundation of the criterion as the orthodox Fathers used it.[27] Defenders of the faith such as Tertullian, Clement of Rome, Dionysus of Alexandria, and Novatian, all held to this "rule of truth" or "canon of truth" as they defended the orthodox position. Any book not in harmony with these teachings they deemed unorthodox and excluded it from the list of acceptable works.[28] The evidence suggests that one of the reasons the orthodox won the day was because they stayed closest to the core documents that the nascent church had bequeathed to them.[29]

A second criterion that played a very important part in the acceptance of a writing was its antiquity. The compilers accepted those works
which were known to have originated during the first century. For
example, the Muratorian Canon, an early list of accepted books,
rejected the Shepherd of Hermas, though it was composed well before
the mid-second century and prized by many branches, because it considered the Shepherd too recent a production.[30] Writings that claimed
to originate from the Lord's Apostles drew careful attention from the
orthodox theologians. To make it into the canon, however, the piece
had to have a known link to the past. The compilers rejected those documents known to have never been a part of any collection; they felt that
only previously collected documents that came from eyewitnesses or
careful historians of the past age should have place in the canon.[31]

A third criterion was how continuously used and widespread a text
was. In other words, popularity gave a text additional weight. Little
wonder the core documents were readily accepted; they were known
from an early date and used all over the empire. The compilers were
suspicious of any text they felt was of unknown origin or that only a few
branches accepted. On the other hand, if a document had a good following, its chance of getting into the canon was high. For example, the
eastern church's widespread use of the epistle to the Hebrews pushed
the more skeptical West to adopt it, while the Western church's use of
the book of Revelation highly influenced its acceptance in the East.[32]

The fourth criterion, and closely related to the one above, was a
work's traditional use. If a work meeting the other criteria reflected
what "had always been done" or "what has been believed from the
beginning," it usually qualified as a canonical text.[33] Again, it was the
core documents that supplied the criterion. During the third or fourth
centuries, if a leader brought into an orthodox congregation a work he
claimed was authentic, but no one had heard of it and it contained
materials not in conformity with what was known before, the orthodox
community rejected it. The same was true if a work had been known
from the past but had not been seen as scripture. For example, though
the letter of Clement of Rome was well known, often read in church
services, and reflected proper church order, no congregation ever

considered it to be in the same class as the apostolic writings, and it therefore found no place in the orthodox canon.[34]

The last criterion, and one the compilers found less easy to apply, was the work's tie to revelation. For the orthodox Fathers, revelation meant the action of the Holy Spirit that allowed God's leaders to speak His word. The compilers tried to determine if a revelation from God was the ultimate source of the work in question. All felt this factor was important, but various communities interpreted its expression differently. For example, the West emphasized the apostolicity of a work, while the East stressed its inspiration. Admittedly, the two positions were not mutually exclusive; the West felt that inspiration lay behind the Apostles, while the East felt that the Apostles received inspiration. At heart, both groups felt a work had to be inspired to be eligible for the canon. For example, the book of Revelation does not appeal to apostolic authority, but it does cite the spirit and power of inspiration that came upon its author. Therefore, as noted, many western Christian leaders accepted it, and the weight of their opinion brought it into the canon.[35]

SUMMARY

During the early third century, the orthodox church authorities adopted these five criteria as the litmus test for authenticity. That did not mean, however, that all applied the various criteria in exactly the same way. Some weighed one category more heavily than another; some accepted the word of this or that former leader over others, some felt that acceptance by branches in more prestigious areas made a document more holy even if it was not used in a majority of places. Still, the criteria allowed for the remaining pieces of the New Testament to be gathered with the already extant core material.

The point is, though the fringes of the New Testament canon remained unsettled for centuries, the core documents were in place before the apostolic era closed. The proto-orthodox preserved, used, and passed these works on, leaving the developing orthodox Christians with a standard which they could use to eventually agree upon a complete and accurate canon. It is important to note that these books did not become authoritative because they were formally put into the canon. Rather, the orthodox Christians included them in the canon because they were already authoritative. It was not until the last decade of the fourth century that the orthodox councils codified the New Testament. When they did so, they imposed nothing new on the Church but codified what was already accepted and practiced.[36]

The degree to which these final compilers succeeded can be readily seen by comparing those works that were placed in the Bible with those that were not. The quality, majesty, testimony, and inspiration in those twenty-seven books far surpasses those excluded from the canon, including such popular pieces as 1 Clement and the Didache. That such is the case should not be surprising, given the gift the earliest Christians gave the later Church in the composition, collection, and publishing of those core documents. In so doing, they, along with the inspiration of the Holy Spirit, provided the guidelines for the makeup of the final edition and preserved the Lord's teachings for us today.

NEW TESTAMENT PASSAGES IN THE APOSTOLIC FATHERS

Category A=quoted from original source; B=paraphrase of a source; C=similarity of thought to a source; D=allusion to source.

NT PASSAGE	FATHER(S)	WORK	CATEGORY
Matt. 3:7	Ignatius	Eph. 11:1	D
Matt. 3:15	Ignatius	Smyr. 1:1	B
Matt. 5:5	Didache	Did. 3:7	D
Matt. 5:7	Clement	1 Clem. 13:1f	D
Matt. 5:13	Ignatius	Eph. 11:1	D
Matt. 5:26	Didache	Did. 1:5	D
Matt. 5:28	Hermas	Mand. 4:1:1	D
Matt. 5:35	Hermas	Vis. 3:9:8	C
Matt. 5:39–42	Didache	Did. 1:4–6	D
Matt. 5:44	Didache	Did. 1:3	D
	Polycarp	Pol. 12:3	D
Matt. 5:47	Didache	Did. 1:3	D
Matt. 6:5, 9–13	Didache	Did. 8:1f	C

NT Passage	Father(s)	Work	Category
Matt. 6:12	Polycarp	Pol. 6:1, 2	D
Matt. 6:16	Didache	Did. 8:1f	C
Matt. 6:24	Clement	2 Clem. 6:1f	D
Matt. 7:1	Polycarp	Pol. 2:3	D
Matt. 7:12	Didache	Did. 1:2	D
Matt. 7:15	Didache	Did. 16:3–5	D
Matt. 7:15, 16	Hermas	Mand. 40:16	C
Matt. 7:21	Clement	2 Clem. 4:2	C
Matt. 7:23	Clement	2 Clem. 4:5	D
Matt. 8:17	Ignatius	Pol. 1:2, 3	B
Matt. 9:11, 13	Barnabas	Barn. 5:9	D
Matt. 9:13	Barnabas	Barn. 5:9	D
	Clement	2 Clem. 2:4	D
Matt. 10:10	Didache	Did. 13:1	C
Matt. 10:16	Ignatius	Pol. 2:2	B
	Clement	2 Clem. 5:2–4	D
Matt. 10:22	Shepherd	Vis. 2:2:7	C
Matt. 10:28	Hermas	Mand. 12:6:3	C
Matt. 10:32	Clement	2 Clem. 3:2	C
Matt. 10:33	Shepherd	Vis. 2:2:8	D
Matt. 10:40	Ignatius	Pol. 2:2	B
	Ignatius	Rom. 9:3	B
Matt. 10:41	Ignatius	Rom. 9:3	B
Matt. 11:28	Clement	2 Clem. 5:5; 6:7	C
Matt. 12:31	Didache	Did. 11:7	C
Matt. 12:33	Ignatius	Eph. 14:2	D
Matt. 13:3	Clement of Rome	1 Clem. 24:5	D
Matt. 13:17	Polycarp	Pol. 1:3	D
Matt. 13:20, 21	Hermas	Vis. 3:4:5	D
Matt. 15:8	Clement of Rome	1 Clem. 15:2	D
Matt. 15:13	Ignatius	Trall. 9:1; Phila. 3:1	B
Matt. 16:26	Ignatius	Rom. 6:1	D
	Clement	2 Clem. 6:1f	D

NT Passage	Father(s)	Work	Category
Matt. 18:3	Hermas	Sim. 9:29:1,3	D
	Hermas	Sim. 9:1–3	D
Matt. 18:17	Polycarp	Pol. 11:2	D
Matt. 18:19, 20	Ignatius	Eph. 5:2	B
Matt. 19:9	Hermas	Mand. 4:1:1	D
Matt. 19:12	Ignatius	Smyr. 6:1	B
Matt. 19:23	Hermas	Sim. 9:20:2	D
Matt. 20:28	Polycarp	Pol. 5:2	D
Matt. 21:33	Hermas	Sim. 5:2:1	D
Matt. 22:11–13	Hermas	Mand. 12:1:2	C
	Clement	2 Clem. 6:9	C
Matt. 22:14	Barnabas	Bar. 4:14	D
Matt. 22:19	Ignatius	Magn. 5:2	B
Matt. 22:37	Clement	2 Clem. 3:4	D
Matt. 22:37–39	Didache	Did. 1:2	D
Matt. 22:41–45	Barnabas	Bar. 12:10	D
Matt. 23:34f	Barnabas	Bar. 6:6	D
Matt. 24:10–13	Didache	Did. 16:3–5	D
Matt. 24:13	Hermas	Vis. 2:2:7	C
Matt. 24:24	Didache	Did. 16:3–5	D
Matt. 24:30f	Didache	Did. 16:6	D
Matt. 24:42	Didache	Did. 16:1	D
Matt. 25:14	Hermas	Sim. 5:2:1	D
Matt. 25:45f	Clement	2 Clem. 5:5; 6:7	C
Matt. 26:7	Ignatius	Eph. 17:1	B
Matt. 26:24	Clement	1 Clem. 46:7, 8	D
	Hermas	Vis. 4:2:6	D
Matt. 26:31	Barnabas	Barn. 5:12	D
Matt. 26:63f	Barnabas	Barn. 7:9	D
Matt. 27:14	Barnabas	Barn. 7:3	D
Matt. 27:28	Barnabas	Barn. 7:9	D
Matt. 27:35	Barnabas	Barn. 6:6	D
Matt. 27:52	Ignatius	Magn. 9:3	B

NT Passage	Father(s)	Work	Category
Matt. 28:18	Hermas	Sim 5:6:4	C
Matt. 28:19f	Clement	2 Clem. 17:1	D
Mark 2:16f	Barnabas	Barn. 5:9	D
Mark 2:17	Clement	2 Clem. 2:4	D
Mark 3:28	Didache	Did. 11:7	C
Mark 3:35	Clement	2 Clem. 9:11	D
Mark 4:3	Clement	1 Clem. 24:5	D
Mark 4:18, 19	Hermas	Sim. 9:20:1, 2	D
Mark 6:52	Hermas	Mand. 4:2:1	C
Mark 7:6	Clement	1 Clem. 15:2	D
Mark 8:16	Clement	2 Clem. 6:1f	D
Mark 8:38	Ignatius	Smyr. 10:2	D
	Hermas	Sim. 8:6:4; 9:14:6	
Mark 9:35	Polycarp	Pol. 5:2	D
Mark 9:43	Ignatius	Eph. 16:1	D
Mark 9:50	Ignatius	Magn. 10:2	D
Mark 10:11	Hermas	Mand. 4:1:6	D
Mark 12:1	Hermas	Sim. 5:2:1	D
Mark 12:3–37	Barnabas	Bar. 12:10	D
Mark 12:7	Hermas	Sim. 5:2:1	D
Mark 12:30	Clement	2 Clem. 3:4	D
Mark 12:37	Barnabas	Bar. 12:10	D
Mark 13:13	Didache	Did. 16:3–5	D
Mark 14:21	Hermas	Vis. 4:2:6	D
Mark 14:27	Barnabas	Barn. 5:12	D
Mark 14:38	Polycarp	Pol. 7:2	D
Mark 14:61f	Barnabas	Barn. 7:9	D
Mark 15:17	Barnabas	Barn. 7:9	D
Mark 15:24	Barnabas	Barn. 6:6	D
Luke 5:8	Barnabas	Barn. 5:9	D
Luke 5:32	Barnabas	Barn. 5:9	D
	Clement	2 Clem. 2:4	D

NT Passage	Father(s)	Work	Category
Luke 6:27	Polycarp	Pol. 13:3	D
Luke 6:27–33	Didache	Did. 1:3	D
Luke 6:29, 30	Didache	Did. 1:4–6	D
Luke 6:31, 36	Clement	1 Clem. 13:1f	D
Luke 6:32, 35	Clement	2 Clem. 13:4	D
Luke 6:36	Clement	1 Clem. 13:1f	D
	Polycarp	Pol. 2:3	D
Luke 6:44	Ignatius	Eph. 14:2	D
Luke 8:5	Clement	1 Clem. 24:5	D
Luke 8:14	Hermas	Sim. 9:20:1, 2	D
Luke 8:21	Clement	2 Clem. 9:21	D
Luke 9:25	Clement	2 Clem. 4:1f	D
Luke 9:26	Ignatius	Smyr. 10:2	D
	Hermas	Sim. 8:6:4; 9:14:6	D
Luke 10:3	Clement	2 Clem. 5:2–4	D
Luke 10:7	Didache	Did. 13:1	D
Luke 10:27	Clement	2 Clem. 3:4	D
Luke 11:4	Polycarp	Pol. 4:1, 2	D
	Polycarp	Pol. 1:3	D
Luke 11:49f	Barnabas	Barn. 5:11	D
Luke 12:8	Clement	2 Clem. 3:2	C
Luke 12:35	Didache	1 Clem. 16:1	D
Luke 13:27	Clement	2 Clem. 4:5	D
Luke 14:34	Ignatius	Magn. 10:2	D
Luke 16:10f	Clement	2 Clem. 8:5	D
Luke 16:13	Clement	2 Clem. 4:1f	D
Luke 17:1	Clement	1 Clem 46:7, 8	D
Luke 18:1	Hermas	Mand. 9:8	D
Luke 19:10	Clement	2 Clem.2:5–7	D
Luke 19:13	Hermas	Sim. 5:2:1	D
Luke 20:9	Hermas	Sim. 5:2:1	D
Luke 20:14	Hermas	Sim. 5:2:1	D

NT Passage	Father(s)	Work	Category
Luke 20:41–44	Barnabas	Barn. 12:10	D
Luke 22:17–19	Didache	Did. 11:2	D
Luke 22:69f	Barnabas	Barn. 7:9	D
Luke 23:7–12	Ignatius	Smyr. 1:2	D
Luke 23:34	Barnabas	Barn. 6:6	D
Luke 24:39	Ignatius	Smyr. 3:2	D
John 3:3–5	Hermas	Sim. 9:15:3	D
John 3:8	Ignatius	Phil. 7:1	B
John 3:14f	Barnabas	Barn. 12:7	D
John 4:10, 14	Ignatius	Rom. 7:2	B
John 5:21	Polycarp	Pol. 5:2	C
John 6:33	Ignatius	Eph. 5:2; Rom. 7:3	B
John 6:51	Ignatius	Barn. 6:3	D
John 6:58	Ignatius	Barn. 6:3	D
John 8:28, 29	Ignatius	Magn. 7:1	B
John 10:7, 9	Hermas	Sim. 9:12:1	D
John 10:18	Hermas	Sim. 5:6:3	D
John 11:25	Hermas	Vis. 2:2:8	D
John 12:3	Ignatius	Eph. 17:1	B
John 13:20	Ignatius	Eph. 6:1	B
John 14:6	Hermas	Vis. 2:2:8	D
John 15:16	Polycarp	Pol. 12:3	C
John 19:34	Barnabas	Barn. 11:1ff, 8	D
Acts 1:24	Hermas	Mand. 4:3:4	D
Acts 1:25	Ignatius	Magn. 5:1	D
Acts 2:24	Polycarp	Pol. 1:2	C
Acts 4:12	Hermas	Vis. 4:2:4	D
Acts 4:32	Didache	Did. 4:8	D
Acts 5:41	Hermas	Sim. 9:14:6	D
Acts 7:52	Polycarp	Pol. 2:1	C
Acts 10:41	Ignatius	Smyr. 3:3	D
Acts 10:42	Polycarp	Pol. 2:1	C
Acts 13:22	Rome	1 Clem. 18:1	C

NT Passage	Father(s)	Work	Category
Acts 15:20, 29	Didache	Did. 1:2	D
Acts 20:35	Clement	1 Clem. 2:1	C
	Polycarp	Pol. 2:3	C
Acts 26:18	Clement	1 Clem. 59:2	C
	Polycarp	Pol. 12:2	C
Rom. 1:3, 4	Ignatius	Smyr. 1:1	C
Rom. 1:21	Clement	1 Clem. 36:2	A
	Clement	2 Clem. 19:2	D
Rom. 1:29–32	Clement	1 Clem. 35: 5, 6	A
Rom. 4:3, 10f	Barnabas	Barn. 13:7	B
Rom. 4:17	Barnabas	Barn. 13:7	B
	Clement	2 Clem. 1:8	D
Rom. 6:1	Clement	1 Clem. 33:1	A
Rom. 6:4	Ignatius	Eph. 19:3	C
Rom. 8:26, 27	Hermas	Mand. 10:2:5	D
Rom. 9:5	Clement	1 Clem. 32:2	A
Rom. 9:7–13	Barnabas	Barn. 13:2–3	B
Rom. 9:21	Clement	2 Clem. 8:2	D
Rom. 11:33	Clement	Clem. 40:1	A
Rom. 12:4	Clement	1 Clem. 38:1	A
Rom. 12:9	Didache	Did. 5:2	D
Rom. 12:17	Polycarp	Pol. 5:1	B
Rom. 15:29	Ignatius	Eph. (Inscription)	C
1 Cor. 1:7	Ignatius	Eph. 11:1	A
1 Cor. 1:10	Ignatius	Eph. 2:3	A
1 Cor. 1:11–13	Clement	1 Clem. 47:1	A
1 Cor. 1:18–20	Ignatius	Ep. 28:1	A
1 Cor. 1: 24, 30	Ignatius	Eph. 17:2	A
1 Cor. 2:9	Clement	1 Clem. 34:8	A
	Clement	2 Clem. 11:7; 14:5	D
1 Cor. 2:10	Clement	1 Clem. 40:1	A
	Ignatius	Phila. 7:1	A
1 Cor. 2:14	Ignatius	Eph. 8:2	A
1 Cor. 3:1	Barnabas	Barn. 4:11	D

NT Passage	Father(s)	Work	Category
1 Cor. 3:2	Ignatius	Trall. 5:1	A
1 Cor. 3:15	Clement	2 Clem. 9:3	D
1 Cor. 3:16	Barnabas	Barn. 6:11ff	C
	Barnabas	Barn. 4:11	D
	Ignatius	Eph. 15:3	A
1 Cor. 4:1	Ignatius	Trall. 2:3	A
1 Cor. 4:4	Ignatius	Rom. 5:1	A
1 Cor. 5:7	Ignatius	Magn. 10:3	A
1 Cor. 6:2	Polycarp	Pol. 11:2	A
1 Cor. 6:9	Ignatius	Eph. 16:1	A
	Polycarp	Pol. 5:3	A
1 Cor. 6:10	Ignatius	Eph. 16:1	A
1 Cor. 6:15	Clement	1 Clem. 46:7	A
	Ignatius	Eph. 4:2	A
1 Cor. 6:19	Clement	2 Clem. 9:3	D
1 Cor. 7:10	Ignatius	Trall. 6:1	D
1 Cor. 7:29	Ignatius	Eph. 11:1	A
1 Cor. 7:39, 40	Hermas	Mand. 4:4:1, 2	B
1 Cor. 8:10	Polycarp	Pol. 3:2	A
1 Cor. 9:15	Ignatius	Rom. 6:1	A
1 Cor. 9:24	Clement	1 Clem. 5:1, 5	A
	Clement	2 Clem. 7:1	D
1 Cor. 9:25	Clement	2 Clem. 7:1	D
1 Cor. 9:27	Ignatius	Trall. 12:3	A
1 Cor. 10:4	Hermas	Sim. 9:12:1	A
1 Cor. 10:16, 17	Ignatius	Phila. 4:1	A
1 Cor. 10:24	Clement	1 Clem. 48:6	A
1 Cor. 10:33	Clement	1 Clem. 48:6	A
1 Cor. 12:8, 9	Clement	1 Clem. 48:5	A
1 Cor. 12:12	Clement	1 Clem. 46:7	A
	Ignatius	Trall. 11:2	A
1 Cor. 12:12ff	Clement	1 Clem. 37:5	A
1 Cor. 12:26	Ignatius	Pol. 11:4	A
1 Cor. 13:4–7	Clement	1 Clem. 49:5	A

NT Passage	Father(s)	Work	Category
1 Cor. 13:13	Ignatius	Pol. 3:2, 3	A
1 Cor. 14:10	Ignatius	Pol. 11:4	A
1 Cor. 14:20	Hermas	Sim. 9:29	D
1 Cor. 14:25	Ignatius	Pol. 4:3	A
1 Cor. 15:8–10	Ignatius	Rom. 9:2	A
1 Cor. 15:20	Clement	1 Clem. 24:1	A
1 Cor. 15:23	Clement	1 Clem. 24:1; 37:3	A
1 Cor. 15:26	Ignatius	Pol. 2:1	A
1 Cor. 15:36, 37	Clement	1 Clem. 24:4, 5	A
1 Cor. 15:45, 47	Ignatius	Eph. 20:1	A
1 Cor. 15:58	Ignatius	Eph. 10:2; 20:1	A
	Polycarp	Pol. 10:1	A
1 Cor. 16:17	Clement	1 Clem. 38:2	A
1 Cor. 16:18	Ignatius	Eph. 2:2	A
1 Cor. 16:22	Didache	Did. 10:6	D
2 Cor. 3:2	Polycarp	Pol. 11:3	B
2 Cor. 3:18	Clement	1 Clem. 36:2	D
2 Cor. 4:14	Ignatius	Trall. 9:2	C
	Polycarp	Pol. 2:2	B
2 Cor. 5:10	Barnabas	Barn. 4:11f	D
	Polycarp	Pol. 6:2	A
	Polycarp	Pol. 4:2	B
2 Cor. 5:17	Barnabas	Barn. 6:11–13	B
2 Cor. 6:7	Polycarp	Pol. 4:1	B
2 Cor. 6:16	Ignatius	Eph. 15:3	C
2 Cor. 8:21	Polycarp	Pol. 5:1	B
2 Cor. 9:8	Clement	1 Clem. 2:7; 24:4	C
2 Cor. 9:12	Clement	1 Clem. 38:2	A
2 Cor. 11:9	Clement	1 Clem. 38:2	A
	Ignatius	Phila. 6:3	C
2 Cor. 11:23–27	Clement	1 Clem. 5:5, 6	D
2 Cor. 12:16	Ignatius	Phila. 6:3	C

NT Passage	Father(s)	Work	Category
Gal. 1:1	Ignatius	Phila. 1:1	C
	Polycarp	Pol. 12:2	A
Gal. 2:2	Polycarp	Pol. 9:2	B
Gal. 2:9	Clement	1 Clem. 5:2	D
Gal. 2:21	Ignatius	Trall. 10:1	C
Gal. 3:1	Clement	1 Clem. 2:1	D
Gal. 4:26	Polycarp	Pol. 3:3	B
Gal. 5:11	Ignatius	Eph. 18:1	C
Gal. 5:14	Polycarp	Pol. 3:3	B
Gal. 5:17	Polycarp	Pol. 5:3	A
	Polycarp	Pol. 5:3	B
Gal. 5:21	Ignatius	Eph. 16:1	C
Gal. 6:7	Polycarp	Pol. 5:1	B
Gal. 6:14	Ignatius	Rom. 7:2	C
Eph. 1:3f	Ignatius	Eph. (Inscription)	B
Eph. 1:4	Clement	2 Clem. 14:2	D
Eph. 1:4–6	Barnabas	Barn. 3:6	C
Eph. 1:18	Clement	1 Clem. 59:3	D
Eph. 1:22	Clement	2 Clem. 14:2	D
Eph. 2:1	Hermas	Sim. 9:16:2, 3	B
Eph. 2:2	Barnabas	Barn. 2:1	C
Eph. 2:8	Polycarp	Pol. 1:3	B
Eph. 2:10, 21f	Barnabas	Barn. 6:11ff	C
Eph. 2:15	Ignatius	Eph. 20:1	B
Eph. 2:16	Ignatius	Smyr. 1:1	B
Eph. 2:20	Ignatius	Eph. 9:1	B
	Hermas	Sim. 9:4:3	B
Eph. 2:20–22	Ignatius	Eph. 9:1	B
	Clement	2 Clem. 14:2	D
Eph. 2:21	Barnabas	Barn. 6:11ff	C
Eph. 3:9	Ignatius	Eph. 19	B
Eph. 3:17	Barnabas	Barn. 6:11ff	C

NT Passage	Father(s)	Work	Category
Eph. 4:2	Ignatius	Pol. 1:2	B
Eph. 4:3–6	Hermas	Sim. 9:13:5	B
Eph. 4:4	Clement	1 Clem. 46:4	D
	Clement	1 Clem. 46:7	A
Eph. 4:4–6	Clement	1 Clem. 46:1–4	D
Eph. 4:18	Clement	1 Clem. 51:5	A
	Clement	2 Clem. 19:2	D
Eph. 4:22ff	Barnabas	Barn. 6:11ff	C
Eph. 4:24	Ignatius	Eph. 20:1	B
Eph. 4:25	Clement	1 Clem. 46:7	A
	Hermas	Mand. 3:1	B
Eph. 4:26	Polycarp	Pol. 12:1	B
Eph. 4:30	Hermas	Mand. 10:2:1–2, 4–5	B
Eph. 4:32	Polycarp	Pol. 5:2; 6:1	A
Eph. 5:1	Ignatius	Eph. 1:1	B
Eph. 5:16	Barnabas	Barn. 2:1	C
Eph. 5:23	Clement	2 Clem. 14:2	D
Eph. 5:25	Ignatius	Pol. 5:1	B
Eph. 6:6	Clement	2 Clem. 13:1	D
Eph. 6:13–17	Ignatius	Pol. 6:2	B
Phil. 1:27	Clement	1 Clem. 3:4	D
	Polycarp	Pol. 5:2	D
Phil. 2:3, 5	Ignatius	Phila. 8:2	C
Phil. 2:10	Polycarp	Pol. 2:1	D
Phil. 2:16	Polycarp	Pol. 9:2	D
Phil. 2:17	Ignatius	Rom. 2, 4	C
	Polycarp	Pol. 1:1	B
Phil. 2:30	Clement	1 Clem. 38:2	A
Phil. 3:14	Clement	1 Clem. 5:1, 5	A
Phil. 3:15	Ignatius	Smyrn. 11:3	C
Phil. 3:18	Polycarp	Pol. 12:3	D
Phil. 3:21	Polycarp	Pol. 2:1	D
Phil. 4:13	Ignatius	Smyrn. 4:2	C

NT Passage	Father(s)	Work	Category
Phil. 4:15	Clement	1 Clem. 47:1, 2	D
Col. 1:5, 6	Polycarp	Pol. 1:2	D
Col. 1:7	Ignatius	Eph. 2:1	D
Col. 1:9	Clement	1 Clem. 59:2	D
Col. 1:12	Clement	1 Clem. 59:2	D
	Polycarp	Pol. 12:2	D
Col. 1:13	Clement	1 Clem. 59:2	D
Col. 1:15	Hermas	Sim. 12:2, 3	D
Col. 1:16	Barnabas	Barn. 12:7	D
	Ignatius	Trall. 5:2	D
Col. 1:18	Ignatius	Smyrn. 1:2	D
Col. 1:23	Polycarp	Pol. 10:1 (Latin)	A
	Polycarp	Pol. 10:1	D
Col. 1:24	Clement	1 Clem. 38:2	A
Col. 1:26	Ignatius	Eph. 19:2	D
Col. 2:1	Clement	1 Clem. 2:4	D
Col. 2:2	Ignatius	Eph. 17:2	D
Col. 2:12	Polycarp	Pol. 12:2	A
Col. 2:14	Ignatius	Smyrn. 1:2	D
Col. 3:4	Hermas	Vis. 2:2:8	D
Col. 3:5	Polycarp	Pol. 11:2	D
Col. 3:9f	Barnabas	Barn. 6:12f	D
Col. 3:22	Clement	2 Clem. 13:1	D
Col. 4:7	Ignatius	Eph. 2:1	D
1 Thes. 2:4	Ignatius	Rom. 2:1	D
1 Thes. 5:13f	Hermas	Vis. 3:3:5	D
1 Thes. 5:17	Ignatius	Eph. 10:1	D
2 Thes. 1:4	Polycarp	Pol. 11:4	B
2 Thes. 3:5	Ignatius	Rom. 10:3	D
2 Thes. 3:15	Polycarp	Pol. 11:4	B
1 Tim. 1:1	Polycarp	Pol. 8:1	B
1 Tim. 1:3–5	Ignatius	Eph. 14:1; 20:1; Magn. 8:1	C

NT Passage	Father(s)	Work	Category
1 Tim. 1:12	Ignatius	Smyrn. 10:2	C
1 Tim. 1:13	Ignatius	Rom. 9:2	C
1 Tim. 1:16	Barnabas	Barn. 12:7	D
1 Tim. 1:17	Clement	1 Clem. 61:2	D
	Clement	2 Clem. 20:5	D
1 Tim. 2:1	Polycarp	Pol. 12:3	B
1 Tim. 2:8	Clement	1 Clem. 29:1	D
1 Tim. 3:5	Polycarp	Pol. 11:2	B
1 Tim. 3:8	Polycarp	Pol. 5:2	B
1 Tim. 3:16	Barnabas	Barn. 5:6	D
1 Tim. 4:15	Polycarp	Pol. 12:3	B
1 Tim. 4:16	Clement	2 Clem. 25:1	D
1 Tim. 5:5	Polycarp	Pol. 4:3	B
1 Tim. 5:18	Didache	Did. 13:1	C
1 Tim. 6:2	Ignatius	Pol. 4:3	C
1 Tim. 6:7	Polycarp	Pol. 4:1	B
1 Tim. 6:10	Polycarp	Pol. 4:1	B
2 Tim. 1:3	Ignatius	Trall. 7:2	C
2 Tim. 1:5	Polycarp	Pol. 12:1	B
2 Tim. 1:10	Barnabas	Barn. 5:6	D
2 Tim. 1:16	Ignatius	Eph. 2:1	C
2 Tim. 2:3	Ignatius	Pol. 6:2	C
2 Tim. 2:11	Polycarp	Pol. 5:2	B
2 Tim. 2:21	Clement	1 Clem. 24:4	C
2 Tim. 2:25	Polycarp	Pol. 11:4	B
2 Tim. 3:6	Ignatius	Eph. 17:1	C
2 Tim. 3:17	Clement	1 Clem. 24:2	C
2 Tim. 4:1	Barnabas	Barn. 7:2	D
2 Tim. 4:6	Ignatius	Rom. 2:2	C
2 Tim. 4:10	Polycarp	Pol. 9:4	B
Titus 1:2	Barnabas	Barn. 1:3, 4, 6	D
Titus 1:7	Ignatius	Pol. 6:1	C
Titus 1:14	Ignatius	Magn. 8:1	C

NT Passage	Father(s)	Work	Category
Titus 2:4, 5	Clement	1 Clem. 1:3	C
Titus 2:14	Barnabas	Barn. 14:5f	D
	Polycarp	Pol. 6:3	A
Titus 3:1	Clement	1 Clem. 2:7	C
Titus 3:5ff	Barnabas	Barn. 1:3, 4, 6	D
Titus 3:9	Ignatius	Magn. 8:1	C
Phile. 1:20	Ignatius	Eph. 2:2	D
Heb. 1:2	Barnabas	Barn. 5:5f;14:4;16:9	C
	Clement	1 Clem. 36:2–5	A
	Hermas	Sim. 9:12:2, 3	D
Heb. 2:5–9	Barnabas	Barn. 6:17–19	C
Heb. 2:9	Barnabas	Barn. 5:5ff	C
Heb. 2:18	Clement	1 Clem. 36:1	A
Heb. 3:1	Clement	1 Clem. 26:1	A
Heb. 3:2	Clement	1 Clem. 17:5	A
Heb. 3:12	Hermas	Vis. 2:3:2	B
Heb. 4:1	Barnabas	Barn. 4: 9–10, 13	C
Heb. 4:1–11	Barnabas	Barn. 15	C
Heb. 4:12	Clement	1 Clem. 21:9	A
Heb. 4:13	Ignatius	Magn. 3:2	D
Heb. 5:13	Polycarp	Pol. 9:1	C
Heb. 6:1	Barnabas	Barn. 6:19	C
Heb. 6:4–6	Hermas	Mand. 4:3:2, 3; Sim. 9:26:6	C
Heb. 6:18	Clement	1 Clem. 27:2	A
Heb. 6:20	Polycarp	Pol. 12:2	C
Heb. 7:3	Polycarp	Pol. 12:2	C
Heb. 7:7	Ignatius	Phil. 11:1	D
Heb. 7:19	Ignatius	Phil. 11:1	D
Heb. 7:22, 23, 26	Ignatius	Phil. 11:1	D
Heb. 9:13ff	Barnabas	Barn. 8:1ff; 14:4–6	C
Heb. 10:23	Clement	1 Clem. 27:1	A
	Clement	2 Clem. 11:6	C

NT Passage	Father(s)	Work	Category
Heb. 10:24	Barnabas	Barn. 4:9–10, 13	C
Heb. 10:32–39	Clement	2 Clem. 26:4	C
Heb. 11:11	Clement	1 Clem. 27:1	A
Heb. 11:13	Hermas	Sim. 1:1, 2	C
Heb. 11:37, 39	Clement	1 Clem. 17:1	A
Heb. 12:1	Clement	1 Clem. 19:2	A
	Clement	2 Clem. 1:6	C
Heb. 12:2	Barnabas	Barn. 5:5ff; 14:4; 16:9	C
Heb. 12:6–8	Clement	1 Clem. 56:4	A
Heb. 12:24	Barnabas	Barn. 5:1	C
Heb. 12:28	Polycarp	Pol. 6:3	C
Heb. 13:12	Barnabas	Barn. 5:5ff	C
	Barnabas	Barn. 4:9–10, 13	C
Heb. 13:18	Clement	2 Clem. 16:4	C
Jam. 1:4	Hermas	Mand. 9:6	C
Jam. 1:5	Hermas	Mand. 9:1; Sim. 9:24:1, 2	C
Jam. 1:6–8	Hermas	Mand. 9:1	C
Jam. 1:12	Hermas	Vis. 2:2:7	C
Jam. 1:17	Hermas	Mand. 9:11	C
Jam. 1:26	Hermas	Mand. 12:1:1	C
Jam. 1:27	Hermas	Sim. 1:8; Mand. 8:10; Vis. 3:9:2	C
Jam. 2:5	Hermas	Sim. 2:5	C
Jam. 3:15	Hermas	Mand. 9:11; 11:6	C
Jam. 4:4	Clement	2 Clem. 6:3, 5	D
Jam. 4:5	Hermas	Mand. 3:1; 5:2:5–7; Sim. 5.6:5, 7	C
Jam. 4:7	Hermas	Mand. 12:2:4	C
Jam. 4:11	Hermas	Sim. 9:23:2–4; 12:6:3; Mand. 2:2, 3	C
Jam. 4:12	Hermas	Sim. 9:23:2–4;12:6:3	C
Jam. 5:1	Hermas	Vis. 3:9:4–6	C

NT Passage	Father(s)	Work	Category
Jam. 5:2	Hermas	Sim. 8:6:4	C
Jam. 5:4	Hermas	Vis. 3:9:4–6	C
Jam. 5:7, 8	Clement	2 Clem. 20:2–4	D
Jam. 5:10	Clement	2 Clem. 20:2–4	D
Jam. 5:11	Hermas	Mand. 9:2	C
Jam. 5:16	Clement	2 Clem. 15:1	D
Jam. 5:20	Clement	1 Clem. 49:5	D
	Clement	2 Clem. 16:4	D
1 Pet. 1:1, 2	Clement	1 Clem. Intro.	D
1 Pet. 1:2	Barnabas	Barn. 5:1	C
1 Pet. 1:7	Hermas	Vis. 4:3:4	D
1 Pet. 1:8	Polycarp	Pol. 1:3	A
1 Pet. 1:10f	Barnabas	Barn. 5:5, 6; 6:7	D
1 Pet. 1:12	Polycarp	Pol. 1:3	A
1 Pet. 1:13	Polycarp	Pol. 2:1	A
1 Pet. 1:17	Barnabas	Barn. 4:11f	D
1 Pet. 1:18, 19	Clement	1 Clem. 7:2, 4	D
1 Pet. 1: 20	Barnabas	Barn. 5:6	D
	Hermas	Sim. 9:12:2, 3	D
	Clement	2 Clem. 14:2	D
1 Pet. 1:21	Polycarp	Pol. 2:1; 12:2	A
1 Pet. 2:1	Clement	1 Clem. 30:1, 2	D
1 Pet. 2:6–8	Barnabas	6:2–4	D
1 Pet. 2:9	Clement	1 Clem. 59:2	D
1 Pet. 2:11	Didache	Did. 1:4	D
	Polycarp	Pol. 5:3	A
1 Pet. 2:12	Polycarp	Pol. 10:2	A
1 Pet. 2:17	Clement	1 Clem. 2:4	D
1 Pet. 2:21	Polycarp	Pol. 8:1, 2	A
1 Pet. 2:25	Ignatius	Rom. 5:1	A
	Polycarp	Pol. 6:1; 11:4	A
1 Pet. 3:8	Polycarp	Pol. 5:2; 6:1	A
1 Pet. 3:9	Polycarp	Pol. 2:2	A

NT Passage	Father(s)	Work	Category
I Pet. 3:13	Polycarp	Pol. 6:3	A
I Pet. 3:20, 21	Hermas	Vis. 3:3:5	D
I Pet. 4:7	Polycarp	Pol. 7:2; 11:4	A
I Pet. 4:8	Clement	1 Clem. 49:5; 2 Clem. 16:4	D
I Pet. 4:14–16	Hermas	Sim. 9:14:6; 8:6:4	D
I Pet. 4:16	Hermas	Sim. 8:6:4	C
I Pet. 4:19	Clement	1 Clem. 2:2	D
I Pet. 5:2	Ignatius	Rom. 5:1	A
I Pet. 5:5	Clement	1 Clem. 30:1, 2	D
	Ignatius	Eph. 5:3	A
I Pet. 5:7	Hermas	Vis. 3:11:3; 4:2:4	D
I Pet. 5:9	Clement	1 Clem. 2:4	D
	Hermas	Mand. 12:2:4	C
I John 4:18	Clement	1 Clem. 49:5; 50:3	D
Jude 1:22f	Didache	Did. 2:7	D
Apoc. 1:7, 13	Barnabas	Barn. 7:9	D
Apoc. 7:14	Hermas	Vis. 2:2:7	C
Apoc. 21:5	Barnabas	Barn. 6:13	D
Apoc. 22:10	Barnabas	Barn. 21:3	D
Apoc. 22:12	Barnabas	Barn. 21:3	D
	Clement	1 Clem. 34:3	D

NOTES

1. Bruce M. Metzger, *The Canon of the New Testament: Its Origin, Development, and Significance* (Oxford: Clarendon, 1987), 1.

2. See David R. Peck, "A History of the Book of Moses to Its Canonization" (master's thesis, Brigham Young University, 2002), 48–95.

3. Metzger, *Canon of the New Testament*, 7.

4. In the late 1800s, scholars from the University of Tübingen in Germany, under the influence of F. C. Baur, concluded that the Gospels and other works that found their way into the New Testament were written no earlier than AD 130 and were the product of much wishful thinking on the part of these later Christians. The classic study from the school is that of Walter R. Cassels,

Supernatural Religion (London: Longmans, Green, 1875), which remains important reading on the subject to this day. His conclusions were rebutted by John B. Lightfoot in his work, *Essays on the Work Entitled "Supernatural Religion"* (New York: Macmillan, 1889), which gathered into one collection the materials he published in *Contemporary Review* between 1874 and 1877.

5. The great and abominable church founded by the devil, whose work is mentioned in 1 Nephi 13, seems to have done much of its damage prior to the period under consideration in this paper and therefore receives only this mention. Being recognized as scripture and also collected, however, did not prevent apostolic writings from later tampering. The short and long endings of the Gospel of Mark and the account of the adulterous woman in John, found in some renditions and not in others, are two examples. However, as the core documents became public property, it was harder for entities to make sizable changes in them (see Larry W. Hurdato, *Lord Jesus Christ: Devotion to Jesus in Earliest Christianity* [Grand Rapids, MI: Eerdmans, 2003], 536). For Latter-day Saints, a very helpful overview is Thomas A. Wayment, "The Story of the New Testament," in *The Life and Teachings of Jesus Christ: From Bethlehem to the Sermon on the Mount,* ed. Richard Neitzel Holzapfel and Thomas A. Wayment (Salt Lake City: Deseret Book, 2005), 21–47. Wayment notes that though scribes did change the text, "the stories of Jesus' life and the activities of the Apostles are largely unassailable. . . . The New Testament Gospels appear to be complete documents without major gaps or interpolations" (44–45).

6. Eusebius' account of the desertion of Jerusalem by the Christians in AD 66 suggests that the prophecy was known and heeded (see Eusebius, *History of the Church,* 3.5).

7. For an exhaustive study of the dating of the New Testament documents, see John A. T. Robinson, *Redating the New Testament* (London: S.C.M., 1976). Taking on those who argue for a later date of composition, Robinson argues that all the documents which became part of the New Testament were written before AD 70, including John's Gospel and the book of Revelation. Though his well-reasoned and carefully articulated arguments appeal to me, he has not convinced me in every case. Some of the writings—for example, 1 John, Jude, and Revelation—fit better toward the end of the first century. Even so, Robinson's work commends itself for careful study and convincingly argues that much of the material had been around in written form a long time before the earliest collections were made.

8. Eusebius, *History of the Church,* 2.15.1–2.

9. Many scholars believe Luke and Matthew used a "sayings source," often referred to as "Q," short for the German word *Quelle,* meaning "source." There is scholarly disagreement as to when Christians began to write down Jesus' words and just what those words were. A number of more liberal scholars taught the Gospel of Thomas, found among the Nag Hammadi materials, as proof of their position, and even place this very Gnostic and late book ahead of the Gospels, insisting it better reflects the historical Jesus. Hurdato has convincingly countered this view, insisting that the earliest Christians had a well-developed christology and understanding of the central message and mission of Jesus (see *Lord Jesus Christ,* 219–48, 256–57). For a balanced treatise on the subject of Q, see C. M. Tuckett,

THE EARLIEST "NEW TESTAMENT"   289

Q and the History of Early Christianity: Studies on Q (Edinburgh: T. and T. Clark; Peabody, MA: Hendrickson, 1996).

10. This makes sense, given the importance that the early Christians placed on the Lord's teachings. Some have suggested, however, that though this sayings source preserved the pure form of the Gospel message, it was amplified and embroidered for and by later copyists and compilers such that much of the original message was distorted and thereby lost. Scholars who have developed theories about the content of Q work on the assumption that it was strictly a sayings source that viewed Jesus as a great teacher and one who heralded the coming kingdom of God. They do not, however, view Him as the Christ or His death as redemptive (see Hurdato, *Lord Jesus Christ,* 217–18).

11. David Trobish, *First Edition of the New Testament* (Oxford: Oxford University Press, 2000), 3–43. Trobish believes "that the New Testament was created not by a long and gradual process, but in a single action." His thesis goes against a long-prevailing view held by Bruce M. Metzger and Bart D. Ehrman, *The Text of the New Testament: Its Transmission, Corruption, and Restoration,* 4th ed. (New York: Oxford University Press, 2005), and more especially Wilhelm Bousset, *Kyrios Christos: A History of the Belief in Christ from the Beginning to Irenaeus,* J. E. Steely, trans. (Nashville: Abingdon, 1970), who believe that Christianity and its writings developed in discrete unilinear layers or stages over a period of nearly two centuries. Trobish's work presents strong evidence that there was a very influential collection of core Christian writings very early, but he seems to be pushing his evidence too far in making the claim that this collection contained exactly the same writings, albeit not in the same order, that are in the current canon. For a review of his work, see D. C. Parker, "Review of Books," *Journal of Theological Studies* (April 2002), 298, and J. Wright, "Book Reviews," *Choice* (October 2001), 329.

12. Specifically: Barnabas, Didache, 1 Clement, Ignatius, Papias, Polycarp, Shepherd of Hermas, Letter to Diagetus, 2 Clement. The dating of some of these works is uncertain, but all were written before AD 140. For details, see J. B. Lightfoot, *The Apostolic Fathers* (Grand Rapids, MI: Baker, 1970).

13. See "A Committee of the Oxford Society of Historical Theology," *The New Testament in the Apostolic Fathers* (Oxford: Clarendon, 1905), i–iii, 2.

14. See the chart at the end of this chapter that gives the scriptural reference for those phrases the Apostolic Fathers used to identify the core materials, where they are found in the Fathers' writings, and to which category they belong. The chart is derived from Committee, *The New Testament in the Apostolic Fathers.*

15. Ignatius does refer to Onesimus but does not cite Paul. He uses the Pauline word *onaimēn* (aorist optative of *oninomai,* "have joy in or benefit from," found in Philemon 1:20), but one word is not sufficient to show that he had access to Paul's letter (see Ignatius, *To the Ephesians,* 2.2).

16. A very helpful study is Committee, *The New Testament in the Apostolic Fathers.*

17. See Wayment, "The Story," 29–31, who argues that John's Gospel was written very early and therefore provides an excellent eyewitness account of the Savior's ministry. His argument that dating it late lessens its validity has some merit, but the Lord had promised John and others of the Apostles that the Holy

Ghost would "bring all things to your remembrance, whatsoever I have said unto you" (John 14:26). It could be argued, therefore, that a late date for the Gospel does not invalidate its accuracy.

18. Second Clement also makes reference to "the gospel," and seems to have more than a single source in mind (see 12.2). He also refers to writings he calls "the books and the Apostles," suggesting he was aware of two groups of sacred works (14.2). For a discussion, see F. F. Bruce, *The New Testament Documents: How Reliable Are They?* (Grand Rapids, MI: Eerdmans, 1943), 23.

19. So few fragments from Papias have been preserved that drawing conclusions from his material is tenuous at best.

20. Hurdato, *Lord Jesus Christ*, 491. By the time of Irenaeus, the fourfold Gospels had been marked off to the extent that he could refer to them as a closed body. On this development, see Martin Hengel, *The Four Gospels and the One Gospel of Jesus Christ* (London: SCM, 2000), 1–33.

21. The earliest lists evaluating the various writings held by Christian churches shows such a variety. For example, the Muratorian Canon mentions two epistles of Paul, Laodiceans and Alexandrians, along with the Book of Wisdom, as being held authentic by some but rejected by most. It also notes that the Shepherd of Hermes was well accepted but not by all. For various ancient lists with their evaluation of books circulating among the Christians, see Metzger, *Canon of the New Testament*, 305–15.

22. Sinaiticus contains the Letters of Barnabas and the Shepherd of Hermas while Alexandrinus included 1 and 2 Clement. Because Vaticanus breaks off at Hebrews 9:14, it is unknown what other materials it contained (see Bruce, *Canon of Scripture*, 205–7).

23. See Thomas A. Wayment, "False Gospels: An Approach to Studying the New Testament Apocrypha," in this volume.

24. Bart D. Ehrman, *The Orthodox Corruption of Scripture* (New York: Oxford University Press, 1993), 19.

25. Ehrman, *Orthodox Corruption of Scripture*, 19.

26. Metzger, *Canon of the New Testament*, 252.

27. Hurdato, *Lord Jesus Christ*, 2–3, 24–26.

28. Metzger, *Canon of the New Testament*, 252, Bruce, *Canon of Scripture*, 260–61. Some have pushed the idea that the early Church did not have a clear conception of what was orthodox and what was not (see Walter Bauer, *Orthodoxy and Heresy in Earliest Christianity*, ed. Robert Kraft and Gerhard Krodel [Philadelphia: Fortress, 1971]). Bauer argued that earliest Christianity was not composed of a single harmonious unit. The harmony suggested by Eusebius and promulgated by orthodox Christianity for centuries, he believed, was little short of propaganda. Instead, the church was fragmented by competing factions and divergent forms with no standard by which to judge which was correct. Bauer's methodology has been questioned, and, though scholars admit that early Christianity was not monolithic, they insist that it did have core beliefs intact. For a list of books and articles evaluating Bauer's work, see Ehrman, *Orthodox Corruption of Scripture*, 33–34n16. Hurdato, *Lord Jesus Christ*, 520–21, has shown that Bauer's work simply has not

withstood the test of time. He argues effectively that the earliest church had a strict sense of who Jesus was and what He taught. The proto-orthodox continued to trust that sense and used it as the criterion for judging what was true and false (see Hurdato, *Lord Jesus Christ*, 1–11, 259–62).

29. See Hurdato, *Lord Jesus Christ*, 259–347.

30. Ehrman, *Orthodox Corruption of Scripture*, 19.

31. Metzger, *Canon of the New Testament*, 253; Bruce, *Canon of Scripture*, 259–60. According to Eusebius, Origen argued for apostolic authority for any writing to be considered holy (see, for example, Eusebius, *History of the Church*, 6.12.1–6).

32. Ehrman, *Orthodox Corruption of Scripture*, 19; Metzger, *Canon of the New Testament*, 253, Bruce, *Canon of Scripture*, 261–62.

33. Bruce, *Canon of Scripture*, 262–63.

34. Bruce, *Canon of Scripture*, 262–63.

35. Bruce, *Canon of Scripture*, 263–65.

36. Bruce, *New Testament Documents*, 27.

17

FALSE GOSPELS: AN APPROACH TO STUDYING THE NEW TESTAMENT APOCRYPHA

Thomas A. Wayment

Unfortunately, the term *apocrypha* is not used consistently to describe one body of material or collection of texts. Generally, the designation *the Pseudepigrapha* describes Old Testament noncanonical writings, whereas the term *New Testament Apocrypha* usually indicates noncanonical writings authored after the New Testament period. Even though these designations are arbitrary, they have become the most common means of differentiating between Old and New Testament–period noncanonical texts. More specifically, the term *the Apocrypha* has been used to describe a collection of books contained today in Catholic Bibles, and during Joseph Smith's day in most printings of the King James Version. Among those books are 1–2 Esdras, the Wisdom of Solomon, and additions to Esther and Daniel. To add to the confusion, all of the books are written pseudepigraphically (written in someone else's name) and have been designated as apocryphal (purportedly containing hidden or secret materials). The focus of this chapter will be on the collection of New

---

Thomas A. Wayment is an associate professor of ancient scripture at Brigham Young University.

Testament apocryphal materials that have not previously been included in the Bible.

The confusion in terminology is due in part to the recent discovery or rediscovery of many texts from antiquity which added to the originally small number of apocryphal texts. But these discoveries are not alone to blame for the imprecision in our terminology. Indeed, our earliest surviving index or list of canonical books, the Muratorian Canon (named after L. Muratori, who discovered the list in an eighth-century manuscript), includes the names of books that are now deemed apocryphal.[1] Presumably, the canon list is a copy of a similar list from about AD 200, although it could be as late as the beginning of the fourth century AD.[2]

In the list, the author enumerates all of the canonical books of scripture, which are very similar to the twenty-seven-book canon of the modern New Testament. However, toward the end of the list, the author differentiates between genuine writings of the Apostles and writings that were forged in the Apostles' names: "There is current also (an epistle) to the Laodiceans, another to the Alexandrians, forged in Paul's name for the sect of Marcion, and several others, which cannot be received in the catholic Church."[3] Interestingly, the author of the list recognizes several other books as authoritative that have in our day been excluded from the canon. He lists the Wisdom of Solomon, the Revelation of Peter, and the Shepherd of Hermas, with the understanding that the latter is a recent composition.

The Muratorian Canon speaks to the heart of the debate over the New Testament apocrypha's value because it shows that books were included in the scriptural canon even though a work was written in the postapostolic era. At times, scholars imply that including the apocrypha in modern Bibles or collecting extrabiblical materials is a modern practice.[4] However, nearly all canon lists from the first centuries after the Apostles include texts that are not part of our modern New Testament.[5] The simple fact that the early Church leaders could differentiate between canonical texts and others that were written for various purposes is encouraging, because it demonstrates a living doctrinal trajectory within the Church. Leaders were not deceived by many of these works but rather may have viewed them much as we do today: "There are many things contained therein that are true, and it is mostly translated correctly; there are many things contained therein that are not true, which are interpolations by the hands of men" (D&C 91:1–2).

Comparatively, there are likely three or four apocryphal texts for every book of scripture in the New Testament. They are not all of a single genre; they include gospels, collections of sayings, acts of individual Apostles, collections of apostolic teachings, revelatory dialogues, and apocalypses. Within these general categories are subcategories, such as infancy gospels and Gnostic gospels, for example. We sometimes treat this vast body of literature, which was composed over several centuries in places as diverse as Europe and North Africa, as a single unit. To properly understand any document within the collection of New Testament apocrypha, we must place it in its proper compositional setting, understand who used it and why, and seek to discern its impact on those who used it.

The value in exerting effort to understand apocryphal literature is twofold: first, once we understand the compositional situation surrounding an apocryphal text, we can then ascertain its potential to preserve credible information about Jesus or the Church that He founded. Second, once we understand how the document impacted Christian communities, we can begin to discern the historical development of the Apostasy within those communities. For example, it is easy to pick up a Gnostic document and read about the journey of the soul from its premortal existence through its heavenly progression without realizing that the text actually presents a significant Gnostic corruption of Christian doctrine.[6] And even though the doctrine might initially resonate with us today, it preserves traces of the Apostasy in action. The following categories, developed to encourage study into the apocrypha in light of the Restoration of the gospel, may perhaps help us use this body of literature in new and meaningful ways.

DOCUMENTS COMPOSED TO REDIRECT CHRISTIAN BEHAVIOR

In a groundbreaking study on the apocrypha from a Latter-day Saint point of view, Stephen E. Robinson looked at the issue of "lying for God" as a means of understanding the purpose and function of some of the intertestamental apocrypha. In that study, Robinson proposed that deception played a significant part in the production of many apocryphal texts.[7] The study is a model of careful scholarship, but its limited scope makes it applicable only to a very narrow set of apocryphal texts: those that seek to alter normative Christian and Jewish practices.

A considerable body of New Testament apocryphal texts originates from a period when the divergence between mainstream Christianity and its many branches was still quite recent, enough so to cause confusion between the various Christian communities. At the end of the first century, and particularly into the second and third centuries, a variety of Christianities—or groups professing divergent beliefs about Christ and His gospel—sought for converts among both Gentiles and other Christian communities.[8] In their efforts to win converts, Christian communities were faced, much as they are today, with conflicting arguments based on the same Christian texts. To help differentiate themselves, some circles of Christians, particularly Gnostic and other marginalized Christian communities, forged documents to further their claims. Some excellent examples of this type of writing survive today, including the recently published Gospel of Judas, a late-second-century forgery which appears to have been written in an effort to validate and promote Gnostic doctrines.[9]

Another example is the Coptic Gospel of Thomas, which contains a subtle correction of apostolic traditions as they are preserved in the canonical accounts, while at the same time it advances new beliefs and ideas in the name of the Apostle Thomas. In logia ("saying") 13, Jesus says, "Compare me, tell me whom I am like. Simon Peter said to him: You are like a righteous angel. Matthew said to him: . . . You are like a wise philosopher. Thomas said to him: Master, my mouth is wholly incapable of saying whom you are like."[10] The passage is built upon the canonical account found in Matthew 16:13–19, but the rephrasing of what transpired both denigrates Peter and Matthew, whose names were associated with the first Gospels quite early, and elevates Thomas.[11] Moreover, the Gospel of Thomas endorses the literary figure of the Apostle Thomas through a claim that he received special esoteric knowledge: "These are the secret words which the living Jesus spoke, and which Didymus Judas Thomas wrote down. . . . And he said: He who shall find the interpretation of these words shall not taste of death."[12]

Some of the salient features of this type of document are (1) a subtle correction of the Synoptic or Johannine accounts; (2) the elevation of a single person, usually an Apostle; (3) preservation of the sayings of Jesus, almost always in new forms or contexts; (4) the preservation and transmission of secret teachings; and (5) a suppression of the humanity of Jesus or His mortal traits as they appear in the scriptural Gospels. A short list of documents that fall into this category are the Gospel of Thomas, the Dialogue of the Savior (although late), the Gospel of the Egyptians, Papyrus Oxyrhynchus 840, the Apocryphon of James, the Gospel of Philip, the Gospel of Judas, the Freer Logion, and many other texts that circulated under the names of the Apostles.[13]

This tradition is characterized by an effort to promote previously unknown teachings and sayings about Jesus because the authors needed to present a credible argument in order to effect changes in what came to be considered orthodox positions.[14] If their works were immediately recognized as forgeries, they would be readily dismissed. However, through careful manipulation of already established sayings of Jesus and the possible discovery and codification of oral traditions, these authors were able to present a seemingly valid contribution. It is not impossible that these texts preserve some lost sayings and traditions about Jesus, yet they must certainly be used with care and with a distinct methodologically proven approach for discerning early and late traditions. In order to make these forged texts more credible, authors sought out forgotten or esoteric traditions about Jesus that preserved an air of familiarity or truth.

IN-GROUP DIALOGUES AND DISCUSSIONS

Whereas many texts were created with the aim of correcting the established orthodox positions of the Church, some documents were created for the purpose of in-group consumption. As in the orthodox tradition where lectionaries, sermons, and homilies were written and disseminated to teach the truths of the gospel in a coherent system, nonorthodox communities created new texts for the same purposes. The Nag Hammadi discovery makes it clear that there were texts in circulation with the sole purpose of teaching Valentinian cosmogony, for example, and were not directed at correcting or attacking the New Testament Gospels in any coherent way.[15]

These in-group texts derive from both orthodox and nonorthodox communities, who produced them for private edification and parenesis, or personal exhortation. Within nonorthodox traditions, these texts are readily identifiable through their completely divergent doctrines and practices. For example, a text within the apocryphal Thomas tradition can be identified easily through the presence of the five ordinances: baptism, chrism, eucharist, redemption, and bridal chamber. These texts are extremely important for reconstructing the wide diversity of Christian traditions in the second and third centuries, in the context of what Latter-day Saint scholars would associate with the period of apostasy.

However, these in-group texts were also developed within orthodox Christian circles for the same purposes. Early canon lists specifically mention these in-group texts by name, and many of the early Church Fathers recognized that they were not as valuable as the canonical texts.[16] Even the Muratorian Canon discerns between this type of writing and the canonical accounts.

Within the orthodox tradition, some of the most important works in this genre are the Shepherd of Hermas, the Epistle of Barnabas, the Apocalypse of Peter, the Epistula Apostolorum, the Didache, and the Wisdom of Solomon. Although not comprehensive, this list helps define the parameters of the orthodox in-group apocryphal tradition. On the other hand, nonorthodox communities produced a series of gospels under the names of well-known heretics, such as Apelles, Bardesanes, Basilides, Cerinthus, Marcion, and Mani. Moreover, a host of other documents fall into this genre, such as the Second Treatise of the Great Seth from Nag Hammadi, the revelations of Hermes Trismegistus, the Pistis Sophia, and the Gospel of Truth.

Before texts such as these can be mined for historical deposits of truth or fact, they must be placed accurately within a distinct religious trajectory, and then we must evaluate that tradition's potential to pre-serve legitimate historical information.

FICTIONAL TEXTS WRITTEN FOR ENJOYMENT

The modern academic mindset has led us to believe that all or at least a significant part of the apocrypha was believed to be historically reliable and that people generally approached them in antiquity as cred-ible sources. This assumption, however, does not hold up after careful scrutiny. The early Church never elevated the apocryphal texts to a sta-tus similar or equal to the canonical texts. Instead, they were able to distinguish between literary fictions and potential nonfiction writings. There was not a large body of fictional works in circulation among first- and second-century Christians, and therefore Christians wrote romances, legendary accounts, and fictional acts of the Apostles to sat-isfy this need. Perhaps some of them even contained a grain of fact, but for the most part it is impossible to believe that Christians did not rec-ognize texts such as the infancy narratives of Jesus as purely fictional literature.

For example, according to one legend, as Joseph and Mary entered a cave on their way to Egypt, they found that it was inhabited by inhos-pitable creatures. Jesus' parents, afraid, were about to flee when Jesus stepped forward and said, "'Have no fear, and do not think that I am a child; for I have always been and even now am perfect; all wild beasts must be docile before me.' Likewise lions and leopards worshipped him and accompanied them in the desert."[17] To amplify the legendary char-acter of the story, the author notes that previous to His encounter with the wild beasts in the cave, the infant Jesus had been sitting on His mother's lap.

These texts need to be discussed in their own context and evalu-ated in relationship to other works in the same genre. Some of them are good fiction, such as the Acts of Pilate, while other texts within this genre are sometimes absurd. Indeed, these texts will probably reveal more about the Christian mind-set in the second century than about first-century beliefs and practices. But they can answer important and interesting questions, such as, What types of literature were early Christians interested in? What emotional and spiritual needs did these documents fill? Did all Christians feel the same about this type of literature?

Christians in the first and second centuries may have been offended at the questionable morality contained in some of the fictional literature then circulating in the Roman Empire. Therefore, they may have sought to produce their own texts for private consumption. One defining feature of this genre is that the gaps left in the canonical texts are consistently filled. For example, Mark mentions that Jesus had brothers and sisters, but he does not provide the names of Jesus' sisters. Later apocryphal texts invent the names of these sisters as well as those of Jesus' grandparents and other unnamed disciples.[18]

THE CHRISTIAN APOCALYPSE

The genre of apocalyptic literature, as in the book of Revelation, was relatively popular in the first few centuries after the death of Christ. While some Christians struggled to accept the book of Revelation as a canonical text, others received it wholeheartedly. Both the Stichometry of Nicephorus (eighth century AD) and the Catalogue of Sixty Canonical Books (seventh century AD) omit the book of Revelation from their lists of acceptable books of scripture.[19] These lists, which originate in the Eastern churches, reflect a general malaise about the authenticity of the book of Revelation in the East, even though the Western churches openly accepted the book of Revelation.

Perhaps as a result of the persecutions of Christians in the Western empire, apocalyptic works were written during the second and third centuries which promised the glorious return of the Savior and the ultimate vindication of the Saints. They became a popular form of expressing hope in the Second Coming, promising vindication to the oppressed.[20] Much of the literature in this genre is quite colorful, and at times it appears that the authors intended to make explicit reference to civic leaders and officials, the details of which are helpful in dating these apocryphal texts.[21]

It may appear that this body of material could be used to determine specific Christian beliefs and expectations about the Second Coming of the Lord, but experience has shown that its focus is probably aimed at satisfying the needs of an oppressed people rather than preserving

Christian traditions about Jesus' return in glory. This body of literature probably holds the keys to unlocking how Christians viewed the Roman Empire, how they felt about being a persecuted people, and how a marginalized group continued to exist alongside a larger, dominant society.

Some of the most important Christian apocalypses are the Apocalypse of Peter, the Apocalypse of Paul, the Shepherd of Hermas, and the Ascension of Isaiah. Unfortunately, the line between canonical apocalypses and noncanonical apocalypses is very faint, and no distinct lines have been drawn. The tumultuous history of the book of Revelation perhaps encouraged the breakdown of the boundaries. Further research into the genre of apocalyptic writing will hopefully result in critical methodologies that will enable us to more decisively differentiate the noncanonical apocalypses and determine their origins.

SUMMARY

Unfortunately, many study apocryphal literature hoping to find previously undisclosed secrets of Christian history and practice without realizing that these texts are universally late and secondary. The books of the New Testament are generally decades, if not centuries, older. Therefore, to argue that an apocryphal text contains more reliable information than the canonical texts, we must first determine whether a given text has any claim to preserve historically dependable information. Moreover, some genres of apocryphal literature are more likely to hold such treasures, but when taken out of context, these facts can have only a very limited impact. The apocryphal tradition is not a smorgasbord of historical and legendary information that can be haphazardly drawn from in order to make firm historical conclusions.

It is safe to say, based on current research, that every apocryphal text that claims to preserve the teachings of a New Testament figure was forged. The same cannot be said of the canonical texts, which indicates that the early Church was quite successful at separating the wheat from the chaff. At the same time, however, the apocryphal literature can inform us about the development of the Church in the postapostolic era.

Early Church leaders faced the threat of outsiders, posing as insiders, who attempted to redirect the affairs of the Church through the creation of forged gospels and letters.[22] Without the aid of the Apostles, those early Church leaders had to distinguish between forgeries and the genuine letters and Gospels of Jesus' disciples. Within the Church, regional leaders also wrote circular letters wherein they sought, like the Apostle Paul, to answer questions and settle disputes among the branches. Several of these letters have been preserved, and while they should not be elevated to the status of canonical texts, they do preserve the second or third generation of Christian writings.

Other texts were clearly written as fictional accounts of Jesus' life and the Apostles' later careers. To some, this genre of writing seems foreign, but even in our own day many fictional accounts of Jesus' life have been created. These fictional accounts, written to inspire and uplift without any pretension of historical legitimacy, may survive for future generations who will classify them as twenty-first-century apocrypha. Like their ancient counterparts, these modern fictional accounts supply names and events to an otherwise incomplete biography of Jesus. They were written for the enjoyment of the believers.

Finally, perhaps the least understood category of apocryphal writing is the early Christian apocalypse. Filled with fantastic imagery and intentionally difficult symbolism, these apocalypses filled a need in the early Christian communities. They likely reveal an era of suffering and marginalization among the churches. To satisfy the human need to feel or expect vindication, some well-meaning Christian authors forged texts that promised the ultimate triumph of the Saints when Jesus Christ returns in His glory.

NOTES

1. See Wilhelm Schneemelcher, ed., *New Testament Apocrypha* (Louisville: Westminster John Knox, 1991), 1:34.

2. The manuscript in which the canon list was found was written much later than AD 200, but the author refers to the Shepherd of Hermas as a recent composition. Most scholars, therefore, date the Shepherd of Hermas to the end of the second century AD.

3. Schneemelcher, *New Testament Apocrypha*, 1:36.

4. See the brief history of the discussion in J. K. Elliott, *The Apocryphal New Testament* (Oxford: Clarendon, 2004), ix–xxv.

5. This list currently includes the Muratorian Canon (c. AD 200), Codex Claromontanus (fourth century AD), the Decretum Gelasianum (sixth century AD), which enumerates books that should be avoided, and the Stichometry of Nicephorus (c. AD 850).

6. The Hymn of the Pearl, a distinct section within the Gnostic Acts of Thomas, is an excellent example. The document derives from the third century AD in Syria and almost certainly contains no credible historical information about the Apostle Thomas or first-century Christianity. Even if the Hymn of the Pearl, which describes the soul's descent from premortal glory, predates the Acts of Thomas, it is still almost certainly a piece of Gnostic propaganda to promote the belief of the divine eternal spark as opposed to the seed of man who is fallen, according to the Gnostic worldview (see Han J. W. Drijvers, "The Acts of Thomas," in Schneemelcher, *New Testament Apocrypha,* 1:380–85; cf. John W. Welch, "The Hymn of the Pearl: An Ancient Counterpart to 'O My Father,'" *BYU Studies* 36, no. 1 [1996–97]: 127–38).

7. Other scholars had certainly recognized Pseudepigraphical and pseudonymous writing, but Robinson looked at the phenomenon in the context of Latter-day Saint scholarship (see Stephen E. Robinson, "Lying for God: The Uses of Apocrypha," in *Apocryphal Writings and the Latter-day Saints,* ed. C. Wilfred Griggs [Provo, UT: Religious Studies Center, Brigham Young University, 1986], 133–54).

8. This is the thesis of Bart D. Ehrman, *Lost Christianities: The Battles for Scripture and the Faiths We Never Knew* (New York: Oxford University Press, 2003).

9. See Rodolphe Kasser, Marvin Meyer, and Gregor Wurst, eds., *The Gospel of Judas* (Washington, DC: National Geographic, 2006).

10. Beate Blatz, "The Coptic Gospel of Thomas," in Schneemelcher, *New Testament Apocrypha,* 1:119. A convenient English translation is John S. Kloppenborg, and others, *Q Thomas Reader* (Sonoma, CA: Polebridge, 1990).

11. See Thomas A. Wayment, "Christian Teachers in Matthew and Thomas: The Possibility of Becoming a Master," *Journal of Early Christian Studies* 12 (2004): 289–311.

12. Blatz, "The Coptic Gospel of Thomas," 1:117.

13. Ron Cameron sees a similar division of texts, which he uses to establish the dating of the sayings traditions about Jesus (see *The Other Gospels: Non-Canonical Gospel Texts* [Philadelphia: Westminster, 1982]).

14. I used the term *orthodox* to describe only that branch of Christianity that came to dominate all others, and I do not intend to make any value statement on the accuracy of their traditions.

15. The Nag Hammadi codices were discovered near the town of Nag Hammadi in Egypt in 1945. Twelve codices were found, including fragments of a thirteenth codex, that contained Gnostic Christian writings. The Valentinians were a radical Gnostic sect that advocated the belief that the creator god (the God of the Old Testament) was wicked, and therefore the material realm was fallen and perverse.

16. See Origen, as quoted in Eusebius, *History of the Church,* 6.25, as well as Eusebius' own thoughts on the subject of the canon in *History of the Church,* 2.23–24; 3.3, 25.

17. Oscar Cullmann, "Infancy Gospels," in Schneemelcher, *New Testament Apocrypha,* 1:462.

18. Bruce M. Metzger, "Names for the Nameless in the New Testament: A Study in the Growth of Christian Tradition," in *Kyriakon: Festschrift Johannes Quasten,* ed. Patrick Granfield and Josef A. Jungmann (Münster: Aschendorff, 1970), 79–99.

19. Schneemelcher, *New Testament Apocrypha,* 1:41–43.

20. Pliny's letter to Trajan (*Epistles,* 10), which documents regional persecution of Christians in Bythinia, offers a counter to the thesis that suppression of Christianity in the west helped promote interest in apocalyptic literature.

21. Philipp Vielhauer and Georg Strecker, "Apocalypses and Related Subjects," in Schneemelcher, *New Testament Apocrypha,* 2:542–68.

22. See 2 Thessalonians 2:2, "That ye be not soon shaken in mind, or be troubled, neither by spirit, nor by word, *nor by letter as from us,* as that the day of Christ is at hand" (emphasis added), which indicates that forgery was already a problem in Paul's day.

18

JOSEPH SMITH AND THE NEW TESTAMENT

Robert J. Matthews

My topic is how the teachings of the Prophet Joseph Smith offer significant and insightful information about the New Testament. My approach to the subject is that of one who trusts the Prophet Joseph Smith's teachings as being correct and of eternal significance, and my conclusions are based on faith in the evidences brought forth by Joseph Smith.

I believe that the forces that caused the apostasy of the Lord's church and left the world without an adequate church also engaged in altering the manuscripts from which our present New Testament is translated. And since no originals are known to be in existence today, the world lacks an adequate collection of manuscripts. Concerning the original New Testament documents, the highly respected Sir Frederick Kenyon said: "The originals of the several books have long ago disappeared. They must have perished in the very infancy of the church; for no allusion is ever made to them by any Christian writer."[1] The loss of priesthood, doctrine, ordinances, covenants, and inspired prophets

---

Robert J. Matthews is a professor emeritus of ancient scripture at Brigham Young University.

characterizes the great apostasy and also sets the stage for a great Restoration. If every essential that was lost is not made available, then we do not have a Restoration. We do not need the original manuscripts as much as we need the vital information they contained, much of which we have received by revelation to the Prophet Joseph without the manuscripts.

My view is that through the Restoration we have a pattern of doctrine and procedure showing that other dispensations functioned in a manner similar to the New Testament period and to the dispensation of the fulness of times. Indeed, Joseph Smith said as much when he stated, "Now the purpose in Himself in the winding up scene of the last dispensation is that all things pertaining to that dispensation should be conducted precisely in accordance with the preceding dispensations."[2] The Prophet said that the Lord wanted the ordinances to remain the same in every dispensation; "therefore He set the ordinances to be the same forever and ever, and set Adam to watch over them, to reveal them from heaven to man, or to send angels to reveal them."[3] Joseph Smith's contributions provide meaningful information and patterns that are not available from any other known source.

In this chapter, I use the expression "Joseph Smith's teachings" to include all that came through him: the Book of Mormon, the Doctrine and Covenants, the Pearl of Great Price, the New Translation of the Bible, as well as the Prophet's personal writings and discourses.

JOSEPH SMITH'S CREDENTIALS

Latter-day Saints accept Joseph Smith's teachings as having a bearing on the writing and compilation of the New Testament. Several factors make using the Prophet's utterances not only legitimate but desirable and very rewarding.

The established order of the Lord's church and kingdom is that men do not appoint themselves but must be called of God by revelation, and they speak as moved by the Holy Ghost. Further, the nature of the heavenly plan is that it can be understood only through the aid of the Holy Ghost, and the ordinances of salvation can be administered only by the authority of the holy priesthood. New Testament Apostles and prophets had the necessary qualifications and were "insiders."

Joseph Smith had the same qualifications from the same Lord Jesus, and he was at least of the same stature as they. As such, he had an edge in relating to the New Testament writers, especially since he had been visited by some of them. He was an "insider."

Among the qualifications to understand the scriptures, none is more necessary than inspiration from the Holy Ghost. Paul explained that since the "natural man" has not received the Holy Ghost, he cannot know the things of God "because they are spiritually discerned" (1 Corinthians 2:14). The Prophet Joseph Smith wrote: "If one man cannot understand these things but by the Spirit of God, ten thousand men cannot; it is alike out of the reach of the wisdom of the learned, [and] the tongue of the eloquent."[4] In other words, in gospel research, no other success can compensate for failure to have the help of the Holy Ghost.

Joseph Smith had practical experience with the operation of the Holy Ghost. After he and Oliver Cowdery were baptized and ordained by priesthood authority, they received the Holy Ghost and were able to better understand the scriptures: "We were filled with the Holy Ghost, and rejoiced in the God of our salvation. Our minds being now enlightened, we began to have the scriptures laid open to our understandings, and the true meaning and intention of their more mysterious passages revealed unto us in a manner which we never could attain to previously, nor ever before had thought of" (Joseph Smith–History 1:73–74).

Learning to use the Holy Ghost is a growth process. Elder Orson Pratt reported the following conversation he once had with Joseph Smith: "[Elder Pratt] mentioned that as Joseph used the Urim and Thummim in the translation of the Book of Mormon, he wondered why he did not use it in the translation of the New Testament. Joseph explained to him that the experience he had acquired while translating the Book of Mormon by the use of the Urim and Thummim had rendered him so well acquainted with the Spirit of Revelation and Prophecy, that in the translating of the New Testament he did not need the aid that was necessary in the 1st instance."[5]

Joseph Smith was the greatest gospel restorer of all time, for the Lord had "given him the keys of the mystery of those things which have been sealed, even things which were from the foundation of the world"

(D&C 35:18). As leader of the dispensation of the fulness of times, it was in the very nature of his calling to be able to discuss in authoritative detail the conditions and function of all previous dispensations, including the time of the New Testament. He understood the New Testament better than anyone since Peter, James, John, and Paul.

"ONE LORD, ONE FAITH, ONE BAPTISM"

Joseph Smith declared emphatically that the fulness of the gospel, with a focus on Christ as Creator and Redeemer, accompanied by priesthood, ordinances, covenants, and callings, was instituted in heaven before the foundation of the world. This complete gospel plan was preached in the name of Christ in every dispensation beginning with Adam. Sacred records and histories were kept by the authorized servants of God in each dispensation. The New Testament dispensation was unique in that it included the Lord's birth, earthly life, death, and resurrection, but the doctrines and ordinances of salvation would of necessity be the same as in all other dispensations.

Joseph Smith taught, "All that were ever saved, were saved through the power of this great plan of redemption, as much before the coming of Christ as since; if not, God has had different plans in operation (if we may so express it), to bring men back to dwell with Himself; and this we cannot believe, since there has been no change in the constitution of man since he fell."[6] And "the gospel has always been the same; the ordinances to fulfill its requirements, the same, and the officers to officiate, the same; and the signs and fruits resulting from the promises, the same."[7] It is evident, therefore, that Paul's concept of "one Lord, one faith, one baptism" (Ephesians 4:5) is not confined to Paul's time only but should be seen as the prevailing rule throughout the entire scope of the gospel anywhere and anytime on earth and in heaven. This principle is not clearly taught in the Bible, although there are hints, but the facts are abundantly attested in the teachings of Joseph Smith. Inasmuch as all dispensations had the same plan of salvation, the records of those dispensations are able to make known some of the concepts not clearly stated in the New Testament record. As taught in 1 Nephi 13:32–40, much truth was lost from the New Testament.

Without the Restoration and the Prophet Joseph Smith, we would not realize how incomplete the current New Testament record is.

Joseph Smith gave us a larger, wider, and more comprehensive view of the Lord's work on this earth than we could have imagined from the Bible alone. The scope of operations is worldwide rather than focused on the Near East as the Bible would suggest. Anyone who has read, understood, and believed the Book of Mormon can hardly avoid the wider view and can never again look at the New Testament in the same light. Revelations showing the wider activity of the Lord Jesus and his personal visits to several different groups in addition to the Jews in Palestine in no way denigrate the New Testament or the Holy Land of the Near East. Rather, they enlarge our view of an active and caring Savior who is God of the whole earth and not an absentee landlord to most of it. In light of Doctrine and Covenants 88:46–61, we see that Jesus is also Lord of the Universe, visiting the inhabitants of many worlds as their only Redeemer, with the same plan of salvation we know on this earth.

THE NEW TESTAMENT PORTRAYAL OF JESUS

Latter-day revelation informs us that the New Testament is a true account of the Lord Jesus Christ, although it is occasionally ambiguous and often incomplete. We may accept as sound doctrine and historical fact the New Testament messages that Jesus was the Son of God in the flesh, born of Mary, baptized by John the Baptist, and that He received the Holy Ghost and performed many miracles including casting out evil spirits and restoring the dead to life. He chose twelve Apostles and commissioned them to teach and baptize all nations. He promised to come again to the earth and establish a worldwide kingdom. He shed His blood in Gethsemane, died on a cross, atoned for the sins of mankind, rose from the dead with a body of flesh, and ascended into heaven. Furthermore, the witness of Christ given in the book of Acts, the Epistles, and the Revelation of John is verified by Joseph Smith's teachings, including his revelatory translation of the Bible.

Every major concept regarding the mission of Jesus Christ can be verified by latter-day revelation very quickly by perusal of the Topical Guide in the appendix of the Latter-day Saint edition of the King

James Version. For instance, under the heading "Jesus Christ" beginning on page 240, fifty-eight subheadings delineate various aspects of His ministry, presenting passages from the Old Testament, New Testament, Book of Mormon, Doctrine and Covenants, and Pearl of Great Price. No better instrument exists on earth to show how marvelously latter-day revelation sustains the New Testament presentation of Jesus. The Topical Guide presents nineteen pages of scripture references to support the fifty-eight subheadings.

In addition to the Topical Guide, hundreds of statements about Jesus are on record as coming from Joseph Smith, of which the following is one example: "The fundamental principles of our religion are the testimony of the Apostles and Prophets, concerning Jesus Christ, that He died, was buried, and rose again the third day, and ascended into heaven; and all other things which pertain to our religion are only appendages to it. But in connection with these, we believe in the gift of the Holy Ghost, the power of faith, the enjoyment of the spiritual gifts according to the will of God, the restoration of the house of Israel, and the final triumph of truth."[8]

A GROWING TREND OF UNBELIEF

For most of the past century, a growing trend has developed among many biblical scholars casting doubt on the historical accuracy of the New Testament. It is popular in some circles to make a distinction between "the Jesus of history" and "the Christ of faith," alleging that the divine and atoning Christ who is worshiped and trusted by many faithful Christians never existed as such a person. This view has been the subject of many publications, but it is not especially shared by the majority of Christians. But I believe the trend is growing.[9] The trend of skepticism was described as a warning by Elder Harold B. Lee:

> Fifty years ago or more, when I was a missionary, our greatest responsibility was to defend the great truth that the Prophet Joseph Smith was divinely called and inspired and that the Book of Mormon was indeed the word of God. But even at that time there were the unmistakable evidences that there was coming into the religious world actually a question about the

Bible and the divine calling of the Master himself. Now, fifty years later, our greatest responsibility and anxiety is to defend the divine mission of our Lord and Master, Jesus Christ, for all about us, even among those who claim to be professors of the Christian faith, are those not willing to stand squarely in defense of the great truth that our Lord and Master, Jesus Christ, was indeed the Son of God. So tonight it would seem to me that the most important thing I could say to you is to try to strengthen your faith and increase your courage and your understanding of the place of the Master in the great Plan of Salvation.[10]

When we realize that the Lord has known from the beginning that the modern world would in many instances reject divine revelation and be immersed in unbelief and that the Bible would be rejected by many, we begin to understand why the Lord prepared for such an emergency. We read in 1 Nephi 13 that soon after the time of Christ, "many plain and precious things" and "many covenants" would be deliberately taken out of the records of the twelve Apostles of the Lamb (see verses 27–28, 39–40). We read also that "because of these things which are taken away out of the gospel of the Lamb an exceedingly great many do stumble" (1 Nephi 13:29). The Lord, however, promised to correct this situation: "Neither will the Lord God suffer that the Gentiles shall forever remain in that awful state of blindness, which thou beholdest they are in, because of the plain and most precious parts of the gospel of the Lamb which have been kept back by that abominable church, whose formation thou hast seen" (verse 32).

As a remedy, the Lord brought forth the Book of Mormon and "other books" to convince Jews, Gentiles, and Lamanites "that the records of the prophets and of the twelve apostles of the Lamb are true" (1 Nephi 13:39). The angel of the Lord declared: "These last records, which thou hast seen among the Gentiles, shall establish the truth of the first, which are of the twelve apostles of the Lamb, and shall make known the plain and precious things which have been taken away from them; and shall make known to all kindreds, tongues, and people, that the Lamb of God is the Son of the Eternal Father, and the Savior of the world; and that all men must come unto him, or they cannot be saved" (verse 40). Please note the emphasis on the New Testament and that it would be in need of some repair and restoration.

The tone of latter-day revelation, including the Prophet Joseph Smith's translation of the Bible, shows Jesus to be very straightforward in His speech. As an example, one notable ambiguity in the New Testament is when Pilate asks Jesus, "Art thou the King of the Jews? And he answering said unto him, Thou sayest it" (Mark 15:2). This passage is vague both in the Greek manuscripts and in the King James translation. The Joseph Smith Translation is clear: "I am even as thou sayest."[11]

PHRASES AND DOCTRINAL CONCEPTS

Certain phraseology and doctrinal concepts which were unique to the New Testament when men had only the Bible are shown by latter-day revelation to be characteristic of other dispensations also. For many years I have noted that the Book of Mormon and the books of Moses and Abraham have phrases and ideas similar in word order and content to the New Testament. But until recently, I had not sensed the historical significance. The following examples will illustrate three different categories.

1. *Situations in which the Book of Mormon and the New Testament contain parallel passages after Jesus had personally ministered among the Jews and the Nephites.* In the first table on page 312, note the similar wording of the completely separate discourses by Paul and Mormon on the topics of faith, hope, and charity, each presumably unaware of the other's treatise, and separated by three hundred years and about ten thousand miles.

Sidney B. Sperry's conclusion was that Jesus probably had discoursed on charity to both the Jews and the Nephites, and it was in the writings or traditions of each church, and Paul and Mormon obtained the words independent of one another from those sources.[12] A second possibility is that both Paul and Mormon received the wording by direct inspiration from the Holy Ghost.

FAITH, HOPE, AND CHARITY

1 CORINTHIANS 13:2, 4–8	MORONI 7:44–46
[If I] have not charity, I am nothing. . . . Charity suffereth long, and is kind; charity envieth not; charity vaunteth not itself, is not puffed up, doth not behave itself unseemly, seeketh not her own, is not easily provoked, thinketh no evil; rejoiceth not in iniquity, but rejoiceth in the truth; beareth all things, believeth all things, hopeth all things, endureth all things. Charity never faileth . . .	He must needs have charity; for if he have not charity he is nothing; wherefore he must needs have charity. And charity suffereth long, and is kind, and envieth not, and is not puffed up, seeketh not her own, is not easily provoked, thinketh no evil, and rejoiceth not in iniquity but rejoiceth in the truth, beareth all things, believeth all things; hopeth all things, endureth all things. Wherefore, my beloved brethren, if ye have not charity, ye are nothing, for charity never faileth.

Another example, but of different subject matter, is seen in the teachings of Mormon and John:

SONS OF GOD

1 JOHN 3:2–3	MORONI 7:48
Beloved, now are we the sons of God, and it doth not yet appear what we shall be: but we know that, when he shall appear, we shall be like him; for we shall see him as he is. And every man that hath this hope in him purifieth himself, even as he is pure.	Wherefore, my beloved brethren, pray unto the Father . . . that ye may become the sons of God; that when he shall appear we shall be like him, for we shall see him as he is; that we may have this hope; that we may be purified even as he is pure.

Yet another example can be seen by comparing Philippians 2:12 with Mormon 9:27.

2. *Situations in which the Book of Mormon passage was previous to Jesus' earthly mission, but the New Testament passage was during Jesus' earthly mission.* One example is Alma (about 83 BC) compared to John the Baptist (about AD 30).

Alma states that the Spirit told him what to say, and I am certain that John the Baptist was inspired by the same Spirit:

THE AXE AT THE ROOT OF THE TREE

ALMA 5:52	MATTHEW 3:10
The Spirit saith: Behold, the ax is laid at the root of the tree; therefore every tree that bringeth not forth good fruit shall be hewn down and cast into the fire.	And now also the axe is laid unto the root of the trees: therefore every tree which bringeth not forth good fruit is hewn down, and cast into the fire.

Note also the following statements of Nephi, son of Helaman (about 30 and 23 BC) as compared with Jesus in the Sermon on the Mount in Galilee and again in Bountiful, about fifty years after Nephi had spoken.

TREASURES IN HEAVEN

HELAMAN 5:8; 8:25	MATTHEW 6:20 (ALSO 3 NEPHI 13:20)
Do these things to lay up for your-selves a treasure in heaven, yea, which is eternal, and which fadeth not away; . . . instead of laying up for yourselves treasures in heaven, where nothing doth corrupt, and where nothing can come which is unclean.	But lay up for yourselves treasures in heaven, where neither moth nor rust doth corrupt, and where thieves do not break through nor steal.

Compare the teachings of Captain Moroni and Jesus:

FIRST CLEANSE THE INWARD VESSEL

ALMA 60:23	MATTHEW 23:26
God has said that the inward ves-sel shall be cleansed first, and then shall the outer vessel be cleansed also.	Thou blind Pharisee, cleanse first that which is within the cup and plat-ter, that the outside of them may be clean also.

It is to be noted that Captain Moroni states that he is quoting what "God has said," which gives an impression that the passage might already have been in the Nephite scriptures.

An interesting situation is seen in the use of the words *jot* and *tittle*. Jesus used these words in His Sermon on the Mount among the Jews and also in the similar sermon in Bountiful. Surprisingly, they appear twice before that time, even as early as 74 BC by Amulek, suggesting that they may have been in use among the Nephites at that time.

JOT AND TITTLE

ALMA 34:13	3 NEPHI 1:25	MATTHEW 5:18
Then shall the law of Moses be fulfilled; yea, it shall be all fulfilled, every jot and tittle, and none shall have passed away.	The law was not yet fulfilled, and that it must be fulfilled in every whit; yea, the word came unto them that it must be fulfilled; yea, that one jot or tittle should not pass away till it should all be fulfilled.	For verily I say unto you, Till heaven and earth pass, one jot or one tittle shall in no wise pass from the law, till all be fulfilled.

3. *Situations in which the Book of Mormon passage is prior to Jesus' earthly ministry, but the New Testament passage is after Jesus' earthly ministry; that is, from the books of Acts through Revelation.* Note the words of Peter as compared to the words of Nephi (545 BC) and King Benjamin (124 BC), each independently speaking about Christ:

NO OTHER NAME FOR SALVATION[13]

2 NEPHI 31:21	MOSIAH 3:17	ACTS 4:12
This is the way; and there is none other way nor name given under heaven whereby man can be saved in the kingdom of God.	There shall be no other name given nor any other way nor means whereby salvation can come unto the children of men, only in and through the name of Christ, the Lord Omnipotent.	Neither is there salvation in any other: for there is none other name under heaven given among men, whereby we must be saved.

Another example is Helaman and Pahoran (about 57 BC) writing about the liberty given by Christ. Compare Paul's similar statement more than a hundred years later.

STAND FAST IN THE LIBERTY OF CHRIST[14]

ALMA 58:40	ALMA 61:9, 21	GALATIANS 5:1
They stand fast in that liberty wherewith God has made them free.	My soul standeth fast in that liberty in the which God hath made us free. . . . God will deliver them, yea, and also all those who stand fast in that liberty wherewith God hath made them free.	Stand fast therefore in the liberty wherewith Christ hath made us free.

How widespread is parallel phraseology in the scriptures? How many parallels are there, and where do they occur? I found at least seventy-five examples distributed widely throughout the scriptures. My analysis shows they occur in at least nineteen of the twenty-seven New Testament books, with Matthew, 1 Corinthians, and Hebrews having the greatest number. At least eleven of the fifteen books in the Book of Mormon have passages parallel to the New Testament. I did not include the Doctrine and Covenants or the Pearl of Great Price in the analysis. Parallel passages occur in the words of all the authors of the books of the New Testament plus John the Baptist and Jesus. Book of Mormon personalities include Lehi, Nephi, Jacob, Enos, Benjamin, Abinadi, Alma the Elder, Amulek, Captain Moroni, Alma the Younger, Nephi son of Helaman, Samuel the Lamanite, Mormon, Moroni, and Jesus.

It is also my observation that parallel or near-parallel passages occur most frequently in preaching or revelatory situations in which the Holy Ghost is involved or when a prophet is citing what an angel had told him. Aside from Jesus, individuals probably were not aware that their utterances closely resemble what others in a different hemisphere and time had said or would yet say.

EVIDENCES OF A DIVINE PATTERN

Earlier in this chapter, I made the point that the complete gospel plan was in place before the foundation of the world and that the gospel has been the same in every dispensation. I propose that revelations from heaven in every dispensation would follow the preordained pattern. There is a sequence and a fixed order to the principles and ordinances of the gospel, and they were very probably revealed in clusters or patterns, like a formula, in every dispensation. Nephi, Jacob, Benjamin, Amulek, Alma, and Samuel the Lamanite said they were repeating what an angel had told them. Ministering angels would know the fixed, preordained plan and would reveal the gospel in the proper order and cluster.

Order and sequence are demonstrated in a variety of situations. Jesus declared a priority when he said that "the first and great commandment" is "Thou shalt love the Lord thy God with all thy heart, . . . soul, . . . and mind" and that "the second is like unto it, Thou shalt love thy neighbor as thyself. On these two commandments hang all the law and the prophets" (Matthew 22:37–40). The same priority occurs in the Ten Commandments: the first four pertain to a person's relationship to God; the remaining six to relationships with other people (see Exodus 20:1–17). Additional meaning is manifested when we recognize not ten unrelated statements but a wholeness and intelligent order.

The same pattern occurs in the Beatitudes, especially as presented in 3 Nephi 12. The earlier Beatitudes speak of faith in Christ, repentance, baptism, receiving the Holy Ghost, and a remission of sins (see 3 Nephi 12:1–6). The others speak more specifically of relationships between people—being a peacemaker, what to do when you are persecuted, and so forth (see verses 7–11). It is noticeable that the Beatitudes in the New Testament lack the early statements about faith, repentance, baptism, Holy Ghost, and remission of sins (see Matthew 5) and thus do not fit the established pattern that is so well given in 3 Nephi by the same Jesus. Fortunately, the complete list is restored to Matthew 5 in the Joseph Smith Translation.[15]

The pattern thus displayed in a wide selection of scriptures is supported by the words of God to Nephi: "I speak the same words unto one nation like unto another" (2 Nephi 29:8).

WRITTEN BY COMMANDMENT

Latter-day revelation infers that the New Testament authors wrote by command of the Lord. This may support earlier compilation and lend credence more to traditional authorship than is asserted by those scholars who base their conclusions on literary analysis.

From Adam to the present, the Lord has commanded his prophets to write and preserve scripture. Adam and his immediate family kept a "book of remembrance . . . , in the which was recorded in the language of Adam" things that were given "by the spirit of inspiration. And by them their children were taught to read and write" a "language which was pure and undefiled" (see Moses 6:4–6). Years later, Enoch used this "book of remembrance" in his ministry (see Moses 6:45–46).

The Book of Mormon is our strongest source for declaring that the Lord wants certain things to be written and preserved. It also tells why the Lord wants such records available to the people. The whole of 2 Nephi 29 dwells on this subject and contains words of the Lord declaring that "the testimony of two nations is a witness unto you that I am God," and "I speak the same words unto one nation like unto another . . . and I do this that I may prove unto many that I am the same yesterday, today, and forever" (verses 8–9). Furthermore, the Lord has said, "I command all men . . . that they shall write the words which I shall speak unto them; for out of the books which shall be written I will judge the world" (2 Nephi 29:11). The Lord says still more: "I shall speak unto the Jews" and "to the Nephites," and "to the other tribes of Israel," and "they shall write it." Eventually, each shall have the books of the others (see 2 Nephi 29:12–14).

With such strong declaration and affirmation, it is strange that of the twenty-seven books in the New Testament, only the Revelation of John contains any statement of a command to write (see Revelation 1:11, 19, and fourteen other instances, all in Revelation). In my view, it is unlikely that the Lord would command only one of the New Testament Apostles to write when commandments to write are so prominent in the other dispensations. Why would it not be so in the New Testament? It is my opinion that the Lord did command the Apostles to write and the fact that the command does not appear in our New Testament is evidence of the leanness and inadequacy of the record. It is a glaring omission, conspicuous by its absence.

Jacob, son of Lehi, made an informative observation that writing on metal was limited "because of the difficulty of engraving," but metal was durable and would remain, whereas what was written on other materials would "perish and vanish away" (see Jacob 4:1–2). Since the Lord knew long beforehand that the New Testament books would be altered and shortened, with the loss of "plain and precious things" and also "many covenants," we see the Lord's wisdom in having the Nephites write on metal and bury the record in the ground out of the reach of men. This way it would remain unchanged and could testify of Christ and of the original truth of the New Testament and also supply doctrinal concepts missing from the New Testament manuscripts (see 1 Nephi 13:32–40).

The Lord's sensitivity to written records was shown when He noticed that the fulfillment of a particular prophecy spoken by Samuel the Lamanite was not included in the official Nephite record. The Lord commanded that it be included (see 3 Nephi 23:7–13). Among other purposes of the written scripture, it has "enlarged the memory of this people" (Alma 37:8), and it keeps the "commandments always before our eyes" (Mosiah 1:5; compare Mosiah 1:4).[16]

I assume that since the Lord commanded the twelve Apostles to write, they surely would have done so, and thus the books of the New Testament, especially Matthew, Mark, Luke, and John, would have been composed earlier than some scholars think. The Joseph Smith Translation might offer some help when it changes the titles from "The Gospel according to . . ." to "The Testimony of . . ." in the case of Matthew and John. Such a change is at least an affirmation of authorship, and it is consistent with Doctrine and Covenants 88:141, in which the Lord refers to the "thirteenth chapter of John's testimony concerning me." It seems probable that each "testimony" began with the words of the original author, but through the years unauthorized changes were made so that current copies vary from the originals and are neither as accurate in detail nor as complete as the originals. There seems an ever-present tendency for some persons to alter the word of the Lord, for there are at least seventeen scripture references with warnings against alteration, citing both intentional and unintentional variants.[17]

Perhaps some feel that since the Prophet Joseph was not a textual critic in the current usage of the term, having not studied the biblical documents, that he might not have been aware of questions of authorship and dating and simply spoke in the traditional context of the day when he discussed the New Testament. However, Joseph Smith did engage in a number of activities characteristic of a deep comprehension of textual backgrounds. (1) He translated an original parchment written and hidden up by John. This is now Doctrine and Covenants section 7. (2) He raised questions about the accuracy of the translation of the Bible, as in the eighth Article of Faith. (3) He was fully aware of 1 Nephi 13, saying the New Testament has suffered many losses of precious material. (4) He judged the Song of Solomon to be not inspired.[18] (5) He spoke of the Apocrypha as being partly correct (see D&C 91:2). (6) He wrote that the Jewish rulers had taken away the fulness of the scriptures before Jesus' day (see JST, Luke 11:53). (7) He wrote that many words were taken out of the writings of Moses (see Moses 1:41). (8) He said that "many points touching the salvation of men, had been taken out from the Bible or lost before it was compiled."[19] (9) He took issue with details in the books of Daniel and Revelation.[20] (10) And he said the Bible did not always agree with the revelations of the Holy Ghost to him.[21]

But Joseph Smith never, so far as I have seen, made even a suggestion that would cast doubt on the authorship of any of the books of the New Testament. My feeling is that the Prophet's calling as seer and translator far outweighs his possible lack of formal training with manuscripts. I think that if the original manuscripts and other documents of the early Church were available today, we would see that they would support the Prophet's decisions in every particular and that the question of doubt raised by some scholarly research is the consequence of imperfect manuscripts and also not having the divine calling that the Prophet Joseph had. Who can match the high level of a seer? A greater spiritual gift "can no man have" (Mosiah 8:16).

NOTES

1. Frederick Kenyon, *Our Bible and the Ancient Manuscripts* (New York: Harper and Row, 1962), 155.

2. Joseph Smith, *Teachings of the Prophet Joseph Smith,* comp. Joseph Fielding Smith (Salt Lake City: Deseret Book, 1938), 168.

3. Smith, *Teachings of the Prophet Joseph Smith,* 168.

4. Smith, *Teachings of the Prophet Joseph Smith,* 205.

5. Minutes of the School of the Prophets, Salt Lake City, January 14, 1871. Manuscript in the Historical Library, The Church of Jesus Christ of Latter-day Saints, Salt Lake City; in Robert J. Matthews, *"A Plainer Translation": Joseph Smith's Translation of the Bible—A History and Commentary* (Provo, UT: Brigham Young University Press, 1985), 40.

6. Smith, *Teachings of the Prophet Joseph Smith,* 59–60.

7. Smith, *Teachings of the Prophet Joseph Smith,* 264; see also 308, 320, 324.

8. Smith, *Teachings of the Prophet Joseph Smith,* 121.

9. A 1929 study of Protestant clergy showed that younger ministers were less accepting of traditional beliefs than older ministers (see George Herbert Betts, *The Beliefs of Seven Hundred Ministers* [Chicago: Abingdon, 1929]). The so-called "Jesus Seminar" of the 1980s and 1990s concluded that only 18 percent of the sayings of Jesus were actually from Jesus, that Jesus did not think of Himself as the Messiah, that He did not promise to return to earth in glory to set up a world kingdom, nor that He commissioned His disciples to convert and baptize the world or establish a church. The Gospel of John was branded the least authentic of all the records. The report casts doubt on Jesus' miracles, His bodily resurrection, and His Atonement for the sins of the world (see Robert W. Funk and Roy W. Hoover, eds., *The Five Gospels: The Search for the Authentic Words of Jesus* [New York: Macmillan, 1993]).

10. Harold B. Lee, LDS Student Association fireside, Institute of Religion, Logan, Utah, October 10, 1971, unpublished typescript in author's possession; in Robert J. Matthews, *Selected Writings of Robert J. Matthews* (Salt Lake City: Deseret Book, 1999), 375.

11. New Testament Manuscript 2, folio 2, page 42. Scott H. Faulring, Kent P. Jackson, and Robert J. Matthews, eds., *Joseph Smith's New Translation of the Bible: Original Manuscripts* (Provo, UT: Religious Studies Center, Brigham Young University, 2004), 355.

12. Sidney B. Sperry, *Book of Mormon Compendium* (Salt Lake City, Bookcraft, 1968), 487–88.

13. See Moses 6:51 for a similar statement originally spoken by God to Adam after he was cast out of the garden of Eden.

14. For additional examples on a different subject, compare 1 Corinthians 15:55 with Mosiah 16:8 and Alma 22:14. Also Philippians 4:13 with Alma 26:12–13.

15. The pattern is further displayed in the Articles of Faith. The earlier articles pertain to the Godhead, the Atonement, and the first principles of the gospel. Remaining articles deal with Church polity and relationships between people, governments, doing good to all men, and so forth. The pattern is also seen inasmuch as the Lord launched the dispensation of the fulness of times with the First Vision, with a visit from the Father and the Son. A specific sequence of principles and ordinances is given in the fourth article of faith: first, faith in Jesus Christ; second, repentance; third, baptism; fourth, laying on of hands for the gift of the Holy Ghost. Not surprisingly this is the order given to Adam (Moses 6:52) and taught

by Noah (Moses 8:23–24), Nephi (2 Nephi 31:4–17), Peter (Acts 2:37–39; 8:14–17), and Paul (Acts 19:1–6).

16. Our present dispensation has also received the charge to keep an accurate sacred record, as given in Doctrine and Covenants 21:1; 47:1–4; 69:1–8; 76:28; 85:1–11; 127:6–7; 128:1–7.

17. *Do not add to or take from:* Deuteronomy 4:2; Proverbs 30:5–6; Revelation 22:18–19; Doctrine and Covenants 20:35. *Intentional removal of material:* 1 Nephi 13:20–41; 14:20–27; Moses 1:23, 40–41; Jeremiah 36:1–32; JST, Luke 11:53; Doctrine and Covenants 6:27. *Other intentional alterations:* 2 Corinthians 2:17; Mormon 8:3; Doctrine and Covenants 3 and 10. *An unintentional omission:* 3 Nephi 23:6–13.

18. See Old Testament Manuscript 2, page 97; Faulring, Jackson, and Matthews, *Joseph Smith's New Translation of the Bible,* 785.

19. Smith, *Teachings of the Prophet Joseph Smith,* 10–11.

20. Smith, *Teachings of the Prophet Joseph Smith,* 290–91.

21. Smith, *Teachings of the Prophet Joseph Smith,* 310.

INDEX